T0381072

Journey into Time

George Richards

iUniverse, Inc.
Bloomington

Journey into Time

iUniverse books may be ordered through booksellers or by contacting:

iUniverse
1663 Liberty Drive
Bloomington, IN 47403
www.iuniverse.com
1-800-Authors (1-800-288-4677)

ISBN: 978-1-4620-1497-2 (sc)
ISBN: 978-1-4620-1498-9 (ebk)

Printed in the United States of America

iUniverse rev. date: 04/28/2011

Authors Biography

The author was born in Dublin Ireland in 1930 and immigrated to England in 1946 where he began his career in the construction industry. Over the coming years his job took him to Nigeria and Ghana on the West Coast of Africa, and later on to Saudi Arabia. He returned to England in 1973 and immigrated to Canada with his wife and four children in 1973 and continued his career as Project Manager in the oil industry from which he retired in 1987. He now resides in Fort Saskatchewan Alberta with his wife Joan and enjoys golfing, reading, and music.

Cover design by my Granddaughter Emma Louise Dake photographs taken from the Wikipedia Free Encyclopedia.

The Great Pyramid of Giza, Egypt
Photographer Berthold Werner

The Temple of Teotihuacan, Mexico
Photographer Michael Wassmer

The Temple of Stonehenge, England
Photographer Gareth Wiscombe

The Great Sphinx of Giza, Egypt
Photographer Ryan Postlethwaite

The Temple of Newgrange, Ireland
Photographer Richard Gallagher

Salisbury Cathedral Salisbury England
Photographer Andrew Dunn

The Burial Mask of Tutankhamon
Photographer Myk Reeve

A Rainbow
Photographer Eric Rolph

Dedication

To my wife Joan for her unwavering love and devotion.

Acknowledgement

To my daughter Ruth Elizabeth Kuik my grateful thanks for her invaluable help and encouragement

PREFACE

As we approach the end of the Astrological Age of Pisces to enter into a new cycle of time, with the arrival of the Age of Aquarius), the political and religious turmoil in the middle East that saw the beginning of the Age of Pisces in the year 63 BC has once again surfaced to bring it to a close.

During this cycle, we have come through an age of deception in which the lie has obscured the truth. Consequently, the question asked so many years ago, "What is truth?" continues to be out of the reach of humankind. For this reason, we will go on a journey into history and revisit those areas that may be of interest and question what has been purported to be the truths of history.

For an age that was to be one of peace for the human family, through some unknown quirk in the natural order we are experiencing a repeat of history. The arrival of the Roman General, Pompey the Great, into Jerusalem in 63 BC that ushered in the Age of Pisces, the world has come through a period of unprecedented killings of civilian populations. Commencing with the rise of the Roman Empire and their dominance of the then known world, to the present with the dominance of the United States of America, never before in the history of humankind has the world experienced such abuse of power by those who would purport to act in the name of peace and freedom.

The conflicts around the globe that began, the twenty- first century indicates that the new millennia will not be an age of peace as hoped for by mankind but one of conflict and turmoil. The terror and horror attributed to the Roman armies in the early years of its creation will pale in comparison to the New World Order that is about to descend on this planet. The cry of "who will protect the innocent" will be heralded throughout the world as never before heard by the human ear. What we are about to see and experience will put the weaker nations of the world into fear, and those nations with the resources will arm themselves as a means of protection. What has yet to be experienced is a tyranny that will evolve from these and future conflicts.

The emasculation of the Russian Republic and the confusion created in its efforts to change from a socialist society into a free market economy has for the moment placed Russia at a disadvantage, however, emerging nations such as China and India will be among those who fear most the domination of the Western powers, especially of America. Over the years, the use of misinformation and propaganda through the news media has been the weapon effectively used in order to pervert the truth. The recent conflicts in Europe have demonstrated its effectiveness in arousing national feelings. The newer form of colonialism by America will not be unlike that of previous years. In times past, it was the gunboat and cannon. However, this time around it will be far more powerful weapons that will dictate policy, weapons that know no boundaries and do not discriminate as to who should die. If it is the belief that power corrupts, and absolute power corrupts absolutely we have a nation today that exhibits all the characteristics of a nation that believes in its own invincibility. Under the guise of creating a world market for the free exchange of goods, its prime purpose is to control world trade to the detriment of the world's nations. What has not been acknowledged is the reliance that is placed upon trade and the resources of the world, which is used as a means of financing its ever-increasing welfare state.

For those who would question its policies, disagree with its brand of democracy, or in any way resist, are ostracized. Like the bully in the schoolyard, there are those other nations in the Western hemisphere who support and readily acquiesce to this form of blackmail. Our news media is inundated with a barrage of propaganda and misinformation in order to distract from the true purpose. Branding those whose political philosophy differs from their brand of democracy as rogue nations, they impose their will by the imposition of sanctions in trade and political limbo. Yet, this powerful nation lives in fear of those who are capable of inflicting harm within their society.

Therefore, in order to sustain its military superiority it must have an adversary, real or imaginary. In the month of March / 2001, America launched the largest and most powerful Aircraft Carrier ever to grace the seven seas. Carrying a compliment of six thousand personnel and eighty of the most modern aircraft it has been equipped with the most destructive weapons known to man. Named after a former President; Ronald Reagan, it was referred to by presiding president, George W. Bush as an Ambassador of Democracy. One can appreciate the irony of this remark against the backdrop of world politics. The word 'Democracy' has been toss around about and prostituted by those who would have us belief that they are the guardians of the truth. Whereas, they have subverted the truth in order to pursue their political and military activities for world trade domination. In the process, justice has ceased to have any meaning.

The voices of the innocent who cry out for justice are greeted with a stony silence from those who swore to uphold the law. The gathering of the world bodies under the auspices of the United Nations is an affront to all civilized people. Those nations who, being the stronger and richer have corrupted the members that make up this body have the ability to punish those who would disagree with their policies. Therefore, in their efforts to curry favor they have sacrificed their integrity and principals on the altar of political expediency by becoming partners in the policies of America. Suffering from the delusion that they are the New World Order, the New Rome, protectors of the worlds democracies, their actions speak otherwise. Those who protest the actions of this body in the world of commerce and banking are considered subversive for expressing their views.

Was it planned this way, definitely not? The founding fathers of America had the wisdom to look back into the past and see all that was evil when men aspire to power. Taking all that was good from the various political systems, they evolved a government of checks and balances that would ensure equal rights for all.

One would expect nothing less from these great men and the fraternity to which they were members. This is no leap of imagination; one has only to look at the structures that serve to house the various arms of this democratic government for it to become apparent as from where these great men developed their ideas that was to bring this nation to greatness. The names given to their buildings evoke memories of an order of men who aspired to the creation of a just society. Their affiliation with the ancient orders was the binding force behind all their actions. What a wonderful opportunity it was for men with great minds to mould a system of government that would last longer than that of Rome. Therefore, in order to prevent the rule by the few, they initiated a democratic society in which people could enjoy the benefits of free speech and equality among their fellows.

That was the dream; Polybius, the Greek historian many years ago, foresaw the reality in his commentary on the different forms of government when he stated. "But as soon as a new generation has succeeded and the democracy falls into the hands of the grandchildren of its founders, they have become by this time so accustomed to equality and freedom of speech that they cease to value them and seek to raise themselves above their fellow-citizens, and it is notable that the people most liable to temptation are the rich. So when they begin to hanker after office, and find they cannot achieve it through their own efforts or on their merits, they begin to seduce and corrupt the people in every possible way, ---. The result is that through their senseless craving for prominence, they stimulate among the masses both an appetite for bribes and the habit of receiving them, and then the rule of democracy is transformed into a government of violence and strong-armed methods. By this time they have become accustomed to feed at the expense of others, and the prospects of winning a livelihood depend upon the property of their neighbors; then as soon as they find a leader who is sufficiently ambitious and daring, but is excluded from the honors of office because of his poverty, they will introduce a regime based on violence--.[1]

There are many parallels in history from which we can draw a picture of the future that will see the downfall of the western democracies. If the past is any reflection of the future, this nation of America will ultimately go the way of all societies that rose to greatness by imposing their will on others only to find that the enemy was not outside, but within their own society.

There is an ever-increasing imbalance in the ethnic populations in the major nations of the western democracies. Over time, the many diverse ethnic groups will over shadow the dominance of the white Anglo-Saxon. Disenfranchised and mostly comprised of the poorer classes, their need for recognition will increase as their numbers multiply.

---

1   *Polybius Greek Historian 200-118 BC 'The Rise of the Roman Empire' Translated by Ian Scott-Kilvert Published Penguin Books*

We have seen the propaganda juggernaut spread the across the airways and in the news media with a message to the world which stated, "If you are not our friend, you are our enemy" either you are with us or against us.[1] Fear and the suppression off free expression have led those nations who are dependent on the handouts they receive from their benefactor to conform. The basic freedoms that we take so much for granted, freedom of expression, freedom of assembly and the right to question the role of government will be the price paid in order to survive. Propaganda, misinformation, obfuscation of the news fill our airways and news media's. Those who have an agenda for world dominance have drowned out reason such that the rule of law has all but disappeared in the affairs of man. The last twenty-one hundred years have been ones of turmoil and conflict; politically and religiously. Will future generations question events of the twentieth century, or will they like their predecessors blindly accept the views of their governments under the guise of 'country right or wrong'?

A New Age is about to dawn upon this planet, and one wonders whether man will realize the damage and destruction he has brought on his environment and take the necessary steps to correct the imbalance before it is too late. With any luck, there may be those few who searching for the truth will reject the status quo and question the truths of history; however will this be sufficient to bring about change?

What I write may not bring about change, nor will it matter in the vast scheme of life, however, I am hopeful that if sometime in the future the words I write may influence one inquiring mind, if so the task has been worthwhile.

George. C. Richards.
Fort Saskatchewan
Alberta. Canada
Thursday, 16 May 2002

---

1   *George W Bush President of the United States of America 2000-2008 in his response to the 9/11 attack on the Twin Towers in New York*

INTRODUCTION

Generally, people look upon traveling to or moving into unfamiliar surroundings as a kind of an adventure. In the majority of cases a feeling of inner excitement gives play to one's imagination. Likewise, for those who possess a fertile imagination, the mind conjures up all forms of imaginary situations, especially on the impressionable minds of the young. Perhaps the reason for moving may be the result of a career change or a permanent relocation to another country. Whatever the reasons, it will evidently be a challenge to their abilities, allowing them the opportunity to meet people of different backgrounds and interests, perhaps become involved in cultures far removed from their previous environment.

Regardless of how experienced we may wish to appear, there is always the initial feeling of excitement and a sense of nervous anticipation as to what the future may hold. There is also, a common characteristic that affects all who are about to move into a new neighborhood or relocate to another region of the country; these are the fears and apprehensions that accompany the decision to leave familiar grounds that has been a part of one's life. Yet despite all of these misgiving are people quickly settle in and meld into their new communities.

This however, changes for those who embark on a journey into areas viewed as being off limits to the general traveler. As when traveling to foreign countries, they will perhaps experience a feeling of excitement when visiting the local market places they perceive as having a reputation for intrigue and mystery. These imaginary feelings may in part be due to the influence the cinema and television has on the minds of the public.

Perhaps when traveling into regions of a strange country, the mind conjures up a myriad of imaginary situations, which tend to generate a feeling of apprehension that people conceal behind a mask of bravado. This is usually the case for those tourists traveling in the Middle and Far East, who see their surroundings through the eyes of Hollywood rather than through the mind of reason and common sense.

Despite the circumstances or reason for their journey, each one of us, irrespective of our station in life, experience and exhibit different feelings when separated from our culture. Consequently, the fears and apprehension that accompany the decision to leave familiar grounds can be a daunting at the best of times.

This particular journey we are about to take will be into the past and the realms of ancient history. The intent is to look at history from the peripheral edge of life and question what has been imposed upon our generation as the truths of history. Along the way, our travels will take us into the myths and legends of various ancient cultures, including some world events that have occurred within living memory. It would be true to say this field of knowledge is a veritable jungle of preconceived beliefs and taboos, held sacred by the majority of contemporary people

In the course of our travels the views and opinions expressed are not found on the popular television shows that deal with the ancient past, when one considers that these programs are generally for dramatic effect rather than the accuracy of the truths of history. Therefore, for those who embark on a journey into the past with the intention of analyzing and commenting on various aspects of religious and political history their fears and anxieties are increased. Quite recently the authorities prosecuted those who expressed their opinion regards events in Europe relative to the Jewish question, for articulating what to them was the truth of these events during the war of 1939-1945.[1]

Additionally, as the topics will cover a wide range of historical, political and religious subjects, it is extremely important to avoid expressing opinionated statements that may offend some segments of society, as it is to offer an explanation on those areas that may be open to question. One also has to consider with some concern the responsibility in approaching these sensitive subjects. It would not be exaggerating to say that an exercise of this nature has the potential of being fraught with pitfalls for those who question people's beliefs, held as established truths down through the centuries.

They may also, during questioning what is deemed established truths, subconsciously feel that the task will be a test of their capabilities in dealing with these oversensitive subjects considered by some to be the domain of scholars and academics[2]. Yet, those who set out on a task of this nature, do so in the hope that something new will emerge, offering a new insight, perhaps a different interpretation or explanation that may generate discussion among those interested in the subject.

This hope is not without foundation, as I have found, when reading of the ancient past, something new appears at each turn of a page that compels one to study that particular period and subject. There are many metaphors, which could describe this experience when browsing through the pages of history. From a personal perspective, this feeling maybe described as when walking down a country lane, with its twists and turns, each bend in the lane brings something new that compels one to stop and admire the landscape and scenery. In this sense, the joy of seeing and meeting the unexpected can be an exhilarating experience and an adventure in itself.

---

1   Kestera James a school teacher in the Province of Alberta Canada who in his role as a teacher questioned the Holocaust of the Jewish people which occurred in Germany during the 1939-1945 war. He was entitled to his opinion however the venue in which he chose to express his opinion were inappropriate

2   Examples can be found in the writings of the more noted Roman historians, especially the works of Tacitus and Sutonius, also in the writings of the Sicilian historian Diodorus Siculus and the Greek historian, Herodotus.

So it is with the writings of ancient historians, similar events narrated by various writers differ in content and interpretations, requiring one to pause, study, and compare, in this context, historians may view historical events from different viewpoints. One can be confident that the intent of these notable historians was not to deceive or misrepresent history. Much like witnesses at an accident, who see the same incident from different perspective? It would be reasonable to suggest that this may perhaps be attributed to their religious and political believes or perhaps social standing in society.[1] Perhaps, it is because of these reasons history abounds in nooks and crannies of contradictions that leave more questions than answers.

It is hoped that in the process of examining the past, our journey may highlight areas of history that appear ambiguous within the supposed religious and historical truths as we know them to-day. Moreover, the comments and the point of views expressed may engender other areas for those who share a common interest in the study of the past. What follows is not intended to be an all encompassing review of the past but a commentary on those areas that are of interest.

In approaching this task, I will be calling into question some of the established orthodox beliefs in religion and history that are the holy icons in contemporary society. Moreover, as the subjects in question cover a wide range of historical, political and religious matters, the views and opinions expressed rests upon the accounts of ancient historians, including information available in the fields under discussion and their related disciplines.

Consequently, the views and opinions expressed are solely with the purpose of finding possible answers to vexing questions that have been a puzzle to the writer and not out of disrespect to any one culture or people. Further, it must, be stressed that this is not a search for truth, (if such should exist), but to weave together what would appear to be unrelated facts and events that perhaps will develop theories based on logic and reason which will satisfy an inquiring mind.

Today we live in a world that is excessively sensitive to any form of criticism on the subject of religious and political beliefs. It is therefore extremely important to avoid any form of prejudice that would give offence to people's sensibilities. As a result, I have found it expedient to be circumspect when responding to questions from those who are sensitive towards these subjects.

Generally, the majority of people exhibit very little interest in the past, except for the few who have academically studied these subjects. Lately, it has reached the point that when being questioned on my activities; I have found it profitable to be prudent by being non-committal in my response to their inquiries. It has also led me to conclude that if given the choice, people prefer to keep their opinions private and tend to veer away from subjects that may expose religious or political beliefs.

---

1   *Publius Cornelius.(AD 55-Ad 117) the Roman historian alluded to this when speaking of his contemporaries and their passion for flattery and bias in their recording of historical events. 'The Histories' Translated by Kenneth Wellesley. Penguin Classics*

It is however, the opinion of those few with whom I have discussed religion and ancient history that, "Religion, History, and Politics should not be matters for general discussion. Being personal preferences, they tend to create acrimony" among those who may have different views on these matters. As an excuse to avoid discussing the matter, some say the nearest they got to the ancient past did not extend beyond the late Roman period and was extremely superficial,' however, sufficient to satisfy examination requirements".

Other than the religious and history lessons that are the standard fare in all educational establishments, it's doubtful if the subject of ancient history form's part of the general curriculum in our present day school system. Where it so, it may give our children a better insight into human behavior. This view was expressed by a noted Roman historian when he stated, "The study of history is the best medicine for a sick mind; for in history you have a record of the infinite variety of human experience plainly set out for all to see; and in that record you can find for yourself and your country both examples and warnings; fine things to take as models, base things, rotten through and through, to avoid."[1]

When one views our modern society and its troubles, time and distance have not changed.

Over the years I have found it dangerous to blindly accept without question the views of those who would attempt to mould public opinion. History has proved the dangers that exist when people allow themselves to become automated in their views and susceptible to ever changing opinions and fads.

World events that shaped our century have shown us that conditions of this nature ultimately lead to the stagnation of the mind and a life of subservience.[2] The indoctrination of a people through political propaganda has a limited time frame. History has shown that over time people begin to question their leader's motives, which inevitably lead to their downfall. So when world leaders, such as we see in America, endorse the slogan, 'country right or wrong' to justify illegal actions, it only is a matter of time before we see a drastic change in the political spectrum.

It is amazing the trust people place in the veracity of the statements emanating from the news media. This unquestioning trust negates any thought of manipulation through subliminal, misleading information in the political and advertising field. Accepting as true, what they hear and see as the truth, it is extremely difficult to convince people that what they see and hear may not be the truth, but a semblance of the truth.

This is demonstrated by the public opinion polls that appear to drive the political agendas in the majority of our Western Democracies. It is within this context of not taking anything on face value, whether in history or religion that I approach this task, in the believe that there may be another explanation to the firmly held views as taught in our educational system. As

---

1   *Titus Livius., 59 BC-17 AD Roman Historian Early History of Rome Translated by, Aubrey De Selincourt. Penguin Classics*

2   *The advent of Communism in Russia and China*

one well-known author stated, "It's only by questioning traditional beliefs can those beliefs be either re-affirmed or modified."[1]

This process of questioning those doubtful areas that have demanded answers can be best described as having layer upon layer of membrane removed from the mind until the sterility of reality remains. The purpose is not to prove or disprove the veracity of history or enter contentious areas that are perhaps beyond my abilities to defend. Nonetheless, being, from my youth interested in history and religious and events of the past, I decided to question those areas that have over the years, created doubts. I would however stress that the opinions and views expressed developed through the process of questioning what has been purported to be historical truths.

---

1   Theiring. Barbara 'Jesus and the Riddle of the Deep Sea Scrolls' Published by Doubleday Canada Limited

Chapter 1

The ultimate mystery that confronts humankind is the question of life, its beginning and ending. From what can be determined all known advanced cultures have questioned what would appear to be the unanswerable, at what time in the life of this planet did life commence and is there a continuation beyond which is the aspiration of all cultures. Will it end with what some say was its beginning, with a 'Big Bang' at which time this energizing force that has sustained all life return to its source? We have to accept the fact that the purpose of all species is to ensure their continuance; can we apply the same to this planet which is a living organism?

In contrast to the many species that accept the vagaries of nature, humankind thinking they are the superior species, spends time and effort trying to avoid the inevitable, always with the hope that they can prolong the allotted time allowed by nature and when they depart this world it is with the belief that it will be to a place of supreme happiness, an eternity spent in the company of the gods. Because of this belief it is not in the nature of the humankind to envisage a total cessation of life.

Believing they possess an immortal soul, cling to the hope that this self created paradise promised to them by their religious leaders awaits them when they die. The fear of not realizing this dream has created a self induce fear that has been exploited by those who consider themselves the appointed representatives of some unseen God delegated with the powers to determine man's destiny. As a result the many religions that have evolved over the millennia have created a world of hatred and intolerance between the many cultures that populate this planet creating an aura of fear; whereas life was never created to be lived in fear, but enjoyed in all its wonders.

Today there are major problems being experienced by people on all continents; with wars, famines, and religious conflicts. We are living in an age when life has lost its meaning, an age when humankind has invented weapons that kill much faster and at a greater rate. In these conflicts the death of civilian populations referred to as 'collateral' damage is counted as of no consequence.

The word itself removes any sense of guilt from the conscience of those who order these atrocities and also those who carry out these evil deeds. The death of thousands of civilians in these conflicts has ceased to have any impact upon the conscience of mankind. The question arises, has this been the way of the world from the beginning or is it of recent era?

So we ask a question, was there a time in the life of man when the mystical 'Garden of Eden' was a reality, not in a religious sense, but a way of life that existed and now only exists in the sub-conscience memory of man? To determine this question would mean delving into the past and questioning what has been considered the truths of religion and ancient history as taught in our institutions. Would we, after such a long search, find a vestige of the 'Elysian Fields' the human family continually pray for, this Paradise on Earth?

Religion tells us that this idyllic paradise is not to be found in this life, but a place to be aspired to, subject to their allegiance to whichever particular faith they follow. However, each religious sect has its own interpretation of what this paradise will be for those who gain this mystical paradise. Nevertheless, for those of the Judaea/Christian religions, this mystical paradise will be attained at great cost, resulting in the destruction of those who do not belong to or practice the beliefs of the Islamic/Judo/Christian religion. Each in their fanaticism to their respective gods will endeavor to annihilate the opposing faction. What we see today had its beginning in centuries past and is continuity of past animosities.

On many occasions opinions expressed would appear to lay the matter to rest when there are those who say, 'what has the past to offer too modern society? Why look back, there is no profit to be gained by dwelling on events that are long since dead. Their arguments appear to have some validity when they cite as examples the progress made in medicine, nuclear science and space travel that within a short span of thirty year's man may have perhaps landed man on the Moon[1] and reached out to the stars. One has to admit their point of view has logic, which is based on sound reasoning. Man has made great strides over a short period of time, but at what cost? The wars that have been inflicted upon mankind over the last two hundred years have become progressively more destructive resulting in enormous loss of life of civilian populations.

It has been stated by the experts that on the cessation of the conflict that engulfed Europe during the war of 1914-1917, that this was the war to end all wars. However, this has not been the case. Man has still yet to learn from the past. As long as the human family subscribe to resolving their problems through the use of force, suffering, death, and destruction is the end results. In this respect the past does have relevance if one can use the lessons of the past to shape the future. But the simplicity of such an action is lost upon the modern politician who is more concerned with his own interest rather than those of the populace.

A famous Roman historian once stated. "I shall find antiquity a rewarding study, if only because, while I am absorbed in it, I shall be able to turn my eyes from the troubles which have for so long tormented the modern world, and write without any of that over anxious consideration which may well plague a writer on contemporary life, even if it does not lead him to conceal the truth".[2]

---

1   *Recent events has brought into question this claim which many say was the greatest hoax perpetrated by America in order to compete with Russia.*

2   *Livius Titus. 59 BC-17 AD The Early History of Rome Translated by Aubrey de Selincourt Penguin Classics*

We can appreciate his sentiments when we read of the political upheavals that Rome was experiencing during his lifetime. The same could be said of our times with the political conflicts that are creating turmoil around the world.

Nevertheless, great advances have been made, some for the good, others that can only be classed as bad especially in the fields of weapons of mass destruction. Such technological progress has never been accomplished during man's existence over the millennia. Modern science contends that no other civilization has made such rapid technological advances as modern man. However, when scientists delve into the ancient past they come across questions that even today with the advances made in science and technology, modern man has yet to find answers.

Who is to say what advances were made by ancient man? Could it be the discoveries today are the memories of what was, and that man is discovering nothing new but what is stored in his memory from the past?[1]

There are also those within the seats of learning who pride themselves on the knowledge accumulated over the years. Nevertheless, when viewed against the surrounding universe and nature, the sum total knowledge gained is minuscule continually subject to correction. We live in an age of hypothesis with each expert expounding his views as the absolute truths.

The amount of time and money spent by our educational institutions in their efforts to solve the Mysteries of the Universe far exceeds the funds expanded in trying to unravel the mysteries of the Planet we call home.

This criticism is not to question the efforts of the scholars who devote their lives to acquiring knowledge for the benefit of future generations for those who are not skilled enough to read the works of the ancient historians in their original language and are dependent upon the scholars who devote their lives to translating the work of these great men. Their efforts have fed the soul of the many, and enabled them to increase their knowledge and develop their intellect; however, those who reference their works do so trusting that the translation is a true and precise reflection of the original works.

The probability exists of modern day scholars impose their own views and interpretations when translating the literature of the past, which tends to bastardize the text from what the mind and thoughts were of the original author. As expressed by one author who stated, "Did not aim at producing a precise translation." Introducing, as he himself points out, "sentences of explanation, omitting passages which do not seem to help the sense, and 'turning sentences and sometimes even groups of sentences, inside out".[2]

When one turns to literature as a means of reference, the approach must be one of confidence and not of one of trepidation. Although it may suit the mentality of the modern age, actions of this nature do a disservice to those who attempt to understand the past, creating doubts in the minds of those who reference their work.

---

1   *Great Dialogues of Plato Meno Translated by W. H. D. Rouse Published by The New American Library*
2   *Michael Grant in his forward to Robert Grave's translation of the 'Twelve Caesars, Suetonius.published by Penguin Classics*

There are also those who professing to be the worlds leading experts within their field of expertise, propound theories and speculate to the point of absurdity. The theories and hypothesis developed are based upon nothing more than opinion, and by a process of embellishment expound their theories as established truths.

Chapter 2

What the professed experts in the various fields of learning have taught as the truths of history are in most part conjectural and open to question. However, to view history from the most momentous period that shaped our Western culture and thread backwards into the past may be more beneficial than trying to determine when man first appeared on this planet, the age of the planet, or for that matter, the age and size of the Universe; none of which is beneficial to man, other than increasing his pool of knowledge. The subjects themselves are prone to speculative thinking among the intellectual establishment, none of which can agree, each contending his position regarding his theories. In most cases their conclusions are conjectural and at times downright ridiculous lacking basic logic.

They fail to keep in mind the good advice once given by an ancient prophet who stated, "Do not try to understand things that are too difficult for you, or try to discover what is beyond your powers. You have no need to worry over mysteries. Do not meddle with matters that are beyond you, for many have been misled by their own presumption". [1] This sound piece of advice could apply to my own puny efforts.

Therefore, keeping within the limitations of my background and educational skills, the intent is not to rewrite or try to change that which is already established by the various institutions as the truths of history, a task beyond my capabilities, but to ask the age old question one receives from a child when their curiosity is not satisfied. The why and how in the hope that there may be others who have asked the same questions and have yet to find answers to the 'Why' which is inevitably followed by the 'How' and the 'When'? My aim will be to question and generally comment on those areas that appear to have left many important questions unanswered.

For example, the believe that man was ignorant of the true Astronomical workings of the Universe until the discovery of the telescope in the 17th century[2] is belied by what is now known of the early ancient civilization of China, South America, Sumeria and Egypt. Yet,

---

1   *New Jerusalem Bible. Ecclesiastics: 21-24.*
2   *Galilei Galilo. (1564-1642 Italian Astronomer, Mathematician and Physicist It has been the long held belief that Galileo invented the telescope, which is not the case. The Telescope was invented in the Netherlands in 1608, but improved upon by Galileo who applied it to Astronomy and his discovery of the heliocentric system regards the rotation of the Planets.*

when we read of the extensive knowledge known to the ancient civilizations, especially that of Egypt, a different picture emerges of a civilization whose political and religious philosophy was based upon the movement of the heavenly bodies. We take for granted this sea of astronomical knowledge known to these ancient civilizations. But the experts have never answered the 'how' and the 'when'. Nonetheless, there are those who have ventured into this dormant world in their search for answers to the many enigmas.

This is best illustrated in the work of Schwaller de Lubicz in his writings on ancient Egypt in which he states. "Before the "Greek miracle" there is indeed a very long period with a civilization possessing an elevated science on which the entire Mediterranean region has drawn. --- It is not the world in general that began six thousand years ago, but the historical Pharaonic Egypt, which begins toward the year 4240 BC, the date at which the establishment of its calendar and system of Sothic cycles can be placed---.[1] Even this conclusion reached by this eminent scholar may not be true, perhaps in the case of the calendar, but questionable regards the longevity of Egypt. There is sufficient evidence to suggest that the Egyptian civilization exceeded 40,000 years.[2]

One has to speculate and wonder on the vagaries of mans progress down through the ages and ask the question," what if". What if this sea of astronomical and mathematical knowledge held by the Egyptians transcended time in its purest form, would mankind have progressed at a much faster rate, instead of receding into an age of darkness and ignorance? It was left to the argumentative Greeks to completely cloud this area of knowledge. Scholars would rather refer to the Grecian period as an age of enlightenment, rather than an age of speculation and superstitious ignorance. The transference of knowledge suffered a major blow with the rise of the Roman Empire and later that of Christianity.

It was with the rise of the Roman Empire, the diffusion of Hellenistic knowledge was interrupted, which was further compounded by the rise of the Christen sect in the first century AD, followed by the autocratic Catholic Church in the fourth century AD.

It was this institution that created confusion in the fields of science by denying that what had been the belief from ancient times, and replaced it with a superstitious religious belief that has been a yoke to the mind of man. As the Roman Empire contributed nothing to the fields of science, except perhaps in the field of jurisprudence, we could say that mankind wallowed in a field of darkness from the 2nd century BC, until the 18th century AD.

It may also be true to say that had it not been for the religious reformation in the 16th century, which released the minds of our great thinkers, it is doubtful if we would have seen the technical, and scientific progress that catapulted man into space. The world no doubt would still be living in an age of intellectual stagnation dominated by the Church of Rome.

Concerning the flow of knowledge, it has been remarked by a dear friend of mine that. "One has to look at the history of Europe and the peoples of European decent. It is a history of

1   *Ibid*
2   *Lubicz R.A. Schwaller de Sacred Science The King of Pharaonic Egypt' Published by Inner Traditions International N.Y*

knowledge, science, technological progress, and a steady betterment of human life. It was not Christianity that made this possible, but the Hellenistic culture that made possible all the virtue, all the value, all goodness, all greatness, and all the wealth of knowledge that has ever existed on this earth. And no other culture that has remained untouched by the Greek culture has ever produced any science, technology, and therefore no wealth---only misery and starvation. Such was the case of Christianity until the reformation after which the human mind was once again permitted to come out of hiding and get to work".[1]

Denying the works of the great minds of Grecian intellects the Catholic Church condemned Europe to an age of intellectual deprivation. Those brave men of the middle Ages, who pitted their minds against the teaching of the Church, paid the ultimate price for their boldness.

In the field of Astronomical science the heliocentric theory developed by Nicolaus Copernicus[2] and the works of Galileo, the Church deemed that the Earth was the center of the world, and not the Sun, and those who would question this belief were condemned, as was the case of Galileo Galilei in 1633.[3] They evolved arguments to justify their reasons for expounding these views.

It was this level of thinking by those, who lacking the fundamental intellectual skills, fettered the minds of those who appreciated the wonders of the Universe.

Within the twentieth century, our knowledge of the more ancient civilizations is emerging and becoming somewhat clear. From what we know of these ancient people, it is obvious that as our Western culture was to Rome, as Rome was to Greece, as Greece was to the Egyptian civilization, each borrowing from the preceding culture.

In essence, the knowledge obtained by the Greeks from the Egyptians, was in turn co-opted by the Roman. From this, we can say that other then becoming a military power within the Mediterranean Basin, there is little to be attributed to the Romans by way of discovery or invention. As expressed by one author, "The limited medieval vision of humanity's history is no longer acceptable to-day"[4]

It was not until the scientific and intellectual development of the 17th century fostered the belief in natural law and universal order and confidence in human reason that spread to influence the 18th century society which resulted in a natural and scientific approach to religious, social, political, and economic issues which promoted a secular view of the world.[5]

The views and hypothesis propounded by the 18th century historians obviously lacked sufficient knowledge of the Far East and Near Eastern civilizations to allow them the means

---

1   *Seda Josef PHD PE This opinion was expressed by my friend Josef Seda when discussing the dissemination of knowledge across the Western civilization.*

2   *Nicolaus Copernicus, born February 1473 in Poland, died May 1543. Copernicus concluded that the Planets moved in a uniformed motion around the Sun which was stationary at the centre of the planetary system; therefore the Earth was not the centre of the Universe.*

3   *Galileo*

4   *Schaller de Lubicz R A' Sacred Science' 'The King of Pharaonic Theocracy'*

5   *Age of Enlightenment Encyclopaedia*

of rendering true opinions regarding the extensive field of knowledge that is now attribute to these ancient people. The perplexity created in one's mind when reading the works of these historians and scholars leave a myriad of unanswered questions. Yet, there are those in the academic world who despite the overwhelming evidence refuse to acknowledge the age and greatness of Egypt. This may perhaps be due to their religious upbringing and the mistaken belief in their intellectual pre-eminence in the world of academia. It could also be attributed to their ignorance and belief in their superiority that developed during the colonial expansion of the Anglo Saxon in the eighteen century.

There was no Greek miracle in learning. In fact there is every reason to believe that the Greek people were in a sense ignorant of anything but the basics of life, which was controlled by a multiplicity of Gods who controlled every facet of their lives. However, in their childhood ignorance they endeavored to unravel the mysteries inherited from the Egyptian culture.

We speak of the Egyptian culture in the thousands of years, and the Greeks in the hundred's. The earliest Greek writing attributed to Hesiod[1] who composed the 'Theogony' in the eight century B.C and was a contemporary of the Greek poet Homer [2]r is the furthest we can delve into early Greek writing.

What is evident is that the knowledge resided in Egypt. What is also apparent as one reads the early Greek writing is that they lacked the necessary intellectual skills to understand the knowledge available. However, there is no doubt that a level of astronomical existed in the days of Hesiod as we read in his 'Works and Days' where he makes reference to the stars Sirius[3] the Pleiades[4], Orion[5], and the star Arcturus.[6]

It would appear that our modern day scholars find it extremely difficult to accept the ancient cultures of Sumeria and Egypt as intellectually superior to Greece or Rome, viewing these cultures as being barbaric and ignorant, much like the British who looked upon the peoples of the colonies as barbaric and ignorant. In reality the ancient cultures of Sumeria and Egypt knowledge of the Universe and the Astronomical workings of the Solar systems was far in advance of anything that was known in the seats of learning in Europe until the 20th century.

The superstitious belief of the Church was the criteria for the 18th century scholars. Obviously they were more intent on attributing all scientific discoveries to the Greek and Roman cultures rather than to the Egyptians. Whereas, this opinion is far from the truth dispute the many claims of academia. They were In fact a superstitious lot who when not in battle with other and those adjoining cultures produced a few who grabbled with the truths that were already known

---

1   Hesiod. Greek poet of the eight century B.C. Composed the 'Theogony of the Gods' and 'Works and Days'
2   Greek poet of the eight century B.C. composed the 'Iliad' and the 'Odyssey', which were based upon the Trojan Wars' and the destruction of the city of Troy.
3   Sirius is a binary star in the constellation Canis Major and is the brightest star in the night sky.
4   Pleiades or Plough In Greek mythology the seven daughters of the God Titan Atlas/
5   Orion One of the most conspicuous constellations
6   Arcturus One of the brightest stars in the night sky

to the Egyptians for many thousands of years. What followed down through the centuries was continuous turmoil of war and conquest by the Roman armies.

It's preposterous to think that the turmoil we see in our society has always been the way of life. If we accept this hypothesis, we reduce ourselves to the level of animalistic predators. However, if we believe that the human family has a special function to perform, believing ourselves to being of superior intelligence, it follows that our function and responsibility is of a higher order.

Was there a time in the history of the human race when there may have existed civilizations that believed they had a close personal relationship with what they considered to be their God, devoid of the fear of retribution? A relationship fostered on love and trust, not only for their fellow human beings, but for all created life out of the love for their creator. However, due to man's propensity to fear the shadows of life and inclination to evil, the existence of such a society or culture it would be difficult for twentieth century man to accept such a hypothesis.

Humanity has the capacity to love and protect. However, as its mind has been distorted by religious beliefs that has fostered hate, bigotry and intolerance, all attributes that have been the principal cause of wars and killings over the centuries. It's only natural that we think it inconceivable that such a civilization could have existed on this planet.

And yet down through recorded history there have been men and woman who divorced them from the mainstream of life, to live singly or in religious communities devoting them to prayer and good works. These special people created a microcosm of the society of which we speak and by discipline and prayer aspired to this union with their creator.

That a civilization, isolated by its location, developed a society of balance and harmony may not be as far-fetched as one would imagine. There is no valid reason to doubt that this close spiritual relationship may have been a reality that existed in former times between the creator, created and nature. This purity of spirit that man believed to be his inheritance can be clearly discerned when reading the Rig-Veda[1], the most ancient sacred religious writings to come out of the Indian Continent.

Having this knowledge leads to the question. Where did it all start? Has this always been the way of the world or was there a time when the human family tolerated each other's presence on this planet, living in an environment of peace and relative harmony with a common belief in a universal creator or God. The myths and legends of old indicate such a time of spiritual religious harmony may have existed in the life of man.

What events occurred that brought on this change in mans relationship to each other? Where and by whom did this intolerance and bigotry first manifest itself whereby people and governments would kill and persecute those who were not of their religious or political beliefs, but most importantly why? How far back in history does one travel to address these questions

---

1   *Rig Veda. A collection of sacred hymns composed in archaic Sanskrit of ancient India, probably 1400 B.C., Translated by Ralph T H Griffith Published by the Book of the Month Club NY*

or would this prove an impossible task? Perhaps the answers are to be found much nearer to our own times rather than in the ancient past.

To find the answers to these questions and others it will be necessary to look for beliefs and religious practices that tended to segment and creates divisions among people and cultures. This search will not only apply to religion but to all other aspects of history that shaped our way of thinking and relationship with those not of our culture or religious beliefs.

We will go back in time to those religions that saw the demise of the Roman Empire and the people who played a major role in the events that were to follow its disintegration and shape our Western culture. But before we go along this road of inquiry it may prove beneficial to look a little further back in time to the religions and cultures that shaped our Western civilization and to a large extent, of the world.

One could become extremely dissatisfied in searching to find the purpose of life and its meaning, creating an aura of fear of the unknown. It is this fear that has driven the human family to the excesses of destruction that has been the hallmark of humanity for the last three thousand years. Life was created to be enjoyed in harmony with the gifts of nature that has been humanity's inheritance.

This has not been the case, as proven by events in today's society and those of the recent past. When our western culture blindly accepted Christianity it reduces humanity to a position analogous to a beast of burden, existing in a vacuum, devoid of will and reason. By submissively accepting without question the doctrines of this establishment meant we limit the scope of our minds by looking at what is at our feet instead of gazing to the horizon.

As children we were taught of a period in the life of humanity when this mystical 'Garden of Eden', we read and hear so much about in our religious teachings, a reality, not in a religious sense, but a way of life that only exists in the memory of man. Or was this belief a concoction of the religious institutions as a means of deluding humanity into the idea of a physical life after death, supposedly in the presence of a supreme godhead.

Personally, I believe that this planet we call home was the original Garden of Eden in its entirety. Not in the idyllic sense as advocated by the Church and religious institutions, but an existence in which humanity was just another species competing to survive among its competitors. There was no evil, no sin as propounded by the Church,

Believing in such an idyllic environment tends to warp one's view of life, as nature itself presents a different picture that is at variance with our idealistic religious view. There is no doubt; there exists a unique balance and harmony in the Universe to which humanity should pay more attention for its common good. It's also beyond question that within this harmonious environment there is a subtle energy force that controls the intricate workings of the Universe. This force has been recognized by the most primitive of cultures and transcends all religious beliefs known to humanity. All life on this planet is encompassed with this life form, and upon death, the energy of the body return to its source.

Having been weaned away from the truths of nature by the religious taboos, of Christianity modern societies live in ignorance of these forces, failing to recognize the importance they have on our existence. Nevertheless, in some mysterious manner there are moments when the senses catch a glimpse of this presence, resulting in a surge of emotional feeling that momentarily overwhelms the body, only to disappear leaving a sense of unexplainable loss. Those in love momentarily experience feelings of this nature.

It's been the belief of many ancient cultures that this present life is transitory. That beyond this life there is another purpose; not necessarily, as proscribed by our religious institutions, but of a more subtle nature. This can be detected, especially in the writings of the ancient cultures of India and Egypt.

However, despite the spiritual teachings of the ancients, with the exception for the urge for self destruction [1] the behavioral pattern of the human family is no more different from those species in nature that are interdependent on each other for their survival.

In this context, the human family, especially those of our Western civilization, having no major predators, except themselves, have spread across this planet like some parasitic fungus, creating a path of environmental destruction. Whereas all other life forms take only that which is necessary for their survival, man's propensity to pollute, kill and destroy for the sake of destroying, is the hallmark of his species.

This outstanding characteristic will eventually lead to the poisoning of the natural environment and a slow disintegration in his manner of living and way of life. Recognizing that humanity has lived on this planet for millions of years and will continue to do so, it will survive its best efforts at self-destruction, but at what cost?

The forces that govern the Universe and this planet belie the idea of a 'Garden of Eden' as envisaged by the religious institutions. This carrot of expectancy is the umbilical cord that holds the allegiance of people to the various religious cults. But within this flux of Universal change there have been societies in recent memory who have experienced this ideal way of life within the natural order until the disruption of their society by our Western culture. There are also those cultures of the ancient past, who suffered sudden cataclysmic upheavals that destroyed their cultures,

---

1   *Lemming. A species of mouse like rodents, who when they undergo a population explosion, are said to commit mass suicide.*

Chapter 3

One does not have to reach too far back in time to catch a glimpse of pristine cultures that were unspoiled until the arrival of the Europeans. Among the many we can count the peoples of South America and the Aborigine of Australia. These people lived in relative harmony until the arrival of the Europeans, which has led to the destruction of their culture and way of life.

There are those who maintain that with the arrival of the European and Christianity, the souls of these innocent people were saved from damnation may dispute this view. How can person who had no concept of sin be guilty and subject to damnation for what to them was a natural way of life. However, the Christian conviction that it was more important to save the soul than the body was the criteria used to justify the barbarity inflicted upon these innocent people. How could the Church who professes to be men of God find justification for such barbaric behavior?

The poverty and extreme living conditions under which these people labor today are the scars that remain of this forced conversion carried out by the Catholic Church. This forced conversion to Christianity led to a life of slavery, superstition and poverty that exists today. As was expressed by the Mexican revolutionary leader Pancho Villa when speaking on the Church's role in Mexico stated that, "They (The Catholic Church) thrust on us the greatest superstition the world has ever known. They (the Priest) ought to be killed for that alone."[1]

Despite all the wonderful accomplishments claimed by man, the ills that plague mankind have not been eradicated or diminished; in fact they are greater today than ever in the past. We see this on the Continent of Africa among those nations who gained their independence from their colonial masters. These nations are beleaguered with wars and revolutions resulting in poverty, hunger, and disease. [2] Conditions of this nature are being experienced across the continent of Africa and are unique to our time.

Scholars contend that no other civilization has made such rapid advances as modern man has in the last two hundred years, Believing that such technological achievements have never

---

1   Tompkins. Peter 'Mysteries of the Mexican Pyramids" Published by Harper & Row NY Pancho Villa the Mexican Generals response to the American Consul who questioned his expulsion of Spanish nationals from his territory.

2   Among these nations are the Republic of the Congo, Liberia, Ivory Coast, Ghana, Nigeria, Zimbabwe, Burundi, are but a few who are experiencing economic and political turmoil.

before been accomplished during man's existence on this Planet, maintain that the lifestyle of our Western civilization has reaped the benefits.

Outwardly, the statement may appear to have some truth, if one is possessed of a narrow view of life. However, when we delve into the ancient past, there are questions that today, with all the advances made in science and technology, modern man has yet to find answers. The excessive amount of time and resources spent by these learned scholars in trying to unravel the mysteries of the Universe would be put to better use in trying to solve the problems that beset mankind.

Likewise, those scholars who translate the works of the ancient historians that allow an insight into a world that would remain closed were it not for their efforts. For those who enjoy reading ancient history, their work is of extreme importance. It's this small group of people whose main occupation is an interest in the ancient past who are totally dependent upon the scholars who devote their lives to translating the works of the ancient historians.[1]

Although doubts may appear to exist they are more inclined to rely on conjecture rather than facts that would give credence to their finds For example, a comparison can be drawn between the teachings of the Christian Church whose doctrines have been developed down through the ages, and that of the Communist party of Russia. In both cases the manipulation of history, or what is purported to be history, conditioned the minds of people in so far as they became willing subjects to the will of the Church or State as the case maybe. This process of indoctrination, which began at a very early age, subverted the truths of history in so far that black became white and white became black depending upon the political climate at that particular time.

Within the Church through the initiatory process of Sin, Baptism, Confession, Forgiveness and Redemption, the individual is tied to the Church from the moment of birth to his/her death. Today this is not so much a problem, as one can choose one's religious affiliation without fear of recrimination. However, during the Middle Ages when the power of the Church was at its height, any deviation from Church Doctrine was noted and reported and should the individual not conform, punishment was swift and severe.

Using the same principals, it would appear that those who developed Communism incorporated the methods of the early Church on which to base their doctrine of submission. As with the Church, adherents of Communism were subject to the Party and monitored by the membership for any signs of deviation from established political doctrine. Should signs of an anti-social behavioral pattern be detected and appeared directed against the State, the result was the loss of party membership and in some cases imprisonment. In the majority of cases Party Commissioners, who were responsible for political correctness, carried out the task of monitoring party members. This process was made possible with the assistance of the general public, who participated by reporting their neighbors to the authorities should they detect any form of anomaly in their behavior.

---

1   *Michael Grant in his forward to Robert Grave's translation of the" Twelve Caesars". By Suetonius The Roman Historian*

One must not assume that my views are meant as an endorsement for the idea of Communistic ideology introduced into Russia as the result of the Russian Revolution in 1917.[1] Far from it, however, one has to admit that the idea had its merits during the early emancipation of the Russian people. Any political system that would free people from a life of poverty and serfdom, that was the common lot of the Russian people, was a welcome change from a life that was less than that of an animal. The idea of communal living must not be confused with the form of Socialistic Communism that evolved in Russia, in which one became a slave to the State rather than a free individual in a community.

Communal living, in which all goods and possessions are held in common, was not a new concept as this system was prevalent in Palestine during the first century BC and the first century AD.[2] This form of lifestyle, whereby all goods and possessions were held in common was a system adopted by the early Christian sect. Evidence of this can be found in the Christian New Testament Acts of the Apostles.[3] It's quite possible; the practice was adapted by the early Christians from a religious sect known as the Essenes who lived in Judah at the time of Christ.

There are communities in to-day's society who successfully practice this form of communal life style, and have done so for a considerable number of years. Here in North America there are those who have formed farming communities, with each community sharing and holding everything in common.

One such group of people, the Hutterian Brethren of North America, a body of Christians known as Anabaptists originated in Europe, practices a strict form of Communism based on religious principals. This particular group of people, around 20,000 are said to be the only group who practices this way of life.

Founded in Moravia by Jacob Hutter, they adapted the principle of common ownership as was practiced by the early Christians. Being persecuted by the Church of Rome, their leader Jakob Hutter was burnt alive as a heretic in Innsbruck, Austria in 1536 by the Roman Church; a most horrible death.

From this and many other cases of a similar nature, it is obvious that it was dangerous to practice a pure form of Christianity or oppose any doctrine of the Church.

The religious leaders of this movement, whose radical views placed them in opposition to Church doctrine, were peace loving and moderate in their views. Nevertheless, like all other religious reformers of the sixteen-century, 'they hoped for religious, social and economic reforms

---

1   *Russian revolution of 1917*

2   *The religious community known as the Essenes who lived in Palestine at the time of Christ. See Flavius Josephus. 'The Jewish Wars' Translated by William Whiston A M Published by Ward Lock and Company London*

3   *Acts of the Apostles. 4: 32-35. 'The whole group of believers were united, heart and soul; no one claimed for his own use anything that he had, as every thing was held in common. None of the members was ever in want, all of those who owned land or houses would sell them, and bring the money from them, to present to the apostles; it was then distributed to any member who might be in need.' The New Jerusalem Bible*

and the separation of Church and State. In their beliefs great stress was placed upon individual conscience and private inspiration. Perhaps their most outstanding characteristic and most influential belief was their concept of a church as a voluntary association of believers.[1] In the early days of the Church those who would question the authority of the Church suffered the severest of punishment, but now that the Church has lost its authority they have reversed their policy and are more conciliatory towards those who oppose their authoritarian rule.

In the Catholic Church, the process of monitoring the behavior of the congregation was the function of the Priest with the help of Church Members. Having firsthand knowledge of the system I can truthfully attest to this statement.

For us children there were occasions when other activities were more attractive than going to Church on Sunday. But by some strange coincidence, the Parish Priest would call to the house on the Monday morning and inquire why we had not been to Church. How he detected our absence was always a mystery. But as we had been taught that we were at all times under the scrutiny of our Guardian Angel, (who was our protector): and the ever-watchful eye of God. The fear engendered by this knowledge added some spice of adventure to our lives but it was not without cost. There was always the obstacle of confession and the displeasure of our parents.

In the simplicity of our young minds, we believed that the Priest was in direct communication with our Guardian Angel or God as there was no other way by which he could have known of our absence. This belief controlled our everyday activities, always we lived in the fear of offending God by committing some sin. There were many occasions when I went to bed trembling with fear thinking that I had inadvertently committed some sin during the day and should I die in my sleep, go straight to hell. One's allegiance to the Church was not fostered through love, but fear of everlasting punishment. It was not until many years later we found the priest had his lines of information well established among our school friends that enabled him to keep a close watch on our activities.

---

1   *Columbia. New Illustrated Encyclopaedia*

Chapter 4

That we should in later years come to doubt and question our religious beliefs would come as no surprise. To those who were strong in their faith, having this knowledge presented no problems. But to those who resented being manipulated by this religious system, at times resulted in a complete rejection of the religious beliefs as taught by the Church.

However, the rejection of Church doctrine did not necessarily result in total rejection of the belief in a supreme power or energy force that is obviously permeates all that exists within this Universe; a force that maintains and controls all life; and is the evolutionary force from which all life emanates. This force is not of a tangible nature, which can be grasped by the hand and observed; it's like one is observing a rose or the beauty of nature. 'He who sees that all work, everywhere, is only the work of nature, and that the Spirit watches this work-he sees the truth'.[1]

To become aware of its presence one has to rely on the psyche. As it is written in the Bhagavad-Gita,[2] "I am the one source of all; the evolution of all comes from me. I am the soul that dwells in the heart of all things. I am the beginning, the middle, and the end of all that lives. They say that the power of the senses is great. But greater than the senses is the mind. Greater than the mind is reason; and greater than reason is the spirit in man and in all."[3]

As the mind will see what it wishes to see, and the ears what they wish to hear; so it is with the senses when at rest, they become aware of a power beyond understanding. There are those who say that this energy force is intangible "remote and unknowable" [4] Yet if one allows the mind to rest in silence, it will be realized that this force permeates all life form. Though it is unknown in the sense of being definable, it can be seen and recognized in the workings of nature: it affects every aspect of life on this planet and by inference within the universe; be capable of, under certain conditions, be experienced by the senses. However, the Planet we inhabit is surrounded with invariable sound waves of every description that must have an adverse effect upon the human psychic and in general that of all life forms.

---

1   *Ibid*
2   *Bhagvad Gita The Song of God A dialogue between the warrior Arjuna and Krishna, the Lord of the soul on the battlefield of life.*
3   *Bhagavad-Gita. Chap's 3. 42. & 10. 8 & 20. Translated by Juan Mascaro. Published by Penguin Classics.*
4   *Philo of Alexandria 15 BC-AD 50 Jewish Historian Excerpts from Cromptons Interactive Encyclopaedia*

There are many individuals from diverse religions and cultures who have devoted their lives in search for this "remote and unknowable" force the ultimate goal being the union of the conscience soul to that which they refer to as "a living Absolute."[1]

Admittedly, for one to attain a level of contemplative consciousness through a process of spiritual exercises would be extremely difficult in to-day's environment. Humanity no longer enjoys an environment of peace and serenity that in times past was conducive to a life of spiritual contemplation. For those who have attained this union, we can only imagine the feelings of excitement, fear, and apprehension created in the mind at the initial encounter with this force. The joy and quietness experienced by these special souls would come with familiarity and training of the mind. But to attain this goal it was necessary they reduce this energy force to the level of understanding acceptable to the religious establishment and needs of society. Therefore endowing this force with the attributes of humanity, made it possible to metamorphosis the intangible into tangible.

Thus by defining and quantifying this presence, the senses can now discern matter to which it can relate. So if the name God, Yahwah or Lord Krishna is ascribed to this force as a means of identification, it must be acknowledged that its presence is inclusive to humanity and not the sole property of any one race or religion. This was expressed by the Greek poet and religious thinker Xenophanes when he stated, "—if oxen or lions had hands, and if they could draw and fabricate as do men, the oxen would depict the gods like oxen, and the horses would depict the gods like horses; they would present them with bodies according to their own form".[2]

It therefore follows that man, out of necessity must have a God in his own likeness. Such has been the case since time immemorial. This energy force that sustains the human family has been given human characteristics in order to satisfy mans need for a god.

Now that this invisible force has been defined and quantified, man can converse with this power, to which he refers to as God or as those of the Indian continent would refer to as the Lord Krishna.[3] Therefore, by extension, attributes all things, all beginnings to a God, to whom he can identify by clothing him in flesh and blood; thereby reducing this energy force to the level of humanity. Having reached this stage of his metaphysical development, it would be only natural, as a means of power and control to become the intermediary in voicing the thoughts of God to his fellow men. This belief engendered in the consciousness of the human family has deprived them of their spiritual inheritance.

It is only through ignorance, and fear of the unknown that compelled man to embody this energy force with substance and give it form. As this idea evolved it became a means of controlling cultures and societies, by giving power to an elite segment of society, whose purpose

1   Underhill. Evelyn 'Mysticism' Published by New American Library
2   Xenophenes (560 B.C-478 B.C Greek poet and religious thinker Taken from 'Sacred Science' the King of Pharaonic Theocracy by R.A. Schwaller de Lubicz Published by Inner Traditions International NY
3   Bhagavad-Gita Translation and Commentary by Maharishi Mahesh Yogi Published by the Penguin Group

was the manipulation of the minds of humanity. This idea engendered in the consciousness of people has allowed the mind to be imprisoned in an envelope aura of superstition and fear.

Among the many Pagan cults and religious sects existing during the latter stages of the Roman Empire the religious sect known to us as Gnostics were to be the rivals of the new Christian sect for the minds of the people. In the early days the duty of keeping their congregation true to Church doctrines was generally the responsibility of the local Bishops. This was to change in the early middle Ages when a tribunal was established for the suppression of heresy, which was then becoming a major problem in Europe.

Although initially controlled by the Bishops, this system was to change when Pope Gregory 1X[1] formally established the Papal Inquisition[2] that was to become the scourge of Europe during the middle Ages.

It was this institution, which brought so much pain and suffering upon those who questioned or deviated from the doctrines of the established Church. In their efforts to suppress any form of criticism or deviation regarding these doctrines, this institution was formed in order to defend the Church against what the authorities considered a mortal danger[3] from those who had the temerity to question and exercise their right to reject these doctrines, which they found consciously objectionable. Despite the death of thousands and the total ruin of many more during the life of this organization, its failure to stem the tide of dissent is evident by the success of the divergent religions within today's society.

However, the instruments of torture may have been removed, and the prisons closed, but the work of this organization continues under a different name. Now known as the Holy Office, it continues defending the Church doctrines, as is well demonstrated by the silence imposed upon those theologians who would question its teachings.

One has a sense of revulsion when reading the Church Authorities justification for their actions during this dark period, when they state. 'The justice dispensed by the Inquisition was comparable to the civil courts of the time the defendant was denied council and cruel tortures were often used to extort confessions.' Sentences of death by being burnt at the stake was the rule rather than the exception, though the Church would have historians believe otherwise, accusing them of being prejudiced should they disagree with the Church's account of this period. Asserting that, "There were many examples of justice, mercy and gentleness on the part of some of the inquisitors." An example of the Church's hypocrisy is clearly evident when they state, 'The principal of the Inquisition may be justified on the grounds that the Church was thereby defending against what she viewed as mortal danger. The cruelties and injustices which sometimes resulted from the application of the principal reflects upon the mentality of the age and are quite irrelevant to the validity of the Church's

---

1   *Pope Gregory 1X. 1227-1241.*

2   *Founded by Pope Gregory 1X in 1233 to intensive the crusade against the Albigenses also known as the Cathari, a religious movement located in the South of France.*

3   *The Catholic Dictionary.*

dogmatic teaching'[1] For those who would defend the actions of the Church authorities in this matter are as guilty as those who perpetrated these crimes in the name of God. How could any organization professing to be God's representative invoke his name and make him a partner to such heinous crimes.

Whether it is the death of one person, or a million, is of equal weight in the eyes of the Creator. The killing of even one human being in defense of Church doctrines can never be justified for whatever reason, however laudable. What fear was it that drove the Church to such draconian measures in order to protect its doctrines is beyond understanding? It cannot be that they were protecting the Word of God, who is viewed as God of love, being all powerful and man's protector, who is by extension beyond the need of man's protection.

It is also illogical to suggest that they were protecting the doctrine of their founder Jesus Christ, whose doctrine was one of love and compassion. The doctrine of love and charity to one's neighbor would not justify the use of torture, murder and armies to impose this wonderful doctrine on people by force of arms.

However, if the doctrine were one of a lie, under these circumstances the use of suppressive measures would be justified to ensure that the lie remained unexposed. It is those doctrines, which are purported to be true that are open to question and needs defending.

---

1   *The Catholic Dictionary.*

Chapter 5

We are entering the twenty-first century, and those who fear that their religious/historical beliefs are in danger of attack, exert political pressure on Governments and Civil Authorities to prosecute those who would question what they purport to be the truth.

In the days of the Inquisition one's life was at stake and when lost, brought the matter to an end. To-day, those who would question or deny the beliefs of others may not lose their lives, but are exposed too much greater punishment by being tried in the civil courts, and if found guilty, deprived of their standing in the community or threatened with possible assassination as in the case of one author who offended the religion of Islam.[1]

However, in the majority of cases those who come into conflict with these religious groups generally suffer being deprived of their professional standing, but more importantly suffer character assassination and inevitably hounded by the authorities.[2] This constitutes what would amount to cruel and unjust punishment for having the temerity to question the doctrine of religious faiths or supposed historical truths.

Our view of Christianity has been fostered upon myth perpetrated and propagated by the Judo/Christian establishment. Over the years the doctrines invented have evolved to the point that facts and fiction have melded to obscure the truth. However, in regards to the Jewish Holy Books, which are fabricated from many ancient sources, were mainly concerned in establishing laws and codes by which people could survive in a hostile environment. [3] However, the development of Christianity from the fourth century AD onwards was directed towards loftier ambitions. For those few men of the early Church who saw fragmented religious communities spread around the Mediterranean Basin, (stretching from Italy to Jerusalem), it was an ideal opportunity to create another Empire to replace the one that was in the throes of disintegration.

The Christian New Testament, the foundation on which the Church of Rome was built is an amalgam of myths that may not be factually true and probably have no basis in fact.

---

1   *Salman Rustie (Check this out.)*

2   *A case which has drawn much attention in Canada concerns the trial of a school teacher, who despite being found not guilty by the courts; continued to be retried on the same charge by the authorities until he was found guilty. (This requires expanding in details).*

3   *The first five books of the Christian Bible, Genesis, Exodus, Leviticus, Numbers, and Deuteronomy*

What can be asserted with any degree of confidence is that in the early years of Church history the main actor's involved in the unfolding drama were actual people and not figments of someone's vivid imagination, which has often been the case in religious history. However the supernatural acts attributed to these people, are in all likelihood pure fiction, developed and propagated to enhance the reputation of the leading characters as a means of impressing the superstitious minds of the pagan communities within the Roman Empire.

It has been hypothesized that the actual events surrounding the life of Jesus were narrated in the New Testament is a form of hidden language, a code, known only to a chosen few, but believed to be miracles by the general public. [1]. However to attribute the formulation of this complex and sophisticated code to Jesus and his Apostles is difficult to accept in light of what is known of their background.

Considering the religious and political confrontations that were taking place between the Jews and the Romans during this period, it would be natural for the Jews to develop a code as a means of identification among their followers. A similar situation as one would find among the Royal Order of Freemasonry,[2] that when the occasion warrants can by the use of a certain sign, a grip, and a word, identifies themselves to fellow members.

This same principal would apply to the Essene religious sect who was prominent during this period. In this context there appears to be no valid reasons for disbelieving the theory as postulated by the author Barbara Theiring[3] and every reason why it should be accepted when viewed against the times in which the events occurred. However to develop this complex means for concealing the truth regarding the life of Jesus is at best conjectural.

It is a common belief that the coming of Christianity in the 1st century AD resulted in a massive surge of adherents to the new sect that was later to become the Christian Church.[4] This has been the perception fostered by the Church historians and the accepted view of the majority of Christians concerning the early days of the Church.

What tends to confuse matters is the use of the word 'Church' which defined a building, as we know it today. The impression given is of an evolving organization, spreading out over the Near East and Asia Minor establishing buildings as places of worship whose members were willing to sacrifice their lives for this new found belief, whereas in the early days they were actually isolated groups of people without any defined place of worship. Generally, their simple

---

1   *Thiering. Barbara. 'Jesus and the Riddle of the Deep Sea Scrolls.' Published by Doubleday Canada Limited*

2   *Although Freemasonry would have us believe their roots extend to the time of King Solomon, this is more wishful thinking than reality. The second assertion is that they found their beginning on the founding of the Knights Templars. This too is open to question, however, may bear some truth. What may be true is the resurgence of the old Templars traditions during the 18th century to be named the Order of the Temple.*

3   *Ibid.*

4   *The New Jerusalem Bible. Acts 2: 41.*

services were held in the homes of members, and quite willing, in the majority of cases, to deny or compromise their new faith if it meant saving their lives.[1]

In fact in the early years Christianity was just another disparate religious sect among many, each feeding from the other, developing their different Theologies, in trying to define the nature of God. In reality 'the early Christians were an ill defined and divided movement each group differing in the interpretation of the teachings of Jesus.'[2], 'In the three centuries before the reign of Constantine[3] it is harder to find anything resembling one mainstream church; instead of a mainstream, one finds many tributaries.'[4]

Nevertheless, within this amalgam of confused beliefs that abounded within the Roman Empire, there was a religion, organized and established, that was the foundation on which Christianity was built. It's to these people we have to turn if we are to have any understanding of our culture and the problems, which are now being experienced within our Western society.

What was to be a unifying church, in which people would experience peace and stability, became a church of dissension and division that has brought nothing but chaos and misery to the world and continues to do so to-day.

The numerous cults that formed people's religious beliefs between 100 BC and 400 AD, the Monotheistic religion of Judaism, was (at this period in history), the only cohesive religion within the Roman Empire: separate and unique in its beliefs and practices.. To some extent the Hebrew people were, unique in this stew of cultures and religious sects that abounded in the Middle East. However, Judaism was not immune from the religious turmoil that was sweeping Palestine. Within their own community there were differences of opinions regards the arrival of the Messiah. Among the many fractious elements was the religious sect of the Essenes, whose documents were recently discovered in the area of the Dead Sea,[5] the beliefs of the members of this body was to form the foundation for the early religious sect, who later came to be known as Christians.

To have some understanding of the events that led to the formation of the Christian Church, one must look at history objectively, completely free of prejudices. It is therefore, important we gain some knowledge of the events that occurred during the centuries leading up to the period, which involved the activities of Jesus and the Apostles. To achieve this aim we must go back to the time of the Patriarchs and Prophets as narrated in the Hebrew books

---

1   *Pliny the Younger (Caius Plinius Caecilius Secundus) AD 62-AD 113 Was Consul in Pontus-Bithynia 100 AD? Letter from Pliny the Younger to the Emperor Trajan about 112 AD seeking advice on the treatment of Christians Information taken from' The Antiquities of the Jews' by Flavius Josephus. Jewish historian 37?-100 AD. Translated by William Whiston M.A*

2   *Roland. Paul. 'Revelations. The Wisdom of the Ages.' Published by Carlton Books Limited London*

3   *Constantine the Great. 288-337 AD.*

4   *Layton. Bentley. 'The Gnostic Scriptures.' Doubleday N Y.*

5   *The Dead Sea Scrolls. First discovered in 1947 by a Bedouin shepherd It is the opinion of the experts that the documents found had been deposited by a Jewish sect which we know as the Essenes, a sect of Jewish ascetics who resided as a community at Qumran which was relatively close to where the documents were found*

of the Pentateuch,[1] and look at the history of Palestine and its peoples before the dawn of Christianity.

It has been said that the "more things change the more they stay the same."[2] This saying is as relevant today as it was three thousand years ago. When we read ancient history, the complaints of the parents and those in authority, they are largely the same we hear today. This situation not only applies to the political arena, but also to the religions in our Western culture. Some believe that the moral decline we see in our society is a harbinger to the world's destruction as foretold in the books of the Bible, both the Old and the New Testaments. But to accept this hypothesis on divine intervention in the affairs of man by some unseen god is to revert to an age of ignorance.

There are a number of sects and religions in our Western society who, supporting their predictions on the teaching of the Judo/Christian Bible, believing that the world will see a major clash of civilizations come the next millennium between the forces of good and evil.[3] With the rise and diffusion of Islam around the world there is every reason to accept this hypothesis as they like their Jewish cousins believe they will eventually rule the world.

Among these is the religious organization known, as Jehovah's Witnesses[4] believe this planet, will end in the next millennium as a result of a great battle that will be fought at a place called 'Armageddon.'[5] In this conflict the forces of good, assisted by the armies of heaven will be victorious over the 'beast and all the Kings of the earth and their armies'[6] which will herald in a new earthly paradise ruled by God and his saints.

Whether this coming battle will be one of mass destruction as envisaged by the various religious cults, or a battle for the minds of humanity is a point worth debating. That this coming battle may bring about a new age and a more balanced society may merit some consideration. Nevertheless, it is ironic that only those who are members of this organization will form the new society of saints with the privilege of participating in the new earthly paradise. Those who are not members or sinners will be cast into the fires of hell.[7] Not a very pleasant experience to look forward too by the majority of the world's population.

Members of this sect believe the Biblical prophecies contained in the Book of Revelation as the literal truth written by the hand of God for the benefit of mankind: their very existence is dependent upon these prophecies. For those who wish to believe in the reality of this prophecy, one is compelled to respect their religious aspirations and the power they hope to attain.

---

1   *Ibid*

2   *Unknown.*

3   *Calculated as occurring in 2028 AD, which will be the completion of the Astrological Age of Pisces and the beginning of the Age of Aquarius. Jehovah's Witnesses Also known as the International Bible*

4   *Students Association Protestant fundamentalist founded in U.S.A. about 1879 by Pastor C.T. Russell 1852-1916. And developed by Judge J.F. Rutherfor 1869-1942*

5   *New Jerusalem Bible. Revelations. 20: 1-15.*

6   *New Jerusalem Bible. Revelations. 19: 11-21.*

7   *New Jerusalem Bible Book of Revelation 19: 19-21*

In contrast to this belief of the total destruction of man, there is also the belief of the Jewish people who view this coming battle in a different light. They believe that this coming conflict will see the resurgence of the Jewish race, and the subjugation of all the worlds people to the Jewish nation. In this scenario Jerusalem will become the capitol of the world to which all nations will pay due homage. [1].

In their belief this coming battle will involve all major nations, they differ from the biblical texts found in the writings of the early prophets of the Pentateuch[2] that confines this coming conflict to Israel, and it's neighboring nations.[3] It's not until we read the prophecies of the prophet Isaiah (740 BC) that the idea of a world conflict emerges.[4]

In the prophecies of Amos,[5] the earliest known member of the Hebrew prophets, the message to Israel is more concerned with the moral behavior of the people and the lack of sound religion among the rich. His condemnation of corruption, social injustice self-indulgence and immorality, forms the main thrust of his message from God. Nowhere in his message do we find any reference to a world conflict that we see later on in biblical writings by those prophets who followed in his footsteps. His message was not one of earthly conflict between nations, but a form of chastisement from God on the Hebrew people for their sinfulness. When he speaks of 'this day of Yahwah,'[6] a time when God will enact his punishment on the Hebrew people He speaks of a day of gloom and darkness, a day of lamentation and mourning among the people of Israel, when they are driven into exile.

The Hebrew people's failure to keep the statutes, commandments and ordinances of God, as articulated by the prophets, will result in the nation being cursed and destroyed by its enemies. The form of punishment is graphically described in the Book of Deuteronomy where it says, that the siege will be carried out on their cities.

"During the siege and in the distress to which your enemies will reduce you, you will eat the fruit of your body, the flesh of those sons and daughters that Yahwah has given you. The tenderest and most fastidious among you will glower at his brother, even at the wife he most cherishes and at all the children that are left to him, grudging them a share in the flesh of those children of his that he is eating. The tenderest and most fastidious of woman among you will glower at the husband she cherishes, even at her son and daughter, and hide from them the afterbirth of her womb and the child she bears to eat them."[7]

---

1   *It is the belief of the Jewish people that from @Judaea will go forth destined to rule the world@ Tacitus, The Histories. The Jews Translated by Kenneth Wellesley Published by Penguin Books*

2   *Ibid*

3   *New Jerusalem Bible Book of Prophets Amos 5: 15. (783-743 BC)*

4   *Isaiah. 13: 1-6. 24: 21-23*

5   *Amos Hebrew Prophet. Preached in the Northern Kingdom of Israel during the reign of Jeroboam 11.793-753 BC*

6   *New Jerusalem Bible Amos 5: 18.-20. Zephaniaih 1: 14. Malachi 2: 17. Joel.1: 15. 2: 1. 10-11.*

7   *New Jerusalem Bible Book of Deuteronomy 28: 54-57.*

The option of a life of peace and prosperity should the people keep the commandments, or death and disaster should they fail in the observance of the Law is a choice given to the Hebrew people by Moses.

Whether this was a memory of an actual event from the historic past would be a matter of conjecture. As there is an element of truth in all legends, an event of this nature occurring is not impossible. If biblical narratives are to be believed, there were many occasions in the history of the Hebrew people that speak of dire famines,[1] which in some cases involved cannibalism.[2]

We tend to forget that these people were just as barbaric in the practice of their religion, as were those other cultures that occupied the regions of Palestine in the ancient past.

There are many recorded incidents, in which the Hebrew people sacrificed their children as a votive offering to the Gods,[3] (a subject of which we will speak of later). How long this practice continued is difficult to say, however, pagan worship and idolatry was common in the Palestine regions up to the time of King Josiah[4] who instituted religious reforms during his reign.[5] To say that it continued and for how long would be speculation.

There are however, references made by the prophet Ezekiel[6] to human sacrifice and idolatry continuing during in his lifetime. There was also a period in history when King Antiochus 1V[7] abolished all Hebrew Laws and reintroduced pagan worship into the Temple of Jerusalem.[8] Although it was of a short duration, except for a few who refused to adhere to the pagan rituals,[9] evidently the majority of Hebrew people conformed to the new laws.

Whether the Prophet Ezekiel was speaking of the past or present is difficult to determine, but it would be safe to assume that religious beliefs and rituals that had been practiced for generations and ingrained in a people's psyche would be difficult to eradicate within one generation.

When we compare the paganism found in Europe and the British Isles,[10] during the middle Ages, and the difficulties experienced by the Catholic Church in their efforts to eradicate these beliefs and practices, we have some idea of the depth these beliefs have on people and how much they control their lives.

1   *New Jerusalem Bible Genesis 12: 10-11. 26: 1-2. 2nd Samuel 21:1. Genesis 47: 4 47: 13-14 & 41: 25-32*

2   *New Jerusalem Bible Deuteronomy 28: 53-57. Leviticus 26: 29-30. +44-45. 2nd Kings 6: 24-31. &28-30*

3   *New Jerusalem Bible Exodus 13: 1-2, 12, 14-16. 22: 29-30. 34: 19-20. Leviticus 18: 21. 20: 2-5. Deuteronomy 12: 2-3, & 31. 1st Kings 10: 5-8. 16: 19, 32, 34. 2nd Kings 16: 3-4. 17: 10-12, &41. 21: 6. 2nd Chronicles 28: 1-4. 33: 6 Ezekiel 20: 25-31. 16: 20-21. Hosea 9: 3. Jeremiah 8: 30-31. 9: 5-6. 32: 35 52: 3. Micah.6: 8*

4   *King Josiah. 640-609 BC.*

5   *New Jerusalem Bible. 2nd Chronicles. 34: 3-7.*

6   *Ezekiel 592-570BC*

7   *King Antiochus Epiphanes 175-163 BC*

8   *New Jerusalem Bible 2nd Maccabees 6: 1-9*

9   *2nd Maccabees 6: 18-31. The Martyrdom of the Priest Eleazar during the persecution in the reign of King Antiochus*

10 *Frazer. J G D C L. LL.D. Litt. D 'The Magic Art and the Evolution of Kings 'A study in magic and religion' 3rd Edition Part 1 Vol. 11 Published by MacMillan and Company Limited London 1911*

Even today shadows of these age-old beliefs are still to be found in the villages and hamlets of the countryside, though modified to remove the more gruesome aspects of the age-old rituals.[1] Yet this message to the Hebrew people is not without hope for those who will be saved and restored to the land promised to their ancestors.

This theme of punishment, by near annihilation, dispersion among the nations, and eventual restoration is a theme that is consistent throughout the writings of the prophets. In fact the first reference is to be found in the Book of Leviticus[2] in very graphic in detail. It would be safe to assume that this theme was adapted and embellished by the early Prophets, especially the prophecies of Amos, whom the prophets Isaiah and Jeremiah[3] may have used as a reference in developing their ideas on a future apocalyptic battle.

As the restoration of the Hebrew people is contingent upon this coming battle, perhaps we should explore the origins of the idea of a world conflict between the forces of good and evil first. These references to a major battle, and the arrival a great leader or prophet would appear to be the basis on which later prophets developed the idea of a Messiah and a future world conflict. It could also be construed from their writings, that this coming battle would have the direct intervention of God. However, the idea of a major battle between the forces of good and evil cannot be supported by the writings of the Pentateuch.[4]

---

1   *Ibid*
2   *New Jerusalem Bible. Leviticus. 26: 14-46. 26: 30-33. 44-45.*
3   *New Jerusalem Bible. Books of the Prophets.*
4   *Ibid.*

Chapter 6

It is not until we read the works of the prophets, Isaiah and Jeremiah, that we detect a new development in the relationship between God and the Jewish people, especially in the writings of Isaiah.[1] Though the trends of his writings are much the same in tone as his predecessors, we see a new religious approach developing in which God will rule over the nations of the world as Priest/King.[2] Perhaps the writers of the Isaiah prophecies were influenced by the ancient Pharaonic theocracy of Egypt whose people believed that the Pharaoh "is a God because he is a Priest, but he is only a priest inasmuch as he is the son of the God".[3]

Reading the Bible is to a large extent dependent upon the individuals understanding of the text and the interpretation they place upon the wording. Whether scholar, King or pauper, each person approaches the works for their own reasons, some for spiritual comfort, while others search for historic knowledge. In all cases each will find whatever he/she is searching that will support their individual needs and religious beliefs.

This logic applies not only to the prophets of the ancient past but also to those who today study the Bible for their spiritual well-being each viewing it from different aspect, dependant on their religious upbringing. Our effort is centered on the question regarding the belief by some that the end of the world is imminent and how they came to acquire this belief. But what is this 'end of the world'? The expression is so loose that it defies logic. Are we to believe that the planet earth will disappear and all life or will all life on this planet be transformed.

One can appreciate the aspiration of those who hope for a better world away from the turmoil that is now prevalent within our society. This hope is more or less as valid as the hopes and aspirations of the people of ancient times who looked forward to a new world of peace and tranquility. It's not the words used that lead to misunderstanding on the part of those who are seeking knowledge, but the manner in which they are placed in context. Words wrongly used or placed tend to create a contentious environment, provoking arguments and controversy. In

---

1   *Isaiah,. Hebrew Prophet 765-? BC In 740 began his preaching during the reign of Kings Jotham Ahaz and Hezekiah.*

2   *New Jerusalem Bible. Isiah. 2: 1-5.*

3   *Lubicz R.A., Schwaller de 'Sacred Science the King of Pharaonic Theocracy Paragraph Concerning Theocracy Note A. Moret Du caractère religieux de la royantè pharaonique (Paris, 1902). Pp 320-321.*

developing a hypothesis on the reasons behind the belief regarding the eventual destruction of the world, many other questions arise, which if one does not exercise caution may create the wrong impression.

Nevertheless, we must accept the premise that the God depicted by the ancient writers of the Pentateuch is not the universal God that evolved from the writings of the prophets. In fact the God conjured up by the minds of the ancient writers was a vengeful and jealous God,[1] unique to the Hebrew people, to the exclusion of all others. Comparing the attributes of the God of the Pentateuch to the God that slowly emerges from the writings of the prophets, it would appear the ancient prophets "passed through a course of moral evolution"[2] whereby the image of the God of old seemed to be less jealous and more caring for his people. It was this image that was later adopted by the new religious Christian sect.

The Hebrew's expectation of a Priest/King/Messiah, as developed by the prophet Isaiah was probably based on the promise given by Moses when he said, 'God will raise up for you a prophet like myself from among yourself to him you must listen.'[3]

Perhaps this was alluding to the request made by Moses when he asked God to appoint a leader of the community, "so that the community of God may not be like sheep without a shepherd". God, in granting this request, instructed that Joshua be anointed by the priest Eleazar to become the leader of the community, sharing all authority with Moses.[4]

This was not a prophecy concerning the future but to address a need for a leader who would lead the community in a situation of war that was about to develop in the coming conflicts. This may have become the principal idea surrounding the prophecies concerning the Messiah/King/Savior as developed by the prophet Isaiah that was later repeated by succeeding prophets and adapted to suit the Christian Church.

The prophet Isaiah takes the hope of restoration of the Hebrew people to new heights when he speaks of a virtuous King who will be of the family tree of David.[5] His arrival will usher in a new era for the Hebrew people. The virtues or characteristics attributed to this King are such that it's easy to see why later generations looked forward to his coming with anticipation.

Obviously, his reference to the house of Jesse,[6] who was the father of King David, was not lost upon those who were conversant with the writings of the prophets, as we note by the writings of the prophet. We notice this in the writings of the prophet Jeremiah[7] that this future King whom Isaiah refers to as "a shoot springs from the stock of Jesse a scion thrusts from his

1   *Exodus. 22:20. 23: 13. Leviticus. 26:1-2. 27: 29.*

2   *Frazer. J.G. The Golden Bough A Study in Magic and Religion. Part 11 Taboo and the Peril of the Soul 3rd Edition. Published by MacMillan and Company Limited London 1911*

3   *New Jerusalem Bible. Deuteronomy. 18: 15-19.*

4   *New Jerusalem Bible. Numbers. 27: 17-23.*

5   *New Jerusalem Bible. Isaiah. 4: 2. 11: 1-10.*

6   *Jesse. Father of King David Purported to be the ancestor of Jesus Christ. See the Gospel of Matthew. 1: 1-16*

7   *Ibid*

roots. That day the root of Jesse shall stand as a signal to the people. It will be sought out by the nations and its home will be glorious."[1]

For those who made it a practice to study the Book of the prophets, it was the spark that kept alive the hope of the Jewish people. In their minds, the arrival of this Priest/King and the promise made by Moses, would, by association point to the coming Messiah.

Later this theme is taken up by Jeremiah who wrote "See the days are coming when I (God) will raise a virtuous Branch for David, who will reign as true King and be wise.[2] This is a cry of hope, not confined to any definite period in time; it could be today, tomorrow or any time in the future. We will see later on how this hope for the future became associated in the minds of people with a wide world conflict. The earliest known prophet, Amos, speaks of the day of 'Yahwah'; a day of darkness, 'without a single ray of light' when God will make the Sun go down at noon and darken the earth in broad daylight.[3] There is no mention of a Messiah or of a world conflict.

This will be a day when God's anger will manifest itself to punish the Hebrew people for the crimes they have committed against God. It's a prediction that first makes its appearance in the Book of Leviticus [4] and takes up the greater portion of the Books of the Prophets.

Perhaps those writers who compiled the Book of the Prophets built and expanded their prophecies based on these two sources; this may have been the case when the Book of Isaiah was written. From where did this belief of an impending world disaster develop and by whom, and for what reason?

A possible answer is found in the writings of Isaiah, one of the more renowned prophets found in the Bible. It's in the writings of Isaiah that we find the first reference to a world conflict directly involving God as the leader of the heavenly warriors. But, was Isaiah speaking of his times in the hope of a better future for the Hebrew people, or was he as some believe speaking of a time in the distant future? Again, this depends on the intentions and beliefs of those who would treat the Book of the prophets as a prophecy for the future. For those without hope it is good that they should have some means, some thread on which to hold on to that may lead them into a brighter to-morrow.

This coming battle, to which the Prophet Isaiah refers to as the 'Oracle on Babylon,' has been interpreted by many in various epochs in history, depending on their religious beliefs. Early Christian attributed the oracle to the fall of the Roman Empire during the 3rd century AD, whereas the religious sect known to us as the Jehovah Witnesses, believe this oracle refers to the fall of the Church of Rome in the next Millennium which they view as an evil organization.

The Hebrew people in the 1st century BC and early Christians of the 2nd century AD believed that the world was about to be destroyed by a major conflict between the forces of good and evil, it should come as no surprise: that this belief is prevalent within today's society.

1   Ibid
2   New Jerusalem Bible. Jeremiah. 23: 5. 33: 15-16.
3   New Jerusalem Bible. Amos. 5: 18-20. 8: 9-10.
4   Leviticus. 26: 14-46.

In fact, by some strange coincidence, the prophecies of old somehow appear to meet the needs of all those who suffer under various forms of oppression, whether it be yesterday, today or perhaps two thousand years from now.

The Oracles itself has all the earmarks of a major battle; whether this is to be an actual or a spiritual battle is difficult to determine. Again it is subject to one's interpretation.

In his discourse, Isaiah speaks of an oracle, in which he has seen future events concerning Israel, for he says,

"On a bare hill hoist a signal, sound the war cry. I on my part, issue orders to my sacred warriors. I summon my knights to serve my anger, listen to the din of kingdoms, of nations mustering. It is Yahwah Sabaoth marshalling the troops for battle. They come from a distant country from the far horizons to lay the whole earth waste. How!! For the day of Yahwah is near, bringing devastation from Shaddai That day, Yahwah will punish above, the armies of the sky, below the kings of the earth; they will be herded together, shut up in a dungeon, confined to a prison and after long years, punished. The moon will hide her face, the sun is ashamed, for Yahwah will be King on Mount Zion, in Jerusalem, and his glory will shine in the presence of his elders@.[1]

One can see in this description the account as described in the New Testament Book of Revelation, which more than likely based upon the prophecies contained in the Book of Isaiah and all the prophets that followed in his footsteps.

The prophecies of Isaiah have been the torch and beacon of hope for the Hebrew people down through the ages. They see in them old promises being fulfilled, when they will be restored to the land of their Fathers to become a great nation, ruling the world from the Temple of Jerusalem. They believe 'God will restore the judges of old, and then you (Jerusalem) will be called City of Integrity, Faithful City.[2] This promise of a new King/Messiah[3] will be their sustaining hope for the future, when it will be said: 'See, this is our God in whom we hoped for salvation.'[4] Therefore, it's understandable how people can, by being selective in their reading of the Books of the Prophets, see in it what they wish to see, and by doing so, misinterpret its true meaning.

---

1   *New Jerusalem Bible. Isaiah, 13: 1-6. 24: 21-23.*
2   *Isaiah. 1:26. 2: 2-5. 11:1-9*
3   *Isaiah. 9:1-7*
4   *Isaiah 24: 6-12.*

Chapter 7

There are numerous religious cults within to-day's society who are influenced by the religious texts of the Bible regarding the impending destruction of the world. Believing that this war is imminent, many have opted to leave this world by committing mass suicide,[1] rather than wait to see the outcome of this supposed religious conflict.

In this respect they are no different than the Jewish people of the Near East who fostered a similar belief at the dawn of Christianity, two thousand years ago. Because of this misconception, the eyes of humanity have been blinkered to the realities of the natural environment and surrounding Universe.

A common misconception shared by those professing the Christian faith pertains to the authorship of the Pentateuch.[2] As they believe it to be the inspired word of God, they are not unduly concerned regards who wrote it, or where: and since it is the word of God, these questions are of little concern. It therefore comes as a surprise for them to be told that modern study suggests its composition to be 'an amalgam of four documents issuing from four different places.' These studies have also revealed a 'variety of style, lack of sequence and repetitions in narrative that makes it impossible to ascribe the whole work to a single author.'

Progress in historical knowledge of other civilizations, and those of the Middle and Near East, shows that many of the laws, institutions, and moral codes found in the Jewish Pentateuch, were borrowed from more ancient peoples and were not indigenous to the Hebrew people. As a result of extensive studies, 'It is now beginning to appear that these sources are very ancient indeed.'

Archaeological progress and our growing knowledge of the history of neighboring civilizations in the Middle East have shown that many Pentateuch laws and institutions had

---

1   *Among the many cults who have resorted to mass suicide were those of a religious cult whose leader was Jim Jones. In 1978 at Jonestown Guyana 900 members of this cult committed suicide, while others may have been murdered. A similar incident occurred in 1995 in Switzerland and Canada where members of a religious cult known as the Order of the Solar Tradition committed mass suicide, and like the circumstances surrounding the suicides in Guyana, some of the members appeared to have been murdered. Widely discussed in all world wide media news outlets.*

2   *The first five Books of the Bible Genesis, Exodus, Leviticus, Numbers, and Deuteronomy*

their non-biblical counterparts long before the dates assigned to the 'documents'; they have shown that not a few Pentateuch narratives presuppose conditions different from and more primitive than those in which the 'Documents' are said to have been written.'[1]

Among these 'more primitive' ancient civilizations would be the advanced cultures of Egypt and Sumeria from whom those who compiled the Pentateuch may have 'borrowed' the greater part of their narrative.

Of these two most ancient cultures, the culture of Sumeria, may have had the greater influence in the compilation of the Pentateuch. The famous Code of Hammurabi [2] may well have influenced the Hebrew writers when developing the Mosaic Laws. There are valid grounds for believing the truth of this theory, as the story of Creation, the fall, and the Flood is found in the legends and myths of this most ancient civilization.[3]

Evidently, what some believe to be the inspired words of God were actually borrowed from more ancient pagan civilizations by the authors of the Pentateuch;[4] who correlated and compiled this information to reflect the religious views of the new religion of Judaism?

This criticism does not, nor is intended to impugn the historicity of Moses, (a subject that will be discussed later). Suffice to say; as there is an element of truth in all legends, we can be confident that Moses was an actual person in history. What is in question is the period in which he is purported to have lived. It must be said that the Bible makes interesting reading, but is it true?

It would be wonderful if scholars had had other historic literature that would support the claims of the Bible. But what is most extraordinary is that there is no mention of the Jewish people in ancient historical writings. Nowhere in the writings of Sumeria, Babylon, Greek or Egypt do we find any reference to the Jewish people. It is also most extraordinary that in an age of learning, no Jewish literature exists that could substantiate their claim to antiquity. What we learn of their culture is found in the first five books of the Pentateuch.

Notwithstanding the events that were to occur with the destruction of the temple, it is obvious that that Jewish people were not of the majority, but a fractious religious minority. If they were who they purport to be, why do we not find more extensive mention of the Jewish culture in the historic writings of the Greek, and Roman historians?

Herodotus, the Greek historian traveled extensively throughout the Middle East. In the course of his travels, he speaks of meeting many different cultures and people. Among the many were the people of Syria, and Phoenicia whom he said resided in Palestine, nowhere in his writings do we find a reference to the Jews or the country of Israel.

What better opportunity existed for a country to win renown than to be involved in a vast enterprise, one that would go down in the annuals of men's memory? The invasion of

1   *New Jerusalem Bible Introduction to the Pentateuch*
2   *King Hammurabi 1792-1750? BC Babylonian King whose code of Laws is one of the greatest legacies from the ancient past.*
3   *Epic of the King Gilgamesh of Uruk. 2500-1500 B C*
4   *Ibid*

Greece by the army of Xerxes would have been such an occasion.[1] Writing on the subject, Herodotus speaks of all those countries and people who were involved in this vast expedition. Of the armada of 1207 ships (Triremes), we are told that the "Phoenicians, with the Syrians of Palestine", furnished 300.[2]

To get around this lack of written records, the Jewish author, Flavius Josephus states, "we have not an innumerable multitude of books among us---but only twenty-two books, which contain the records of all the past times, which are justly believed to be divine: and of them five belong to Moses, which contain the laws, and the traditions of the origins of mankind till his death".[3]

Returning to the practice of borrowing from other religions and cultures to develop new philosophies and religions it would be naive of us to believe that this is of recent origin. History confirms this has been the practice in all ages and cultures. Therefore, Judaism is no exception; neither are the religions of Christianity nor Islam. In fact many offshoot religions within modern society had their beginnings from such a practice.

An example of this borrowing and adapting can be detected in all major religions around the world.[4] Most authorities confirm it and it is the common belief of the experts, that the idea of one God can be directly attributed to the religion of Judaism: from which Christianity and Islam borrowed, and adapted the principal of Monotheism on which to base their religious tenets. But even this hypothesis can be questioned in light of what is known of the Egyptian civilization.[5]

As all other religions in our Western society were developed on much the same principle, this practice of borrowing and adapting is not unique. Among those churches that have ascribed to this policy, the Church of the Latter Day Saints[6] would be an example.

As opposed to the belief in one God, there is Polytheism, which is a belief in many Gods as was later practiced in ancient Egypt, Greece, and Rome. But are these statements true? Perhaps in the case of Greece and Rome, whose people believed their every waking moment to be in the hands of the Gods, who controlled all their actions? However, can we make the same statement for the people of Egypt? The experts would have us believe that this is the case concerning the

---

1   Xerxes .484-430 BC, King of Persia, Invasion of Greece 480 BC

2   Herodotus 'The Histories' Book V11. Chap 86-92. Translated by George Rawlinson. Published by J.M.Dent & Sons. London

3   Josephus. Flavius 'The Works of Flavius Josephus' Against Apion. Book 1. Translated by William Whiston. A.M. Published by Ward, Lock& Co. London

4   Frazer. J.G. D.C.L. LL.D. Litt.D. 'The Golden Bough' a study in Magic and Religion. 3rd Edition. Vol 1-6. Published by MacMillan and Company Limited London 1911

5   Budge Wallis E A The Egyptian Book of the Dead Published by Dover Publications Inc N Y gives a clear indication regards the concept of there being only one God (Monotheism)

6   The Church of Jesus Christ of the Latter Day Saints founded in 1830 by Joseph Smith., Their believes is primarily based upon the Bible and the Book of Mormon. The Book of Mormon recounts the early history of people in America from 600 BC-420 AD.

religious beliefs of the Egyptians, attributing to them the worship of animals and a Pantheon of Gods like those found in the Greek and Roman cultures.

This may have been true of Egypt in the latter days of its empire, when its religion and culture may have degenerated into a period of superstition and religious myths through the influence of the Greek, and eventually the Roman cultures. But, was this true for the ancient past? Obviously not, as in the opinion of one eminent expert Egyptologist, "The dwellers in the Nile Valley, from the earliest times, knew and worshipped one God, nameless, incomprehensible, and eternal."[1]

The author goes on to state. "The unity of a supreme and self-existent being, his eternity, his almightiness, and external reproduction thereby as God; the immortality of the soul, completed by the dogma of punishments and rewards; such is the sublime and persistent base which, notwithstanding all deviations and all mythological embellishments, must secure for the beliefs of the ancient Egyptians a most honorable place among the religions of antiquity".[2]

It was the firm conviction of Dr. Brugsch that the Egyptians "believed in a self-existent God who was one being, who had created man, and who had endowed him with an immortal soul. The Egyptian religion is pure Monotheism, which manifested itself externally by a symbolic polytheism.[3] Clearly, "the evidence inscribed during a period of over four thousand years, ancient Egypt did not have a 'religion' as such; it was religion in its entirety".[4]

When one contrasts the attributes ascribed to the God of the Pentateuch, as seen through the eyes of the Hebrew people, and the God as described in the Pyramid Text,[5] of Egypt, the characteristic of both these entities are so divergent that they may be complete opposites as one would find in the Gnostic Scriptures.[6]

The beauty expressed in the Pyramid Texts far exceeds that which is found in the Pentateuch. While the latter epitomizes all that is evil in mankind, inducing allegiance through fear and intimidation, with the eventual hope of rewards, the Pyramid Texts describes beauty, harmony and balance associated with God. From this it can be acknowledged that over the years, Judaism, and its counterpart, Christianity, have been uneconomical with the truth. Both entities based their teaching on fear rather than piety.

---

1   Budge.E.A.Wallace, *The Egyptian Book of the Dead. Introduction. 'Ideas of God' Opinion attributed to Dr, Brugsch, de Rougè, and other eminent Egyptologists.*

2   As quoted from the *'Egyptian Book of the Dead'* by E.A.Wallis Budge Attributed to--**Études sur le Rìtuel Funèraire des Anciens Égyptiens (in Revue Archèologique),Paris,1860,p,72.**

3   Rouge. Emmanuel, vicomte de 1811-1872.French Egyptologist.,Égypte,PARIS, 1839, p245, col 1. Taken from the *'The Egyptian Book of the Dead'* Translated by E.A. Wallis Budge.

4   Lubicz. R.A. Schwaller de *'Sacred Science' the King of Pharaonic Theocracy Inner Traditions International*

5   Brugsch. Dr. Religion and Mythology. Pp96-99. Taken from the *'The Egyptian Book of the Dead'* Translated by E.A.Wallis Budge

6   The Gnostic Scriptures. Translation by Bentley Layton. Doubleday.

It can be clearly construed from the wording of the texts that the Egyptian people believed in 'One infinite and eternal God who was without a second'[1] Therefore, to attribute to the Hebrew people the development of a Monotheistic religion would be to deny all available evidence to the contrary.

This evidence can be found in the selected texts as translated by Dr. Brugsch[2] and quoted by E.A. Wallis Budge[3] in his translation of the Egyptian Book of the Dead. From these passages Mr. Budge selected the following to support the theory of the Egyptian's belief in One God, as described in the Pyramid Texts:

"God is one and alone, and none other exists with Him—God is the one who hath made all things—God is a spirit, a hidden spirit, the spirit of spirits, the great spirit of the Egyptians, the divine spirit—God is from the beginning, And he hath being from the beginning, He hath existed from old and was when nothing else had being. He existed when nothing else existed, and what existed He created after He had come into being. He is the Father of beginnings---God is the eternal One, He is eternal and infinite and endures forever and aye---God is hidden and no man knoweth His form. No man hath been able to seek out his likeness; He is hidden to God's and men, and He is a mystery unto his creatures. No man knoweth how to know Him—His name remaineth hidden; His name is a mystery unto His children. His names are innumerable, they are manifold and none knoweth their number—God is truth and liveth by truth and He feedeth thereon. He is the King of truth, and He hath stabilized the earth thereupon—God is life and through Him only man liveth. He giveth life to man, He breatheth the breath of life into his nostrils---God is father and mother, the father of fathers, the mother of mothers. He beggeth, but was never begotten; He produceth, but was never produced; He begat himself and produced Himself. He createth, but was never created; He is the maker of His own form, and the fashioner of His own body---God Himself is existence, He endureth without increase or diminution, He multiplieth Himself millions of times, and he is manifold in forms and in members—God hath made the Universe, and He hath created all that therein is ; He is the Creator of what is in this world, and of what was, of what is, and of what shall be. He is the Creator of the heavens, and of the Earth, and of the deep, and of the water, and of the mountains. God hath stretched out the heavens and founded the Earth—What His heart conceived straightaway came to pass, and when he hath spoken, it cometh to pass and endureth for ever---God is the father of the Gods; He fashioned men and formed the Gods---God is merciful unto those who reverence Him, and He heareth him who calleth upon Him. God knoweth him that acknowledgeth Him, He rewardeth him that serveth Him, and He protecteth him that followeth Him."[4]

---

1   *The Egyptian Book of the Dead Translated by E.A. Wallis Budge. Published by Dover Publications Inc N Y Introduction. Note 4. Le Panthèon Égyptien. Paris. 1881. P.4.*

2   *Ibid*

3   *Ibid*

4   *The Egyptian Book of the Dead Translated by E.A.Wallis Budge. Published by Dover Publications Inc N Y Note.1.Brugsch, Religion und Mythologie. P 96-99.*

In the Pyramid Texts we see a continuity of life unhindered by fear and intimidation by one's creator, a life to be lived in love and harmony, devoid of fear.

Can there be any doubt in the minds of scholars regarding the religious beliefs of the ancient Egyptian? Scholars may enter upon a quest from the podium of intellectual pursuit by schematically dissecting the word 'God' to find its origins. An exercise of this nature would be stimulating for the intellect, but of little value, as 'God' is not found in the intellect, but in the spiritual soul of man. It would be fundamentally wrong to hypothesis that Monotheism derived its beginning from Polytheism, as it would be to assert that Christianity had its origins, and developed from Communism.

Therefore, it's reasonable to suggest that the early writers were cognizant of Egyptian religious beliefs as well of those of Babylon and the neighboring countries. By adapting and modifying these beliefs into what is now the Pentateuch they used the name of God as a tool to justify their actions in their relationship with the neighboring tribes. One could rightfully say that the Jews invented themselves, along with their sacred books in order to authenticate their claim to antiquity.

When the characteristics of the God of the Pyramid Texts and the God of the Pentateuch are compared, there are no similarities. Whereas the God described in the Pyramid Text is a God of love, beauty, harmony, and balance, The God of the Pentateuch is jealous, demanding, and destructive. But why change the character of the God if it is not to create an aura of fear, which leads to the control of the mind.

Notwithstanding the views held to the contrary, there is nothing pleasant about a God who would advocate the murder and destruction of a whole community of people. It is written. 'Strike down Amalek. Do not spare him but kill man and woman, babe and suckling put all the people to the sword. [1] From this it is easy to see why the killing of the Palestinian people comes easy on the conscience of the Jewish people.

When he supposedly instructs the Hebrew people to kill 'all the male children, including the Mothers and those women who had slept with a man'[2] he demonstrates the same characteristics as the Gods who were revered by the surrounding tribes in their demands for human sacrifice. Using the name of God to instill fear and intimidation in the conquest of the surrounding tribes is a practice that is prevalent in to-day's society.

The God of the Pentateuch, or should we say the God of Moses, is on par with those gods found in the most primitive societies, who in the opinion of most experts, , were cruel and savage in their religious practices.

That the Hebrews believed in one God was not to their credit. If we are to take the bible literally, their religious practices and behavior towards other people were no different than those of other tribes living in the regions, perhaps even more barbaric A great deal of what is found

---

1   *The New Jerusalem Bible 1st Samuel. 15: 3, 9.*

2   *The New Jerusalem Bible Exdous.11:5-7,12. 13: 2, 13-16. 20: 3-6. 24-25. 34:19-20. Leviticus. 26: 16-45.*
     Deuteronomy. 7: 1-6. 20: 10-18. 28: 53-68 Numbers. 31: 17-18.

in the Pentateuch and the books of the Prophets, including the New Testament was probably, if not actually taken from the ritual religious texts of more ancient cultures and surrounding nations of whom the Hebrews were cognizant. This observation can also be attributed to the sayings of Jesus, as many of his sayings are similar to those found in more ancient texts.

In many ancient societies similar practices existed and were practiced through the auspices of the priests acting as God's representative. Invoking the name of god was a tool and a means of control in their demands for blood sacrifices from their subjects.

Notwithstanding the criticism which historians have leveled against the Egyptians for their polytheistic belief and supposed practice of animal worship,[1] nothing of such a barbaric nature, as is found in the Hebrew Pentateuch, has been found in Egyptian religious beliefs or practices in fact quite the contrary. The Egyptian people were the most devout of people in their way of life and religious practices.

People who had developed this barbaric behavior, as a means of expanding their authority over others through fear and intimidation, would by necessity develop a psychological hatred towards those who were not of their religious beliefs and by extension place little value on the life of those who were not of their faith or political persuasion.

The pages of history are strewn with innumerable incidents of this nature, including those of recent times that attest to this fact. Humanity has allowed its mind and conscience to be corrupted by this idea of a god who generated hate and bigotry while at the same time professing love and compassion for those who would follow his precepts.

The events as described in the Pentateuch, whether an amalgam of legends, myths or fiction, or the product of the imagination of the writers who compiled these religious books, for those who read and believe the teachings of the Pentateuch, the Book of the Prophets, and all they contain, may perhaps be the reason why the mind of humanity is sub-consciously sick.

---

1   *Polytheism The belief in the plurality of gods in which each deity is distinguished by his special function as is found largely in the religious practices of the Egyptians. The key word is 'function' that would be in keeping with the believes of the Egyptians and the part that the gods play in the ritual of the dead and the weighing of the soul. The Egyptians believe that the soul of man is immortal would negate the hypothesis that the Egyptians were prone to worship animals as gods. Budge. E.A. Wallis. 'The Egyptian Book of the Dead' Published by Dover publications Inc N Y*

Chapter 8

In what follows the questions will be centered, not so much on the 'why', as I am sure that the majority of societies could manufacture a myriad of valid reasons for their actions, as history can testify, but on the 'how' and 'when, questions that the majority of people find exasperating when trying to fend off the incessant' questions of the young who look to those in authority for guidance.

How often in life have we received a response to our questions believing the answers to be true on what is purported to be the facts, only to find out later what had been offered was an opinion or firmly held beliefs. Situations of this nature made one look more closely and question the information received in all its aspects. With this view in mind it's important, before we proceed, to look closely at the period in question and the people that shaped the future of our Western culture.

Generally, the common belief regarding the animosity and intolerance which led to the persecution of the Jewish people by those of the Christen faith had its beginning during the second century of our common era. However, this may not the case, as the problems within the Jewish communities had more to do with the various sects within the Jewish religion and their interpretation of the Judaic Laws.

The questions surrounding these contentious issues involved only those of the Jewish faith, as we know from the writings of Paul of Tarsus,[1] in his mission to the Jewish people in Asia Minor and Rome. The persecution of the Jews and those other sects who would not embrace the new Christian religion was to come at a much later date when the persecuted became the persecutor.

In the early days of his missionary work, Paul's message was directed to the Jews who had settled in Asia Minor and Rome. Those who were not of the Jewish faith may have heard his message; but his missionary work was primarily to those Jews. It was not until his return to Jerusalem in 49 AD and the confrontation with Peter[2] that it was determined as to who would

---

1   *Paul of Tarsus, born in Cilicia around 10 AD. A Jew of the tribe of Benjamin, who was also a Roman citizen. Educated in Jerusalem by the famous teacher Gamaliel who was a member of the Jewish Sanhedrin and a doctor of the Law. See Acts. 5; 34-41. 22; 1-5*

2   *The New Jerusalem Bible. Acts. 10; 1-48. Galatians; 1-14.*

be included in the new kingdom. The outcome of this confrontation resulted in an agreement to preach the Gospel to the gentiles. It would be reasonable to suggest that the problems between the Jewish people in the early years, was one of interpretation of the Laws, which if the present can be used as an example, would be extremely acrimonious when debating its finer points.

We can only envision the upheaval caused between the various Jewish religious fractions with the emergence of this new form of teaching. To some it would appear that their world was coming to an end, as the conflict of conscience would be psychologically devastating to those Jews who lived by the letter of the Law.

We have an indication of this during the reign of the Emperor Claudius[1] who,' Because the Jews of Rome caused continuous disturbances at the instigation of 'Chrestus', he expelled them from the city.'[2] This is supported by the account recorded in the Acts of the Apostles where it is written, "After Paul left Athens, he went to Corinth where he met a fellow Jew and his wife who had recently left Italy because of an edict by Emperor Claudius that had expelled all Jews from Rome.[3]

The event as recorded by Suetonius,[4] is supported by the account narrated in the Bible which authenticates the expulsion of the Jewish communities from Rome during the reign of the Emperor Claudius. This edict would have continued during the life of Claudius until his death in 54 AD.

As we know from the writings of St. Paul, the Jewish communities had re-established themselves in Rome during the reign of the Emperor Nero.[5] There is no reference to this expulsion to be found in the writings of Flavius Josephus,[6] the Jewish historian, in fact quite the opposite.

According to Josephus, the Emperor Claudius issued an edict restoring all rights and a privilege to those Jew's who resided in the city of Alexandria and to all who resided within the Roman Empire.[7]

Obviously the account narrated by Josephus is not in accordance with the known facts, which bring into question not only this event, but also all other similar edicts and special privileges granted to the Jewish people by the Roman authorities recorded by Josephus in his major works.

It is doubtful if the Roman authorities looked upon the Jewish people with any kind of special favor that would warrant them being treated as equals.

---

1   Emperor Claudius.41-54 AD.
2   Suetonius. 'The Twelve Caesars' 'the life of the Emperor Claudius' Translated by Robert Graves. Penguin Classics.
3   The New Jerusalem Bible.Acts of the Apostles. 18; 1-4. This gives a possible date of 49/50 AD as the time of the expulsion.
4   Gaius Suetonius Tranquillus. (AD 69-140).
5   The New Jerusalem Bible.Acts of the Apostles. 28: 17-22
6   Josephus. Flavius. Jewish Historian of the 1st century A.D.
7   Josephus. Flavius. 'Antiquities' Book X1X.-Chap.VI. Translated by William Whiston. M.A.

If we look a little more closely into history we find that the problems experienced by the Jewish people had commenced at a much earlier period in history. This coupled with the rise of Christianity has seen the continuation of a policy of animosity and persecution down through the ages into our own era, culminating with the events of the twentieth century that saw the near annihilation of the Jewish people in Europe.[1]

However, this continuous harassment and persecution is not unique in their history, as they have suffered similar precautions in the past. Not because of who they were, but of what they were, a people who had set themselves apart from the rest of mankind as special to the Creator. Their claim to be the chosen of God and future rulers of the world was not a philosophy that would sit well with the Roman authorities.

The great persecution[2] that occurred in 167-164 BC[3] is well documented within biblical texts[4] and the writings of Flavius Josephus[5]. He records the efforts by the Syrian King Antiochus to assimilate the Jewish people with those of other surrounding cultures by the process of Hellenizing the population of Judea into a single people. Requiring each community to renounce their particular religious customs and adopt those pagan practices as dictated by the King.[6] The Jewish people met this with stiff resistance and their refusal to comply led to a persecution of extreme barbarity.[7]

We must, however differentiate between the two forms of persecution. One was an effort to assimilate a people into one cohesive whole by blending them into the surrounding cultures. These efforts were brought to an end when it was obvious that the plan would not work. The exercise was abandoned after a period of three years, and the Jewish way of life resumed as normal.

In the case of the Catholic Church the persecution lasted for centuries with the sole purpose of converting the Jewish people to the Catholic Faith. Failing to achieve their purpose, the Church turned to the systematic persecution with the aim of eradicating their religion and culture. Had the same conditions suffered by the Jewish people been applied to any other culture, they would have willingly assimilated to avoid the pain, suffering and ignominy that the Christians associated with the Jewish race. Given the period of time in which these events took place in 167- 164 BC,[8] the process of combining an amalgam of peoples of diverse political

---

1   *The imprisonment of the European Jewish communities by the German Authorities during the 1939-45 war.*

2   *Antiochus Epiphanes.1V. (175-163 BC). His attempt to suppress the Jewish faith and Hellenise the Jewish people lead to a persecution of extreme severity.*

Josephus. Flavius Antiquities. Book V11. Translated by William Whiston. M.A. Published by Ward Lock and Company London I

New Jerusalem Bible. 1st Maccabbs. 1: 29-67. 2nd Maccabees. 6: 1-31. 7: 1-42.

3   *During the reign of King Antiochus Epiphanes 1V. Of Syria.*

4   *The New Jerusalem Bible 1st and 2nd Maccabees.*

5   *Josephus Flavius. Jewish historian. AD. 37-95?*

6   *Antiochus 1V Epiphanes. (175-163 BC)*

7   *The New Jerusalem Bible. 2nd Maccabees. 6; 1-31. & 7; 1-42.*

8   *The Great Persecution. (167-164 BC).*

and religious beliefs into one cohesive society would be an easy task. Apparently this was not the case when it came to the Jew's.

The attempted coercion into the Christian faith was until recently the dream of succeeding Popes. But with tenacity and a single sense of purpose that defies explanation, the indomitable spirit of these people helped them to survive the abuse, hate, and ostracism of the Christian world to maintain their unique individuality in the face of overwhelming odds. A people of a lesser spirit would have willingly surrendered their freedom in order to avoid the adverse conditions that formed the life of the Jewish communities down through the centuries.

Their belief that they are chosen by God, to perform his will on earth set them apart from the rest of society, and would make the process of assimilation impossible. Although there may have been those who readily accepted the edict, for those who refused to conform, the persecution that followed, (which lasted approximately three years), was extremely severe in its barbarity. The persecution and attempted reform of the Jewish people was ended by an outbreak of war in Upper Asia and the death of the King Antiochus 1V [1] allowed the Jewish people to practice their faith as of old [2] with the purification of the Temple and the renewal of the sacrifices according to the law.[3]

The arrival of the Roman General Pompeii's into Jerusalem 63 BC resulted in the Eastern Provinces[4] being reorganized into vassal states, subject to Roman rule. It would appear the Roman authorities liberality towards those of other religious sect's was condoned as long as they conformed to the general practice of making offerings to the Gods. Therefore, there was little or no interference in the religious practices of communities within the Roman sphere of influence. The respect the Romans had for the Gods, enabled the Jews to practice their faith unhindered as it was with all those other religions under Roman rule without undue interference by the Roman authorities. It could be said that the Roman Authorities were the most tolerant when it came to the question of religion.

This view is supported by the behavior of Pompeii the Great[5] who according to a Jewish historian,[6] describing the his arrival into Jerusalem states; "When Pompeii entered the Temple in Jerusalem and saw the treasures of money and golden ornaments refrained from any sacrilegious act that would profane the Temple in fear of offending the Gods. "There was in that Temple the golden table, the holy candle sticks, and the pouring vessels, and a great quantity of spices:

---

1   Ibid

2   Josephus. Flavius. 'Antiquities' Book X11 Translated by William Whiston. M.A. Published by Ward Lock and company London Maccabees 1: 6. 18-27

3   The New Jerusalem Bible Chronological Tables.

4   64 BC The middle East was re-organized by Pompey the Great during his campaign in the East whereby Pontus, Syria, and Cilicia became Roman Provinces; Armenia, Cappadocia, Galatia, Colchis and Judea became Roman vassal states.

5   . Cneius Pompeius Magnus. (106-48 BC) Roman General. Sometimes called Pompey the Great.

6   Flavius Josephus.

and besides these there were among the treasures two thousand talents of sacred money: yet did Pompeii touch nothing of this on account of his regard for religion".[1]

Although nothing of this incident is mentioned in the life of Pompeii,[2] or by any other Roman historian of the same period, one can appreciate the reverence in which the Romans in general held for their Gods and the belief in their power over the affairs of man. For those who have studied contemporary politics know (from our own historical experience) of some who have held the reins of power, but are not of the same religious mind. There have also been those who have challenged and defied the powers, which in some unknown way control the natural course of events in the life of man.

Later on we are told by the same author of a Roman Genera General Crassus [3] who on his way through Judea to campaign against the Parthians carried off the money[4] that Pompeii had left in the Temple.[5] Obviously, this particular person had less fear of the Gods than Pompeii when it came to money if he was willing to sacrifice his religious scruples in the acquisition of riches. However, from the historical accounts of this man's actions were in accordance with his character as it appears he was a person of a mean and avaricious disposition whose life was devoted to the accumulation of wealth.[6] Therefore, to pillage the riches of the Temple would be in keeping with what is known of his greed. However, as in the case of Pompeii the Great and his visit to the Temple in Jerusalem there is no mention of these incidents recorded by Roman historians which would verify the statements made by Josephus.

Historians relates that Crassus campaign in Parthia was a total failure which resulted in the loss of the greater part of his army and eventually his life[7] During the turmoil created by the rout of Crassus forces, Cassius[8] took possession of the treasure and fled to Syria.[9]

---

1   *Ibid*

2   *Plutarch. (AD 46?-120) 'Fall of the Roman Republic' Translated by Rex Warner. Penguin Classics.*

3   *Marcus Licinius Crassus. A member of the first Triumvirate--Crassus, Pompey, and Caesar. Undertook an unsuccessful campaign against the Parthians, in which he lost the majority of his army, after which the leader of the Parthians treacherously murdered him.*

4   *According to Josephus, Crassus on his way to campaign in Parthia came into Jerusalem and carried away all the gold that was in the Temple. Flavius Josephus. 'Antiquities' Book XIV. Chap. Translated by William Whiston. M.A.*

5   *Josephus. Flavius. 'The Antiquities' Book XIV. Chap; VII. Translated by William Whiston. M.A.*

6   *Marcus Licinius Crassus. Died 53 BC.*

7   *Plutarch. 'The fall of the Roman Republic' Translated by Michael Grant. Penguin Classics*

8   *Caius Cassius Longinus. Who along with Brutus were the leaders in the conspiracy and assassination of Jules Caesar 44BC?*

9   *Flavius Josephus. 'Antiquies' Book XIV.-Chap, VII. The account as narrated by Josephus regarding the treasure states that Cassius took possession of the treasure "As he fled from Rome to Syria" Josephus may have Cassius going in the wrong direction from the field of battle According to Plutarch, 'The fall of the Roman Empire' 'The life of Crassus.' After the battle of Carrhae, Cassius deserted Crassus and rode of to Syria with 500 cavalry. It would be safe to assume that if Crassus had taken the treasure, he was making sure that it did not fall into the hands of the Parthians.*

We can however place credence on the narrative recounted by Josephus when he relate a similar situation that raised a major disturbance among the Jewish people during the time of Pontius Pilate[1] who used the Temple funds in the construction of an aqueduct to bring water to Jerusalem.

These moneys contributed to the Temple were substantial when one considers the amount received as Temple offerings from Jews living inside and outside Jerusalem. The Temple tax of a half-shekel was mandatory and paid by all Jews without exception, as recounted in the Bible This poll tax was the result of a command given by Moses to the people of Israel when he said, "Everyone subject to the census, that is to say twenty years or over must pay half a shekel this half shekel shall be set aside for Yahwah will be the ransom for your lives" [2]

We know from available historical documents the reverence in which the Romans held their Gods being extremely superstitious regarding religion and individual standing with these invisible powers. However, this situation changed when the Emperor became one of the Gods, as in the case of those Emperors who were deified by the Roman Senate[3] and placed among the Gods for due homage by Roman citizens and all people who were subject to Roman rule. Apparently the religious freedom enjoyed by the Jewish people came under attack when the Roman authorities attempted to introduced the statues of Emperor Gaius Caesar [4] into the Temple in Jerusalem.

. This was not the only occasion on which the Roman authorities attempted to impose their religious beliefs into the Jewish Temple. During the reign of Emperor Tiberius attempts were made to introduce the standards and shields of the serving regiments, including the statues of the Emperor into to the Temple by the Roman Governor of Judea, Pontius Pilate[5] , an act so abhorrent to the Jewish people that it caused riots in the city.[6] Their continued resolve resulted in Pilate rescinding his order, by having the standards and shields returned to Caesarea. Yet, through all this religious turmoil, the Jewish people were not persecuted for their religious beliefs as was to be the case later on during the rise of Christianity

When one views the Roman Empire at this moment in history and the power it exercised over its conquered people, having to contend with what they viewed as a small group of religious fanatics had to be an exasperating experience. This long-standing acrimonious relationship between Rome

---

1   *Pontius Pilate. Roman Procurator of Judea during the time of Jesus Christ.*

2   *The New Jerusalem Bible. Matthew. 17: 24-27. The temple tax paid by Jesus and Peter. Mark. 12: 41-44. The Widows Mite.*

Also Exodus. 30:11-16. God spoke to Moses and Said, "When you take a census and make a register of the sons of Israel, each is to pay God a ransom for his life.

3   *Julius Caesar, Augustus, Claudius, Vespasian, and Titus.*

4   *Gaius Caligula. 39 AD*

5   *Josephus. Flavius. 'Antiquities' Book XVlll.-Chap. Translated by William Whiston. M.A.*

6   *These two attempts by the Roman authorises to treat the Temple of Jerusalem as they would any other Temple within the Roman domains resulted in the removal of the standards and shields by Pontius Pilate, and in the case of the statues of Caligula, time and distance prevented this order being carried out by the death of Caligula.*

and the Jewish people had existed over an extended period, involving some of the leading figures in the Roman political world. It therefore comes as a surprise that a noted historian who is viewed as the leading authority on Roman history could be so lacking in detail regarding the history of the Jewish people. As his works are standard texts within our educational system, his views and opinions can and do affect the opinions and views of those who read his works. If his works were used as a sole reference without availing to those historians who were his contemporaries, his prejudices and narrow-minded views would transmit themselves to the student.

To demonstrate this point we will make reference to two incidents that occurred involving the Jewish population living in Rome which if taken on face value would give the impression that the Jews were a persecuted race under the Romans, but this was not the case. Both of these incidents were recorded by Tacitus[1] and Suetonius[2] that show a marked difference in context. As Tacitus[3] was the earlier of the two, we will narrate and compare his version to that of Suetonius.[4]

In his efforts to correct the morals of Roman society Tiberius[5] had the Senate pass laws against immorality and prostitution by the wives of Roman citizens. Among those decrees passed one involved the expulsion of Jewish and Egyptian religious rites/cults from Rome. This incident is covered extensively in the writings of the Jewish historian Flavius Josephus in his works on the 'Antiquities 0f the Jews.'

As Tacitus[6] was a contemporary of Josephus[7], being about forty years of age at the time of Josephus death in 95 AD, it is probable that Tacitus used the works of Josephus as a reference when compiling his works on the 'Annuals of Imperial Rome'.

What is surprising is the main ingredient of the version, as told by Josephus has been diluted by the two historians to the point of being contradictory, making it difficult to determine as to which version is correct. It would seem that both Tacitus and Suetonius copied the work of Josephus in relating this particular incident. Of the three versions, that which is described by Josephus should be taken as being the true sequence of events. In narrating the story as described by Josephus, it will be necessary to abbreviate his story, yet maintain the essentials without diluting the important elements which are as follows.

"There was in Rome a woman whose name was Paulina, a member of a very distinguished family; known for her virtuous manner of living. Being very rich and beautiful had a great reputation, yet led a life of modesty. She was married to Saturninus who was equal to her in

1   *Ibid*
2   *Ibid*
3   *Ibid*
4   *Ibid*
5   *Ibid*
6   *Ibid*
7   *Flavius. Josephus. Jewish Historian. The Works of Flavius Josephus Translated by William Wiston A M Published by Ward lock and Company London*

character. A Roman Knight, Decius Mundus, who was high up in the Equestrian Order fell in love with this woman. His efforts to seduce her by an abundance of presents, even with the offer of two hundred thousand Attic drachmae[1] for one night was of no avail. Being denied her affections, and unable to bear his misfortune, decided to die by depriving himself of food. Now Mundus had a freed woman whose name was Ide, grieved at the young man's resolution to kill himself devised a plan by which the young man would achieve his purpose and sleep Paulina for one night.

So she went to the Priests of the Temple of Isis and with a bribe of twenty-five thousand drachmas she informed them of the young man's passion and got their agreement to partake in the plan. Accordingly, the oldest of the priests went to Paulina and told her that the God, Anu had fallen in love with her and enjoined her to come to him. On hearing this news she went to her husband and told him of the message she had received from the Priest and the Gods wish to sup and lie with her, so he agreed to her accepting this offer, being confident in his wife's chastity. Accordingly she went to the Temple and supped there and when it was the hour to go to sleep, the Priest shut the doors of the Temple putting the lights out. Decius Mundus came out from where he was hiding and pretending to be the God Anubis got into the bed with Paulina and did not fail of enjoying her, leaving Paulina before daybreak, to avoid being recognized. Paulina went to her Husband and told him how the God Anubis had appeared to her. She also told her friends of her adventure who were amazed at what had happened, but were not convinced by what Paulina was telling them, refrained from making any adverse comments in fear of offending Paulina. On the third day after what had happened Mundus met Paulina, and said, "Nay, Paulina, thou hast saved me two hundred thousand drachma, which sum thou mightiest have added to thy own family: yet hast thou not failed to be at my service in the manner I invited thee. As for the reproaches thou hast laid upon Mundus, I value not the business of names; but I rejoice in the pleasure I reaped by what I did, while I took to myself the name of Anubis."

When Paulina realized the grossness of what she had done she told her husband of the horrid nature of this wicked act perpetrated on her by Decius Mundus. At the request of his wife, Saturnius reported the matter to Tiberius who had the case investigated. On proving the allegations true, he ordered the Priests to be crucified as well as the freed woman Ide. He also had the Temple of Isis demolished and the statues of the Goddess (Isis) thrown into the Tiber banning the practice of the Egyptian cults in Rome."

The second story of which Josephus speaks is an incident that happened around the same time and relates to the expulsion of the Jews from Rome. This incident involved a confidence trickster masquerading as a Rabbi and a woman, who was a convert to Judaism and extremely rich. The events described by Josephus are as relevant today as they were in that remote

---

1   As the Roman drachma was equivalent to approximately 0.12 oz of silver, the total weight would be around 240.000 oz's. A quarter shekel.

period; leading one to believe that very little has changed in life when it involves confidence tricksters.

One would assume that as society progresses, people become more aware and less gullible. This however is not the case, as is illustrated in the tale as told by Josephus.

Again as before, we will abbreviate the story and retain the most pertinent parts to avoid confusion. The story as narrated is as follows.

"There was a man who was a Jew that had been driven from Israel for transgressing the laws. On his arrival in Rome he professed to be a teacher in the wisdom of the Law of Moses, and procured the services of three other men as his partners. These men persuaded a woman by the name of Fulvia, who had embraced the Jewish faith to religion tosend purple and gold to the temple in Jerusalem. On receiving the gifts from Fulvia, they sold them and used the money themselves. When the husband of Fulvia reported this to the Emperor Tiberius he had inquiries made and in finding the facts to be true ordered all the Jews to be banished from Rome.

At this time the Consuls listed four thousand men out of the Jewish population and sent them to the island of Sardinia; but punished a greater number of them, who were unwilling to become soldiers on account of keeping the laws of their forefathers. Thus were the Jews banished out of the city by the wickedness of four men?"[1]

Relating the same events Tacitus states, "Another discussion concerned the expulsion of Egyptian and Jewish rites. The Senate decreed that four thousand adult ex-slaves tainted with these superstitions should be transported to Sardinia to suppress banditry there. If the unhealthy climate killed them, the loss would be small. The rest, unless they repudiated their unholy practices by a given date,[2] must leave Italy."[3]

These same incidents described by Suetonius is as follows, "He abolished foreign cults at Rome particularly the Egyptian and Jewish , forcing all citizens who had embraced these superstitious faiths to burn their religious vestments and other accessories. Jews of military age was removed to unhealthy regions, on the pretext of drafting them into the army. The others of the similar beliefs were expelled from the city and threatened with slavery if they defied the order."[4]

Each of the versions have a common trend as to the foreign cults being expelled from the city of Rome; the enrolment of the four thousand into the army and subsequent posting to Sardinia. Though each differs in the telling, i.e. the drafting of four thousand to which Tacitus refers to as ex-slaves, whereas Josephus and Sutonius refers to them as military draftees. Each

1   Flavius Josephus. 'The Antiquities' Book XV111.-Chap. Translated by William Whiston. Published by Ward Lock and Company London

2   This event occurred in 19AD the year Germanicus died.

3   Tacitus. Cornelius. (55-117 AD) 'The Annuals of Imperial Rome' Translated by Michael Grant. Penguin Classics.

4   Suetonius. 'The Twelve Caesars' 'The Life of Tiberius' Translated by Robert Graves. Penguin Classics.

devises a different motive for both agree to their being sent to Sardinia, which was to be their ultimate destination. It is doubtful if Tacitus is correct in classing them as ex-slaves.

As Judea was a Roman province, it would be natural that like all other provinces would be called upon to furnish a given number of personnel to the armed forces.

If one were to be in ignorance of the writings of these famous historians, the expulsion of the Jews from Rome could be misconstrued and seen as a form of religious persecution carried out under Tiberius. As Christianity had not yet appeared in Rome as a major religious sect, it would be natural to assume that this could be construed as a form of religious persecution, which may not be the case.

Perhaps there is another explanation, which may fit in with the events, around this particular time. It is more in keeping with the times to state that the expulsion of the various religious sects from Rome had more to do with the breakdown in the social order by the upheavals created by the Jewish communities.

From the time of Pompeii arrival in Jerusalem in 63 BC until it's destruction by Titus in 70 AD[1], the Jewish religious sect was a thorn in the side of Rome.

An example of how this narrow minded religious prejudice is transmitted through the educational system is to be found in the writings of Cornelius Tacitus (AD 55-117 AD) the Roman historian.[2] Though little is known of his personal life, we can infer from the positions he held within Roman politics and his marriage[3] that he came from a leading Roman family. We can also surmise that he had to be a man of special qualities to survive through to reign of nine Emperors, possible ten, as he may have lived to see Emperor Hadrian (117-138)[4] in power, and from what is known of Roman history, to survive the political intrigues during this period was no mean achievement.

It was during the reign of the Emperor Domitian[5] that a general persecution was carried out, not only against Jews and Christens and members of the Roman Senate, but also those of the leading families of Rome and the Imperial household.[6]

In Tacitus we see a man of high education, politician, diplomat, obviously a man of discernment, who guarded his privacy and that of his family to survive in the political climate that was Rome during the reign of the Emperor Domitian. The first of his works, which was

1   Titus. AD 39-AD 81. Roman Emperor (AD 79-AD 81) Son of the Emperor Vespasian.
2   Tacitus. Cornelius. (55-117 AD) 'The Histories' Translated by Kenneth Wellesley. Penguin Classics.
3   He married the daughter of Cneius Julius Agricola. (AD 40-93). Roman General who was consul and governor of Britain (AD 77-85). of whom Tacitius wrote a biography in which he expressed his admiration for his father-in-law.
4   He was born in the reign of the Emperor Nero (37-68 AD). His political career as a senator covered the reigns of the Emperor's, Vespasian (AD 69-79), Titus (AD 79-81), Domitian (AD 81-96), and Nerva (AD 96-98).
5   Emperor Domitian, Emperor of Rome 81-96 AD.
6   Suetonius. 'The Twelve Caesars' The life of Emperor Domitian. Translated by Michael Grant. Penguin Classics

a discussion on oratory,[1] demonstrated why the elite of Roman society celebrated him as an eloquent speaker.

We can also gather from his writings that he was of a sensitive nature, and as one would expect from a historian of his stature, a seeker of truth. It is also apparent from his writings that he was not easily fooled by flattery. Being a man of letters and a historian he would have ready access to the leading families in Rome, but most importantly, the Senate archives for his research and information.

It is therefore more than surprising to find that his information on the Jewish people is so lacking in substance, being a motley of truths, half truths and in the majority of cases the result of a vivid imagination, leading one to believe that his work had been written without recourse to any historical documents or bona fide external sources of information.

His description of the Jewish people, their origins and religious practices is so convoluted; it is difficult to accept that a person of his standing could have been the author of such nonsense.

It would also appear from his description of the Jewish people, his information was gleaned from the gossip of the market place rather from reputable historical sources which were extent during the period in which he wrote the 'Histories' of Rome; did he faithfully consult those written sources'[2] that were available to him, obviously not, otherwise his description of the Jews and their religious practices would indicate a conscientious approach to detail and have a ring of authenticity. As one author so aptly puts it, "The account of the Jews is a fascinating faggro of truths and lies."[3]

In order to establish the truth of this statement we have to refer to the writings of Flavius Josephus the Jewish historian who wrote and published two great works[4] on Jewish history during the lifetime of Tacitus. Because of the people involved and the statements made by Tacitus it is obvious that he had not read these works or, if he had knowledge of their existence, refused to accept the information as authentic, which would bring his credibility and integrity into question.

On the other hand are we to take the works of Flavius Josephus as truthful accounts of events, or an attempt to embellish and authenticate the Jewish people as a nation rather than one tribe among many. Obviously Josephus had his own agenda regards his heritage and may perhaps have been prone to exaggeration. Was there such a war as described by Josephus, or was this just another attempt by the Jews to annoy the Roman authorities, which ultimately led to their expulsion from Jerusalem and subsequently from Rome.

---

1   *Tacitus. Cornelius. 'Dialogues'. A discussion of oratory in the style of Cicero. (106-43 BC) Roman orator, politician and philosopher who was put to death by Anthony in 43 BC.*

2   *Ibid*

3   *Kenneth Wellesley. In his introduction to 'The Histories' by Tacitus.*

4   *Josephus. Flavius. 'The Antiquities of the Jews.' & 'The War of the Jews.' Translated by William Whiston. A.M., Published by Ward Lock and Company London*

When one views the antagonist in this affair, for the Jews to say they were a cohesive fighting force against the might of Rome is best left to one's imagination.

These two works by Josephus which deal extensively with the history of the Jewish people and their war with the Roman authorities, that eventually lead to the destruction of Jerusalem were published in 75 AD and 93 AD respectively.[1]

Josephus takes great pains to praise the behavior and character of the three Emperors[2] to whom he not only owed his life but his future well being. Tacitus has made the same statement when he refers to the same three Emperors and the important part they played in his life and the furtherance of his career. This in itself appears strange for two men who were contemporaries. If both of these men were so close to the Emperor, why were they unknown to each other?

Tacitus, being a professional historian, would have known of Josephus, even if it were through the gossip that permeated the Emperor's household.

In the preface to his work on 'The Antiquities of the Jews,' Josephus speaks of a personal friend whom he classes as "A lover of all kinds of learning, but principally delighted with the knowledge of history." History tells us that this special person, known as Epaphroditus, who was a former freed slave of the Emperor Nero[3] had advanced to the position of private secretary to the Emperor Domitian, (who later had him executed in the 14th or 15th year of his reign).[4]

The close relationship between all of these people would suggest that Tacitus knew them because of their proximity to the Emperor. It is also interesting to find the name of Epaphroditus appearing in the letter of St. Paul to the Philippians[5] in which he refers to this gentleman as his helper. Despite views to the contrary, it is obvious that St. Paul was under arrest in Rome during the reign of the Emperor Nero at the time of this correspondence.

The question that has not been answered, was this the same Epaphroditus who was the friend of Josephus?

---

1   *Josephus wrote his seven books on the Jewish Wars long before he wrote on the Antiquities of the Jew's. His seven books on the War's was published about 75 AD, and those on the Antiquities about 93 AD. Taken from the Preface of the Antiquities, note 3. Translated by William Whiston. M.A.*

2   *Vespasian, Titus, and Domitian.*

3   *Epaphroditus who is said to have guided the hand of the Emperor Nero to commit suicide*

4   *Epaphroditus. A freed slave of the Emperor Nero. See Tacitus 'The annuals of Imperial Rome' Penguin Classics Introduction by Michael Grant Suetonius. 'The Twelve Caesars' Translated by Robert Graves Published by Penguin Books in which the same person is referred to as the secretary to the Emperor Nero. By the same author Epaphroditus is referred to as the secretary to the Emperor Domitian whom he had executed because he had helped Nero commit suicide, possible the year 95 AD. There would appear to be some confusion regarding this gentleman's man as it appears again in the life of the Emperor Tragan 98-117 AD This may be a coincidence as certain types of names are popular. This name also occurs in the letters of St. Paul to the Philippians in which he speaks of Epaphroditus as being his helper in Rome, who when sending greeting to the Philippians, sends them on behalf of himself and those of the Imperial Household. This is significant as it implies there were Christians within Nero's household. See Philippians 2: 25-30. & 4: 18*

5   *Ibid*

Josephus in writing on his relationship with the Emperor's family relates much the same loyalty as expressed by Tacitus when he says, "I had great care taken of me by Vespasian; for he gave me an apartment in his own house. He also honored me with the privilege of a Roman citizen and gave me an annual pension; I also received from Vespasian no small quantity of land as a free gift in Judea."

We can accept the truth of his statement as one Roman historian refers to Josephus when he states, "Also a very distinguished Jewish prisoner of Vespasian's, Josephus by name, insisted that he would soon be released by the very man who had now put him in fetters and who would soon be Emperor."[1]

On the death of Vespasian, his son Titus succeeds to the Government of Rome. In his reference to the future Emperor Josephus states, "Titus kept up the same respect for me which I had received from his Father, and Domitian who succeeds Titus still augmented his respect to me. He also made that country I had in Judea tax free, and Domitia, the wife of Caesar continued to do me kindness".[2]

If Josephus is correct, and we have no reason to doubt his honesty, He was living in the residence of the Emperor at the time he was writing the 'Antiquities of the Jews', and possibly his other works as well.[3]

It is reasonable to suggest that others of the Emperor's household knew the composition of these works. This is supported by his reference to Epaphroditius,[4] secretary to the Emperor, of whom Josephus writes. " A man who is a lover of all kinds of learning, but is principally delighted with knowledge of history, and this is on account of his having been himself concerned in great affairs and many turns of fortune."[5]

These few words of Josephus as to this man's character speak volumes about the high esteem in which he was held by those who knew him. Obviously, he was a man of great intelligence and extraordinary abilities, possibly at one time in his life a person of wealth and position. Josephus freely admits the influence this particular person has on his work when he says, "I yielded to this man's persuasions that always excite such as have abilities in what is useful and acceptable to join their endeavors with his." This encouragement to Josephus to apply himself to the work of compiling the history of the Jews was recognition by an equal of the importance of this work.

It is also apparent that others were aware of the religious history of the Jews, as he says, "I found that the second of the Ptolemies was a King[6] who was diligent in what concerned

1   Suetonius. 'The Twelve Caesars' Translated by Robert Graves. Penguin Classics.
2   Josephus. Flavius. 'The life of Flavius Josephus'. Translated by William Whiston. A.M.
3   'The Life of Flavius Josephus', 'The Jewish Wars', and 'Against Apion'.
4
5   Josephus. Flavius. 'The Antiquities of the Jew's'. Translated by William Whiston. M.A.
6   Josephus is referring to King Ptolemy 11.(306-246 BC) who was King of Egypt in (285-246 BC) a member of the Macedonian family.

learning and the collection of books, that he was ambitious to procure a translation of our laws. Accordingly the books of the law were sent to Alexandria by the Priest Eleazar for copying by the Egyptian King." [1]

If the account describe by Josephus is correct, and there is no reason why we should doubt his word, the religious history of the Jewish people were extent during the time of Tacitus.

Why Tacitus did not avail himself to this corpus of information is a mystery. However, this may not be the case as has been demonstrated. He was a man of deep intellect, perception and honesty. This can be seen in the opening chapters of his work,[2] much the same words as Josephus, when he states; "My official career owed its beginning to Vespasian its progress to Titus and its further advancement to Domitian I have no wish to deny this, but partiality and hatred towards any man are equally inappropriate in a writer who claims to be honest and reliable".[3]

And yet in his work[4] he expresses his intolerance and hatred towards the Jewish [5] race in such an invective manner it would lead one to question the motives behind his vitriolic comments and ask why, for what reason? Why does he demonstrate such bias on this one subject, against these particular people?

In the appendix to his translation of the works of Flavius Joseph,[6] William Whiston treats this question at length, In his summation he tends more towards Tacitus hatred of the Jews and the new emerging Christian sect' as a reason for his animosity. He is however correct in stating that Tacitus had to be conversant with the writings of Josephus, and being a man of religion, it is natural that he should attach this animosity to the question of religion.

This view is supported by his statement when he states," Since Tacitus was so bitter against the Jews and knew that Christ and his followers were Jews, he also knew that the Christian religion was imported into Rome from Judea--it is no wonder that his hatred and contempt of the Jews extended itself to the Christians".[7]

It would appear that the Church Fathers manipulated church history and attached a decree of importance to the early years of the new emerging sect that may not conform to historic facts.

---

1   Josephus. Flavius. 'The Antiquities of the Jew's' Translated by William Whiston. M.A. The books of the law was sent to Ptolemy 11 by the priest Eleazer who was put to death during the great persecution in the reign of Antiochus 167-164, see 2nd Maccabees 6: 18-31.
2   'The Histories'. Translated by: Kenneth Wellesley.
3   Tacitus. Cornelius. Book 1.Translated by: Kenneth Wellesley. Penguin Classics.
4   'The Histories' Book V. Translated by Kenneth Wellesley.
5   Tacitus. Cornelius. (55-117? AD). 'The Histories" Book V. 'the Jews' Translated by Kenneth Wellesley. Penguin Classics.
6   'The Antiquities of the Jews'. 'The Life of Flavius Josephus'. And 'The War of the Jews'. Translated by William Whiston. M.A. (1667-1752). Appendix. Dissertation 111. Observations upon the passages taken out of Tacitus.
7   Whiston. William. The Works of Flavius Josephus. Appendix. Dissertation 111.

Rome, as the center of the known world was beset with a myriad of different religions and sects. Religion was, as it is today, big business, used to influence the affairs of state and the daily life of the people. Just as in our society today, religious sects appeared and disappeared depending on their popularity with the people. The arrival of one more sect on the scene would not unduly worry the Roman Authorities.

There is every reason to believe that the arrival of the sect, which became known as 'Christians' would, became popular as a topic of conversation among the upper classes of society. In fact its arrival on the scene could be compared to the religious sects that appeared in North America in the early 1800's the founding of the Church of Jesus Christ of the Latter Day Saints by Joseph Smith in 1830, and the Theosophical Society by Madame Blavatsky in 1831 are examples.

Today there are different religious groups being formed, and after a time disappearing, sometimes voluntarily and at times by the pressure of the State. There are also numerous sects scattered throughout Europe and North America that have survived over time and are thriving communities within society.

Two of the more successful of these communities is that of the Hutterian Brethren and Mennonites who practice a strict form of Communism based on religious principals. Therefore to assert that the early Church was a vibrant thriving institution is not in agreement with what is known of the first two centuries of Church history.

What Tacitus motives were not so difficult to define? His honesty and integrity are not in question; as he was a man of his own generation whose judgment may have been clouded by the events surrounding the new sect that was creating so much discord in Rome, and as a means of self protection enveloped him in a blanket of ignorance. To find an answer to this question we would have to take a closer look at this man and his times to give us some indication for his animosity towards the Jews and the reasons for his invectives.

As we are discussing education and the importance history has in shaping the mind of the young, reading the works of this famous historian, and lacking an in-depth knowledge of events associated with this period, his views and opinions of the Jewish people would have a lasting effect upon a young impressionable mind that would be difficult to eradicate. Human behavior being what it is, subliminal impressions planted into the sub-conscience of the young would create and harbor aversion to whose presence, both from a business and social aspect.

This animosity and bigotry shown to the Jewish people in our Western society can be directly attributed to the writings of the early historians and the teaching of the Catholic Churchh, as it blamed the death of Jesus on the Jewish people.[1]

---

1   *According to the account as narrated in the Gospel of Matthew after being questioned by Pilate, Jesus is shown to the crowd who demand the release of Barabbas and the crucifixion of Jesus. When being told by Pilate that he was "Innocent of this mans blood" The people shouted back, "His blood is on us and on our children" thereby assuming collective guilt. The New Jerusalem Bible. Matthew. 27: 11-26.*

Reading of the event bears all the signs of a dramatic moment in time, which one could envisage, with the storming of the Bastille, or the siege of Stalingrad. Drama at its best, but was it true?

From what is known of his career Tacitus was a member of the Roman elite Senate and later a substitute consul under the Emperor Nerva (AD 30-98)[1] who on succeeding the Emperor Domitian, appointed him Proconsul to Asia Minor [2] which is present day Turkey.

As Proconsul he would be in sole charge of the army, wielding full judicial powers, with the overall responsibility of administering the province on behalf of the Emperor and the Senate, (his power while holding this office being equal to that of the Emperor). In his capacity as the sole Roman authority in Asia Minor his office would bring him into contact with both the political and religious fractions within these regions.

This particular period in Roman history, saw what was later to be known as Christianity, spread out from Jerusalem into Rome, has been viewed as nothing short of miraculous. This supernatural phenomena being attributed to the work of God, but the reality of the times tell a different story, which is more in tune with historic fact and has a lot to do with Astrology and the precession of the Equinox rather than religion. However, when one considers the harsh conditions of life that people were living under, any respite that would relieve them from this yoke of servitude was welcome.

It is not to be wondered that the general public received a religion that taught the doctrine of equality whereby all people, irrespective of their station in life were equal in the sight of God and as such deserved a level of dignity with open arms. It's no wonder the Church grew at such a rapid pace, but there was a price to be paid in the persecutions that were to follow for the next three centuries until the edict of Milan (in 313 AD) by which Constantine granted religious toleration to the Christian Church.

During the life time of Tacitus (55-55 117 ADAD 117 AD) the Apostles had written the four Gospels (by the year 90 AD), and St. Paul had had traveled extensively throughout Asia Minor, Greece and Rome spreading the teachings of the new sect and establishing communities of Christian's. We also know from St. Paul's Epistles that the young church was thriving and growing rapidly.

1   *The New Columbia Illustrated Encyclopaedia. Nerva. Marcus Cocceius. (30-98 AD) Roman Emperor (96-98 AD). Who succeed as Emperor on the death of Emperor Domitian? (81-96 AD).*

2   *Present day Turkey. Known during Roman times as Asia Minor consisted of, Cappadocia, Bithynia, Cilicia and Lycia. According to Biblical accounts St. Paul was born at Tarsus in Cilicia about 10 AD. St Paul preached extensively in this area during the early days of his missionary work on behalf of the fledgling church. All of the early Ecumenical Councils held by the Church of Rome, were convened in Asia Minor starting with the Council of Nicaea in 325 AD. With most of them being in or near Constantinople, the former Byzantium, which Emperor Constantine had renamed for himself and made his capitol. The Catholic Bible. Ecumenical Councils. According to Church records it is the opinion of the Church authorises that the Gospels had been completed by 90 AD. St. Paul had travelled extensively throughout this region spreading the Gospel during his ministry for the Church. Later he was to meet his death in Rome in AD 67 during the reign of the Emperor Nero.*

In the few short years of his ministry, the new pagan converts were becoming a force within the various communities. However, in this new found environment of hope and expectation there was conflict between those who were seeing the abrogation of the old Jewish laws and the introduction of a new covenant that would see the end of Temple worship later events would prove to be true when the Temple was destroyed by the Romans (in 70 AD).

With the new converts, it would appear that God had left the Temple and in doing so rejected the people of Israel. The conflict of conscience among the Jewish people had to be one of sorrow and lament. Conditions of this nature would be the ideal conditions that would create friction between those Jews who had embraced the new religion, and those who retaining the old religion, looked upon those converts as apostates

By the time of Tacitus arrival in Asia Minor to take up the duties as Proconsul, the new sect of Christians was well established. However, the acrimony between the Jewish communities, those who had retained the old beliefs, and those who had embraced the new belief was a contentious issue that would involve the Roman Authorities.

It is therefore reasonable to suggest that Tacitus was intimately involved with the various religious factions within his area of administration. Taking all these facts into consideration, it would seem that Tacitus had reasons to deny his knowledge of Jewish history and vent his spleen if he were a convert to the new faith and a strong supporter.

From his comments regarding the Jewish people and their origins, Tacitus knowledge would appear to be superficial, which is strange for a historian of his stature and the positions he held within the Roman administration. No historian worth his salt could be so ignorant of a culture that had been part of Roman history, since Judaea was first occupied in 63 BC.

It may be suggested that this show of ignorance was deliberate and not so difficult to determine when his life and times are examined a little more closely. For a historian to be so wrong in his description of a people who within his life time were to play a major role in the events that were to shape Europe's religious and political institutions is more than surprising.

I say this in light of what is known of this particular period in Roman history. This period brought about the destruction of the Temple in Jerusalem, the dispersion of the Jewish people, the rise of Christianity, and the beginning of what was to be the end of the Roman Empire.

Chapter 9

Reading the works of the ancient historian's, a clue to their character can be found is not what they say, but what they don't say, that is of importance. This alone would be reason enough to look for what is not there as a means of determining their motives. In this context, what is remarkable in Tacitus's major work 'The Histories' is the absence of any reference to the new emerging Christian sect that was creating so many problems for the Empire?

This alone would be reason enough to look for what is not there as a means of determining his motives. What is remarkable in his major work 'The Histories' is the absence of any reference to the new emerging Christen sect?

Additionally, his position as Proconsul in Asia Minor by virtue of his office would bring him into close contact with the new sect and its leaders in resolving the many squabbles that ensued between the Jew's and the new emerging Christian sect.

His silence is even more telling when we look at his other historical work in which he writes about the persecutions of the Christian sect that was carried out by the Emperor Nero (54-68 AD).[1]

As a member of an elite family he had to be aware of the daily happenings within Roman society. When writing on the great fire that destroyed Rome in AD 64 he is the first Roman writer to make reference to the newly emerging Christians when he writes, "Nero fabricated scapegoats and punished with every refinement the notoriously depraved Christians (as they were popularly called). Their originator, Christ, had been executed in Tiberius's reign by the governor of Judaea, Pontius Pilate".[2]

It is interesting to note, this is the only direct reference made by a Roman historian to the person of Jesus Christ and the crucifixion. Notwithstanding the above comments regarding the new sect, it is obvious that he had discussions with members of the Christen sect to obtain the information regarding Jesus or had been party to discussions regarding the matter.

This hypothesis is based on the premise that the new sect, during its infancy, became an underground movement to avoid persecution by the Roman authorities. Like all secret organizations, it would be difficult to obtain information unless one was a friend to be trusted.

---

1   *Cornelius Tacitus. (56-117 AD) 'The Annals of Imperial Rome'. Translated by Michael Grant. Published by Penguin Classics.*

2   *Ibid*

As he goes on to say, "Despite their guilt as Christians, and the ruthless punishment it deserved, the victims were pitied. For it was felt that they were being sacrificed to ones mans brutality, rather than to the national interest." We can sense a feeling of sympathy for the brutality being shown to the Christian.

What is also remarkable is his silence regarding the persecutions that were carried out by the Emperor Domitian and Titus against the Christians in Rome and the Near East. Though not of a long duration, nevertheless they were just as brutal as the persecutions carried out by the Emperor Nero. Perhaps his silence is understandable and self-serving. As a protégé of Domitian and the son-in-law of a famous General, it would be courting disaster to criticize the ruling families.

Being a senator and high official, he would be familiar with the Emperors family and knowledgeable of the gossip surrounding his mentor, and by inference, would be involved on a social level with the ruling families. Yet, his silence is all the more remarkable regards the persecutions and the events leading to the death of the Emperor Domitian by Stephanus, the servant of Domitian's niece, Domitilla. We can assume that by adopting the attitude of ' discretion being the better part of valor' he secured the safety of his immediate family, therefore, his policy of hear nothing, see nothing, and say nothing achieved its purpose.

As we are endeavoring to determine the cause of Tacitus's hate and bigotry towards the Jewish people, we can with a degree of certainty say that either he had been converted to the Christian faith or was a sympathizer and fellow traveler. This hypothesis can be deduced from the events surrounding the death of the Emperor Domitian and his assignment as Consul to Asia Minor by the Emperor Nerva, successor to Domitian. To have a sense for this period in history we must realize that the new emerging Christian religion was no slow lumbering giant, but a spreading flame that swept across Asia Minor and those areas bordering the Mediterranean.

We can speak the words, but our mind cannot grasp the force that saw the spread of Christianity. It was as though people of the Roman Empire were waiting for a liberator to free them from the bonds of slavery. Anyone or anything that would alleviate their suffering was a welcome guest. This feeling not only applied to the ruling classes, whose life was prone to fear, not knowing when they would lose it (on the orders of the Emperor), but, also to those who had life was one of bondage and slavery. By the year 54 AD, the year Nero succeeded Emperor Claudius, Christianity had reached the innermost circle of the ruling families of Rome.

Therefore, it should come as no surprise to find that members of Emperor Domitian family had converted to Christianity. Tacitus had to be aware of the circumstances surrounding the death of Flavius Clemens, (whom Domitian had executed) and the banishment of his wife Domitilla to a desolate island of the coast of Campania. [1] There exists little information by the Roman historians as to the cause of this action by Domitian against the members of his own family.

---

1   *Gaius Suetonius Tranquillus. 'The Twelve Caesars'. Translated by Robert Graves. Published by Penguin Classics.*

Piecing together the fragments of information that are available, and coupling these with the events recorded by the early fathers of the Church, concerning the reign of Domitian, it is obvious that the persecution carried out by the Emperor, directly involved, not only his immediate family, (Flavius Clemens, and his wife Domitilla) but also leading families of Rome on the charge of being members of the Christian sect.

It is recorded that during this persecution many of the leading families lost their lives, while others were banished from Rome which resulted in the loss of citizenship, and the confiscation of their property. What is certain is that Flavius Clemens, and his wife Domitilla were Christians as they were later honored by the Church of Rome as among the first martyrs to sacrifice their lives for the new faith.[1]

Tacitus is silent on the subject, as he is, on the circumstances surrounding the death of the Emperor Domitian. However, a Roman historian of a later date who makes reference to the execution of Flavius Clemens, attributes his death to "some trivial pretext" thought up by his cousin the Emperor Domitian, also describes the events, which lead to the assassination of the Emperor by Stephanus, a steward of the Emperor niece, Domitilla.[2]

There is also his silence on the atrocities carried out by Domitian on the Christian and Jewish communities in Rome, and also the brutality by his brother Titus in Caesarea.

It is recorded that Titus: in celebration of his brothers (Domitian) birthday had 2500 people die in fighting wild beasts, by crucifixion, as human torches, and in the arena, fighting each other to the death. There is also the occasion, when on proceeding to Berytus in Phoenicia, to honor his father's (Vespasian) birthday; he held another show in which an equal number of people lost their lives.[3]

The silence of the Roman historians is understandable when we consider that the use of slaves, criminals, and those who were viewed as enemies of the state were used in the arenas as a means of entertainment. In a culture that placed little value on life, the gladiatorial shows, in which animals and people were used to entertain the general population, were of no more or no less importance than what the present day sports, with their weekly football or hockey game. Therefore, occurrences of this nature would be of no interest to the Roman Historian, nor would it interest historians in today's society.

Other Roman historian's writing on the life of the Emperor Nero, pay only passing reference to the punishment inflicted on the Christians to whom they referred to as being a "sect professing a new and mischievous belief". However, there is no evidence of the Christians being

1   Edward Gibbons. 'The Decline and Fall of the Roman Empire' Published by Bison Books London Gaius Suetonius Tranquillus, AD 69-140. 'The Twelve Caesars'. Translated by Robert Graves. Published by Penguin Classics.
2   Ibid
3   Flavius Josephus. 'Antiquities of the Jews' 'The War of the Jews' Wars'. Book V11. Chap 111. Translated by William Whiston, M.A.

responsible for the fires that devastated Rome, as described by Tacitus unequivocally states it was Nero who instigated the burning of Rome.[1]

Perhaps his invective remarks concerning the Jews can be attributed to the hatred and animosity that existed between the Christians and the Jewish communities in the latter part of the first century. It is also probably that the writings of Tacitus fuelled the fires of animosity towards the Jewish people by the newly converted Christians, which gave rise to the persecution that has been inflicted upon the Jewish race that to some extent continues today.

Although the Church of Rome has made some effort to rectify its position regarding its moral teaching concerning the Jews, it's impossible to eradicate the mindset that has been created over the centuries. Due to the lack of direction by those who are responsible for teaching moral behavior to the young, we fail to look upon each other as human beings, whose destiny is intertwined, as is all life, having the same beginning and destined for the same end, irrespective of our birth or the circumstances under which we were born.

I have spent some considerable time on the subject of religion to show how religious teachings imparted to us, in our formative years, can have a telling effect upon our way of thinking. This in turn influences our behavior towards others whereby we can look upon their suffering as being of no consequence. This lack of respect and feeling breeds a sterility of conscience that negates any sense of compassion for life. There was a time when the loss of life aroused in each of us a feeling of personal loss. On hearing of a death or accident, our natural inclination was to say a silent prayer and feel a sense of remorse. Today people are inundated with death through the news media to the point that the death of one person, or a million, is of no significance. The numbers have ceased to have any meaning.

I am reminded of the comments made on the same subject by a noted author when he stated. "With every approach to knowledge guarded by a formidable array of experts and bibliographies, the aspirant must possess sharp wits and unnaturally developed skepticism if he is not to fall victim to one or the other of the rival schools of dogma, secular and ecclesiastical, which, though mutually exclusive, unite instinctively to frustrate any attempt to avoid altogether the established orthodoxy's".[2]

"Nowhere is the tyranny of the pedant more evident than in the study of human origins and the sacred history. Most books on the ancient past rely on their authority on nothing more substantial than the preconception of their authors, inevitably influenced by the mis-applied theories, and the corrupt traditions of the Christian Church. We are conditioned at an early age to accept a narrow, linear view of history, according to which civilization is a recent and unique development, now for the first time becoming universally established".[3]

1   *Gaius Suetonius Tranquillus. Roman Historian, 69-140 AD. 'The Twelve Caesars' Translated by Robert Graves. Published by Penguin Classics.*
2   *Michell John. 'City of Revelation' Published by Ballantine Books. NY.*
3   *Ibid*

We are brought up in a secular society, which imposes the strict limitations of thought and language necessary for its own survival. Few people have the time or inclination to examine evidence, which might disturb the settled convictions to which they have grown accustomed. The majority must rely for information on the opinions of the professional critics, who are naturally inclined to tend to their own gardens, to preserve therein the neatly angled hierarchies of familiar ideas, and to weed out all that fails to accord with the prevailing order. It is not an easy matter to question the ideas into which one is educated from infancy, to doubt the pretensions of currently fashionable authorities: neither is it desirable for anyone whose way of life depends upon the favors of the literary or academic world that he should do so".[1]

His criticism concerning the educational system may not meet with the approval of the majority of people, nevertheless, when evaluated against the established beliefs held to be true within the educational system in our society today; his opinions must be respected... I have quoted extensively from this writers work to support some of the views and comments that will be made concerning the beliefs that are sacrosanct within today's religious and scholastic environment.

---

1   Ibid

Chapter 10

It is painful to see man tearing his soul asunder by his actions towards his fellow men, and more so, towards his environment. The widespread turmoil, and misery that exists on our planet today reminds one of the dire predictions prophesized in the Bible, and in the legends of South America that speaks of the destruction of the world.[1]

There are widespread ideological and religious conflicts between nations, as there are between people and their Governments. Our society appears to be a world of continuous wars and conflicts, and it is difficult to find a single country where peace exists. It should therefore come as no surprise that this generation long for a world that can offer some form of stability and order.

Because of the disorder, we are seeing death and destruction inflicted upon civilian populations on all continents; it's difficult to differentiate between our society and those of the historic past. Whether this is due to some form of psychosis is difficult to determine. However, when one listens to the world news, the predictions regarding the destruction of the human species is all too evident.

Much like the behavioral pattern of a species of Lemming, who are said to commit suicide, when they experience a population explosion. Man, as a species, with the power he controls, appears bent on destroying himself, and along with life on this planet. However, what we can be certain off; earth will survive as it has in the past, with perhaps a remnant of life to start the cycle all over again. Let us hope that those who survive will learn a lesson from the past and create a world of peace and stability.

When we look back in history, we are reminded of the events that led to the decline and destruction of ancient cultures and civilizations. As we trace our steps back into the ancient past we find similar situations existed within the more advanced cultures to which we will reference.

It is no coincidence that each of these civilizations saw their rise to power and eventual decline under one of the Astrological signs that act as a time clock in the affairs of this planet.

---

1   Vaillant. G.C. 'Aztecs of Mexico'. Publish by Penguin Books London The Toltecs of Tula. Aztec mythology tells of the creation of the world and the four eras through which life will survive. The world has gone through three stages; the fourth era in which we live today is called the 'Fire Sun'. This era will be destroyed by a general conflagration. Myths of a similar nature can be found in most South American cultures.

Knowing the part that Astrology has played in the lives of our ancient ancestors, it would be a grave error for our modern society to ignore the events of the past.

The literary works of the great Roman historians clearly demonstrate the importance that the Romans people, who were extremely superstitious, placed upon their Astrologers priests before embarking upon any enterprise. There are many occasions in their recorded history when a major enterprise was postponed due to unfavorable omens being predicted by the priests.

One famous General refused to go into battle until instructed by certain oracles, who would tell him the right time and place for victory. To ensure instant communication with the powers that control the destiny of man, he relied upon the services of a prophetess who accompanied him during his campaign against the German tribes, who were attempting to cross into Italy.[1]

It is extremely difficult for those of us who divorce our self from such superstitious beliefs to believe the importance the Romans placed upon the most innocuous signs. One historian states, "Before the victories, two vultures were always to be seen flying above the Generals armies following them on the march. These birds could be recognized by the bronze collars on their necks, for the soldiers had once caught them, fitted on the collars, and let them go again. Afterwards, whenever they recognized the birds they used to greet them gladly, and the sight of them when they were marching out used to make them confident of their victory".

It is obvious that the writer had had little knowledge of this particular bird's behavior. We could say that the Vultures had a personal stake in the outcome of the pending battle, in that they were looking forward to a hearty meal at the end of the day, therefore, their presence was self- serving. Continuing, with his narrative, he goes on to say, "Many other prodigies appeared at this time. Most were of the ordinary type. ---There had been seen in the sky at night flaming spears and shields that signified victory for the Romans". [2] It is clear that this particular historian possessed a very creative mind for the occult.

Modern society would question the sanity of these people, and their superstitious beliefs in the supernatural, forgetting that the reading of one's Astrological horoscope in the daily news papers is a daily occurrence for the majority of people, as it was for our ancestors in the past.

In today's environment any magazine or newspaper that you open will contain your personal horoscope, by which one can develop a future plan to avoid possible misfortune. Like the soldiers of the past, people are looking for some form of reassurance in their lives.

Titus Livius, the Roman historian stated when compiling his history of the Roman Empire, "I am aware to, that most readers will take less pleasure in my account of how Rome began, and in her early history; they wish to hurry on to more modern times, and to read of the period, already a long one, in which the might of an imperial people is beginning to work to its own ruin".

---

1   *Plutarch. Greek historian. (AD 46-140). 'Makers of Rome'. The life of Gaius Coriolanus. Translated by Ian Scott Kilvert. Published by Penguin Classics.*

2   *Plutarch. 'The Fall of the Roman Republic. Translated by Rex Warner. Published by Penguin Classics.*

He goes on to say, when speaking of the situation that existed in Rome, "My own feeling is different; I shall find antiquity a rewarding study, if only because while I am absorbed in it I shall be able to turn my eyes from the troubles which for so long have tormented the modern world".[1]

When we view the world today, it appears history is about to repeat itself. The decline and disintegration of a world power, is not in this case political in nature, but religious, as it concerns the power of the Church of Rome. Over the coming years we will see a gradual decline in the teaching and power of this institution, and eventually its disappearance from the world stage. However, its ability to accommodate to changing circumstances has been well demonstrated over the years, and may well serve it in the future. To survive, it may have to align itself with one of the major religions now in existence. In this regard it well may align itself with the major Evangelical organizations in America, as a bulwark against the religion of Islam, which is gaining ground throughout the world.[2] Alternatively they may perhaps return to the Judaic roots from which they originated

As we are approaching, what people believe is the end of the Millennium, we see the spread of Islam exerting its belief around the globe. Within the last fifty years, the world has seen Islam demand recognition to separate statehood, not based on political, but on religious agendas.

Unlike Christianity, the Muslim's do not consider themselves as others, owing allegiance to the country of their birth. Their allegiance is to the God established in the Koran, as preached by Mohammed, and like the Christen Church in ages past, when they gain supremacy it is only a matter of time before they exert their authority by suppressing those who will not embrace their belief.

The dream of old is fast becoming a reality in Europe with the creation of Islamic states west of the Bosporus. The Islamic dominance over those not of their faith is currant in those areas of Europe, where with the help of America, and its western allies, the Islamic states of Bosnia-Herzegovina, Kosovo, and Macedonia have been creates to the detriment of Yugoslavia.

Similar events are occurring in Russia within those provinces, which are predominantly Muslim. One has to be conversant with the wording of the Koran to recognize the singleness of purpose exhibited by those of the Muslim religion in their efforts to propagate the doctrine of Mohammed.

It is inconceivable for us to think that the turmoil we see in our society has been a way of life down through the ages. Was there a time in the history of the human race when there may have existed a civilization who believed that they had a close personal relationship with what they considered to be their God, devoid of fear and retribution, a relationship of love and trust, not only for their fellow human beings, but for all created life, out of love for their creator.

---

1   *Titus Livius. (BC 59-AD 17) 'The Early History of Rome' Book 1. Translated by Aubrey de Selincourt Published by Penguin Classics*

2   *I would like to take credit for this most obvious of theories however this theory was first voiced by Gioacchino da Fiore a Cistercian monk (1130-1202 AD) who predicted the downfall of the present Church hierarchy and a new Age of the Holy Spirit when Christians would unite with infidels in an Order of the Just.*

That would be the dream, but due to mans propensity to evil, it is extremely difficult for twentieth century man to accept such a hypothesis, as his mind has been distorted by religious beliefs, continuous wars and conflicts over the centuries. However, it is conceivable that such a civilization could have existed on this planet in ages past. Memories and traditions, which are the leaves of history, indicate to us that such a society may have populated the planet in ages past.

This affinity to the belief of a benevolent creator has resulted in some to divorce themselves from the mainstream of life, to live singly, or in religious communities, devoting themselves to prayer and good works. These special people, who by discipline and prayer aspired to this union with their creator, created a microcosm of the society of which we speak. That a civilization, isolated by its location, developed a society of balance and harmony may not be as far-fetched as one would imagine.

There is no reason to doubt that this close spiritual relationship may have been a reality that existed in former times between the creator, created, and nature. This purity of spirit that man believed to be his inheritance can be clearly discerned when reading the Rig-Veda, the most ancient sacred religious writings to come out of the Indian Sub-Continent.[1]

---

1   'Rig Veda .Translated by Wendy Doniger O'Flatherty. Published by Penguin Classics.

Chapter 11

One can sense mans wonder and amazement at the beauty the Universe , that surrounds him and we can appreciate the questions he asks we hear our ancient ancestor asking the same questions, which are as relevant to-day as they were those thousands of years ago.

"There was not then what is now nor what is not. There was no sky and no heaven beyond the sky. What power was there? Where? Who was that power? Was there an abyss of fathomless water? Darkness was hidden in darkness. All was fluid and formless. Who knows the truth? Who can tell us whence and how arouse this Universe. The gods are later then it's beginning. Who knows therefore whence comes this creation? Only that god that sees in the highest heaven: he only knows whence this universe comes, and whether it was made or uncreated. He only knows or perhaps he knows not"?

We can also visualize our ancient Priest standing in the immensity of time looking into space and wondering as to why and for what purpose he is on this earth. In his introduction to the 'Bhagavad-Gita Gita' Juan Mascaro refers to the joy and beauty of this planet and universe by saying "In the Vedas we see man watching the outside world with joy and wonder. He feels life and prays for victory in life. He watches the beauty of the dawn and the glory of the sun and he feels that fire and air, and the waters and the winds are living powers: His life depends upon nature, and he knows that between nature and he there is not an impassable gulf. Man loves this beautiful creation and he feels that his love cannot but be answered by a greater love".[1]

The sentiments expressed in this excerpt are to be found in the beliefs of a majority of ancient civilizations and native cultures, especially by the native North American Indian and his love for the land and nature.

Unlike modern man who is forever trying to find mechanical answers to spiritual questions, these people accepted their place within the order of the universe without question.

They found no need to question the gifts that nature provided. In their religious beliefs, they viewed their purpose in life as being the custodian of the land and the creatures that existed

---

1   *The Bhagavad-Gita Gita. Tran: Juan Mascaro. Introd. Published by Penguin Books*

within their environment as a responsibility imposed upon them by the Great Spirit whom they believed to be the supernatural power that permeates all life.

Science are still looking and asking the same questions that made these ancient people look up to the heavens and question their place in the universe. However, unlike these people of old, the modern method of scientific quest being more mechanistic rejects the idea of a spiritual energizing force as the progenitive source of creation.

Whereas, our ancestors in their quest for knowledge detected the energy force or soul that is the essence of all life and spiritually aligned themselves with what they believed was their creator. In contrast modern man has been weaned away from this most natural of relationships to believe in a god who demands their allegiance. A relationship of this nature is one of trepidation rather than of expectation.

In these beautiful Vedic hymn can be detected the deep religious nature of these writings and appreciation of man's efforts to find answers as to how the solar system and universe were created. The above excerpt taken from the collection of the Vedic Hymns of India, are the most ancient religious texts found in the Indo-European language, reputed to date back to around 1500 BC, or earlier.

Although history attributes the Vedic literature to an Aryan race who migrated[1] into NW India from South Russia and Turkistan around 1500 BC,[2] the possibility exists that they may have been written at a much earlier period during the Harappa civilization that occupied the Indus valley (2500-1800 BC)[3] and became religious doctrine in successive generations of immigrants into the Indus Valley region over a long period of time.

Who were the people who composed these hymns?

Tradition ascribes the authorship to inspired seer-poets.[4] However, it is more likely that these hymns were the work of a religious priesthood and orally taught to the young neophytes on their entry into the priesthood over an extended period of time. As the hymns were written in Sanskrit, a language which scholars attribute to an Indo-European origin, the probability exists that these hymns were in existence and an integral part of the Harappa civilization prior to the arrival of these new Aryan immigrants. This would suggest that Sanskrit may have been the language of the original inhabitants of the Indus Valley civilization, although there is no hard evidence to support this hypothesis.

It is however, reasonable to suggest, in evaluating the information that is now available about these cultures, a picture may emerge to indicate that the new immigrants may have been absorbed into the new society. Perhaps being more prolific then the indigenous people, over

---

1   *Atlas of World History Vol 1 Hermann Kinder/Werner Hilgemann The Early Empires/India (3000 BC-c A.D. 700) Published by Penguin Books*

2   *Ibid.*

3   *Ibid*

4   *The New Columbia Illustrated Encyclopaedia.*

time adapted their culture and way of life, increased in population to the extent that the ruled became the rulers.

Historically there would appear to be some confusion and contradictions regarding the history of this region.

The Indian sub-continent contains some of the most ancient civilizations that existed in this region more than 4500 years ago[1] yet little was known of this continent until the arrival of the British East Indian Company in the seventeenth century.

The knowledge developed by these early colonel traders of the people and regions, in general was more imaginary then actual historical fact, distorted by myths and legends leaving many questions unanswered.

It was not until the late eighteen century that efforts were made to translate the main body of Indian classical literature that a history of these Aryan people began to emerge.[2].This was not based upon historical or archaeological evidence, but largely on the translation of the Rig-Veda's, a collection of Vedic hymns purported by the scholars to be the classic religious literature of these Aryan people.

Up to the 1920's it was hypothesize by the experts that this Aryan culture was the only civilization that existed from ancient times within the Indus Valley.

Based upon this premise they developed the theory that the source of our superior Western civilization derived its beginning from this race.

This view was clearly demonstrated by the German Government during the 1930's by which German descent was traced back to this Aryan culture that they classed as a master race.

Taking advantage of this theory, efforts were made by those in power to introduce the concept of a pure genetic race that would restore the greatness of the Germanic race. One would like to think that the defeat of Germany would put an end to this nonsense, but this has not been the case. The same view is held to be true by many in our Western culture, especially in North America where the question of race is still a very contentious issue.

It is nothing short of remarkable how this nation of people, who have no real racial or cultural identity, classes themselves as superior. With the exception of those few families who have maintained their Anglo-Saxon roots, the majority of the American people are an amalgam of people from all nations on this planet. Genetically they are far from being superior, and it would be questionable if they are intellectually superior as they claim.

This pursuit for ones identity has lead man to look at the surrounding beauty of this universe and questions his existence and his place in the order of nature. His efforts to explain its origin and workings can be compared to the ongoing scientific efforts to explain the Biological interaction between the cells that make up the total human being when in the womb.

---

1   *The Atlas of the World Vol 1 By Hermann Kinder/Werner Hilgemann Penguin Reference Books*
2   *Ibid*

In this field of research the development of the human fetus and of the brain from the moment of conception is a mystery that defies explanation. By the same token, the intricate formation and working of the brain is just another mystery to science as is the workings of the Universe, or for that matter nature itself. In their efforts to explain these mysteries that are beyond our comprehension, they tend to indulge in all types of fantasies to support their theories, meanwhile tend to forget the realities that are readily discernible.

Chapter 12

The hypothesis put forward by the scientific communities on the origins of the Universe, and of life, has as much validity as the believes held by the most primitive peoples.

Even the ever-broadening scientific knowledge of modern times has brought no unanimous agreement about the exact origin of the earth and the solar system. The general theory that as a result of a cosmic explosion the solar system began as a finely dispersed mass of gas and dust, rotating and concentrating gently under gravitational forces[1].

As the volume decreased, the rotation became more rapid. In time, when the centrifugal force at the equator of the nebula equaled the pull of gravity successive rings of matter separated from the outer part of the disk until the diminished nebula at the center was surrounded by a series of rings. Out of the material contained in each ring, through a centrifugal process of shrinking, the gasses matter condensed to form the Earth, and the Planets that presently orbit the Sun. [2] Such a theory defies explanation, however, in the absence of any other explanation, was accepted by the scientific community.

In their efforts to explain the mysteries of the solar system, science based their theories on hypothetical conjectures that leave more questions than answers. The more one evaluates the theories postulated by the various experts the more improbable it becomes that a solar system of order and harmony could evolve through a process of chaos. The theory of matter being condensed through the gravitational forces in space to form the sun and surrounding planets not only is improbable but impossible due to the many questions that remain unanswered. "The origins of the planets and their satellites remain unsolved. The theories not only contradict one another, but each of them bears within itself its own contradictions. If the sun had been unattended by planets, its origin and evolution would have presented no difficulty."[3]

It is interesting to read the theories propounded by the experts regarding the origins of the Universe.

---

1   *History of Man The Last Two Million Years. Published by the Readers Digest.*
2   *Laplace. Pierre Simon. Exposition du systeme du Monde*
3   *Velikovsky. Emmanuel. Worlds in Collision. Published by Pocket Books N Y*
Jeans, Astronomy and Cosmogony, ₚ.395.

"It is hard enough for us to work out what is on this Earth laborious to know what lies within our reach. Who then can discover what is in the Heavens".[1]

The wisdom and logic in this statement is as valid today as when written thousands of years ago by some scribe who unlike our present day scientist recognized the limitations that nature imposes upon man and our human families place within the order of the Universe. His observations should act as a lesson to our scientist when they set out to unravel the secrets of the Universe that is our heritage.

Although scientist have increased their knowledge in many fields, and advanced technology to a height undreamed of fifty years ago, to the extent that man acquired the ability to leave this planet and reach out to the stars. Yet with all these amazing scientific breakthroughs, scientists are no nearer to solving the mysteries of nature to day as they were in the early years of scientific development.

It would appear that science approach the mysteries of nature with a sterility that prevents the mind from seeing the beauty of the inherent inner spirituality that is unique to the human family. It is this uniqueness that separates the human family from all other creatures living on this planet.

This spirituality is not to be confused with religion as is known to day whose aim is to govern personal conduct in life and the salvation of souls.[2] The animated spirit that lies dormant in the soul of the human being, which at times manifests itself to the astonishment of the scientific community, is the living creative force that energizes the universe and all life on this planet.

Opposed to this science would have us believe that man is but a living phenomenon without origin or continuity, a physicochemical accident.[3] This fear of not knowing his origins make the human being susceptible to all kinds of fears and phobias. It is this aura of superstitious fear of the unknown and uncertainty of the future that man created a God to whom he could identify, thus allowing the priests and shamans the means to play upon the fears of mankind in controlling human behavior.

The shamans that controlled the minds and personal lives of our ancestors are still with us today, albeit they have changed their manner of dress and form of worship but their aims and purpose have not changed. The close relationship that existed in former times between the Creator, Created and Nature, the purity of spirit that was mans inheritance has been contaminated by a guilt complex that has been fostered by the various religions down through the ages to their advantage.

The idea of original sin as postulated by the Christen Church separated man from his Creator, thus paving the way for the injection of a supplementary Godhead as a means of redeeming mankind from the supposed sins of their first parents.

1   *The New Jerusalem Bible. Book of Wisdom. 9-16*
2   *De Lubicz. R.A. Schwaller. Sacred Science Translated by André and Goldian VandenBroeck. Published by Inner Traditions International NY*
3   *De Lubicz. R.A. Schwaller. Sacred Science.*

This animated spirit that is the controlling energy force of the universe was part of the human psychic at the dawn of time, as it is today. It is this energy force that brings order and harmony to this Planet.

The elements that make up the human psychic are an elusive mystery yet to be solved by the scientists in their continuous search for knowledge. However, this knowledge will not be acquired through the process of mechanistic science, but by the science of transforming consciousness and the acquisition of psychic spiritual powers.[1] What are these spiritual powers of which we speak that today we refer to this as the soul of man?

The information gathered by Anthropologists and Historians from the worlds remaining primitive societies lead us to belief that our ancient ancestors had a deeper understanding of the mysterious forces that motivate the human psychic then do our modern scientific communities. For when the various theories propounded concerning man and his environment are evaluated, one indisputable fact emerges that is beyond any question of doubt and that is the antiquity of man and the world he occupies. However, there needs to be a clarification when we speak of antiquity.

We are not referring to a period that consists of a mere five thousand years before our common era, which appears to be the period that most scientist attribute to as our historic past, but, to a period of time that has not yet been clearly defined by the experts. For amid the convolution of dates propounded, what is uncertain, and has yet to be answered is how long has man existed on this planet and from where did he originate?

Up to the 1st century these questions posed no problems for the various cultures. In the simplicity of their religious belief our ancestors had arrived at a simple answer that satisfied their needs and gave them an unquestionable assurance of their immortality.

The fatalistic believe in a God as their creator and protector removed all the uncertainties and vagaries that life had to offer. This belief in a supreme God in one form or another was universal, but with the introduction of Christianity, his place in the life of mankind was modified and refined. No longer was he a God who demanded continuous sacrifices, quick in venting his anger should his demands not be met. He was now transposed into a compassionate and loving God, a father to mankind, and a shepherd to his flock.[2] This is the belief that has been the foundation on which the majority of cultures have based their creeds for the last two thousand years. However, over the centuries the various religious bodies have placed a multitude of impediments in the way of this idyllic relationship to the detriment of those who would seek a relationship of love. The demands placed upon the psychic conscience of the human family as a prerequisite to this love has been a yoke on the conscience of the human family.

It was not until the age of intellectual and scientific development, that in the modern sense of the term, came into being in the 16th and 17th century, an age that fostered the belief in natural law and universal order that man emerged from the darkness of intellectual sterility.

---

1   *De Lubicz. R.A. Schwaller. Sacred Science.*
2   *The New Jerusalem Bible. John. 10; 1-18.*

When one looks at mans progress, it is a history of knowledge, science, technological progress, and a steady betterment of human life. It was not Christian, but Hellenistic culture that made possible all its virtue, all its values, all goodness, all greatness, and all the intellectual wealth that has exist over the last millennia. No other culture, as long as it remained untouched by thinking the Greek way has ever produced any science, technology, and therefore no wealth only misery, stagnation, and starvation. Such was the case with Christianity for the first 800 years of its existence, until the human mind was permitted to come out of hiding and get to work".[1]

The confidence generated in human reason spread to influence the 18th century that resulted in a rational and scientific approach to religious social, political, and economic issues which promoted a secular view of the world.[2] This was the age when society's intellects broke free from the restrictions that had been imposed upon their freedom of expression by the religious intolerance of the Church of Rome, a freedom that allowed man to question the existence of his God and begin the search for his origins.

However, in their haste to find the cause and effect of mans being, the theories developed by the early scientists were as questionable as those postulated by the various religious bodies concerning mans origins, as were the beliefs of our ancient ancestors.

By analogy, scientists look on the picture of our pre-historical past and select those areas of time and events that are prominent in the foreground.

This approach leads them to formulate theories that will explain what can be determined by visual inspection. Scant attention is paid to what lies in the background, as the details are shrouded in mist and shadows. The picture presented by the background is confused because of its different shades of color, which can change according to the perspective of the viewer, and in the majority of cases is open to unlimited interpretations.

This is evident by the various views expressed by the experts concerning the origins of man and the Universe. As was expressed by one author, "Time is the dimension in which history exists. Even though one learns the facts and interpretations of history, the men and events, the great civilizations and great periods, no one can approach mastery of the subject without comprehension of the time relationship involved."[3]

It therefore follows that in order to avoid offending the moral and religious sensibilities of the establishment and of those cultures who are sensitive to religious criticism, those who write upon these subjects, must, out of reverence somehow involve the Godhead in the evolutionary process, and all other aspects of mans endeavors. This superstitious fear of offending God as we have said before, places modern man on par with the most primitive societies.

---

1 *Seda. Josef. PhD. PE*
2 *Columbia New Illustrated Encyclopaedia.*
3 *Wallbank Walter T. Civilization. Past and Present 4th Edition Vol 1.(1960). Chronology of Civilization Published by Scott, Foresman and Company NJ.*

The invocation of God in the actions of man is a common trait found in all ancient and modern cultures, whether this is out of a subconscious fear of retribution or reverence is difficult to determine.

Thus it would appear that for the same reason, the theories postulated by the various bodies are influenced by the specter of this unseen God. This fatalistic tendency, by which all that occurs in the affairs of the human family is the will of God, is a characteristic of all religions, more so the major religions of our Western civilization, being more predominant in the Islamic and Indian cultures of the Far East.

To show by example an incident of this nature it will be necessary to refer to a recent event that occurred in the former Yugoslavia when an American aircraft was shot down after completing a bombing mission over the city of Pale, the capitol of the Serbian forces.

The pilot, who ejected safely from his aircraft, landed in a very heavily wooded area and was lost for a period of six days, after which time he was rescued by his comrades. On his return he attributed his safety to the intervention of God by stating that "Were it not for the love he had for God and God's love for him his rescue would not have been successful,"[1] claiming his safe return as a miracle.

As this pilot had been on a bombing mission in, which it is believed quite a number of civilians lost their lives, including women and children. It would appear that our existence is subject to the whimsical will of a capricious God, who is selective in who should live, and who should die.

There is no doubt that those who died equally loved the same God nevertheless; God saw fit to save the pilot at the cost of their lives. It is highly probable that the community, who suffered at the hands of this pilot, may have been informed by their religious leaders that it was the will of God that their loved ones should die, and should eagerly accept their loss as an offering to God.

The idea of offering up ones pain and suffering for the greater glory of God, is the philosophy practiced by the Christen Church The justification for this idea can be found in the writings of the founders of the early Christen Church, being based on the premise that if God offered up his only son Jesus Christ as a sacrifice for the sins of mankind, therefore any suffering experienced by man pales in comparison to this ultimate sacrifice.

Christens have from the conception of their religion been taught that "Suffering is part of their training."[2] References to the doctrine of accepting ones trials and tribulations in life as a prerequisite to ones entry into the heavenly kingdom are contained in the Holy Bible of the Christen Church where it is said "When the Lord corrects you, do not treat it lightly for the Lord trains the one that He loves and punishes all those that he acknowledges as his son's,"[3] "I am the one who reproves and disciplines all those I love."[4] "You will always have your trials

---

1   *O'Grady. Capt. U.S.A. Naval Air Force. June. 1995.*

2   *The New Jerusalem Bible. Heb. 12-7.*

3   *The New Jerusalem Bible. Proverbs. 12. 5-7.*

4   *The New Jerusalem Bible. Revelations 3. 11.*

try to treat them as a happy privilege, even though you may, for a short time has to bear being plagued by all sorts of trials your faith will have been tested and proved like gold."[1]

From this it can be determined that the doctrine of fatalism was the doctrine of the early Church in teaching the people to accept what life had to offer and join their suffering to that of God's for the salvation of mankind. The development of this moral philosophical idea may be attributed to the eradication of offering to God the human sacrifices that were demanded by the religious priests in former times as an atonement for mans transgressions.

This God who was "The hand that from formless matter created the World, made man imperishable, and made him in the image of his own nature,"[2] is to be feared, loved, and pacified by personal offerings of prayer and good deeds to appease his anger. Failure to do so is to suffer during one's lifetime on this earth and being denied God's presence on departing this world, or as Christens are taught in their religious doctrine, the soul being cast into a state of darkness. Therefore it is imperative that the Christen be forever mindful of what awaits him should he stray from the straight and narrow path outlined for him by his religious superiors.

As God is viewed as the Supreme King and Jesus Christ the Son of God[3] as the supreme high priest appointed by God to offer himself as a sacrifice for the sins of mankind was the greatest gift God bestowed upon man. "No one could represent the King in his divine character as his son, who might be supposed to share the divine afflatus of his father. No one, therefore, could so appropriately die for the king and, through him, for the whole people, as the king's son."[4]

This idea of offering up ones son as a sacrifice in atonement for mans transgressions was adapted by the Apostle Paul in his letters to the Jewish communities who lived outside Palestine in the early years of his ministry in Asia Minor and Europe. In his letter to the Hebrews he talks extensively on the subject of Temple sacrifice as required under the Law of Moses. Comparing the sacrifices carried out by the Temple Priests to that of Jesus Christ who offered up his life for the sins of mankind.

The language of human sacrifice used by Paul was understandable to the Jewish people, as it was part of their heritage.

The practice of Kings offering their Son's as sacrificial victims was common prior to the event of Christianity as there are numerous instances in recorded history of Kings offering their son' or subjects as sacrificial victims to the Gods or to appease the Gods anger.

This form of sacrificial sin offering on behalf of the people was not unique to any one people or culture,[5] but was the practice in the majority of cultures around the world. It was also the

---

1   *The New Jerusalem Bible. James. 1. 2-3. 1st Peter. 6-7.*

2   *The New Jerusalem Bible. Book of Wisdom. 11.18. 2. 23.*

3   *The New Jerusalem Bible. Matthew. 3: 17. 4: 3. 14: 33. 16: 17.*
     Luke. 9: 35-36.
     John. 1: 34. 3: 16-18.

4   *Frazer. J G. D. C. L., LL.D., Litt. D. The Golden Bough.3rd Edition. Part 3. (1911)The Dying God.*

5   *Frazer. J G. D. C. L., LL.D., Litt. D. The Golden Bough.3rd Edition. Part 3. (1911) The Dying God Published by MacMillan and Co Limited London 1911.*

practice for the common people to offer their first born as a sacrificial offering to the God's as a gift offering.

Whether the killing of human beings as an offering to God was a practice that has always existed in the life of man cannot be determined by modern historical research. However, there are sufficient written records to prove that the practice was prevalent among the Semitic races of the Middle East within historic Biblical times.[1]

Numerous cases are documented in the Bible regarding this repugnant of religious practices which was an integral part of the Semite cultures. "Thus Philo of Byblus, in his work on the Jews, say's; "It was the ancient custom in a crisis of great danger that the ruler of a city or nation should give his beloved son to die for the whole people, as a ransom offered to the avenging demons; and the children thus offered were slain with mystic rites. So Cronus, whom the Phoenicians call Israel being King of the land and having an only begotten son called Jeoud (for in the Phoenician tongue Jeoud signifies 'only begotten') dressed him in royal robes and sacrificed him upon an alter in a time of war, when the country was in great danger from the enemy."[2]

A similar event occurred in the expedition of Israel and Judah against Moab, "When the king of Moab saw that the battle had turned against him, he mustered seven hundred swordsmen in the hope of breaking his way out and going to the King of Aram (Edom), but he failed. Then he took his eldest son who was to succeed him and offered him as a sacrifice on the city wall."[3]

As the Judo/Christen Bible has molded the religious thinking of the twentieth century. It may be beneficial to look at the idea of Monotheism, which was the foundation of the Jewish nation, and also of our Western culture, as opposed to the religions that existed in Palestine prior to the arrival of Moses from Egypt.

In general people tend to look upon the Bible as the factual history of the Hebrew race, with God or Yahweh as the central character in molding the peoples thinking according to his dictates. This would be wonderful if it were true as it would prove the existence of God and the Jewish race as the world's primer people destined to rule the world as Gods chosen people[4].

1   *The New Jerusalem Bible. Genesis. 22; I. 31; 13. Exodus. 13; 1. Leviticus. 18; 21. 20; 25. Deuteronomy. 18; 10. 1st Kings. 16; 34. 2nd Kings. 3; 27. 12; 1-3 16; 3. 17; 17, 31. 23; 10. Judges. 11; 30. Micah. 6; 7. Isaiah. 57; 5-9 2nd Chronicles. 3; 1. 28; 1-4. 33. 1-6. Ezekiel. 16; 20-21, 31. Jeremiah. 7; 31. 32; 35. !St Machabees.1. 46; 52.*

2   *Frazer. J G. D.C.L., LL.D., Litt.D. The dying God. 3rd Edition. Part 111. (Philo of Byblus, quoted by Eusebius, Praeparatio Evangelii, and I. 10. 29 sq.)*
     The New Jerusalem Bible. 2nd Kings. 3; 26-27.
     Tacitus. Cornelius. (55-117AD) The Histories. Book V. 1-13.
     The New Jerusalem Bible. Genesis. 11; 31.
     The New Jerusalem Bible. Chronological Table

3   *The New Jerusalem Bible. 2nd Kings. 3; 26-27.*

4   *Tacitus. Cornelius. (55-117AD) The Histories. Book V. 1-13.Translated by Kenneth Wellesley Publish by Penguin Classics*

This however is not the case, although our Western civilization owes a depth of gratitude for the moral teachings that are found in the Books of the Bible, a moral philosophy that has shaped our culture, acting as one would say as a brake on man's tendency to evil. Nevertheless, to believe that God who is depicted as being the essence of good would bring about an evil act to shape the future of the world by the destruction of peoples and nations to achieve his aims is evil within itself. Therefore to attribute these actions to God is morally wrong.

The use of God's name in granting divine favor to rule is not unique in the history of mankind, but has been a long-standing tradition among many civilizations. The divine rights of Kings were a practice that was in existence until quite recently, and did not come to an end until the early part of the twentieth century. However, in the transition from a Monarchical system to that which in the most part is Democratic, the world has come through a dramatic period in its history.

Within this new Democratic system there are those in our present society who believe that it is their divine right to rule in a new society to which they allude to as the New World Order in which the political and economic policies developed will be adhered to by all nations irrespective of their political or religious believes. As this new order has more to do with trade rather than religious ideology, its success will be dependent upon the speed by which the natural resources of this planet are depleted.

The idea of a God granting the right to rule to a select group of people forms part of the Biblical history of the Jewish people and begins with the migration of Abraham from Ur of Chalda to the land of Canaan. It is recorded in the Bible that when Terah the father of Abraham left Ur of the Chaldaeans with his family to settle in Canaan their journey took them to Haran in South East Turkey,[1] where they resided until the death of Terah. On the death of Terah, Abraham took his wife, his nephew Lot, and those people that he had acquired while living in Haran.

Quite possibly these were slaves or workers who had attached themselves to his household, a custom that is still prevalent in the Middle East, and set off for the land of Canaan, where he arrived around 1850 BC.[2]

On his journey he passed through the land as far as Shechem's holy place, the Oak of Moreh,[3] which is today identified with Nebi Dahi, South of Mount Tabor. From there he made his way by stages to the Negev desert in the Sinai Peninsula region.

This journey was a formidable undertaking considering the distance travailed and the territory in which they had to traverse. One can imagine the families, the camp followers and herds of animals slowly wending their way down through the different regions of Palestine, grazing their animals on what land was available or negotiating with the local people for permission to graze and water their flocks.

---

1   *The New Jerusalem Bible. Genesis. 11; 31.*
     There are no sources in the current document.
2   *The New Jerusalem Bible. Chronological Table*
3   *The New Jerusalem Bible. Genesis. 12; 5-6.*

As water was of vital importance and remains so even to to-day to these people, it would be an important aspect for their survival to gain the good will of the local authorities before entering their territory. This same scenario has been played out over thousands of years by the Bedouin tribes in their treks across the desert from one water hole to the next, continually searching for sufficient grazing on which to feed their flocks.

For those with a poetic mind this form of living would appear to be idyllic, whereas it is for those who still practice this life style is and was a hard and demanding life. However, with the event of modern technology that has brought a major road system to the desert regions, it is likely that the modern Bedouin moves his flock by transportation rather than by the old ways of walking from oasis to oasis.

This old form of lifestyle among the Bedouin is being slowly erased by modern technology and better living conditions.

As Abraham, the progenitor of the Hebrew nation is the central figure in the Biblical saga that was to follow his entry into Canaan, it would be beneficial to look beyond Abraham and take a brief look at what was happening within the regions of the Middle East during the period in question.

But before we can delve into this it's essential that we remove the specter of this unseen God who suddenly appears to tell Abraham, "I will make you a great nation. It is to your descendants that I will give this land."[1]

What better way of acquiring land to the detriment of the indigenous people then to convince ones followers and others that God has given it to you and your descendants. In all likelihood this claim is as spurious as all those areas in the Bible concerning the Godhead and his dealing with the people of Palestine.

As the beliefs found in the early books of the Bible are an amalgam of the myth and legends that were the religious believes held by the Semitic peoples. The idea of a supreme God was not unique, as this concept of a God of the heavens, a supreme deity was the belief of the Indo-Europeans,[2] and prevalent in all countries around the globe. Although there was a hierarchy of Gods to which homage was paid, the majority of cultures recognized the existence of one supreme figurehead.

Little is known of Hebrew history other then what is contained in the Books of the Bible. Notwithstanding the archaeological finds that have been unearthed over the years that clearly indicates the presence of people and historical events down through the ages.

There is no clear evidence that would substantiate the claims postulated by the Jewish historians [3] regarding the culture known to us to-day as Israelites. Although the word Jew and Hebrew are look upon today as being synonymous, this may not have been the case in early

1   *The New Jerusalem Bible. Genesis. 12: 2-7.*

2   *Hermann Kinder/ Werner Hilgemann. Atlas of World History vol. 1.Published by penguin Books*

3   *Josephus.Flavius. Against Apion. Trans: William Whiston. A.M. Published by Ward lock and Company London*

historic times. There is every possibility that these were two separate cultures that assimilated into what we know today as Israelites.

The books of the Bible were not compiled until around the 2nd century BC being derived from earlier traditional folklore and historical records, (both written and oral). It is likely that this claim on the land of Palestine was inserted into the body of the Pentateuch to justify the actions that were to follow down through the centuries and as it is today. It is therefore important that when looking into the period when Abraham entered Canaan it must be in the context of looking at history objectively and with an unbiased mind.

If the date given for Abraham's entry into Canaan is correct, it occurred in the Egyptian Middle Kingdom during the 12th dynasty (1991-1780 BC) in the reign of the Pharaoh Sesostris the third, (1878-1840 BC).

It was during this period that Palestine was occupied by the Egyptians whose influence over Palestine and Syria extended along the coastal regions but not the interior.[1]

This is not to imply that the interior was uninhabited or sparsely populated, as there is every reason to believe from the Archaeological work carried out within this region that it was heavily populated by a people of the Semite culture, and not necessarily Hebrews.

These people in the interior were largely nomadic pastoral, as are the Bedouin tribes of today. In contemporary Arabic society Abraham would be classed as a Sheikh, the leader of a family tribe.

Though grouped under the name of Semites, this culture was comprised of, Arabs, Acadians, Assyrians, Canaanites including Amorites Moabites, Edomites, Ammonites, and Phoenicians. There is also the Aramaean tribes to, which the Hebrew race belonged, which was part of this Semite nation of people.[2]

All these different tribes were to some extent directly influenced by the advanced civilizations of Sumeria and Egypt, which lay to the East and West of Palestine. One could say that Palestine was the corridor used by various combatants in time of war, the most famous being the Pharaoh Ramses on his way to the battle of Kadash and the Greek general Alexandria in his conquest of the Middle East.

We can also by inference assume that in times of peace extensive trade was carried out with the trade links that existed between the various cultures especially among the Greek Phoenicians, and Egyptian merchant traders. It would appear that history has come a full circle when one looks at this region today, the problems that existed three or four thousand years ago have resurfaced to be played out by the descendants of the original occupants of Palestine.

It was into this culture that Abraham migrated from Haran with his family and followers.

---

1   *The New Jerusalem Bible. Chronological Table.*
     Brinton, Clarence Crane. A History of Civilization. 5th Edition. Prehistory to 1715 Published by Prentice-Hall Inc Englewood Cliffs New Jersey
2   *Columbia. New Illustrated Encyclopaedia.*

This was no strange land he was entering, nor were the people strange and alien to him. Quite the contrary, these people were related both in culture, language and religious believe. They were also tolerant of the various forms of worship which was based upon a hierarchy of Gods of whom Baal was supreme, as one would find within the Christen communities today when we speak of God as being the supreme ruler and source of life. Baal was to the Canaanites the source of life and fertility, the creator and ruler of the Universe.

There were numerous Temples dedicated to the god in Canaan and the name was added to the names of many localities, some of which can be found within this region to-day. We can assume that these place names signified the location of a Temple that was dedicated to this god, to who worship of prostitution and the sacrifice of children were made.

There was also the god Moloch, the Canaanite god of fire to whom human sacrifices were made, especially children.

A Temple dedicated to this god was located at Tophet in the valley of Hinnom near Jerusalem As these religious beliefs were prevalent throughout the Semite culture, it is obvious that Abraham, being of the Semite race was a follower of this religion. This being so it would be Abraham's religious duty to sacrifice his first born to the God Baal, as was the custom and law the Semite culture demanded.

According to the Bible, Abraham was instructed by God to take his son Isaac to Moriah and offer him as a burnt offering, "On a mountain I will point out to you."[1]

From the Biblical account it took Abraham three days from where he was living, which we are told was Beersheba, to reach the mountain of Moriah, a distance of approximately 57 miles as the crow flies. To-day to travel from Beersheba to Jerusalem presents little problem to the traveler with the road system that is now part of our modern life, but in the days of Abraham to travel 57- 60 miles in three days was no mean achievement as the route of travel was over ancient caravan trails.

The mountain of Moriah, or mount whichever one prefers, was the location on which it is said the Temple of Jerusalem was built by King Solomon. However, inasmuch that there are those who firmly belief that this was an actually historical event, there is no evidence to support that there was such a person as King Solomon. One could say that this is just another instance when the compliers of the Pentateuch allowed their imagination to enhance the Jewish pedigree.

This reference to the Temple can be found in the 2nd Book of Chronicles, 3; 1, which states that "Solomon then began to built the house of Yahweh in Jerusalem on Mount Moriah where David his father had a vision."[2] It is obvious that this particular area was a very special place in the life of the Semite people, and was held in high honor as the dwelling place of the high God and a place of human sacrifice.

---

1   *The New Jerusalem Bible. Genesis. 22; 2.*
2   *The New Jerusalem Bible. 2nd Chronicles. 3; 1.*

It can be inferred from the sayings of the Prophets that Jerusalem was an appointed place where parents burnt their children, both boys and girls to the greater glory of the Gods Baal or Molech.[1]

One would like to believe when reading the story of Abraham that the practice of offering up ones children as a human sacrifice was brought to an end within the family and tribe of Abraham.

This however was not the case, as this vile practice continued on down through succeeding generations and was the practice during the reign of the supposed King Solomon.

Notwithstanding, it is highly probable that at some undefined period in the past, man and all life on this planet lived in a balanced environment of order and harmony. What events occurred that caused these idyllic conditions to change, would be to speculate upon the events of the past that brought this world to near destruction. Whatever it was that brought an end to this pristine way of life, made man fearful of his very existence. The psychological fear engendered by these events created an aura of insecurity and apprehension and a fear of an uncertain future. Conditions as described would be ideal for the creation of a God to whom man could direct his everyday problems and restore his sense of security.

Rather than God being the creator of man, we could say that it was man who formed God from which all religious practices evolved down through time. Therefore, it was not the serpent of evil that disrupted the serenity of this idyllic environment, this mystical Garden of Eden, but the introduction of Godhead into the affairs of man.

It would appear that man uses the name of god as a "sacrificial goat" by attributing all of his actions to the will of God, by these means, abdicates his responsibility and forfeits his inherent gifts of free will, reason, and conscience.   These ideas of a God as being the prime cause for the creation of the Universe and all life on this planet form part of the myths and legends of all ancient cultures and are the fundamental believe of the majority of religions and cultures known to us today. Pre-eminent among the numerous versions describing the process of creation as taught in the Judo/Christen religion as described in the Bible.

The story of Adam and Eve as being the first Man and Woman created by God is the most prevalent version within our Western culture to-day. A religious idea that teaches how God created man "who fashioned him from the dust of the soil,"[2] is the accepted doctrine within the Christen communities around the world.

No man can shape a God as good as himself.[3] A sentiment expressed in many different ways and under various forms by all modern civilizations and cultures, even to the most primitive. Man has held fast to the belief in a supreme God as the Creator of the World and of the Universe. Who, it is said created a Garden of Eden, a world of beauty for man to care for and enjoy.?

1   Frazer. J G. A Study in Magic and Religion. The Dying God. Published by MacMillan and Company Limited London

2   The New Jerusalem Bible. Book of Genesis 2. 6-7.

3   The New Jerusalem Bible. Book of Wisdom. 16-16.

This firm belief of being created in the image of his God has convinced man of his superiority over all other life on this planet and placed him in a special relationship with his creator. It is within this context that man sees himself created for a higher purpose that his presence and purpose on this earth is to be caretaker and guardian of this paradise. Such a belief is prevalent between the North American Indian, and the Aborigine of Australia. And if one researched the matter further, no doubt it would be found that there were many ancient cultures that harbored the same belief. Many have theorized as to the location of this garden of paradise. The general theory held by many religious faiths as to the location of this Garden, that it was somewhere within the basin of the Euphrates and Tigris Rivers in Mesopotamia, that is known to-day as Iraq. Excavations carried out within these regions indicate the presence of thriving communities around 5,000 BC.

The date would conform to the periods postulated in the Christen Bible as to the time in which the world was created.

However, there is no evidence, which would support the theory of this region being the cradle of mankind, or being the mystical Garden of Eden. This historic Middle East region, known as the Fertile Crescent, has played a major role in politics and religion from early Biblical times, and is the site of the most ancient cultures and antiquities known to modern Archaeology.

If man would rationalize his thinking, he may come to the conclusion that if this story was to have any credence, rather than this mystical dream being in a fixed location to satisfy the needs of our religious establishments. The Garden for which man searches to satisfy the yearning of his soul is under his feet. This living organic planet that pulsates with life may be the mystical garden into which the Creator placed man and woman.

Having this self-induced close relationship with his creator, man has believed that on his departure from this world he will have the privilege of becoming an integral part of the Godhead by being absorbed into his Divine presence. By paying homage to his Creator and being assured of immortality man developed cohesive communities of tribes and families. This common believes formed the foundation stone of all cultures and civilizations, and the prime reason for man's survival and progress down through the ages.

Countless theories have evolved concerning the origins of man. There are myths found in all cultures, even to the most primitive that attribute mans creation to the Gods. Mans inherent belief in his immortality will not allow him to accept anything less than being created by a God to whom he will return when his life on this earth is complete. This belief transcends time and found in the Mythology of all civilizations and cultures across this planet.

These myths of creation are in man's psychic consciousness, as is his D.N.A hereditary characteristics that identify him as the unique person that nature intended. These are the religious beliefs that have shaped the fabric of our Western culture for the past 1600 years, and that of the Judaic culture since the formation of their race.

It is inconceivable for man to believe that life ceases on his death. Of all the living creatures, it is only man who has developed the idea of a conscience, and an immortal soul, denying these attributes to any other living creature. As energy is the source that maintains all life, if there is such a thing as an afterlife, it is reasonable to believe that all life's energy will return to its source at the moment of death. If we accept this hypothesis, it follows that this would apply to all life without exception, even to the most minuscule.

The Judaic story on the creation as recounted in the Bible, has two versions of the same event that are similar, though slightly different in context to those found in other ancient civilizations. Both narratives tell of a God who created the heavens, the earth, and all they contain by his will to create. However, on the 6th day there is a change, God decides to create man. "God created man in the image of himself, in the image of God he created him, male and female he created them. And so it was, God saw all he had made, and indeed it was very good. Such were the origins of the heaven and earth when they were created."[1]

It is notable in this account, that a second person or a group is present to whom God is addressing, and who apparently assists him in the act of creation. As God say's, "Let us make man in our own image, in the likeness of ourselves."[2]

Although the account of creation narrated in the Bible is similar to the Mythological legends that were prevalent during the period in which the books of the Bible were compiled, those who transcribed the story imply to the presence of two or more people during the act of creation.

Scholars within the Church of Rome and other Christen Churches including the myriad of religious bodies that profess the Christen teaching on creation, have gone to great lengths to explain away this anomaly within the text as translated from the original documents, however, fall short in their explanation.

The idea of man being created by man does not invalidate the religious believe held by the human race down through the ages that formed the basis of to-days religions. By accepting the belief in a Creator demonstrates mans urge to be one with his maker.

The second account of the creation contains the story of the Garden of Paradise is somewhat different to that of the previous version. According to this narrative, when God had made earth and heaven, "there was yet no wild bush on the earth nor any wild plant sprung up, for God had not sent rain on the earth, nor was there any man to till the soil. However, a flood was rising from the earth and watering all the surface of the soil. God fashioned man of dust from the soil. Then he breathed into his nostrils a breath of life, and man became a living being." Then God said "it is not good that man should be alone, I will make him a helpmate. So God made man fall into a heavy sleep, And while he slept, he took one of his ribs and enclosed it in flesh. God built the rib he had taken from the man into a woman, and brought her to the man."[3]

This latter version of the creation is the one popularly known to the Christian communities around the world and is compatible to those versions found in other civilizations that ascribe man being created from clay or dust.

1   *The Jerusalem Bible. Gen, 1:1.26-31. 1:1.2-4-7. 1:1.2. 18-23.*
2   *Ibid*
3   *Ibid*

These mythological tales on the creation were ancient before the compilation of the Hebrew Old Testament. In contrast to the elaborate version of creation as described in the Judo/Christen Bible, there is the more simplistic versions that are the religious fabric of more ancient societies.

The most archaic myths to which we can make reference are those of the Aborigine of Australia. These people lived a very simple nomadic life, "having no knowledge of basic planting, gathering of crops or animal husbandry, but existed by hunting and food gathering from wild plants and roots, or any other form of food that nature could provide.[1]

They were also completely isolated from contamination by other cultures until the arrival of the European's in the 18th century.

In their mythology on the origins of the world, they say the earth emerged from an endless sea, believing that the earth and the sky were there from the beginning of time.

On the origins of man, their mythologies attribute the creation of all living beings to celestial heroes. The sky hero, Daramulan, who is the Father of all Things, they believe to be the master of life and death. Their myth of man's origins, tell of the migration of the cult hero's, which they regard as their first ancestors, emerged from the ground and when they had taught men the social rules that govern the tribes; they sank into the ground to disappear forever.[2]

Other points of interest regards the Australian Aborigine, is their reference to their ancestors, who they say migrated to the island in the distant past, which they refer to as 'Dreamtime'. However, like the majority of ancient people, the Aborigine had no idea of time in the true sense of the word.

For those ancient people who were not in possession of a calendar, the seasons, planting, growing, and harvesting counted time. Their days are controlled by the rising and setting of the sun. This situation is prevalent in Africa, and South America, among those tribes who have not yet been contaminated by European influence. Therefore, to explain time was beyond their comprehensive, to them it was 'Dreamtime, a period in the distant past that required no explanation.

Their idea of believing in a supreme being who created man and all living things places this Stone Age man on par with our sophisticated religious believers of today. This believe in a God having the power of life and death over his creation is the basic tenant of the Christen faith, also of all the different religions on this planet, and as one goes back in time, the same believes is found in all ancient cultures.

These religious myths cover time and distance and are not unique to any one culture, but cover a vast spectrum of cultures across this planet. There are those who deeming themselves sophisticated in the scholarly science, dismiss these myths as superstitious fears that inhabit the mind of the natives.

---

1   *Larousse. World Mythology.*
2   *Ibid*

Therefore being outdated, are not relevant for study in to-days school system. Yet the adherents of the various religious faiths firmly believe in the creation of man as described in the Judo/ Christen Bible. .

During the middle Ages, it was the general practice of the Church of Rome to condemn people to death for questioning the doctrine of creation as prescribed in the Bible.

This belief, so firmly imbedded in the conscience of our Western culture, infuse society with an aura of fear that to deny this precept, would be synonymous to the sin of heresy, and if not deserving immediate death, would result in the soul been dammed to the fires of hell on departing this life.

The idea of mans creation from earth or mud and in one case peat, is not unique to our Western religious culture, as mans curiosity surrounding his origins are an integral component found in the religious practices of diverse cultures around this planet ranging from China, South America, Australia, Middle East India, and Africa.

It would irrational to think that each of the races, on the different continents lived in isolation from each other over thousands of years. It would also be irrational to belief that man evolved from a "drobble of mud", having his beginning in primordial protoplasmic mass, or originating from the sea, or some stagnant mud hole from which he evolved through successive stages of evolutionary adaptation to arrive at the point at which he is today.[1]

These mythological tales transcend time and are from cultures who were unaffected by the Judaic idea of creation as described in the Bible. It has been the view of Anthropologist that the Sumerian culture of 5000 BC is the oldest source of knowledge concerning cosmological myths on the origin of man. Yet this idea of man being created from mud or clay is not found in the Sumerian idea of mans creation or that of the Egyptians, Greeks or India mythology.

The Sumerian myth of creation tells how cosmic order arouses out of primeval chaos, in which the creation of the world was affected by successive emanations. From the primordial sea came the earth and the sky, and the Gods gave man in order to look after their sheep.

The Sumerian culture represented the earliest stage of human thoughts on creation that we know. This may not be true, as the Aborigines of Australia, who were isolated from the rest of the world until the coming of the Europeans in the 18th century, recount a similar version in their account of the creation.

According to these oral traditions, they tell how the earth slowly emerged from the endless sea, also believing in a supreme being, whom they regarded as the "Father of all things"[2] and the master of life and death. It is interesting that the Aborigine worshiped the sun in their religious ceremonies, a practice that was common to all cultures and civilizations.

In the mythology of the Bantu tribe of South Africa, their oral tradition relates a similar version. According to their traditions they speak of their God Unvelingange, "He who pre-

---

1   Wendt. Herbart. 'It Began in Babel' Translated by James Kirkup. Published by Dell Publishing Inc .NY
2   Larousse World Mythology.

exists"[1] who is granted powers of creation by the Supreme Being, to whom they refer to as, "He who arouse from a bed of reeds and from the ground"[2]

In the Chinese mythological version of creation, the story of the goddess Nukua, whom they attribute as the creator of humanity, is of ancient origin.

"One day as she wandered through the newly created world, Nukua yearned for a companion like herself. She came to a river and gazing at her reflection in the water, trailed her hand in the water and scooped up some mud from the riverbed. She kneaded the clay into a little figure, on which she fashioned legs on which it could stand; Nukua was so pleased with her work that she determined to populate the whole world. Nukua realized that to save the human race from becoming extinct when the original people died, divided the humans into male and female, with the ability to reproduce without her assistance."

There are many different versions of this tale; however, the main ingredients of the human race being created from clay remain.

This idea of man being created from clay is in the mythological tales of the Maya and Inca cultures of South America. According to the Incas, Viracocha, the great god of the Incas, had fashioned one race of men from clay, which he had to destroy because of their transgressions.

The Chocoan Indians speak of a race of men whom the Gods destroyed because of their cannibalism. Following this a second generation who were transformed into animals, to be followed by a third version of mankind whom the Gods fashioned from clay.

The geographical range of these common believes in cultures as diverse as China, Australia, and South America would indicate a common source of mythological knowledge, which may have been transmitted to each of the continents through trade or other forms of communication. However, to suggest that this knowledge was spread through the centrifugal diffusion of a single race that migrated from country to country by way of land bridges to populate the world would be irrational. This hypothesis may be valid if the story of Adam and Eve was based on historical fact or if the story of Noah and the Ark were true. However, there is no evidence that would support the Biblical stories. One can only surmise that this was another occasion when ancient tales were adapted for incorporation into the biblical narratives.

There exists a commonality be between the tales of creation that emanates from the various ancient cultures. As our ideas of creation were molded by the teachings of the Judo/Christen faith over the last 1,600 years there is no reason to reject the theory that this belief of man being created out of mud or clay was not spread throughout Asia, South America by the way of travel by other cultures in the distant past. What period is hard to determine, suffice to say that the version attributed to the Chinese Fu-Hsi Dynasty of 2800 BC, is much earlier than the Judaic version.

---

1   *Ibid*
2   *Ibid*

Whether this belief in man being created from clay is fact or on mythological fiction is academic. Man being the thinking creature that he is, must find a purpose for his existence on this planet and in doing so, developed his theory along, which to him, were logical lines.

Metaphysics and philosophy did not enter into the reasoning of our ancient ancestors; the question of existence presented much more simple questions, and demanded simple answers. Just as the average person believes in the story of creation as described in the Christen Bible, it is much easier for our Christen culture to believe that man was created from a drobble of mud molded by the hand of God then it is for him to believe that he derived his beginning from the ape.

No other ancient culture or civilization has propounded the theory in their mythology of man being descended from the ape or from any other form of animal. It would be abhorrent to an Egyptian or a Greek to believe that his ancestor was an Ape. It was their firm belief that they descended from the Gods and made in their image.

The Egyptian versions of creation speak of a period of primeval chaos. In which there existed a conscience principle. The god Atum, who alone and unaided succeeded in fertilizing himself and produced the first couple, from whom a second couple derived from the first. According to Egyptian mythology the God Ptah, maker of the universe had his existence in Nun, the primeval Ocean, and existed before creation of the Universe. This conception of universal chaos is found in the mythology of China and Sumeria.

The idea of believing a supreme being created man and all living things, places the Stone Age man on par with the religious tenets of the Christen Church of today. These believes in a God having the power of life and death over his creation, is the basic tenant of the Christen faith, and all the different religions on this planet, and this belief can be found in all ancient cultures.

How this marvel of creation was achieved, by whom or what is a question that defies all answers by science, as their best efforts are based upon conjecture and speculation.

Like our ancestors, modern man has to find a reason and purpose for his existence. It is within this context that man has invented a God to whom he can look to as the Creator to ensure his well being in this life and continuity in the next, if it should exist?

The similarity between our ancient ancestors and modern man are not so different, as both aspired to the same believe in the hereafter. It is inconceivable for man to believe that life ceases to exist on his death. Thus being associated with a God will assure his immortality.

When we read the myths and legends from ancient times, we find that, even the most primitive cultures have endeavored to find their relationship within the natural order of the Universe. As in all cases, there exists a common trend in the beliefs and relationship to the Gods. Therefore in this respect modern man is not unlike his ancestors who looked to the heavens and asked how this complex diversity and beauty of life were created, spending their lives looking for answers, even questioning their very existence.

The question that requires a response, is not as to the why and the how, but to the question of when? When did man arrive, and from where? How long has man occupied this planet?

This question is not only applicable to man, but to all life. It is extremely doubtful if these questions will find an answer. Those who belief in the existence of a God who created all life, reject any other belief that would deprive them of His companionship, have His assurance that all questions will be answered, reject any other idea of creation that would deprive them of this assurance.

In commenting on the work that has been carried out by our scientific communities in their quest to find answers to the origins of man and the Universe, we could say that the scientist of to-day have discovered nothing new on this planet or the Universe. Although their discoveries would appear to be new to us, in fact they have only found that which is already in existence since the beginning of time, and known to cultures much older than ours is at this point in time.

Mankind's curiosity regards his origins and place in the Universe did not have its beginning in the seventeenth century, but with people of much older civilizations in the distant past. "For the mind wants to discover by reasoning what exists in the infinity of space that lies out there, beyond the ramparts of the world".[1]

The evident truth is that there is not one drop of water or one type of species on this planet that was not here in ages past. How and when this occurred is the mystery that has defied a reasonable answer from the mind of man. However, due to the catastrophic cataclysmic upheavals that this planet has experienced over millennia, continents have vanished into the depths of the ocean, and replaced each other's position across the globe. Due to these upheavals, species have vanished from the face of the earth, never again to be seen by man, as is happening to-day, due to mans abuse of his environment.

Scientist in the field of Cosmology, Paleontology, and Anthropology, has in their studies of the origin of the Universe and the structure and evolutionary process of the Earth, postulated theories that are conjectural. There exists no avenue by which the theories propounded by the different schools concerning these issues can be proved or disproved by conventional methods. There is as much controversy surrounding the origins of this Earth and the Universe, as there is among the experts concerning the origins of man.

These contentious issues have not only created problems in the academic world, but also for the religious bodies in the Western hemisphere who reject the idea of creation as envisaged by the scientific community. Moreover lacking any form of definitive proof by which these issues could be discussed, whereby a consensus of opinion could be reached, results in an exercise of futility, as the points under discussion are based upon personal opinions that are subjective and conjectural, Despite this lack of clear consensus among the experts, Cosmologist are quite definitive in stating the age of this planet as being between 4.5 and 5.0 million years, and the universe as 8.0 to 13.0 billion years.[2]

---

1   Carus. Titus Lucretius. 'On the Nature of the Universe' Translated by R.E. Latham. . Published by Penguin Classics

2   Larousse Encyclopaedia of Archaeology Pre-Historic Archaeology

What is more surprising is the theory that the Universe is 10 billion light years in diameter which would suggest that the Universe is circular and enclosed with limited boundary. [1]

However, if one accepts the 'big bang' theory which hypothesizes that as the result of a cosmic explosion, the planet Earth, and its attending Planets is in continuous motion travelling into unlimited space, implies that the universe is open without boundaries. This theory itself is conjectural and open to question. If such an event as the 'Big Ban g' did occur where would one locate the center or source of the initial explosion?

On the other hand, if one were to accept that the Universe is enclosed, would lead one to belief that we are living on a globe within a globe. Such being the case, simplicity suggest that like the ripples on the surface of a lake, when they reach the shore, rebound to return to the source. However, reason suggests how illogical this hypothesis appears when one considers the uniformity of the planetary system of which we are a part.

If we accept the 'Big Bang' theory as theorized by Professor Hawkins, we must by extension accept the realities of such an event. Explosions, whether man made or Cosmic have certain characteristics that cannot be circumvented. Unless restricted or intentionally directed, explosions do not create a spiraling motion of matter, but dispersed matter in all directions from a central point in an outward circular pattern. One cannot calculate the forces generated by this Cosmic Explosion; any attempts to do so would be purely hypothetical. Where then is this central point of energy?

One could well ask, "How many sides has a circle" and develop a theory which would support their conclusions. What is within the field of logic is the characteristic from the initial moment to its aftermath. From the moment of the explosion, the forces generated within the Cosmos would be beyond our comprehension. Nevertheless, assuming that there existed no impediment in the direction of its travel that would reverse its outward motion, it would eventually slow down, stop, and reach the point of inertia.

The rhythmic pulse of the Universe and the uniformity our planetary system would suggest a system, which is in a continuous circular motion, and not in an outward spiraling motion from a central point. "Granted then that empty space extends without limit in every direction---under the impulse of perpetual motion, it is unlikely that this earth and sky and the surrounding planets are the only created cohesive planetary system. Such being the case one must accept that there exists elsewhere in the vast expense of space, other clusters of matter similar to this one which the ether clasps in ardent embrace. Therefore must acknowledge that in other regions of space there are other earths peopled by various tribes of men and breeds of beasts". [2]

Anthropologist and Paleontologist are also quite definite in their assessment of mans origins, and emergence at the dawn of time on this planet. The time given for this momentous occurrence is given as 14 to 12 million years, a time when man diverged from the Ape, an issue

1   *Larousse Encyclopaedia of Archaeology Pre-Historic Archaeology*
2   *Carus. Titus Lucretius. 'The nature of the Universe' Translated by R.E.Latham Published by Penguin Classics*

that is as contentious as that of the Cosmologist, and their theory relative to the age of this planet, and the Universe.

Reason must play a part in the assumptions put forward by the experts, but can we believe the explanations put forward by the scientific community regarding our historic past. When evaluated against the age of man, modern science is embryonic in its development, how much credence can be placed upon their theories?

Contemporary science has been built upon hypothesis over the last 150 years, and has been in a continuous flux of change. The theories propounded as truths in the early years of scientific discovery were at times based solely upon guesswork and questionable rational.

As this universe and the world on which we live are in a continuous process of change, the same can be said of scientific discoveries in the future. The amount of knowledge that has been accumulated over the last 150 years is minuscule in comparison to what is waiting to be discovered.

The scientific theories of mans beginning, the creation of life and the universe as propounded by the different schools are at a disadvantage, as the belief of the individual come into conflict and are irreconcilable with these theories.

The religious person will look to the heavens and believe that a supreme being or creator was the cause of the universe being created, and feel that among all the life that exists on this earth, he alone is special and has a personal relationship with the Godhead. Thus having this belief is assured of his future happiness and immortality on his departure from this life. He finds no reason to question this belief of what to him is the obvious.

There are also those of the school of Paleontology and Anthropology, who believing that man being descended from the ape, remove the hand of the Creator from the affairs of man, thus depriving those who are religiously inclined of this level of comfort, condemning them to a non-existent future and denying those who belief in a supreme 'Being', the fellowship of their Creator. "[1]

---

1   Huxley Thomas H. *The Origin of the Species. Collective Essays. (1860)*

Chapter 13

The hand that from formless matter created the World, made man imperishable, and made him in the image of his own nature.[1] There are many theories concerning the origins of man. We have the biblical version, which tells the story of Adam and Eve and the garden of paradise. And there are the myths found in all cultures on this planet that attribute mans creation to the Gods.

There are also those who hypothesis that man derived from another planetary system and is a creature of the stars. This is coupled with the theory which states that at some time in the past, extra terrestrials, with a superior intelligence, possessing advanced knowledge in molecular genetics, manipulated the genetic code of what our Anthropologist call a 'pre-hominid' race, whom they say were our ancestors, and first cousin to the Ape.[2]

Be as it may, if we are to use reason instead of emotion, we must however remove from our minds the religious concept of a god being the creator of the Universe and of humanity. This form of thinking puts us on par with the most primitive beliefs of man. Though one must admit that in the absence of any other explanation, the idea of a 'God' as the primary cause of creation satisfies the human need for a super-human being

The question will always remain, where did man originate? Was he the product of an accident of nature, or was he truly a creature of the stars? In this regard, the theories developed by the scientific community are as questionable as those developed by our religious bodies when it comes to explaining this mystery of man.

Man cannot find the answers to the mysteries that is our Universe through reason. In his efforts to find answers to these questions, he created an intermediary as a means of explaining the unexplainable. "Who knows the truth? Who can tell us whence and how arouse this Universe? Who knows therefore whence comes this creation? The Godare later than its beginning".[3]

This idea of a living God as the prime cause for the creation of the Universe and all life is the belief of all cultures on this planet. It could be said that in believing in Godhead as the initial

---

1   *The New Jerusalem Bible. Book of Wisdom. 11.18. 2. 23.*

2   *Von Danikin. Erich. 'In Search of Ancient Gods' Translated by Michael Heron. Published by G.P. Putnam's Son's. NY*

3   *The Bhagavad-Gita Gita. Book 111. 86. Translated by Juan Mascaro Penguin Classics*

form of life, is man's efforts to come to terms with his inner self. God, should he exist as an entity is not to be found in the finite, but in the infinite, which is the creation of all life. There is no mystery concerning the Universe, and life. There is however, the unexplainable whereby man cannot adequately explain his presence on this planet, or the origins of life. In his efforts to explain through logic creates more questions than answers. Whereas, all life accepts their place upon this planet, it is only man who questions his existence and endeavors to find answers in order to satisfy his curiosity and needs.

Among the numerous written versions, the Judaic Biblical version, as described in the Book of Genesis, is most prevalent in our Western culture. This tells the story of Adam and Eve, the first Man and Woman to inhabit this earth, and the creation of a Garden of Paradise, in which they would dwell for all time. A religious view that teaches how God who fashioned man from the dust of the soil" created man,[1]

This is the doctrine that is taught and accepted within Christen communities around the world. Because of these teachings it is mans belief that his presence on this earth was not by accident, and as his Creator, created him in his own the image, his presence was for a higher purpose.

Though expressed in many different ways and under various forms by all ancient civilizations and cultures, the human family has held fast to the belief in a supreme God, who created a world of beauty, who when his work of creation was complete, created man to be the guardian of his creation.

This was the paradise in which the Creator planted man and woman, a living organic planet, pulsating with life, a paradise to care for and enjoy, for all time.

So, when we read the words that were written so long ago, we can say from the description, that this planet Earth was truly a 'Garden of Eden'.

Having this close relationship with his creator, man believed that on his departure from this world he would have the privilege of becoming an integral part of the Godhead by being absorbed into his Divine presence. And it is by paying homage to his Creator and having this assurance of immortality that man has developed a cohesive community of tribes and families that is the foundation stone of all cultures and civilizations from time immemorial, and the reason for his progress down through the ages.

Very little attention has been paid by the establishment to the ignorant and superstitious period in which our western culture languished under for thousands of years, while the schools of learning in Mathematics, Geometry, and Astronomy flourished in the Middle and Far East, South America, China, Egypt, and India.

We must accept the fact that Christianity is to our present civilization another form of idol worship. However, unlike Christianity, which is intolerant to any other form of worship, paganism was tolerant and accepted divergent views of other religions. This quest by man to find

---

1   *The New Jerusalem Bible. Book of Genesis 2. 6-7.*

his origins, is not confined to one culture, but is to be found in the mythology of civilizations and cultures from the distant past.

From the Biblical narrative we are told, "God said, let us make man in our own image, in the likeness of ourselves, and let them be masters of the fish of the sea, the birds of the heavens, the cattle, all the wild beasts, and all the wild reptiles that crawl upon the earth. God created man in the image of himself, in the image of God he created him, male and female he created them. And so it was. God saw all that he had made, and indeed it was very good. Such were the origins of the heaven and earth when they were created".[1]

There is also the controversial theory developed in the 19th century by those, who state that man, through an evolutionary process of change and adaptation, is descended from the primate family of Apes. Anthropologists belief that man has progressed, through an evolutionary process from a primitive beginning, as that of an ape, to his present stage of Homo Sapiens over a period of 2.5 million years. This theory of man being directly descended from the Ape is not in itself a scientific truth, but a hypothesis, developed by two eminent naturalists, Alfred R. Russell (1823-1913) and Charles R. Darwin. (1809-1892).

In the mid 19th century, Charles Darwin published his work on the "Origin of the Species" and the "Descent of Man." The foundation for his hypothesis was based, not upon genetic scientific proof, but on the anatomical similarity that existed between the various species that occupy this planet, a characteristic that is common to all species.

Therefore, because of the anatomical similarities that exist between man and the family of primates, it was not difficult to construct a family tree that would indicate a descending relationship with the primates on this planet. This is evident in the illustrations used by the Anthropologist to demonstrate the different stages of mans progress between ape and man, that is to be found in the majority of publications dealing with this subject. This illustration of mans progression presupposes that the human brain evolved at a similar rate. Should we accept this hypothesis we are presented with a problem regards the Neanderthal species of man. Was he the brutish uncivilized specimen we read off and depicted in the many illustrations? Although scientists have never seen a pre-human, they allow their imagination to develop a picture of what he would act and look like. Can we discard this false hypothesis and see our Neanderthal ancestor as a loving and caring human being who took care of those less fortunate and believed in the hereafter as evidenced by the burial remains that have been discovered and the many cave paintings discovered that indicate that these particular individuals were artistically competent and in tune with nature.[2]

Although there exists a clear anatomical relationship between Man and Ape, as there is among all species of similar characteristics, it does not necessarily follow that man is descended

---

1   *The New Jerusalem Bible. 'The Book of Genesis'.*
2   *Crane Briton/Christopher John B/Wolff Robert Lee A history of Civilization Prehistory to 1715 Published by Prentice-Hall Inc New Jersey USA*

from the Ape. There exists too many gaps in the supposed line of descend to support this theory.

As was stated by one author, "Biologist would dearly like to know how modern apes, modern humans, and the various ancestral hominids evolved from a common ancestor. Unfortunately, the fossil record is somewhat incomplete as far as the hominids are concerned, and is all but blank for the apes.[1] It has also been hypothesized that "Homo sapiens did not emerge from the Ape, but the complete physical being which certain apes represent as the end result of the animal lineage is indispensable for the creation of man".[2] If we are to belief that man was individually created, as was woman, we must by extension belief that all species were created equally, and under the same conditions. But like our ancestors, a reason and a purpose has to be found for our existence. How and who achieved this marvel of creation, is a question that cannot be answered by science.

We should therefore recognize that all species on this planet were individually created with the special gift of pro-creation to ensure its continuity, and are all unique, and when man, in his ignorance is the cause of destroying one of these species, it is gone forever, never to return.

Darwin, in his reference to the transmission of hereditary characteristics, was unknowingly referring to what is known to present day science as the D.N.A., genetic code which transmit the hereditary characteristics within all life forms.

He was astute in his observations as regards the transmission of characteristic traits within a family. At the time when he was developing his hypothesis, he stated that "The laws governing inheritance are for the most part unknown, when any deviation of structure---appears, as we see it in father and child, we cannot tell whether it may not be due to some cause having acted on both."[3]

Scientists have discovered that the transmission of hereditary characteristics is through the actions of the chromosomes found in the cell nucleus that carries the genes in a linear order from both parents.

They also recognized that the abnormalities that appear in all life forms are the results of some malfunction within the genetic chromosomes, and not to the reversion to some primitive state as an ape, as hypothesized by Charles Darwin, who when commenting on the theory of reversion by some members of the human family stated, "The simple brain of a micro cephalous idiot, in as far as it resembles that of an ape, may in this sense be said to offer a case of reversion"[4] [to that of his primitive ancestor].

His reference to these poor unfortunate people, who through no fault of their own, were in most cases the result of incest and continuous inbreeding within one family or group of families, as would be found more frequently in a village environment. In the majority of cases

1   Leakey. Richard. E'The Making of Mankind'.
2   De Lubicz. R.A. Schwaller. 'Sacred Science' Published by Inner Traditions. N.Y.
3   Darwin. Charles. The Origin of Species. (1809--1882)
4   Darwin Charles. The Decent of Man. (1809--1882)

these people were ostracize and incarcerated in an asylum or some other form of institution away from the mainstream of society.

Cases of this nature were frequent in the villages and towns of England and Europe in the middle Ages, more so during the industrial age and in the lifetime of Mr. Darwin. There were numerous cases documented and recorded, as it was the practice of the medical profession to use these people for medical studies during their lifetime and after their death.

To compare them as a throwback to the ape as their ancestor because of their abnormality in order to justify a hypothesis was morally wrong. These two theories concerning man origins were prevalent up to the twentieth century and were the cause of extensive acrimonious debates within the religious communities by those who held opposing views on the subjects.

In the forward to his book, 'The Making of Mankind,' Richard E. Leakey expresses grave concerns regarding those whom he classes as religious fundamentalists who have committed "themselves to the impossible task of discrediting the work of science".

By questioning and denying the theories hypothesized by science on the evolution of man, he appears to express a sense of apprehension that state legislation would require "scientific creationism "Be taught alongside the theory of evolution within the educational system".

Why this concern is difficult to understand, as the theory of "creationism" is not opposed to the theory of evolution, both theories are to a great extent compatible.

The doctrine of creation teaches that all things were ultimately created by God from no previously existing matter: "But Gods action in creating could have been either to bring the world to its present form into being from nothing, or to create from nothing only the first existing matter e.g., the single Cell. To which he gave the power to become by evolutionary development the world as we know it to-day."[1] "That forms now perfectly distinct have descended from a single parent-form".[2] "It is difficult to comprehend the meaning of such facts as these, if we suppose that each species of animal and plant,....was formed and placed upon the surface of the globe at long intervals by a distinct act of creative power; and it is well to recollect that such an assumption is as unsupported by tradition or revelation as it is opposed to the analogy of nature".[3]

This theory would nullify the idea of Adam and Eve as being the first human creation of the Creator, and bring into question the Biblical account of creation, outlined in the Book of Genesis. To have both these ideas discussed in tandem would create the ideal situation for open healthy constructive debate

Notwithstanding, the views expressed by the different schools on this subject, the divergence of opinions that exists between the various bodies are such that there are no avenues by which a consensus could be reached, as both views regarding the process of creation are hypothetical and have not been proven.

1   *The Holy Bible. Edited by Rev. John P. O'Connell. (1961).*
2   *Von Baer. (1859)*
3   *Huxley. Thomas H. Presistent Types of Animal Life. (1859). Lecture to the Royal Institution.*

It is therefore, extremely difficult, if not impossible to disprove that which has not been proven as fact. As was expressed by one author, who when commenting on the "Origin Of Species" stated,"When we descend to details, we cannot prove that a single species has changed, nor can we prove that the supposed changes are beneficial, which is the groundwork of the theory." [1] To state that species do change and have changed as a result of evolution as a fact as "incontrovertible as gravity", "and to talk of the "theory" of evolution as grossly misleading,'[2] is to express one's own point of view, as the statement appears to put the matter to rest and preclude further discussion. Dogmatic statements do nothing to resolve these contentious issues.

When evaluated against those other theories concerning mans origins. The theory of evolution is nothing more and nothing less than a theory, which lacks any substantial supporting evidence. For scientist to speak in absolutes does not lend itself to resolving contentious issues, but rather tends to exasperate those who may find the expressed theory in conflict with their religious or personal beliefs.

At the moment there are no absolute proofs regarding the origins of man, or for that matter, the idea of a god as being the creator of man. Both ideas are hypothetical, with no absolute scientific evidence that would support either of these two theories or beliefs. Both are subjective and open to question and allowed to exist without creating fear and apprehension. Having one Inquisition inflicted upon mankind within our historic past should teach us a lesson.

Twentieth century man would maintain that with the scientific knowledge he now possesses, he has the answers to all questions that has beset mankind, forgetting that what we belief to be to-days answers, may be tomorrow's questions. The Anthropologist of today in his efforts to find mans origins, though his methods may appear to be a little more sophisticated, and his theories a little more scientific. His theories and explanations are no more than and no less as valid as those theories as found in myths and legends of the past.

When one speaks of truth, or as expressed, 'scientific truth', and professes to be its custodian, would do well to remember that like all else in life, truth is subject to the times, personal views, and opinions. Much like the brilliance and color on the facets of a diamond that by analogy is subject to the time of day the intensity of light and the eyes of the person viewing this applies to those in the political and religious arena who, have the ability to influence public opinion.

So it is when we speak of truth, one's idea of what they would call truth may not necessarily conform to and be the view of those who hold the reins of power. History does not allow the scientific community the license of complacency that they are right in their hypothesis of man being descended from the ape, nor genetically engineered for some purpose or for that matter an omnipotent God. All of these theories are equal in weight and are subject to the personal beliefs of the individual.

---

1   Huxley. *Thomas H. Collective Essays. (1860)*
2   Leakey. *Richard. E. The Making of Mankind.*

In the myths and legends from ancient times, it is found that in all cultures, even the most primitive, have all tried to find their relationship within the natural order of the Universe. In all cases there is a common trend in their beliefs, and that is their relationship to the Gods. Whereas, one man may look to the heavens, and ask 'why', another may ask 'how, and both will spend their life looking for answers The question that requires a response is not if man had a common ancestor in the ape, but how long has man been on this earth, when did he arrive, and from where? As there exists a clear anatomical relationship between all species of similar characteristics on this planet, it does not necessarily follow that man is descended from the ape, as there exists too many gaps in the supposed line of descend to support this theory.

However the theory would lend support to the hypothesis of man being developed from another form of species similar to that of man and would conform to the theory of manipulating the genetic code in order to create the species Homo sapiens"[1]

If one were to accept the evolution of man from a primitive primate, one would expect clear evidence of a continuous imperceptible process of change. It is ludicrous to suggest, in order to justify one's hypothesis; evolution is a process of stops and starts, whereby each species totally disappears, only to re-appear at some later time in the guise of a new species.

If there is an imperceptible continuous progressive change to all species, it is logical to suggest that there should be evidence of species that are in the flux of change. Not dead evidence, but living evidence of beings and animals who exhibit characteristics of being somewhere between man and ape. However, to use as an example the theory as hypothesized by Charles Darwin in which he states that, "the simple brain of a micro cephalous idiot as proof of reversion from man to ape"[2] does not fit into this category.

It was stated by one leading Biologist, "Evolution is recklessly opportunistic, when it favors any variation that provides a competitive advantage over other members of an organism own population or over individuals of a different species. For billions of years this progress has automatically fuelled what we call evolutionary progress". No program controlled or directed this progression; it was the result of the spur of the moment decisions of natural selection"

From this statement we can presume that man and all life was brought into existence by a natural event without purpose, and would support the theory of a single cell as being the progenitor of all life forms in nature, including man. As remarked by Richard E. Leakey "In one sense we are the product of a series of chance events, in another; we are the result of a progressive, but not purposeful series of innovations"."[3]

This concept may apply under conditions as one would experience in a laboratory involving biological experiments, which are carried out on a minuscule scale, but does it apply to nature, the Laws of the Universe or for that matter Man. This theory also leaves unanswered the question of intermediaries that should exist if this theory was valid.

---

1   Leakey. Richard. E. The Making of Mankind.
2   Darwin. Charles. The Decent of Man.
3   Leakey. Richard. E. The Making of Mankind.

On the question of natural selection and the struggle for existence whereby the weaker members of a species, unable to compete for a food source die out and cease to exist. Is the basic law of survival and applicable to all life on this planet.

It was believed that the process of natural selection acted very slowly, over extensive periods of time, during which natural events caused the destruction of some species on this planet, also in this process some species who suffered from these catastrophic events were at a disadvantage by their reduced number.

Due to this decrease in population, these species may have become extinct in their fight to survive.

In commenting on this subject, it was said that, "Any form which is represented by few individuals will run a good chance of utter extinction, during great fluctuations in the nature of the seasons, or from a temporary increase in the number of its enemies...for as new forms are produced...many old forms must become extinct. From these several considerations, I think it inevitably follows, that as new species in the course of time are formed through natural selection, others will become rarer and rarer, and finally extinct".[1]

It was the view of one noted biologist, who in responding to Darwin's theory on natural selection commented, "There is no positive evidence at present that any group of animals has by variation and selective breeding given rise to another group which was even in the least degree infertile with the first. The belief in natural selection must at present be grounded entirely on general considerations ...When we descend to details... we cannot prove that a single species has changed through the process of natural selection"[2].

When a species of animal or man become extinct whether through the actions of nature, or man's inhumanity to man, there is no evolutionary process by which a new species can be create or ever was created. "So profound are our ignorance, and so high our presumption, that we marvel when we hear of the extinction of an organic being; and as we do not see the cause, we invoke cataclysms to desolate the world, or invent laws on the duration of the forms of life."[3]

The cataclysms that have occurred over the eons that had a devastating effect upon all life on this planet was not the invention of a fertile imagination, but actual realities as proven by geological evidence. Had it not been for these catastrophes that were the reason for the disappearance of so many species, it is highly probable that the reptilian life of old would be still walking this planet and swimming in our seas, albeit, in reduced numbers.

Accepting as fact that all species on this planet are individualistic, with the special gift of procreation to ensure their continuity and are unique with their special place within the order of the Universe the amount of species alive in our generation are but a fraction of the number that once existed in ancient times. The disappearance of which has been due to numerous cataclysmic

1   Darwin. Charles. *The Origin of Species.*
2   Huxley. Thomas H. '*Origin of Species*'. *Collective Essays (1860).*
3   *Ibid*

events that have inflicted this planet, in addition to the damage that has been inflicted upon all forms of life by isolated natural catastrophes down through the ages.

This destruction of nature's gifts has markedly increased since the event of the Industrial Age, and has dramatically increased in the twentieth century. The destruction of the world's natural resources has adversely affected the worlds wildlife that has led to the total disappearance of thousands of the world's species continues at an alarming rate and has become a major concern in all countries around the world.

The destruction is not the result of some catastrophic or cataclysmic event, but to the action of man, who of all the worlds species is increasing in number exponentially to the detriment of his environment. For those species that survive the ravages of man, will if protected and nurtured increase in numbers to the benefit of all. However, there will be no new replacements from Mother Nature, as propounded by Darwin.

When man in his ignorance is the cause of destroying one of these species, it is gone forever, never to return. As expressed by a noted naturalist, "Each time a species is brought to extinction through the actions of man or causes which are brought about through some natural catastrophe. We will have to see the creation of a new heaven and earth before we will see the species again".[1]

It is the opinion of the scientific community that the probability exists of this planet suffering some form of catastrophic event that will have a devastating effect upon all life. Whether man will precipitate this event with some form of nuclear disaster, or through natural causes, as would occur should a large meteorite impact the Earth, is highly probable. Depending upon the severity and extent of the damage inflicted upon the environment, the human race may find itself in the same situation as occurred 65 million years ago, when Earth suffered its last great upheaval.

One can only speculate as to how future generations will address the results of this catastrophe in their myths and, assuming that there will be a remnant left to record these events. For those species that are destroyed by these disasters, there will be no replacements by Mother Nature or modifications, as propounded by the Naturalist. However, if the survivors are to overcome this calamity, adapting to their new environment, and changing circumstances will be of major importance.

It should be recognized that all species on this planet were created with the special gift of procreation to ensure its continuity and all are unique and special in their individuality. Events of this nature could be compared to those catastrophes that occurred in the past of which it was said, "why in the beginning even while the proud giants were perishing, you preserved the germ of a new generation for the ages to come".[2]

---

1   *This saying may be attributed to the noted Naturalist George Foster. 1754-94. however should be researched.*
2   *The New Jerusalem Bible. Book of Wisdom. 14-6.*

The chronological table compiled by pre-historians that outlines the pre-historic period is based upon very little evidence with which to support their theories, it is in essence, purely conjectural. The time frames attributed to the different periods by the experts is still a controversial issue and is continually being revised as new theories are developed by the different schools of thought who study these particular disciplines. However, despite this lack of clear consensus of opinion among the experts, Cosmologists and Geologist are quite definitive in stating the age of this planet as being between 4.5 to 5.0 billion years of age, and the Universe as between 8.0 to 13.0 billion years.

Anthropologist and Paleontologist are also definite in their assessment of mans origins and emergence at the dawn of time upon this planet as between 14 to 12 million years ago, a time when man diverged from the Ape, A theory that is as contentious as that of the theory relative to the age of the Earth and the Universe.

In the absence of any written records, they rely heavily upon the few artifacts, which have been discovered in various countries around the world. Based upon these finds they develop theories concerning the pre-historic past, which to a great extent are purely conjectural. This is evident from the dates extrapolated by the historians which state that man has made little or no progress over the aeons of time until the emergence of the Neanderthal man of 100,000--40,000 years ago.

This is clearly evident in the theories developed by the Anthropologist, Raymond Dart, who in 1924, discovered in the Transvaal, South Africa the fossil remains of what he classed as primitive hominids, or as it was termed, the missing link between man and ape, dating these artifacts as being in the region of four million years old.

How he arrived at this date has not been explained, as there were no methods available at that time by which the dating of artifacts could be accomplished, and this applies to all pre-historic dating prior to the 1960's, at best this was an estimated guess with no yardstick by which one could make a comparison.

Excavations carried out in 1959 by Dr. Leakey in East Africa discovered deposits, that in the view of Dr. Leakey indicated the presence of man with a suggested date of 2.3 million years. These excavations unearthed deposits containing stone objects, bones of animals that are now extinct, skeletal debris of small vertebrates, early mammals of a large size, and of what was purported to be the skeletal remains of humans, deemed to be pre-human remains.

There was also remains of food and stone implements, which would indicate the refuse of a prehistoric settlement who had discarded it's debris in one particular spot over an extensive period of time, much as what happens to-day.

A detailed examination of the skeletal remains showed certain discrepancies, which could not be explained by any natural causes, and these suggested the intervention of mankind.[1] It was suggested at the time of these discoveries that the cradle of civilization had its beginning in East Africa and not in the Middle East as had been the long held believe of the experts.

---

1   *Larousse. Encyclopaedia of Archaeology. Pre-Historic Archaeology.*

I was living in Ghana. West Africa in the early 1960's during the presidency of Kwame Nkrumah, when the news of Dr. Leakey findings were published which theorized that man had his beginning in East Africa.

A seminar was convened at Legon University to discuss these findings and may have been the cause of the creation of the Organization of African Unity in 1963, which led to the full awakening of the African conscience and its true identity among the nations of the world. But was the hypothesis put forward by Dr. Leakey true? Many historians and scholars refuse to accept such a hypothesis, as little progress had been made by the African people over the millennia.

Until the arrival of the Europeans into East and West Africa in the 15th and 19th century, the manner and lifestyle of these people had gone through little change. In fact they can, to a great extent be compared to the Aborigine of Australia who lived a comparatively serene existence until the arrival of the Europeans in the eighteen-century.

The same can be said of the people of East and West Africa. There are many areas in Africa where the lifestyle of the people has seen little change over the years by way of the most rudimentary technological progress. History tells us that the Egyptians traded extensively with the African people yet did not have any marked effect upon their culture or manner of living. To suggest that modern man had his beginning in the regions of East Africa, is like many theories relative to mans presence on this planet, is grasping at straws. One can appreciate the reasoning behind the theories associating the primate family of apes with that of man, and by extension, Africa, the only region where the species of ape are to be found. Of course there are many other areas around the world in which Anthropologist may yet find answers to some of the outstanding questions that still require answers, however, will it be enough to dispel the theories associating ape and man?

The percentage of finds and the amount of land mass investigated is minuscule in comparison to what awaits investigating. In all likelihood the answers may never be found within this lifetime, or for that matter, future ages, as the destruction of ancient records and the corruption of the myths and legends of the ancient past will have been completed by the religious establishments, and those in the field of academia.

From the description of the skeletal remains, of what is claimed to be pre-human man, and the circumstances in which they were found among the debris of other animals, would suggest that he or she, if it were human, was not a willing participant in the festivities that lead to their demise.

Having spent some time in West Africa, where I became acquainted with some tribes who hunted monkeys and baboons for food, and viewed them as a rare delicacy, it could be inferred that the skeletal remains found may have been those of a species of monkey that has long been extinct. It is also possible; these who lived in the more ancient past may have practiced cannibalism.

As was stated by one authority "If we look back to an extremely remote past, before man had arrived at the dignity of manhood, he would have been guided more by instinct and less by reason then the lowest savages at the present time. Our early sub-human progenitors would not have practiced infanticide or polyandry; for the instincts of the lower animals are never so perverted as to lead them regularly to destroy their own offspring, or to be quite devoid of jealousy. Hence the progenitors of man would have tended to increase rapidly;" [1]

We can assume from this statement that a reference was being made to a species of pre-hominid or the missing link as is classed by to-days Anthropologists. However, was Darwin speaking of one tribe from which man descended, or were there many; each prying upon the other in order to survive?

The stone implements found at the site, would indicate an organized society of people who were established at the same spot over a long period of time. Logic would also suggest that to hunt and kill large mammals required organization and co-operation, if the hunt was to be successful.

Under these circumstances this would indicate a people who were intelligent in planning and co-coordinating their activities. If findings of pre-historic man were to have any validity, it would require that all skeletal remains of what one would term human, needs to be found in conditions that would indicate a form of burial as was found in China at Chou-k'ou-tien north of Beijing or in circumstances by which it could be determined that they had met with an accident, isolated from any other random debris that would indicate a refuse dump that was used for discarding unwanted food and bones.

One can appreciate the reasoning behind the many theories associating the primate family with that of man, however, why must we go through the laborious process of theorizing man's beginning and his evolutionary progress. Each step we take back in time, our answers are met with questions.

When we speak of man's evolutionary progress, the race that springs to mind is that of the European. It would appear that the diversity of the world's people is excluded from the process. But, through a process of imagination and manipulation, scientists have developed a family tree that creates a relationship between man and ape that is non-existent except anatomically. Due to their theories being based upon the premise of man being descended from the ape, it is assumed that this planet was populated by only one species of the human family until the arrival of the species known as Neanderthal Man in around 100.000 BC. Anthropologists deny any form of major development, except in the most rudimentary form, to pre-historic man.

When twentieth century man began his exploration of the stars and outer space, two new theories developed concerning mans place within the Universe. The first of these theories propound that man and all life on this planet derived their beginning from another planetary solar system. To support this theory they refer to the myths and legends of old that appear to have some basis in fact that would account for the diversity of life that exists on this planet.

1   Darwin. Charles *The Descent of Man.*

The second theory proposed is that extra-terrestrials with a superior intelligence, possessing advanced knowledge in molecular genetics, manipulated the genetic code of what Anthropologist call a pre-hominid man,[1] whom they say were our ancestors and first cousin to the Ape.

In essence, another species of the primate family, distinct in features and characteristics as the baboon is from the ape, however, in this instance, more inclined towards the features as that of man, thus making him ideal subject for the experiments that were to follow.

This theory would also lend support to Darwin's theory and account for the missing link that has created so much attention by the work of Richard E Leakey.[2]

Accepting this theory raises more question then answers, as it fails to account for the diversity of life, not only that which existed in the past, but which exists in the present presupposing that all other life existed for millions of years prior to man arrival on this planet.

Any theory or hypotheses concerning life on this Earth must encompass and consider the beauty and diversity of all life, not only Homo Sapiens, for it to be given consideration.

For the purpose of clarity, it will be necessary to place aside, for the moment the theories concerning the origins of man e.g., mans presence being due to a biological accident of nature, whereby man evolved from a single cell which led to the evolutionary process as postulated by the theory of man evolving from the ape.

Accepting this hypothesis would necessitate the acceptance that the same principal would apply to the millions of different species living on this planet, each individual life form having its beginning from a single cell. "Thus living plants and animals are not separated from the extinct by new creations, but are to be regarded as their descendants through continued reproduction."[3]

The theory of man and all that exists, being created by a benevolent Creator or God for some purpose only known to itself, is a simplistic answer to a complex problem. Also the theory of being created by a god is mans effort to find a cause and reason for his existence an idea accepted by the religious institutions and is the belief of most of the worlds religious bodies.

Therefore, let us assume for the moment, that life did in fact evolve from a single cell, with all its complexities as a pre-requisite to humankind's evolutionary progress.

If man has not existed from the beginning, we must presume that he had to arrive from somewhere, perhaps from another planetary system that was in direct communication with this planet. Also, if this planet earth were a mirror image of that which is already in existence in some corner of our galaxy, the diversity of the human race and all life would be explained.

We could theorize and look at the probability of an occurrence of a catastrophic cataclysm that had an adverse effect upon this planet. An occurrence that brought man and all life to near extinction, an event that in all probability severed the communication links between world

1   von Danikin. Erich. In Search of Ancient Gods. Trans; Michhael Heron.
2   Leakey. Richard. E. The Making of Mankind.
3   Verhand. Dr. Schaaffhausen des Naturhist. 1853.

cultures. Such an event may have resulted in our extraterrestrial neighbors taking action to correct the near extinction of the human species.

Such a cataclysmic event may have taken place approximately 65 million years ago an event that is supported by geological evidence. It has been determined it was during this period, the Dinosaurs and a major portion of the worlds' species became extinct. So it is reasonable to suggest that our ancestors suffered the same fate during this catastrophic cataclysm.

There have also been other sporadic isolated occurrences down through the ages that can be recorded by Geological evidence. However, from the legends and myths of the past, this memory of a major cataclysm has been embedded in the conscience of man. To-day the scholar of pre-history has brought to light "the enormous prodigious antiquity of human lineage"[1].

This hypothesis would lend support to the theory of a super intelligence, through the process of genetic engineering restored the human race, thus saving it from total extinction creating in mans psychic conscience the concept of a Creator. In addition would support the theory as expressed by the Anthropologist who state, man descended from the Ape, and also support the theory of man being created by a race who made man in his own image.

The theory of extraterrestrials manipulating the genetic code of these ancient primates, would suggest that man acquired immediate intelligence,[2] and all the attributes and skills he presently possesses to survive.

It would also support the diversity of race we see on this planet. This would eliminate the missing link that Anthropologist has been searching for over the years, and account for the gap that exists between the species, but not necessarily eliminating the theory of man being descended from the ape or his distant cousin, the pre-hominid. However, it could be argued that if this knowledge had been transplanted in man through the process of molecular engineering, somewhere in the region of 6.5 million years ago, why has it taken man so long to arrive at this point in his development?

The knowledge acquired would enable man to progress at an exponential rate whereby his progress would possibly be on the level of our famous Neanderthal species that existed 100,000 years ago. This level of progress may have been achieved, within three or four generations, when viewed against Earth's time scale. Or can we dispense with the theory that our present civilization had its beginning a mere 5.000 years ago in the valley of the Euphrates River or Africa, and look elsewhere for a civilization that existed in the distant past, the memory of which is a shadowy specter in the sub-conscience of man.

The ancient legends of China, South America and the Celts of Europe and many other cultures of antiquity, we find references to a race of giants who were the remnants of a great race that had flourished in the remote past, and had been near exterminated by a world disaster.

Entering into the realm of theories, it could be inferred from the legends, that these people, seeing their race brought to the point of extinction, and being advanced in the field of science

---

1   Unknown. Research?

2   Velikovsky. Immanuel. Worlds in Collision. Published by Pocket Books N Y

and technology, instituted a program of molecular engineering to ensure the continuity of mankind, by manipulating the genetic code of a species of primate, that was far removed from the ape, but possessed a certain physiological compatibility to man.

What time frame would be required to develop a new species of is indeterminate. However, in all likelihood could be achieved within three to four generations by cross breeding in sufficient numbers. Would this experiment be confined to one species or many different types? When one considers the diversity of the human family, it would be necessary to carry out this experiment to many species to create the human family as it is today.

To accept this hypothesis as a consideration, would require that the world as existed in the ancient past could be compared to the world as existed 50,000 years ago to Egypt In this case we have a culture that was much further advanced than any other culture during that period in history. If we are to believe the Archaeologists, while Egypt flourished in the Arts during this period of their development, the rest of mankind were living in very primitive conditions, much as Africa is today.

It could also be raised as a point of interest, to which group of people our pre-hominid ancestor will belong? Will he/she be Caucasian, African, or Mongoloid?

We see the advances made by the Western culture in the fields of Technology while at the same time a large portion of the world's population live in the same primitive conditions as their forefathers have done for thousands of years.

In this environment their manner of life has diminished in that their poverty is more acute. I do not wish to imply that Egypt with all her advances was capable of performing such work as manipulating the genetic codes of the human being. Although there is evidence to suggest that they were conversant with the practice of genetic engineering in the field of horticulture.

The science of manipulating the genetic code is not the sole property of the science fiction writer. A scenario of this nature is not impossible, but highly probable, as science to-day is clearly demonstrating their ability to manipulate the genetic code of the human body. Public opinion appears to have some reservations concerning this practice and have raised strong objections. However, eventually there will be little opposition to stop science from proceeding along this path.

In the ancient legends, it was this race of giants that were eventually brought to total extinction in the respective countries by the indigenous people. The most difficult aspect of this hypothesis is the mind accepting as fact that a race of people, far superior to our own culture in technology and intelligence may have existed in the pre-historic past.

Did such a race of giants exist? If the myths and legends of the past are too be believed, they not only existed, but have been the cause of many of the legends that are part of the heritage bequeathed to us by the Greek and Celtic cultures. Were these the only cultures to which reference could be made, there would exist some room for doubt as to the authenticity one could attach to these stories, when one is aware of the fertile imagination that existed among the storytellers of old.

But when tales of a similar nature are found in such diverse cultures as China and South America, there is every reason to believe that there exist an element of truth within the fabric of these ancient myths. The fact that there have been no substantive proofs offered by way of artifacts, which would prove the existence of such a race, does not necessarily preclude the possibility of such a race being in existence in the remote past.

The knowledge that existed in the Indus Valley, Egypt, China and South America had to have a source, a point of departure to which one could make reference. In this instance the only point to which one can make reference is that of the Neanderthal Man, and if we search further back in time a creature that was somewhere between the two worlds of man and ape. But there are no intermediates. The nearest to the Neanderthal man, is the Aborigine of Australia.

It is much more difficult to accept this theory, and then it is to accept the theory of a superior race that left a legacy of knowledge that was the foundation of our civilization. What is certain is that this knowledge of Astronomy, Mathematics was not the legacy of the Neanderthal culture or for that matter the natives of Africa.

"Tales of giants and monsters which stand in direct contact with the findings of great fossil bones are scattered broadcast over the mythology of the world". Huge bones found at Punto Santa Elena, in the North of Guayaquil have served as a foundation of a colony of giants who dwelt there. The whole area of the pampas is a great sepulcher of enormous extinct animals; no wonder that one great plain should be called the "The field of the Giants" and that such names as the "Hill of the giants," should be a guide to the geologist in his search for fossil bones."[1]

This is not the only occasion whereby fossil remains of extinct animals have been found. For example, the famous Kent's Hole near Torquay in England contained bones of the Mammoth Elephant, Rhinoceros, Lion, Hyena, and Bear; and red asseous breccia, charged with the bones of quadrupeds which have long disappeared from Europe are common in almost all the countries bordering the Mediterranean Sea.[2]

"In Sicily, great quantities of bones of Mammoths, Elephants, Hippopotamuses, and other animals long extinct have been found. Such bones, as we have seen, are often found in limestone caverns and the limestone gorges of Cilicia are rich in fossils".

In Greek mythology, "The Arcadians laid the scene of the battle of the God's and the Giants as related in the legend of Typhon and Zeus in the plain of Megalopolis, where many bones of Mammoths have come to light"[3]

Similar tales of a race of giants can be found in the mythology of the British Isles. Across the landscape of the British Isles there are structures, figures of giants etched into the landscape

---

1   Taylor. E B. *Early History of Mankind. (The Golden Bough. By J G. Frazer.D.C.L LL.D., Litt.D 2nd Edition. Part! V. Adonis Attis Osiris. The God of the Corycian Cave.)*

2   Frazer. J G. D. C. L., LL.D., Litt.D. *The Golden Bough. 2nd Edition. Part 1V Adonis Attis Osiris. The God of the Corycian Cave*

3   *Ibid*

and burial mounds, that traditions tells that when opened, these burial mounds contained the skeletons of people who were in excess of eight feet tall.[1]

In South America, there are numerous localities to be found where the legends of a giant race still remain in the memory of the people. In the British Isles legends attributed to a race of Giants inhabiting these Islands in the distant past is still a part of the psychic of the people, place names such as, the Giants Graves, near Milton Lilbourne, Wiltshire, Halcombe in Somerset, and the Giants Hill near Skendleby, Lincolnshire are some of the main tourist attractions in Britain..

Of the more notable Giant's is that of the Cerne Abbas Giant Dorset, England, and the Long Man of Wilmington. These figures, were carved into the hillside by cutting away the top layer of turf to expose the white chalk underneath, are approximately one hundred and seventy eight (178 ft) and two hundred and thirty one (231 ft) feet tall respectfully.

When these figures were carved into the hillside and by whom is not known, there is no recorded history that would indicate the age of these figures only that which has been handed down in legends and folklore. Many theories have been put forward as to the function these figures had in the life of the people. In the case of the Cerne Abbas Giant, it is said that he had some strong connection to the fertility rites carried out by the local people during the Spring fertility celebrations, which were a common occurrence all over Europe It was the believe that if a woman who was barren were to sleep within the area of the Giant, she was sure to conceive.

The theory with regard to the Long Man of Wilmington is quite different in context to that of the Cerne Abbas Giant. This figure, which is 231 ft tall represents the largest human figure in the world, and is depicted as holding two rods, one in each hand, in an upright position. One can only hypothesis as to its function or what it represents. Many theories have been put forward as to the function of these gigantic figures, each one as valid as the other. Nevertheless, the figures are clearings cut and precise, and can only be seen from an aero plane flying above the area. One author has suggested that it may have been "a signal from Neolithic man to his gods in their airborne craft".[2] Who could deny such a hypothesis for the want of an alternative explanation?

However, unlike our modern day artists, the people of ancient times did not carry out these Herculean tasks for the want of something to do or as make work projects. In Ireland there is the Giants Causeway, located on the north coast of Co. Antrim, which consists of thousands of basaltic columns of volcanic origin. According to legend, the causeway is a portion of a road system that was constructed by a race of giants as a means of travelling, or as some have suggested, a road system associated with the lost continent of Atlantis.

The development of a new type of human being, through the process of selective breeding is not new. Historically, many cultures have practiced this form of control on its people, not only within our own historic past, but within recent history, as in the case of Germany in the 1930s.

1   Bord. Janet and Colin Mysterious Britain.
2   Bord Janet& Colin Mysterious Britain Published by Paladin Books. London.

The philosophy of selective breeding is discussed at great length by Plato in his book, the "Republic." (427?-347 BC.) [1] Although the writings of Plato were purely theoretical, we can accept his reference to the people of Sparta who in the 7th century BC practiced a form of selective breeding.

He explains how the Spartans approached the question of ensuring only those of their citizens, who were physically the best, would be chosen for the purpose of procreation. "If the Government directed them to breed children for the state, they had no scruples in obeying the command". [2]To achieve this, only the best of their men and women, who "would share a common life style", were selected.

We can infer that those chosen were subject to certain standards, which one could presume were related to good health, physical attraction, and intellectual abilities. He goes on to say, "The best men must cohabit with the best women, and as opposite, the worse type of man, presumably those who do not meet the standards, should mate with the worse type of woman, but on a less frequent basis. Also, the physicians, by the use of drugs, will ensure that those of an inferior nature shall not produce inferior children. The children of the best type must be brought up and protected; however, the children of the worse type must be disposed off to protect the tribe being contaminated by defective births".' When a child was born it was submitted to the inspection of the heads of the tribe, and if they judged it to be unhealthy or weak, it was exposed to die on the slopes of Mount Taygetos'.[3]

It is obvious from what Plato tells us that the Spartan society was, on all levels, controlled by its rulers to the point of decreeing the number of children born each year and from what parents.[4] There is every reason to believe that a form of infanticide existed in the past in all societies.

To deny such a proposition is to deny the realities of what life was like for our ancestors, and for those who lived a life of subsistence. Under these circumstances no society could afford to allow the weak, and unhealthy to survive. It was necessary for the survival of the tribe that all its members be capable of supporting its families. There is also no reason to discard the theory that the practice of infanticide continues today in some of our less advanced societies. During my stay in Nigeria, West Africa, it was the common practice that when twins or triplets were born, only one would survive, the rest was disposed of by being exposed to the elements.

Lacking any fast and hard evidence, scholars will not accept the theory that advanced societies may have existed in pre-historic times. Societies that have left faint traces of their passing on the landscape are to be found in the myths and legends that have been passed on from generation to generation.

It is within the myths and legends, if we endeavor to understand the symbolism, a new understanding will unfold, if we are to understand the future, it is imperative we have an

1   Plato. *Great Dialogues of. Book V. Trans; W H D. Rouse. Published by Mentor Books N Y*

2   *Ibid*

3   Plato. *'The Republic'. Introduction Translated by Sir Desmond Lee Published by Penguin Classics*

4   *Ibid*

understanding of the past. And if we are to search for this hidden culture or civilization we must concentrate on the massive stone structures and temples dotted across the planet.

Where are we to look, can we retrace our steps into the ancient past, in order to keep on an even keel and prevent us from entering into the realm of speculation. There would appear to be an unspoken agreement among scholars regarding the earliest known civilization[1], which they date approximately 5,000 BC. They appear to push aside all the evidence that would suggest the human family's prolonged existence on this planet.

Basing their theories on the description narrated in the Bible, it is into this time period that they endeavor to place the cataclysms and catastrophes that have inflicted this earth over aeons of time.

It would be a benefit to our knowledge of the past if historians that study the past, looked at the evidence that is available in all the disciplines and evaluate the whole range of knowledge available. To inject these catastrophes into this short period to authenticate the events as postulated in the Bible does a disservice to those who are looking for answers.

_1_

Chapter 14

One cannot deny that over the millennia some species have become extinct due to catastrophic events and through natural causes. There have been many catastrophic events that may at times brought humankind and all life to near extinction. The periods and dates in which some these events occurred have been extrapolated from fossil remains, ranging from the Triassic, to the Quaternary periods which saw the extinction of the Dinosaurs. However, that no evidence has been found indicating the presence of man in these eras does not necessarily preclude his presence on this planet.

Numerous theories have been put forward regarding the events that were the prime cause for the disappearance and extinction a greater portion of life. Among the many advocated relates to the change in the oxygen-carbon dioxide ratio may have occurred worldwide. It has also been suggested that the Earth has been subject to many periods of unusual cold during its Geological history. Depending upon the source of information, the first of these cold spells, which are classed as Ice ages occurred some 2 billion years ago, and within the last one billion years the Earth has experienced at least six major periods that brought on mass extinction's of some of the world species.

According to the Geological, evidence, major catastrophes occurred during the ages attributed to the various periods in the life of this planet.[1] One such instance may have occurred in the region Sudbury, in Canada,[2] where it is believed, a meteorite of large proportion impacted the earth some thousands of years ago, which may have been the cause of the melded rock that is quite prevalent in that area.[3]

---

1   *Cambrian Age 640 million years, Ordovician Age 425 million, Devonian Age 350 million, Permian Age 240 million, Triassic Age 200 million, years ago.*
    Kinder Hermann. / Hilgemann. Werner. Atlas of World History. Vol 1.
    Summerscale. Sir John. The Penguin Encyclopaedia.
    Lyell. Sir Charles. Principles of Geology
2   *Sudbury. Canada. North of Georgian Bay on Lake Huron Extensive mining operations is carried out in producing, Nickel, Copper, Gold, Silver, Platinum, Cobalt, Sulphur, and Iron Ore.*
3   *Kinder Hermann. / Hilgemann. Werner. Atlas of World History. Vol 1.Published by Penguin Classics*
Summerscale Sir John The Penguin Encyclopaedia

It has also been suggested, that it was during the Cretaceous Age, which they say occurred between 140-- 65 million years ago,[1] when the Dinosaurs became extinct as is proven by the many fossil remains that have been uncovered, this was a worldwide catastrophe affecting all continents.

The meteorite, if it was a meteorite that caused this major catastrophe had to be of an immense magnitude. Such an event would affect all the planets vegetation, which would in turn affect all the worlds' herbivores. Given these circumstances, it would only be a matter of time before all life was affected.

Notwithstanding the views expressed by the Geologist on this matter as to the frequency of the cold spells, that affected this planet, what is confirmed from the Geological evidence is that the Earth has been subjected to at least two periods of unusual cold over the aeon's of time; An event that may have occurred 2 billion to 640 million years, and the other during the Pleistocene Era about 65 million years ago.

The theory for the first of these cold spells has been many and varied. One theory suggests that the Earth may have passed through a cloud of interstellar dust[2] during the Precambrian period, 670 to 4.5 million years ago, which deprived the earth of the sun's heat. Had an event of this nature occurred, the earth would have been subject to a bombardment of interstellar debris and possible meteorites which would, on impacting with the Earth increase the level of dust particles surrounding the planet. As the amount of carbon dioxide in the earth's atmosphere varies, this blanket of dust would have a corresponding adverse effect upon the amount of carbon dioxide in the earth's atmosphere and be detrimental to all plant and mammalian life.

This would account for an extended period of cold over the whole of the planet, but would not account for an ice age as viewed by to-days standards. Due to low temperatures created by these circumstances, the lakes and rivers would over a period of time, freeze over, and perhaps some shallow coastal sea areas, but there would be no general glaciations of deep ice over the land surface, as was the great ice age of the Pleistocene Epoch.

Ingredients, which are a requisite to the formation of an ice age that would conform to the Pleistocene Epoch, are missing e.g. intense heat to account for the evaporation of the vast amounts of water necessary to create the moisture that would form the density of ice as we see at the North and South Poles.

Geological evidence indicates that a catastrophic event of major proportion occurred around 65 million years ago during the Cretaceous period that saw the demise of the Dinosaurs and numerous other species on this planet. What it was that caused these climatic changes has been a matter of debate for many years, as the frequency of these occurrences down through the ages, has never been firmly established.

However, based upon the fossilized evidence accumulated by Paleontologist, it has been hypothesized that the initial destruction was caused by some external force of such magnitude

---

1   *Ibid*
2   *Summerscale. Sir John. The Penguin Encyclopaedia.*

with the capacity to adversely affect and change the world's climate. It has also been theorized, that a combination of catastrophic events brought about major geographic and climatic changes that virtually destroyed the natural habitat and all plant life, which was the main food source of the of the herbivores family of dinosaurs.

The destruction of the herbivores dinosaur, whether through the results of the initial catastrophe and the subsequent lack of a food source, were the main factors which led to their extinction and would inevitably lead to the demise of the carnivores dinosaur, who were the main predator of the herbivores. Deprived of their main food source and due to their size and clumsy gait, the carnivore's dinosaur lacked the ability to prey upon the smaller mammals as an alternate food source. No doubt there were other types of mammals and wildlife that were preyed upon by those dinosaurs that were carnivorous, however, from what we know; their main source of food was the herbivores dinosaur.

Under these circumstances, it would only be a matter of time before the whole family of these species ceased to exist. And contrary to the theory of natural selection and the survival of the fittest, no new species or modifications of this species evolved from these changing circumstances. Therefore the disappearance of the dinosaurs was total and complete by the end of the Cretaceous period.

This was not an abrupt ending, but a slow process, never been determined by the Paleontologist. What can be theorized is that the initial impact had a devastating effect upon all life, both on land and to some extent, in the sea that saw the destruction of much of the sea dwelling reptiles. Fossil remains of these gigantic reptiles have been found in rock strata on all Continents is indicative of their proliferation. Excepting the date on which these events may have occurred, the evidence that they did occur is incontrovertible.

What caused these catastrophes and their frequencies is a matter of conjecture and approximation within a time frame of millions of years. However, the myths and legends of South America tell of five ages in which the earth suffered major catastrophes are well documented.[1] It would be stretching the bounds of probabilities to suggest that the civilizations of China and South America were referring to the catastrophes of 500 to 140 million years ago as those recorded in their legends, though not improbable.

Our Geologist and Paleontologist have already made their determination as to the periods in which these events occurred, that is outlined in the Geological table which is the yardstick of time as we view it today. When we read their theories concerning pre-historic times, the fertile imagination as shown is nothing short of amazing. The description of life as existed around 2 billion to 140 million years ago is so accurate in detail, it would appear that the writers had actually lived in those time periods, or endowed with the knowledge from some hidden

---

1   Vaillant G.C. *Aztecs of Mexico Published by Penguin Books According to Aztec belief, the world passed through four or five ages, or Suns The God Tezcatlipoca was the god of the first era, Quetzalcoatl, the second era, Tlaloc, the third era Chalchiuhtlicue, the fourth era, and Tonatiuh, the fifth era, which is our present age that will be destroyed by earthquakes.*

source for the purpose of transmitting this information to future generations. Therefore there is no reason to reject the hypothesis that ancient people were not capable of making their own determination as to the periodic events, which became part of their folklore and legends.

Like all myths and legends from the past, ancient people, unlike modern man, were not interested in the date on which these events occurred. What was important was that the event had taken place and became the legends that were passed on from generation to generation. To consider such a hypothesis would be to accept the man's presence on this planet much earlier than has been hypothesized by the Paleontologist.

Whether the ancient legends were referring to these particular ages or events that preceded the Cretaceous period or subsequent events, is a matter of speculation. Geologist has determined that the earth has been subject to unusual cold at least twice in its Geological history.

The most recent glaciations occurred in the Pleistocene Age, known as the great ice age, was a period when layers of ice were formed over the surface of the land that was many thousands of feet thick.[1]

Geologist also state that this was followed by four Interglacial and glacial periods when the Earth went through successive warming and cooling stages which saw the ice caps retreat to the positions which they occupy to-day. However, this may not be the case. It has been remarked on how the experts manipulate history in order to substantiate their theories. This may be one of those instances when they have taken free license to account for some anomalies in their theories.

There exist too many gaps that demand answers; as was remarked by one authority, "The Pleistocene history of North America holds ten major mysteries for every one that has already been solved".[2]

There are many disputable facts that have to be considered when evaluating the various theories put forward by the experts when discussing the glacial periods suffered by our planet. In simplistic terms, it involves, the stationary Sun, the circumsolar motion of the earth, and the earth's rotation.

Simple logic suggests that to create the conditions for ice to form to the degree put forward by the experts; the earth had to be deprived of the Suns heat and be inundated with moisture in the form of rain or snow. It is impossible to create the conditions described by the experts without copious amounts of moisture.

For the earth to go through four glacial, and four interglacial periods suggest that the earth was deprived of the sun's rays on four occasions over long periods of time; further suggesting that the rotation of the earth axis around the sun had been interrupted on four occasions by some galactic occurrence.

---

1   *Pleistocene Age is said to have occurred, between 600,000 -540,000 thousand years ago*
2   *Daly.R.A The Changing World of the Ice Age' (1934), p.111.*
    Velikovsky Immanuel 'Earth in Upheaval' Published by Pocket Books. NY.
    'Earth in Upheaval' Published by Pocket Books. NY.

Under these circumstances the earth would not be deprived of the sun's rays. For this to occur there would have to be an intermediary source in the form of volcanic ash enveloping the planet that would prevent the sun's rays reaching the earth's surface. Would this affect the whole of the planet's surface, or only certain sectors? Given the conditions necessary to create a very cold environment, the obvious answer would be that only portions of the planet were affected; otherwise there would be a lack of moisture.[1]

Be that as it may, it has been proven that some "four million years ago Greenland was a sub-tropical region in which forests of exotic plants, including among the species, magnolia and fig trees" grew in a land that is today covered with ice.[2] Logic would suggest that at some time in the past the earth's axis was quite different in its relationship to the sun. How and what occurred to alter this axis has been an ongoing debate among the experts.

It has been remarked that "the historians of climate has chosen a field as hard to master as it is to square the circle.[3] It seems sometimes that the history of climate is a collection of unsolved, even unsolvable, questions. Without drastic changes in the position of the terrestrial axis or in the form of the orbit or both, conditions could not have existed in which tropical plants flourished in Polar Regions. If anyone is not convinced of this, he should try and cultivate coral at the North Pole".[4]

Since there is no way by which the theories put forward by the various experts can be proved or disproved, it has to be assumed, if we accept their hypothesis, our planet has on four occasions been inflicted with some form of cataclysmic disaster.

One could say that the theories put forward by our modern experts is equal to the mythology of the South American and other ancient cultures which tell of the world experiencing four cataclysms in the remote past. Although the versions handed down through the ages differ from those propounded by the experts, it is no coincidence that ancient cultures should retain the memory of these events in their folklore.

Consequently, it can be said that the earth, suffered some cataclysmic event in past ages. Whether this occurred on four occasions, as put forward by the experts, is academic. What has been established is that the earth did suffer some form of catastrophe that brought on the demise of the dinosaurs and a great portion of life on this planet, some sixty-five million years ago.

However, evidence would suggest that our planet suffered two catastrophic events; one of led to the demise of the Dinosaurs, and the other, the great ice age. What can be stated with

---

1   *There is no available evidence to suggest that China went through an ice age. It would therefore follow that those adjacent countries would also have been free of ice.*

2   *O'Hare Flora Arctica Fossils: Die fossile Flora der Polarlander. (1868)*

3   *Lawlor, Robert. Sacred Geometry. Published by Thames and Hudson Ltd. London Squaring the Circle First found in the writings of the Greek philosopher, Plato, in his most famous work on the creation myth in his book Timaeus. Sacred to the Order of Freemasonry Reputed to be associated with the foundation plans for the Egyptian Pyramid of Giza, and Stonehenge at Salisbury in England.*

4   *Velikovsky, Immanuel. 'Earth in Upheaval" Published by Pocket Books. N.Y.*

some degree of certainty is that the demise of the Dinosaurs was due to the obliteration of their food supply by a heat source that destroyed all plant life. Whereas the death of the Mammoth Elephant and the vast herds of "huge elephants, enormous hippopotami, and gigantic carnivores, was suddenly buried under a mantle of ice, covering plains, lakes, seas, and plateaus. Upon the life and movement of a vigorous[1] creation fell the silence of death"?

When we speak of the ice age there is an inclination on the part of the majority of people to think that this condition was worldwide and affected all countries on the planet, whereas this was not the case.

From what is known of this period, the ice cap covered a very limited area which was confined to those areas delineated by Northern Europe, including parts of England, parts of Ireland, North America, including Canada, and Siberia.

This condition is said to have lasted until about 20,000 years ago when the earth's climate began to warm and the level of ice receded and decreased, that to-day the depth of ice found in Antarctica and Greenland is approximately 8,000 feet thick.[2]

Among the ancient legends regarding the many catastrophes suffered by this planet a description is found in the works of the Greek historian, Herodotus, in which there is a passage that has been the cause of considerable controversy down through the ages. [3]

In his writings on ancient Egypt, he records a conversation he had with an Egyptian priest when discussing the history and antiquity of ancient Egypt. In regards to this discussion, Herodotus goes on to say, "They declare that three hundred and forty-one generations separate the first king of Egypt from the last I have mentioned, (Sethos-Seti 1303--1200 BC)--the priest of Hephaestus—and that there was a King and a high priest corresponding to each generation. Now to reckon three generations as a hundred years, three hundred generations make Ten thousand (10.000) years and the remaining forty-one generations make one thousand, three hundred and forty (1,340) years, thus one gets a total of eleven thousand, three hundred, and forty (11,340) years. During the whole of which time, they say, no god ever assumed mortal form, nothing of this sort occurred either under the former or under the later Kings. They did say, however, that four times within this period the sun changed his usual position, twice rising where he normally sets, and twice setting where he normally rises".

It is obvious that the people to whom Herodotus is speaking are people of importance, as Herodotus continuing states, "They took me into the great hall of the Temple and showed me the wooden statues there, which they counted; and the number was what I have said, for each High Priest had a statue of himself erected there before he dies. As they showed them to me, and counted them up, beginning with the statue of the High Priest who had just died, and

---

1   *Agassiz, Louis. Etudes sur les glaciers. (1840) p. 314*

2   *It has been estimated that if the ice caps on the North and South Poles should melt, the sea level would rise 120 feet inundating all of the low coastal regions around the world.*
    Herodotus. (490--425 BC) The Histories. Trans; Aubrey de Selincourt. Publish by Penguin Classics

3   *Ibid.*

going on from him through the whole number, they assured me that each had been the son of the one who preceded him".[1]

The negative opinions expressed by early historians as to the veracity of Herodotus writings have been rejected by today's scholars, who view his works as a major contributor to our knowledge of the past. Admittedly there are, within the works, stories that appear to be less then credible, however, one must admit that he is quite clear in stating as to what he has seen and to what he has been told by others. Also where he has been and where he has not been.

Perhaps there were times when the tales told to him were less then believable as the Hieroglyphics inscriptions which he observed on the side of the Pyramid, were according to the interpreter who read the inscriptions for Herodotus, recorded the amount spent on radishes, onions, and leeks for the laborers. Herodotus is convinced of what the interpreter is telling him, he goes on to state, "and I remember distinctly that the interpreter, who read me the inscription, said the sum was 1.600 talents of silver". [2]

The same situation may have existed in his reference to the Pharaoh Cheops, to whom the building of the great Pyramid is attributed, who being short of money, due to the expense of building the Pyramid, sent his daughter into a brothel with instructions to charge a certain sum for her services. Who in addition to charging for her services, "for with the intention of leaving something to be remembered by after her death, requested each of her clients to give her a black stone and of these stones was built the middle Pyramid of the three which stand in front of the Great Pyramid".[3] Common sense would indicate the impossibility of this tale, but it would appear that Herodotus was susceptible to the tales of the Egyptian storytellers.

It is highly unlikely that an Egyptian King would send his daughter into a brothel or that the Egyptians would profane a structure of this importance. In all probability, the interpreter had no knowledge of Hieroglyphic script. In this respect, Herodotus would be no more than the tourist who visits Egypt to-day or any other country where the natives enjoy taking the tourist gullibility for granted. Some forbearance should be shown as none of us are immune from been taken in by a tall story by those who would profess to be knowledgeable in the lore of the country.

In the case of the interpreter, there would be a reward for his efforts, irrespective in the truth of his statement, whereas, the priest of the Temple had no monetary rewards in mind when imparting the information to Herodotus, other than one scholar imparting information to another. Therefore the story as recounted by the priest as to the rising and setting of the sun is not to be viewed as a tall tale or the boasting of those with excessive pride and vanity.

Unlike the Greeks, the Egyptian religion was devoid of such pretensions as it was based on the concept of Truth. In this regard we can give credence to the statement by the priest. However the statement requires examining as common logic dictates that if the Sun was to

1   Herodotus. *The Histories. Trans; Aubrey de Selincourt. Published by Penguin Classics*
2   Herodotus. *The Histories. Trans; Aubrey de Selincourt.*
3   *Ibid.*

change position from East to West, an event of this magnitude would require that the Earth be thrown off its axis and to some degree, reverse its rotation that would result in major upheavals and disturbances across the planet. However, it is obvious that this was not the case, as the Egyptian Priest assured Herodotus that Egypt was quite unaffected by these events, when he goes on to say. "The Harvests, and the produce of the river, were the same as usual, and there was no change in the incidence of disease and death".[1]

Why the Priest would make this statement is questionable, as logic dictates that life would not be normal and tranquil after such events, but in a state of chaos. Reason would reject such events occurring as being impossible and beyond the bounds of probabilities. Therefore, there must be another meaning behind the statement that was beyond the understanding of Herodotus, as the Priest, respecting the statues of Herodotus as an historian and a guest, assumed that Herodotus was conversant with the subject they were discussing, would find it unnecessary to go into long explanations that may be the cause embarrassment.

In this respect, the Priests statement negates any form of catastrophic upheaval. So it would be wrong in this instance, to read into this statement that which is not there, i.e., "cosmic upheaval in which the South becomes North and the Earth turns over."[2]

This may perhaps be a reference to the magnetic poles that have, based upon geological studies, and varied considerably in location over aeons of time. Recent studies of paleomagnetism indicate that the earth's magnetic field has reversed its polarity many times in the geological past.

Events of cataclysmic nature have occurred in the distant past, as proven by geological evidence that created geographic and climatic changes, which brought on the extinction of the Dinosaurs.

In the case of Herodotus and the Egyptian Priest, we can discount the theory of major catastrophes as it does not conform to the second statement regarding the harvest, the product of the river, disease and death.

To what then was the Priest alluding? Obviously Herodotus is listening and not paying attention or else is listening and fails to understand the import of what's being said. Therefore, in writing up his notes, makes reference to the Sun as being the simpler of the alternatives, rather than the zodiacal constellations processional cycle across the heavens.

There is also a possibility that legends existed within Greek mythology that alluded to the numerous catastrophes that has occurred over time, and was known to Herodotus. However these ancient myths have been lost due to the pollution of Greek legends with that of religion as we see in the Theogony,-a genealogy of the gods, attributed to Hesiod, a Greek poet of the 8th century BC.

However, oblique reference to a catastrophic event in which the world suffered earthquakes and floods in a time when the sun ceased to shine exists in ancient legends. The Greek Myths

---

1   *The Histories. Trans; Aubrey de Selincourt. Published by Penguin Classics*
2   *Velikovsky. Immanuel. Worlds in Collision.Published by Pocket Books N Y*

record three separate tales that may have been one event in ancient times, the Giants Revolt, the conflict between the gods Typhon and Zeus, and Deucalions Flood. Each myth could be construed to refer to a general cataclysm that affects the earth which consisted of earthquakes, volcanoes erupting, and the inundation of the planet, and the near extinction of mankind.

According to the myth of the Giants Revolt, the giants became enraged when Zeus confined their brothers the Titans who had been born from mother earth, The giants, without warning, seized rocks and firebrands and hurled them from the mountain top towards the gods. While Athene went to search for Heracles, the Goddess Hera forbade Eros, Selene, and Helius to shine, while under the feeble light of the stars, Zeus groped about on earth.[1]

In this very bloodthirsty tale the Giants are defeated to the annoyance of Mother Earth, who for revenge gives birth to the Monster Typhon. Apparently the story refers to a major cataclysm that saw the sun disappear from the heavens and placed the world in darkness. A similar myth is told by the Peruvians, in which they tell of the battle between two serpents known as Kaimai and Tren—Tren, who made the waters of the sea rise to prove how great their powers were[2] which may be a reference to the floods and earthquakes suffered by the South American Indians.

In the second of the myths we have the story of the battle between Typhon and Zeus. Again we have a tale of monsters and serpents battling with the Gods, when Typhon, the largest monster ever born is described as, "From the thighs downward he was nothing but coiled serpents, his arms when spread out reached a hundred leagues in both direction, had serpents heads instead of hands, his vast wings darkened the sun, fire flashed from his eyes, and flaming rocks hurtled from his mouth."[3] In the following battle with Zeus there is mention of thunderbolts, mountains being moved, and volcano's erupting, and the darkening of the sun, would lead one to believe that the two related events refer to the same occurrence.

The third myth that deals with the inundation of the earth and is known as 'Deucalions' flood, which in many respects is similar to the story of the flood as found in the Bible. This tells the story of Deucalion and Pyrrha who lived in a time when the earth was inhabited by a violent and vicious race of men. This race of men incurred the anger of the gods who decided to punish them by letting loose a great flood to bring about their destruction. However, the gods decided to spare two just people, who were Deucalion and Pyrrha. On the advice of the gods they built an ark or chest. For nine days and nine nights they floated around in the water, until they came to rest on the mountain in Thessaly.[4]

When condensed, these three myths speak of a time when the world was in a state of chaos and turmoil, a period when thunder and lightning flashed across the sky. Volcano's erupted. The sun disappeared from the heavens, and the land was inundated with a flood of unimaginable

1   Graves. Robert. *The Greek Myths. Bk. 1.*Published by Penguin Books
2   Larousse. *Encyclopaedia of Mythology.*
3   *Ibid*
4   *Ibid*

proportions. A time when many thought the world had come to an end, As to when this event occurred and how many times did the earth suffer, is yet unknown, however, the similarities between the legends of South America, Greece, and those of China are too striking to be ignored.

Many writers, even from the early Greek, and Roman, have down to the present, place their own interpretation upon this statement by Herodotus, attributing various events that would conform to their religious or political beliefs. It has been assumed by many that the early historians of the first century AD and those of earlier dates would have checked their information against the Temple records, which were still extent during this period. However, it appears that these ancient writers followed the version as expounded by Herodotus and continued to make reference of the Suns position to the Earth's rotation, quoting much later historians and writers to support their hypothesis, ignoring the importance of the second statement by the Priest.

It is impossible that an event of such a catastrophic nature could have occurred four times in a span of 11,340 year. Should a single event of this magnitude occurred; at least 75% of all life would be eliminated. Only those who were living in the far North or within area of Antarctica would survive such a catastrophic event. But for it to happen every 2,800 years would see the end of all life on the Earth's surface, as it would be impossible for the Earth and its inhabitants to recover sufficiently to withstand the second onslaught, not counting the third and the fourth.

Therefore, for an event of this nature to occur in the time suggested by Herodotus does not seem reasonable. Evidently, if Herodotus was not conversant with the subject matter, he may have assumed that the Priest was referring to the Sun, and not the movement of the constellations across the heavens, would be the case when viewed against the second statement.

If this hypothesis merits consideration, it would be supported by the hypothesis proposed by R A. Schwaller de Lubicz who stated, when addressing the same problem said. "Instead of condemning this "fairy tale as proof of the Egyptians feeble astronomical knowledge, would it not be better to seek for an understanding of its meaning? Doesn't the rising refer to the vernal point? In modern language, this would mean that the vernal point had twice been located in the same constellation of Aries, and that it also passed twice in the opposing constellation of Libra. This would grant the duration of one and a half processional cycles to the entire historic and prehistoric periods, or approximately 39,000 years.[1]

This would appear a more appropriate explanation and agrees with what the Priest may have being imparting to Herodotus, thus implying obliquely to the antiquity of Egypt. However, this explanation may not fit well with those who maintain that Egypt's historic period is less than 5,000 years BC. Furthermore, as Egypt has been lauded by the ancient historians as a people who kept a strict daily record of all unusual occurrences, events of this magnitude would not go unnoticed, but would be an important part of the Temple records.

---

1   de Lubicz. R A. Schwaller. *Sacred Science. Published by Inner Traditions International Ltd. N.Y.*

A famous Latin geographer, Pomponius Mela of the first century AD had this to say on the matter. "The Egyptians pride themselves on being the most ancient people in the world. In their authentic annuals, one may read that since they have been in existence, the course of the stars has changed direction four times".["][1]

He is quoting from written records; therefore it is obvious he had access to the Temple records. Seeing that this gentleman was a Roman geographer, who published a description of the then known world, he would have traveled extensively in and around the Mediterranean, which of course would include Egypt. Therefore, being a representative of the Roman Government, would receive preferential treatment by the Egyptian Priests, thereby gaining ready access to the Temple records. It is therefore reasonable to suggest that the statement made by Pomponius Mela regarding the movement of the stars, supports the hypothesis postulated by Schwaller de Lubicz.

Amid all the convolutions of opinions that have been expressed on this matter, there may be an element of truth. Let us assume for the moment that the Priest was referring to the processional zodiacal cycles of the heavenly constellations and not to the reversal of the suns position in relation to the Earth's orbital motion. We are left with two problems, one is that Egypt is a lot older then our historians and Archaeologist give her credit for, and two, she was highly advanced in Astronomy.

The legend that speaks of a world catastrophe, is to be found in most of the ancient civilizations around the world, most notably, that of Mexico and Peru. In the legends of Peru, it is said that the world suffered four cataclysms that almost destroyed all living creatures.

The first was a fire, which was the result of a heavenly body striking the earth. This event created tidal waves and heavy rains that caused the rivers to swell and flood the land, and after the great fire there came the long night. People could not leave their homes. The world was plunged into darkness by the disappearance of the sun. There was no food and vast majorities of people, animals, and birds died of hunger.

The Caraja Indians say that at one time "The sun flashed so quickly across the sky that no one could complete any task, there was nothing but dim light on the surface of the earth, and there was no sun". After this, the earth was re-peopled by the few who survived the catastrophe. This event was known to the ancient Peruvians and to several tribes on the East coast of the Andes".[2]

A similar legend can be found in the Book of advice of the Mayas, in which it says. "At that time there was nothing but dim light on the surface of the earth, there was no sun".[3] The famous Aztec Calendar Stone discovered in Mexico City makes mention of a myth known as the four 'suns.

---

1   *Pomponius Mela. (c 50 A D) De Situ Orbis.*
2   *Larousse. Encyclopaediaæidea of Mythology.*
3   *Ibid*

According to the Aztecs, there were four eras known as 'suns, before our era, which all ended in cataclysm.

The first era known as "four tiger"saw the inhabitants of the earth perish, and on the date before "four tiger', the sun disappeared.

The second era known as "four wind" say that mankind was swept away by terrible winds.

The third sun known as "four rain" states that a fearful shower of fire destroyed all beings and things

The fourth sun called "four water" is said to have created a flood that destroyed the world and only one man and woman survived to re-people the earth.[1]

This will be followed by our own sun, known, as "four earthquakes" will see our world destroyed by earthquakes.[2]

The Toltec empires, that predated the Aztec culture, tell how the world creation began, that was followed by the five eras, through which life has survived.

The first era, known as the "water sun' was when the world was created, eventually destroyed by floods and lighting.

The second era, known as the "sun of the earth" saw the world populated by giants, who almost disappeared when earthquakes obliterated the earth?

This was followed by the third era, which was known as the "wind sun" and was when the Olmacs lived on this earth. They were the people who destroyed those of the giants who had managed to survive the world's destruction.

The forth sun, which represents the present era, is called the "sun of fire"which will see our present world end in a general conflagration.

It is highly probable that the different cultures of Mexico were influenced by each other's myth and legends with slight variations. However, as there exists a trend that is common to all, e.g., a consistent reference to the earth being struck by some form of meteorite that brought near destruction to mankind and all life. The disappearance of the sun made it impossible to plant crops, resulting in a shortage of food that caused people and animal life to die of hunger.

What is of interest is that similar events occurred on four occasions within the memory of these people. In accepting the truth of these ancient legends historians are left with one more part of a puzzle in the mosaic of this planets history. What age can be attributed to South America? It is estimated that the first settlers to reach Mexico occurred approximately 40,000 BC, or even longer,[3] however, the legends that have been handed down through the ages would suggest a far greater age then the Geologist and Archaeologist are willing to submit.

A universal legend that was prevalent during the time of Herodotus, of which he must have been aware for him to make reference to the different locations for the rising and setting of the

1   *Ibid.*

2   *Ibid*

3   *Larousse. Encyclopaedia of Archaeology.*

sun, can be found in various other cultures. These legends were known to the civilizations of Mexico, China, and Japan, including the Eskimo people of the Northern regions, and North America Indians. The legends tell of a major catastrophic upheaval that resulted in the planet being thrown out of its natural orbit from around the sun and off its axis.

A catastrophe of this nature would create havoc around the planet and result in the world experiencing a period of darkness. A situation of this nature is expressed in an ancient Chinese legend that tells of a horned monster, Kung- Kung who ventured to fight one of the five sovereigns for the title of Emperor. He was overcome, and in his rage he flung himself at Mount Pu Chou. The column of the sky was broken, and the link with earth was cut. In the North—West the sky collapsed. Hence the sun, moon, and stars slipped to the North- West and the earth tilted towards the South—East."[1]

The Chinese speak of two deities who are placed at the northeast and the northwest of the world with the task of stopping the sun and moon and fixing the length of their course. Furthermore, it is said that the sun rose and set in different places, which were named according to the seasons.[2]

This account is somewhat similar to that as expressed in the writings of Herodotus and those of South America, as regards to the rising and setting of the Sun. It can be inferred from this legend that the Earth suffered a major catastrophic event that saw the Earth tilted off its natural axis and the sun disappear from the heavens. Was this event linked to the extinction of the Dinosaurs, or was it a later event that brought on the Ice Age that saw the extinction of the Mammoth Elephant?

There is sufficient evidence to suggest that continents have disappeared and reappeared over the millions of years. Thus the discovery of marine fossils in the mountain regions should come as no surprise.

On the other hand, when we read the various legends of civilization whose history reaches back in to the shadows of time, although analogous when speaking of fire and flood, and the disappearance of the Sun, nowhere is there a mention of an attending ice age.

To suggest that the disappearance of some species was due to the process of natural selection is pure conjecture. The Anthropologist of today, in his efforts to find mans origins, though his methods may appear to be a little more sophisticated, and his theories a little more scientific, is no more valid than those theories found in the myths of the past.

Why is this knowledge only manifesting itself in the Caucasoid and Asiatic groups and not in the Negroid? It has been hypothesized that man had his origins in Africa. If this had any truth one would expect to find a corpus of ancient myths as we find in other cultures. However, this is not the case; Africa is devoid of any ancient links to the past.

In a recent article on this subject, it has been suggested that the destruction of the Bronze Age civilizations of Egypt, Mesopotamia, and Greece, was the result of a series of natural

---

1   Larousse. *Encyclopaedia of Mythology.*
2   *Ibid.*

disasters in about the year 2350 BC. According to the dynastic list of Egyptian Kings of the old kingdom, this would cover the reign of about twenty Kings, covering Dynasty 3, 4, 5, and 6, between the years 2686 BC to 2345 BC. Among the many famous Pharaohs that reigned during this long period was the Pharaoh, Unas,[1] the last King of the fifth dynasty whose funeral ceremony ritual are so prominent in the Egyptian Book of the Dead.[2]

According to one expert, this worldwide devastation was the result of a "massive meteor storms are the most scientific reason why these ancient societies collapsed".[3] This theory was confirmed by an astrophysicist[4] who claims to have identified a meteor cluster in orbit around the Planet Jupiter, which collides with the earth every 3,000 years. He believes it was this shower that caused the ice age and then returned in a later cycle to prompt the cataclysm of 2350 BC.[5]

It has been said, "To fix a chronological limit for the arts and civilization of Egypt is absolutely impossible".[6] When we speak of Egypt we are lost in time. Nevertheless, the Egyptian culture was many things during its long history, however, its greatest contribution to our knowledge was the copious amount of literature, and both on stone, and on papyrus that was our inheritance.

Therefore, logic would suggest that if such events as put forward regard the extinction of their society, the priests of the Temple would have recorded such a calamity.

In commenting on the work that has been carried out by our scientific communities in their quest to find answers to the origins of man and the universe, it is a paradox that the scientists of today have discovered nothing new on this planet or the universe. In fact, they have only found that which has been in existence since the beginning of time, and known to our ancestors.

While Anthropologist and Paleontologist, much like the Cosmologist, are as definite in their assessment of mans origins and emergence upon this planet, 14 to 12 million years ago, a time when they say that man diverged from the Ape is conjectural, and is as much contentious as that of the Cosmologist and their theory relative to the age of the Earth and Universe. What has been published concerning these subjects change as new theories are developed and will continue into the future?

Geologist basing their theories on the earth's strata, tell of the cataclysms and catastrophic upheavals that inflicted this planet over the billions of years, it would appear that man is a relative newcomer.

---

1   *Dynasty 5. 2494-2345 B.C. Unas, the first pharaoh to inscribe the interior of his pyramid with religious text, known as the Pyramid Text.*

2   *Budge. E.A. Wallis. The Egyptian Book of the Dead. .Published by Dover Publications, Inc N.Y.*

3   *Peiser. Dr. Benny Anthropologist. John Moores University. Liverpool. England*

4   *Clube, Victor Astrophysicist. Oxford University.*

5   *The Sunday Times. London. Meteor showers blotted out man's first civilization, by Rajeev Syal.*

6   *Ibid*

Chapter 15

What is man, he is unique, he is special, and his variability gives him this special place on the planet."No two individuals are alike. We may compare millions of faces, and each will be distinct. That genius that implies a wonderfully complex combination of high faculties tends to be inherited."[1] Scientist can tell something of his biological make-up, but cannot explain his contradictions, his perverse nature, his capacity to love, to destroy, his compassion and hates.

"What is man that you should spare a though for him, the son of man that you should care for him, yet you have made him little less than a god."[2] "If men are capable of acquiring enough knowledge to be able to investigate the world, living among his work's, how can they be so slow to find it's Master?"[3]

The discoveries made over the last one hundred years have been phenomenal, surpassing anything that has been accomplished over the previous two thousand years, or so we are led to believe? Within this short time, Western society has taken a quantum leap with inventions that as little as fifty years ago was the material of which science fiction novels are written.

The field of modern Medicine has advanced in leaps and bounds, to where the transplanting of human organs is now commonplace. In the early years, the risk of failure in this procedure was extremely high whereas now the rate of success is high, with the aid of modern drugs and new advanced surgical procedures, the failure rate has markedly decreased... Today it is commonplace for people to receive triple, and quadruple heart surgery. People, who fifty years ago faced the prospect of death, can now look forward to a relatively full life span.

In addition, the field of Microsurgery has allowed the most intricate of operations to be accomplished with a high degree of success in operations that were impossible a short time ago. People living within those countries that are technically advanced are living longer and enjoying a better standard of life compared to their parents and grandparents.

Also in the fields of Physics and Mathematics there has been an ongoing increase in knowledge since the eighteen century. Man's dream of joining the birds in their flight and possessing the ability to leave this planet has been realized with the help of rocket propulsion.

---

1   Darwin. Charles. The Descent of Man.
2   The New Jerusalem Bible. Psalm 8- 4. 5.
3   The New Jerusalem Bible.Book of Wisdom. 13.--8--9.

He can now view his world from the heavens that surrounds this earth he calls home, and to counteract all of these successes, has become the ultimate destroyer, in that he can now kill and destroy more, with much less and in a shorter time.

With the power he now controls, man may believe he is master of the Universe, as there are little of the Earth's hidden secrets that he cannot solve by the new science. Taking on the role of the Creator, he possesses the power to create life through his advances in the field of Microbiology.

New scientific techniques developed in the field of Cryogenics, allows the male sperm and female ovaries to be frozen for fertilization at some future date is a common practice. The fertilization procedure, which is initiated under laboratory conditions, is used extensively on women who have infertility problems. Once fertilization has occurred, the implantation of the fertilized embryo into the female womb becomes a simple procedure. This method can be applied, not only to humans, but also to all other life on this planet.

From the events that have occurred over the last twenty years or so, one could assume that with the innate curiosity that is mans inheritance; he will eventually take the step that will lead him to experiment in the process of cross breeding different species. If such experiments presented no ethical problems, it would be an interesting experiment if one were to reverse the Darwinian Theory and cross breed man with the Ape. What would be the result? Would the offspring resemble the characteristics of the species known as Ramapithecus, or Australopithecus? There is no reason why one should discard such an experiment happening in the future. If such an experiment is possible today there is no reason to reject the theory that such an event did not occur in the distance past.

The rapid advance made in the field of fertility transplantation allows man with the knowledge he now holds, to create initial life outside the womb. And with the help of new fertility drugs, can determine the amount of human embryos within the female womb and the sex of each child. With such abilities man can and will no doubt control his destiny. Projecting our thoughts into the future the picture we envisage would give one a concern for the future of this planet. The rapid increase in the world's population will eventually lead to a food scarcity. Will there come a time when the world will be unable to support its ever increasing population? Such an event would require that a system of population control be introduced in order to sustain one's life style and avoid mass starvation. Will this be the time when we see a system of selective breeding being introduced in order to control the growth? Will this be the age when we can say that this is truly the age when the "survival of the fittest" becomes the norm rather than the exception?

One would believe that man has reached his chosen goal, to be the master of his destiny, with the power to manipulate life and create his environment, or conversely, bring it to the point of total destruction.

This sudden surge would make one believe that this knowledge has been lying dormant in the sub-conscience of man to manifest it at this point in time, and through the process of remembering, is regaining the knowledge that was known through his psychic sub-conscience.

How do we compare the knowledge of today to that which existed in the past? When we look and read of the ancient civilizations, there are many areas of knowledge that are yet unknown to us. Even today with all of our progress, scientists are unable to find answers too many of these questions. They offer hypothesis, theories, and conjectures, and somehow come up short in their explanations.

In all fields, the enigmas left to us by these ancient people defy explanation. This beautiful living organism of a planet that may be the envy of the Universe, of which man can rightfully say, " I love the beauty of your house, and the place where your glory dwells. I look up at your heavens, made by your fingers, at the moon and the stars you set in place."[1] [2]

The beauties of which astounded the first Astronauts, and continues to do so for those who view it from outer space, see in it the hand of an intelligence greater than man, a Universe of which all things were ordered by measure, number, and weight.[3]

The delicate balance that exists within this Universe is not a haphazard occurrence or an accident of interstellar chaos, as scientists would have us believe. The school of philosophy that teaches the concept of order being created from chaos may apply to politics or civil unrest, but does not apply in this case, as the balance and harmony that exists within the Universe and that of nature itself precludes any form of chaotic beginning.

It is when man through his ignorance, and abuse of power tries to impose his will upon the delicate balance of natural laws, will eventually bring about his own destruction and that of all life on this planet, as man invites destruction through his own actions.

Should this event ever occur, this planet will survive and over time replenish its beauty, slightly modified, but still beautiful. What will be missing will be the beauty of life, as we know it and man"s presence to enjoy its beauty.

As it is written in the Book of Wisdom, "Vain are all men who have not known the Creator and from the good things that are seen, have not been able to discover him, or by studying his works, have failed to recognize the Artificer. Since the very author of beauty has created them and since through the grandeur and beauty of the creatures, we may by analogy, contemplate their Author."[4]

Whether one is inclined to believe in a God or Creator or not, common logic would dictate that life did not just happen, that within the Universe order and harmony is self-evident, which would suggest mans progress through time is controlled by some form of super intelligence. Whether this may be the collective consciousness of man or some form of external force, controlling the workings of the universe, is beyond man's comprehension, and for the moment is a matter of conjecture and speculation.

1   *The New Jerusalem Bible. Book of Psalms. 8. 3--6. 26--8.*
2   *Ibid*
3   *The New Jerusalem Bible Book of Wisdom. 11. 21.*
4   *The New Jerusalem Bible. Book of Wisdom. 13. 1,--2,--5.*

If man is to avoid being the cause of his own destruction, it would be in his best interest to find his place in this order and recognize his relationship within the harmony of nature and his natural environment. However, this is not the case, when one views the world today, it would appear that man is making his best effort to destroy his environment through his abuse of natures gifts and natural resources.

This living organic planet and all life on the land, in the sea, lakes and rivers is being contaminated by chemical waste that is some cases has brought to extinction a greater portion of the worlds wildlife. The destruction of the rain forests across this planet has been the cause of dramatic changes in the weather patterns around the globe, and has been the cause of many species been brought to extinction.

When through the actions of man, a species is brought to extinction, or causes, through some natural catastrophe, we can say, as was expressed by a famous naturalist. "Each time we experience the loss of a species through the actions of man, we will have to see the creation of a new heaven and earth before we see that species again"...[1]

There is nothing extraordinary about the human species when compared to all other species on this planet, even down to the most minuscule atom. Each species have their individual special gifts of survival. However, what makes man unique and separates him from other species is his adaptability and inventiveness.[2]

By his very nature, he is a contradiction in that he can appreciate and create beauty, demonstrating compassion and love. Where he differs from all other species, is his ability to destroy on an unprecedented scale, not only those of his own species, but any that he may perceive to be a threat to his existence or way of life.

It is in this context that he perceives himself as being master of his destiny, and that of all that occupy this planet. This free license to kill and control his destiny and that of all other species has manifested itself exponentially since the 16th century.

This characteristic is equal to all races to varying degrees, some greater than others. But, when we use the expression "Man", It must first be determine to whom we are referring and to what culture and race. When we speak of adaptability and inventiveness it would be a grave error to believe that these attributes can be attributed to all races that inhabit this planet.

There have been cultures that demonstrated amazing abilities and degrees of inventiveness in the course of history. However, in this instance, we are referring to those known to us as Anglo Saxon, the race who, being further advanced than any other culture in Science, Technology, and Industrialization, presently dominates this planet.

Charles Darwin in writing on the Descent of man commented, "Man in his rudest state in which he now exists is the most dominant animal that ever appeared on this earth. He has spread more widely than any other highly organized form; and all others have yielded before

1   Foster. George. 1754-1794.
2   Leakey. Richard E. The Making of Mankind.

him. He manifestly owes his immense superiority to his intellectual faculties, to his social habits, which lead him to aid and defend his fellows."[1]

In general, the world was a peaceful place in the early centuries. Admittedly, there were minor wars and conflicts between countries and tribes that were soon resolved for life to continue at its usual pace. However, this aura of tranquility was to end with the first wave of Anglo Saxon immigrants from Europe to the new worlds.

The expansion off this race saw the destruction and eradication of peoples and cultures unprecedented in the history of man. These wanton acts of murder and rapine as occurred in South Africa with the killing and near extinction of the Bushman of the Kalahari by the Dutch settlers, and subjection of the indigenous tribes were acts of barbarity. In Australia, similar events occurred that saw the near extinction of the native Aborigine, and the total extinction of the native people of Tasmania, by the British settlers through disease, and extermination.

Charles Darwin posed a question, which considering the date and the time in history, was self evident, when he asked, " do races or species of men encroach on and replace one another, so that some finally become extinct". [2] One can assume that at the time of writing, events that were taking place in the Colonies of America, South Africa, Australia and the South Pacific would have answered his question. Probably, the destruction of these native people would have been of no concern, as the mentality of the time classed them as less than human. Looked upon as being devoid of any form of what one would class as intelligence, savages being the common term when speaking of these people, their survival was the prerogative the European settlers.

As Anglo-Saxons spread out across the world they were blight and harbingers of death to many races of people who up to their arrival led a relatively quiet and peaceful life. In addition to the killings there were the overzealous Christen abhorrence to the nakedness of the indigenous people, whom they forced to wear European clothing, which was infected with disease's that brought some cultures to the point of extinction.

In North America the indigenous population suffered immeasurably in the hands of the Christen missionaries, and civil authorities, which at times led to the extinction of tribes of people. The devastation and destruction brought to North America by the early settlers is well documented.[3]

When we view the society that is now America, we see a culture permeated with violence as a way of life. Everywhere within this society, crime abounds on a scale that is unequalled in any other society on this planet. This society, an amalgam of all the worlds' cultures is in a true sense a hybrid culture that has lost its way. Because of its structure, it cannot identify itself with any one culture that would give it some form of authenticity. There is murder, theft, riots, perjury, treachery, corruption, bribery and fraud within its society and governing body. Acts are committed against the natural order in the destruction of the human fetus. Adultery and divorce

---

1   Darwin. Charles. *The Descent of Man.*

2   *Ibid*

3   *Mowett Farley. Desperate People.*

on an unprecedented scale that has led to the breakdown of the family structure that forms the foundation and fabric of a stable society. We see a generation of young people polluted with the use of drugs and corrupted by a society whose duty was to protect and nurture the young.

A society that classes itself as the leader of a new world order would appear to be on the verge of self-destruction from within. It lives in fear of the world and in fear of its ability to destroy. In the belief that their society is invulnerable to attack by any external source, they are contemptuous of those who do not measure up to their standard.

In their ignorance and sense of power, they continually interfere in the internal affairs of other nations. This interference may appear to resolve the issues for a short time, however, in the long term create animosity and distrust, which eventually leads to future conflicts.

Somehow, their politicians have failed to learn from history, that to interfere with the process of political or religious change is to create chaos within a society or culture. This all-important process and its necessity to the well being of people were acknowledged by ancient civilizations. In this process can be seen the rise and fall of the great Empires down through the ages.

An example of such situations can best be seen in the conflicts that existed in Korea, Vietnam, and Israel. The interference by the American and European powers in each of these conflicts did not resolve the issues, but only delayed the inevitable. Eventually these conflicts will be resolved however; the animosity created precludes any form of resolution by peaceful means.

However, had the conflicts been allowed to reach their natural conclusion, there would be peace within these regions today. But, as there was no conclusion to the conflicts, a situation of discord and civil unrest prevails, which will continue into the future until a resolution is found. "It is within these great conflicts to which the ignorance of these nations condemns their lives, that they give such massive ills the name of peace.[1]

The more man delves into the past for knowledge relative to his place in the universe, the more he realizes how little the knowledge he possesses is. Science and the public are beginning to realize the importance of the ecological balance that exists in nature. They are also recognizing the effects of each species in the natural order as it applies to the interdependence of each species and their total dependence on each other for survival.

Within this complex cycle of life and death, if life is allowed to progress within the order as nature intended, balance and harmony is maintained to the benefit of all. However, when one species breaks loose from the main stream of life with the capacity to dominate its environment and control its destiny, chaos and disorder is the result.

Some believe that this planet was inflicted with some form of nuclear explosion in the far distanced past, which caused nature to mutate and created the age of the dinosaurs.

Whether this was, an event caused by man, or from outer space cannot be determined. Whatever may have been the cause, the results are being discovered by the Paleontologist to-day.

---

1   *The New Jerusalem Bible. Book of Wisdom. 14--22.*

Does man possess the capability for self-destruction to the point of destroying his environment? Maybe not at the moment, but given time, should present no problems.

We tend to use the word 'Man' loosely and encompass all humanity in this category, attributing to him all the ills that beset humanity. This may not be true; if we reflect on the matter, what we are really talking about is one race and culture that we class as Anglo Saxon. This segment of the world's community would appear to be the predominant race controlling the destiny of this planet.

How long this situation will exist will be determined by the emergence of those other cultures that have been scientifically and industrially dormant over the last fifty years. The demise of self proclaimed Empires have been well demonstrated in the annuals of history.

Chapter 16

The unique complex characteristics and diversity of the human family are as complex as the molecular genetic code that makes up the human psychic, each molecule having its own identity and intelligence within the framework of the body. It is this uniqueness and individuality of each single person, precludes the lineal theory of evolution. This uniqueness and individuality of the human species is clearly demonstrated in the surgical procedures of organ transplants and the acceptance of the donor's organ by the host body. Generally, should it be donated by a stranger, there is a rejection of the organ. It is only through the help of drugs, that the body is conditioned to accept the replacement organ; however, this procedure is not always successful.

One has only to read of the work that is being carried out in the field if genetics and the manipulation of the genes of man and animals, and for that matter nature itself, to really appreciate how far man has progressed in the last fifty years. His curiosity knows no bounds in his search for knowledge. It would appear that man has now reached the stage in his development when he is inclined to dispense with the concept of a God or a force outside of himself as being the Creator of man and the Universe.

One frightening characteristic of this form of reasoning is when man looks upon himself as the creator of life and sees himself outside the laws of nature. A theory put forward concerns an event that may have had had a devastating effect upon the world sometime in the past. It has been suggested that man overstepped the bounds in molecular genetics and nuclear fission and brought about his own destruction, improbable, perhaps and material for science fiction, but could such an event have occurred?

Could it be that man who has existed from the beginning of time and is sub-consciously regaining the knowledge that once existed in the distant past, as it says in the book of wisdom, "In each generation she (Wisdom) passes into holy soul's"?

Knowledge that may have led to his destruction and near demise and is now beginning to re-emerge to recommence the process that will allow him to find his place in the Universe.

The regaining of knowledge through intuition or memory recall is an integral part of the human psychic. This was demonstrated by the Greek philosopher Socrates (c 469-399 BC) in his discussion with Menon on the question of memory.[1] In his discussion, Socrates through the process of questions, put to Menon's slave Anytos, regarding Geometrical design, demonstrates that knowledge is inherent in the soul of man and lies dormant in the mind and it is through the process of questioning that our memory is titillated into remembering and the knowledge is brought to the forefront of our cerebral intelligence.

In his conversation with Theaetetus, he compares himself to a midwife in delivering knowledge to those who associate with him. In which he states that his pupils, "Not because they ever learn anything from me, the many fine ideas and offspring that they produce come from within themselves. But, the God and I are responsible for the delivery."[2]

This acquisition of knowledge can be initiated through self-inquiry or through some external source, as with Socrates questions to Anytos. Anytos, being a slave to Menon, had not received any form of education that would qualify him to respond correctly to Socrates questions on geometry.

It was reasoned that as he had not received his knowledge in this life, he must have acquired it at some other time, before he came into existence in this life. This infers that like all the great religions of the world, the soul of man is immortal, and it is within the soul that all knowledge is passed from one generation to another. To—day we would equate this with the D.N.A molecule that is responsible for transmitting hereditary characteristics from our parents and is the building block of nature.

In the works Socrates it is evident that he was a believer in the reincarnation of the soul. It was his belief that the soul of man is immortal, has existed from all time, and is never destroyed, and though it comes to an end in the death of the Body, it is born again. As we read in the Book of Wisdom, "I had received a good soul for my lot and being good, I had entered an undefiled soul".[3] "And since the soul is immortal, and often born again, it has seen everything that is on this earth, and there is nothing it has not learned, and since all nature is alike, there is nothing to hinder man remembering and learning from himself".[4].

It is this inherent instinct that man, in his desire to satisfy his curiosity, by the process of questioning and remembering a panorama opens in his search for knowledge.

The Book of Wisdom states, "So I prayed and Understanding was given to me. It was she (Wisdom) that gave me true knowledge of all that is. Who taught me the structure of the world and the properties of the elements? In each generation she (Wisdom) passes into holy souls"."[5]

Continuing his discourse with Menon, Socrates goes on to say, when speaking of the geometrical knowledge that Anytos has acquired through the process of being questioned and remembering. "Yet no one having taught him, only asking questions, yet he will know, having got the knowledge out of himself, and to get knowledge out of one's self is to remember.... Then

1   *Plato. Great Dialogues of. Trans by. W H D. Rouse. Published by Penguin Books*
2   *Plato. Great Dialogues of. 'Theaetetus'. Trans; Robin Waterfield. Published by Penguin Classics*
3   *The New Jerusalem Bible. Book of Wisdom. 2: 6.20.*
4   *Plato. Great Dialogues of. Trans by W. H. D. Rouse. Published by New American library.*
5   *The New Jerusalem Bible. The Book of Wisdom. 6; 24. 7, 17, 27.*

if he did not get this knowledge in this life, he must have learned it at some other time.... Is not that the time when he was not a man (When his soul was not on this earth). Then if both in the time when he is a man,(on this earth) and when he isn't(when his soul is not on this earth) there are to be true opinions of him, which are awakened by questioning and become knowledge, will not his soul have understood them for all time....Then if the truth of things is always in our soul, the soul must be immortal; so that what you do not know now by any chance—that is , what you do not remember—you must boldly try and find out and remember".[1]

From this, we can deduce that it is man's duty to seek out the knowledge that is his inheritance by natural law, waiting to be discovered, for it is by this process of self-discovery that mans progress has advanced so rapidly over the last 150 years.

There have been numerous recorded instances of children, who at a very early age demonstrated a phenomenal aptitude in the Art's, Music and Mathematics, in addition to the professions. Some of these prodigies have been as young as three years of age. These recorded cases are not confined to any one country, continent or period in history, but are a general occurrence around the world. The age of these gifted children, preclude any form of education attributable to their having this knowledge at such an early age.

One could cite many cases to support this statement; however, one case of interest is that of a student who at fifteen years of age has passed the qualifying exams for his Ph.D. The article that appeared in our local newspaper was as follows. "Whiz Kid; He reads math books as most people read novels. He was doing probability by the age five, abstract algebra at 10 and calculus at 12. At 15, when some kids are just starting to think about collage, Alexander Khazanov of New York has already passed the qualifying exams for a Ph.D. Now he is a finalist in the prestigious Westinghouse Science Talent Search contest—for a paper so complex his teachers are worried the judges would not understand it. "Alex presented his paper in my research class—I'm a physics teacher --- and I had tremendous difficulty following it. Said Sam Teitel, who co-ordinates contest entries at a public school for students in math and science".[2]

This is only one of numerous cases that has manifested itself around the world, and is not only applicable to the twentieth century, but may perhaps have been the case over aeons of time, in all ages of mans progress. We can therefore assert that the beliefs of Socrates and of the words of Solomon are based on very firm foundations when they say that the soul is immortal and transcends time, carrying within itself the knowledge of the universe.

It was not until after the religious Reformation in Europe (c 1517) that the public had the opportunity to an education by an increase in private and public schools. In England, the Education Act of 1870 was the basis of free and universal elementary education and by the late 19th century elementary education up to the age of 13 years was compulsory and free in most advanced countries.

---

1 Plato. Great Dialogues of. Menon. Trans; W H D. Rouse. Published by the New American Library
2 The article appeared in the The Edmonton Journal. Edmonton. Alberta. 27th Jan. 1995.

However, prior to the Reformation, the educational system that existed was controlled by the religious Orders of the Church of Rome Although the majority of people lacked any form of education and were to a great extent illiterate, totally dependent upon the Church clergy for guidance and information.

We are inclined to look upon the middle Ages as a period of intellectual stagnation, which did not flower until the 17th century. This would be a wrong assumption, intellectualism was in bloom, but like a bird with its flight feathers cut, lacked the ability to leave the ground due to the restrictions imposed by the religious authorities within the Church of Rome.

Leaving aside for the moment the schools of learning that existed in the Middle East and Spain. There were also the great seats of learning in the Monasteries in Ireland England and Scotland. In addition, the Universities of Paris, Bologna, Oxford and Cambridge were major centers of learning during this period.

However, the restrictions that were placed upon the minds of the great thinkers by the Church authorities did not allow for free expression. For those who were prepared to run the gauntlet and challenge the teachings of the Church ran the risk of imprisonment, and a life of being forbidden to teach or speak, and in the majority of cases, death of a most cruel nature, by being burned at the stake after a period of extensive torture. This suppression of intellect was not to see freedom until the Reformation of the 16th century.

There are documented cases in which the writings of some famous scholars were condemned. In some cases the guilty party, though dead was tried and found guilty which resulted in his bones being exhumed and burned. Even in death, it was difficult to escape the vengeance of the Church.

The list of names of great men and minds that lived in this historical period is extensive. These intellectual giants were no match for the Lilliputian minds that controlled the society of their day. The great Philosopher and teacher, Peter Abelard, (c 1079--1142) being one of the many, regarded as the founder of the University of Paris, whose works were condemned as heretical was tried, found guilty, imprisoned, had his writings destroyed and forced to submit to the rules of the Church.

Another one of these great minds was Pietro Abano (c1250--1316), Physician, Philosopher and Professor of Medicine at Padua in Italy, who's efforts to reconcile Arabian medicine and Greek natural Philosophy was condemned by the Inquisition. Though found not guilty at his first trial, following his death and burial, was tried inabsentia and found guilty. As a result of the verdict, his body was exhumed and his bones burned.

We could add to this list the names of Roger Bacon, Copernicus, and the most famous name, which is known to every schoolboy, Galilel Galileo, who was tried by the Inquisition, sentenced to enforced house arrest and forbidden to teach. These are only a few of the cases out of the many that are on record. For those with the ability to think and reason, the age in which they lived was not conducive to a long life of fulfillment, or the rewards that one would expect from a lifetime of study.

In an age that frowned upon any form of intellectual prowess, should a family of poor circumstances produce a child that showed any marked abilities it was in their interest to restrict the child in his ability to satisfy his curiosity? However, or should they be people of limited circumstances, the boy would be sent to a monastery for his education where his compliance with the tenets of the Church was compulsory. An example of such a situation, of which there were many, can be best illustrated by the life of John Huss, (c 1369-- 1415) the Czech religious reformer, of whom we can say was the forerunner of the Reformation that was to free the minds of free thinkers in later years.

He came from a peasant family and went on to study Theology at the University of Prague, where he was ordained a priest in the Catholic Church, and rose to become Rector of the University of Prague. In his sermons, Huss attached the abuses of the clergy, denounced the Papal Bulls of Pope John XX111, and the sale of Indulgences by the Roman Pontiff and denied the doctrine of Infallibility of the Imperial Pope. All of which earned him the hostility of his peers and the Authorities in Rome which led to his excommunication by the Church of Rome.

Huss presented himself at the Council of Constance (c1414--1418) which was initially convened to resolve the dispute in regard to the validity of the election of Pope Urban V1 in c1378, which resulted in the formation of two rival claimants to the Papacy of Rome -- that of Gregory X11 and John XX111. A Council, held at Pisa in 1409, which elected a third Pope, further exasperated, the situation.

It was within this impossible background of religious and political intrigue that Huss had to argue and justify his views. Against this backdrop of religious bigotry and intolerance, his chances of a fair hearing were remote. The Church had already one schism on its hands and was not about to allow another one to develop, regards the power and established doctrine of the Church.

John Huss presented himself at the Council was arrested and tried as a heretic despite being assured of his safety. The Council condemned his writings and sentenced him to be burned at the stake. (c1415).

Jerome of Prague, a close friend and companion of Huss, had done his studies at Prague University and Oxford, England, defended Huss at the Council, he in turn was arrested and imprisoned. Jerome recanted his beliefs, however, was not released from prison, eventually withdrawing his recantation, was found guilty of heresy and burned at the stake (c1416).

These intellectual giants were to cause the release of the great minds in times to come. The restrictions imposed by the Church of Rome as a State religion adversely affected progress in the field of scientific discovery was to continue until the reformation by Martin Luther in 1517 AD. Had it not been for the work of Luther, it is likely that we would still believe the Sun circled the earth and the planet earth the center of the Universe.

It is only now that modern educators are fully realizing the potential of the young minds that are emerging in to-day's society.

Had the process of self-discovery been allowed free license to develop by the Church of Rome, who is to say how far man would have advanced during this long dark period?

Credit can be given to John Huss and Martin Luther, and those brave souls that followed, had it not been for these great men it is likely that the infamous Inquisition of the Holy Office with the rack and torture would be the controlling factor in our lives to-day, confining man to an age of superstitious fear and ignorance.

The freedom of expression and intellectual license that has been the hallmark of our society since the 17th century has allowed man to fly beyond the bounds of this earth. We are indebted to Sir Isaac Newton (c 1642--1727), Jacob Bernouilli (c 1654--1705) and those other great minds of the 17th and 18th centuries. Had these great minds been subject to the dictates and intolerance of the Catholic Church the world would be wallowing in a trough of ignorance.

How do we account for the extensive field of knowledge that was known to the ancient civilization's, knowledge on which our Western culture has used as a foundation on which to build it's progress over the past 150 years? Little attention has been paid to the ignorant and superstitious period in which Western culture languished under for over sixteen hundred years, while the schools of education in Mathematics. Geometry and Astronomy flourished in South America, China, Egypt, India, the Middle and Far East.

It would be a grave error to believe that our civilization with all it's complexities had it's beginning in 4,000 BC a period when man first experienced a quantum leap in knowledge that lead him into the copper and bronze age and the beginning of his progress to this point in time.

An opinion expressed by one eminent authority of Egyptology states, "At approximately 3,400 BC a great change took place in Egypt, and the country passed rapidly from a state of Neolithic culture with a complex tribal character to (one of) well-organized monarchy. At the same time the art of writing appears, monumental architecture and the arts and crafts develop to an astonishing degree, and all the evidence points to the existence of a luxurious civilization. All this was achieved within a comparatively short period, for there appears to be little or no background to these fundamental developments in writing and architecture."[1] This hypothesis would appear to answer all our questions if it were valid. However, too many historical gaps remain and a myriad of unanswered questions to give this hypothesis any validity.

The chronological table compiled by the experts outlining the pre-historic period is based upon very little evidence to support their theories. In the absence of any written records, they rely heavily upon the few artifacts found in various locations around the world. Based upon these finds they develop theories, which are to a great degree conjectural.

What if the more ancient civilsations that reached beyond 5,000 BC saw no reason to keep written records. What if society was such that all knowledge was memorized and passed on from generation to generation through the priesthood and the ruling class, as was the case in

---

1   *Emery. W.B., Archaic Egypt.*

ancient Egypt, where society was hierarchically structured, whereby each class was imparted the knowledge appropriated to their calling.

Plato, the Greek philosopher envisaged such a society when he was formulating his ideal state in the 'Republic'. It is probable that he was using Egypt as a prototype when developing his theories. It is also possible that an advanced civilization existed in the past, one that that saw no need to keep written records but relied upon the transmission of knowledge through oral teaching, couching their teaching in Myth and symbol, as was the case in Egypt and Greece.

We can infer from the common belief of all peoples on this planet that the ebb and flow of cultures across this planet has been ongoing since man appeared upon earth. It would be naive for us to believe that each of the races who occupy this planet, on all the different continents, lived in isolation over hundreds of thousands, if not millions of years. We would also be naïve to believe that mans common ancestor was the Ape, or that Man evolved from a drobble of mud, having his beginning in a simple primordial protoplasmic mass originating from the sea.

Opposite to these beliefs is the Biblical version, which says that man had his beginning in the Garden of Eden, with the ensuing migratory expansion that led to the planet been populated?

Next came a flood of cataclysmic proportions, which we are lead to believe destroyed the human race, with the exception of Noah and his family, who they say regenerated the human race.

When one considers answers to these beliefs, find that they are too simplistic to stand up to any form of scrutiny. What can be said is that human species, and all life upon this planet, is complex and beyond our understanding. Probably, because of the uniqueness of man, scientists tend to separate humanity from all life forms, whereas, all life form should be viewed as a whole.

That there is inherent Biological characteristics in all species is evident, however, in mans search for answers to his origins, it would appear that he has a tendency to find a simplistic answer to all his questions; this has been the case of the various civilizations that have occupied this planet over the last six million years. The common denominators that are characteristic in all the major races would indicate a commonality between all of the major civilizations in varying degrees, indicating a communication link between these cultures. All believed in a 'God' in varying degrees

Scholars and the experts, would have man travelling over the land, acting like gibbering idiots scratching the ground for grubs and insects to sustain his existence, until eventually he progressed up the ladder of evolution to emerge to what he is today.

The common denominators that are characteristic in all the major races would indicate a commonality between all civilizations in varying degrees, which would indicate a communication link between cultures as we experience in our present industrial age.

We know the civilizations of China, Mexico, Sumeria, Babylon, Egypt, and India possessed a calendar that was equal to, if not better than the one in use today, each of these cultures were highly knowledgeable in Mathematics, Astrology, Astronomy, Geometry, and the Arts.

In addition, the working of metals, i.e. Gold, Silver, Copper and Bronze, indicates a deep knowledge of Chemistry, and Metallurgy. The buildings and structures that still stand are a testament to this knowledge. Compared to these ancient cultures, the cultures of Greece and Rome are quite recent and a product of the Sumer-Babylon and Egyptian cultures as our present culture is a product of Greece and Roman.

The diversity of the human race and its people does not lend itself to the theory of there being a common ancestry or place of origin by which the planet was populated by the process of centrifugal expansion by one race of people, put forward by the Archaeologist and historians.

This theory may be true on the question of knowledge emanating from a single source, as happened with the Industrial Revolution. The Technological advances, made over the last thirty years, are a case in point. Cultures situated in the most remote regions of this planet are in possession of some form of technology, which to them, is an advanced piece of equipment, be it radio, television or bicycle.

People, who at the turn of this century lived in isolation in Africa and the Northern Territories of the North America Continent, or the middle of the Sahara Desert, can now boast of high technology in the form of computers and satellite dishes. Therefore, on the theory that the spread of knowledge may have had a common source would entail there being a communication link between the different countries and cultures.

When writing on the Sumerians, the civilization that occupied the Euphrates and Tigris basin, the theory that the area was unoccupied until the arrival of a group of middle class Indians from the Indus Valley or that the Sumerian civilization was developed by some unknown race from the Asiatic regions,[1] is a hypothesis that is weak and without foundation.

As our European culture of today is the product of the Greece and Roman cultures, now vanished, one could extrapolate and proceed to extend the process in reverse to all other cultures and civilizations that have preceded each epoch. Each civilization being absorbed and changed by each succeeding age, yet maintaining the cultural links that connect them to the past, some by Myths and Legends

As an example, as we look at America today, we can see an amalgam of cultures that has descended upon that country over the last 350 years. The predominant culture being, for the moment, that of the Anglo Saxon race. However, over time, this situation may change with the influx of the Mexicans from the South and marked increase in the number of emigrants from East Asian countries. Due to their high birth rate among these three main groups, i.e. Afro—American, Mexican and Asian, as opposed to the low birth-rate of the Anglo Saxon.

It is a highly probable that America will face a dramatic change in cultural values within the next fifty years, in which the Afro—American and the Hispanic races will combine their strength to dominate the existing order. It is also noteworthy that these new emigrants have, for the most part retained their cultural links, in language and customs, especially the people

1   Wendt. Herbart 'It Began at Babel'. Published by Delta Book NY

originating from Asia and Mexico. Whereas, the Afro—American has not completely identified them with the American White dominated culture seen as an oppressor of the Negro race from the days of slavery, it was not until the 1960's the Negro were given the right to vote by an act of Congress.

Furthermore, when one looks at the Political and Military institutions see that the positions of power held by the Black Afro-American has dramatically increased over the last thirty years. During the 1939-45 World War, the American Negro played a minor role in the conflict. However, the Korean conflict raised the status of the American Negro. It was during this conflict that he was accepted as a combat soldier. From then onwards, his rapid rise to the positions of command was phenomenal, which resulted in an Afro—American being in command of the American Military during the Gulf War. If the present trends continue, and the Afro-American continue to gain power in the Political, Business, and Military areas at the same rate, it is likely that the politics in America will experience major changes. Each of the cultures which now constitute the American society, has to a great extend retained its own cultural and ethnic background. The concept of there being an American culture is nonexistent. The common source from which the American society sprung was the continent of Europe, followed by all other races that live on this planet.

In this vast centrifugal migratory expansion, that has been ongoing since the 17th century, and continues today. Each of the different races imported their own form of religion and customs to the new land, and with the exception of the Anglo Saxon race, have made little progress to integrate with the other ethnic groups. There have been the few exceptions, but overall, most members of the American society, especially between the Black and White fractions, reject intermarriage between the various races.

On the discovery of Australia by the British explorer Captain Cooke in 1788, the estimated Aboriginal population was approximately 300,000, made up from five hundred different tribal societies. To-day that number has decreased to approximately 125,000, consisting of 45,000 aborigines of pure stock, and 80,000 of mixed race through marriage with the arrival of the new settlers.

The substantial decrease in population has been brought about through various causes attributable to the policies adapted by the British Government and the early settlers and also the diseases, which were brought to Australia by the Europeans. It is a matter of history, that through the same policies, the indigenous population of the island of Tasmania was completely decimated to the point of total extinction. It is an historical fact that through this genocide policy, there is not one native Tasmanian on our planet,

A situation of a similar nature is occurring in Brazil, South America. Through the influx of new immigrants and an increasing population, the natural habitat is been destroyed to accommodate the new farms and industrial expansion.

Completely isolated from the twentieth century, this has had an extremely harmful effect upon the indigenous native population who has lived in this pristine environment for thousands of year. Their exposure to the new settlers has had a devastating effect upon their environment and way of life that has resulted in a decrease in population by decease and depredation.

Although there appears to be no clear consensus as to the origins of the Australian Aborigine, many theories have been propounded as to the origins of these people, and of the many that have been postulated, that of the migration of the Aborigine from America to Australia is one of the most interesting.

According to this theory, America was at one time in the past inhabited by an Asiatic race that had traveled across the Bering Straits into Alaska approximately 40,000 years ago. Over the next thousands of millennia, they slowly moved down through the continent to reach the southernmost tip of South America and from there voyaged to Australia.

Based upon the physical characteristics that are common to the North American Indian and those of Australia, It has been theorized that the Aborigine of Australia are the first cousins to the American Indian.[1]

It has also been theorized that their place of origin was in South East Asia from where they migrated about 20,000 years ago, and related to other ethnic groups in South India and Sri Lanka.

Of the two versions, the latter has more a degree of probability then the former theory of expansion from America. However, were we to accept this latter theory, again the question is raised as to why there was no cultural progress among these people over the millennia?

One would assume that in migrating from South East Asia, who was an advanced culture, the aborigine would have retained some vestige of his previous life, both in religious and cultural ties. However, this was not the case, the aborigine of Australia was devoid of the simplest form of intelligent thought by which he would progress his simple life style.

However, when their cultural practices are investigated there appears to be a striking similarity with other world cultures.

When the British explorer Captain Cooke arrived on the shores of Australia, the native Aborigine people were living in a pristine environment. The mythological and legendary tales that had sustained their religious and cultural beliefs over thousands of years had survived untainted by any external influence.

If experts were to have an understanding of these people, it would be beneficial to pay attention to these legendary tales. In them, we may find a commonality with other cultures of the world, which would give credence to their folklore and question long held views, regards their history.

In their mythology, the Aborigines, speak of their ancestors migrating to the island in the distant past, assisted by another culture that they refer to as the celestial heroes. Is it possible that these people were transported to this island in the far distant past for their own protection to save them from becoming extinct and left to develop at their own pace?

---

1   *Larousse. Encyclopaedia of Archaeology.*

Could it be that, a civilization who were culturally advanced, in an effort to protect a minority, a culture, who were disadvantaged by a society, out of compassion and respect, collected together what members of the different tribes remained and transported them to their new homes in Australia, Tasmania and New Guinea?

Could it also be that the people in these lands were the remaining tribes of what was once the Neanderthal man of Europe? This hypothesis pre-supposes that such a civilization existed, and that they had the knowledge and the expertise to carry out this monumental task. It also fits in with the legends and myths of these Stone Age people.

It is also interesting that the Aborigines had an affinity to the Sun in their myths and legends and in their religious practice, as Sun worshippers.

Were we to accept the hypotheses of migrating from the cost of South America to Australia, logic suggests that after such a long period of time, there would be a degree of sophistication in their manner of living, but this is not the case. These people remained in the Stone Age for over 20,000 years, the only tool credited to them being the boomerang, a masterpiece of aerodynamic principals.

These special instruments were for sporting and hunting. It was assumed, until quite recently, that this instrument was indigenous to the Aborigine of Australia, however, ancient boomerangs have been found throughout the world, in Europe, Egypt, and India.

The oldest boomerang discovered was found in Florida some years ago that was at dated as being 10,000 years old, tests were carried out on models of this discovery, and proved extremely effective. Other types discovered in Germany and Denmark in Europe, dated at around 5,000 BC.

It's been suggested that the boomerang was an American invention,[1] this hypotheses would have some credence if it were not for the fact that the aborigine was in possession of this instrument for 20,000 years or longer. His way of life precludes him the honor of having invented this amazing tool, as he lacked the basic skills, i.e., Geometry, Mathematics and Aerodynamics required producing such an instrument.

Based upon this premise, if he had not invented the boomerang, it's logical to assume that the principal of its construction was given to him by some other advanced culture in the remote past, and retaining the method by which this tool was made to memory, had the ability to produce it ad infinitum.

This practice is common among certain tribes in Ghana and Nigeria, West Africa, who are renowned for their wood carvings and gold making. The knowledge handed down from Father to Son through countless generations; also applies to the art of weaving the designs of the different tribal cloths for the chiefs and their wives.

The fact that the boomerang, discovered in such diverse locations should be an indication a communication link between the various cultures over millennia of time. In addition, the

1 *Quest for the Past. Readers Digest.*

similarity in the myths and legends that exists between the different societies across this planet is another indication of the close relationship between the different cultures.

People in ancient times had no need for written records. The myths and legends that were passed on from generation to generation, were not only incorporated into their religious beliefs, but became the realities of everyday life, and the thread by which the tribal society's stability was maintained. There is little to distinguish our present day society from those of the past when one considers how the myths and legends of our past are the binding elements of our society.

However, there are those who would say that these myths and legends are purely superstitious nonsense that man has outgrown and are irrelevant to our modern society. Yet, if we look at to-days society, we find that modern man is not that far removed from his ancestor's superstitious nature and his fear of the unknown. The art of Astrology and fortune telling is more popular today than it has ever been in the past and tends to exert a strong influence on the everyday life of the average person.

One has only to look in any bookstore and view the multitude of literature that is published on this one subject to appreciate its impact upon mans psychic conscience thoughts. It would also be enlightening if we were to monitor our behavioral pattern to appreciate the truth. We may think ourselves too intelligent and sophisticated to believe in such nonsense, but close observation of our everyday actions will come as a shock to our intellect. We will realize that we are not that far removed from our Neanderthal ancestor.

It is a strange phenomenon that were the legends concerning men tend to change in context, by which they are made to appear taller, more manly, more heroic, and all the other attributes that make men more appealing to women. On the other hand the myths and legends concerning women remain in most part unadulterated by time, and have been passed down to us from pre-historic times virtually intact, to the extent that the majority of these myths are in practice today, in some cases slightly modified, but still the fabric that some cultures include within their religious practice.

So when we delve into the past we become aware that there existed a common belief among the people on all continents. The myths and taboos were universal, found in all cultures, even down to our own time. Among the many there were those that concerned the values ancient culture placed upon the importance to the tribe when a young girl reached the age of puberty, experiencing her first menstrual period, and the restrictions which tribal societies place upon women during their menstrual cycle.[1]

Professor J.G.Frazer of Cambridge University, England [2] demonstrated a common belief among the world's people whereby the same practices are analogous to various cultures around the globe. In his studies, he describes some beliefs associated with the Aborigine of Australia, which were analogous to more advanced cultures of the Middle East. This would give some

---

1   *The New Jerusalem Bible Leviticus 15: 19-33*
2   *Frazer. J.G.'D.C.L., LL.D, .Litt.D. The Golden Bough A Study in magic and Religion. Balder the Beautiful Part VII, Vol 1. Published by MacMillan and Co Ltd. London.1913*

credence to the hypothesis that at some time in the remote past there existed a common link between the various cultures.

One such subject relates to the taboos associated with the seclusion of young girls reaching the age of puberty "when it is forbidden for them to touch the ground with their bare feet or see the sun. These two rules are observed either separately or conjointly by girls at puberty in many parts of the world".[1]

Describing the practice of one tribe in Northern Australia, states, "A girl at puberty is said to live by herself for a month or six weeks; no man may see her, though any woman may. She stays in a hut of shelter specially made for her, on the floor of which she lies supine. She may not see the sun, and towards sunset she must keep her eyes closed shut until the sun has gone down, otherwise it is thought that her nose will be diseased". The practice is similar to that of other tribes of Australia. [2]

The ebb and flow of cultures across this planet has been ongoing since man first appeared upon this earth. As to when this event occurred, and how, is one of the many mysteries that modern science is endeavoring to find an answer. However, in all probability, it will continue as a mystery into the future, as there is insufficient evidence of the pre-historic past by which science can lay a firm foundation of facts to arrive at any firm conclusions.

The scientific community agrees that man was walking this earth in the Paleolithic Age six million years ago, are however, hesitant to commit themselves to any firm conclusions regarding these finds from the late Tertiary period, other than classing the find as a pre-hominid.

The scientific community has not established whether this was a true man, or the remains of some animal that had some close relationship with man, as the ape has to man. Fossil remains found in Kenya in the mid 1960s assessed as being 4.0 to 5.0 million years old, but there is some uncertainty and disagreement among the experts regarding these dates.

What has been established is that man existed 2.5 million years ago this date has been disputed among the experts, some suggesting a much later period of 1.8 million years. But when Anthropologists are dealing with time frames of hundreds of thousands of years in offering their hypotheses on the origins of man, it would be extremely difficult to be exact with the limited amount of information available on which to base their conclusions,

Nevertheless, it would be naïve for us to think that each of the races that occupy this planet lived in isolation over hundreds of thousands of years. It would be naïve to suppose that man evolved from a drobble of mud, having his beginning in a primordial protoplasmic mass, or

---

1   *The Australian Aborigine practice of secluding their young women id analogous to other culture in Alaska, British Columbia, North American Indian, South America, Indians of Brazil, Indians of Guiana, Hindu's of India, Cambodia, East Africa and South Africa. Frazer J G A study in Magic and Religion 3rd edition Part 11 Taboo and the Perils of the Soul*

2   *Frazer. J.G. D.C.L., LL.D., Litt.D. The Golden Bough. A Study in Magic and Religion 3rd Edition. Part V11. Balder the Beautiful. Vol 1*

originating from the sea, or some stagnant mud hole from which he evolved through successive stages of evolutionary adaptation to arrive at the point at which he is today.[1]

The concept of humanities creation from earth, or mud, and in one case peat, is not unique to our Western religious culture. Nor is mans curiosity surrounding his origins confined to the 18th century Anthropologist, but is universal, to be found in various cultures, ranging from China, South America, Australia, Middle East, India, and Europe. The mythological tales that transcends time are from cultures who at that stage of their progress were unaffected by the Judaic concept of creation.

The self-evident truth is that there is not one drop of water or one type of species on this Earth that was not here at the beginning of time. However, due to the catastrophic cataclysmic upheavals that this planet has experienced over millennia, continents have vanished into the depths of the Oceans, and replaced each other's position on the face of this planet. Due to these upheavals, species have vanished, never to be seen again by man, as is happening today, not through any catastrophic event, but through to man's abuse of his environment.

It is apparent from the vast quantity of literature, published over the years, which expounded the various theories concerning this planet, the experts have in their quest to determine the cause and effect of the evolutionary process, allowed free license to their imagination in developing their theories.

Anthropologist leapfrog through time to arrive at a point where all of the diverse races of mankind emerge in all their complexities of color and characteristics which make up the human family, (Mongoloids), Africa (Negroid), Australia (Aborigines), and Europe (Caucasoid).

The few skeletal remains discovered which Anthropologist use as a foundation on which to base their theories would appear to be insufficient evidence on which to extrapolate humanities progress across the aeons of time. The areas in which discoveries were made, are to a great extend, with the exception of those discoveries made in China, Siberia and the Middle East, confined to the Western Hemisphere, which forms but a small percentage of the earth's land surface.

There is no explanation as to how this complex selection of color and characteristics came about in the evolutionary process as developed by Charles Darwin. Were we to use the present situation as exists on our planet today, we find a diversity of races and cultures that have occupied their place upon this planet since the end of the Pleistocene age.

When one views the Aborigine of Australia, the Pygmy of the Congo, and the peoples of Africa, we see a people who are still in the process of basic technical development, who have yet to reach the advanced stage of development that has been achieved by our Western civilization. Despite the lack of any hard and fast evidence to the contrary, we should not discount the theory that a similar situation existed in the remote past when this planet was inhabited by various cultures existing on each of the Continents.

---

1   *Wendt. Herbert. 'It Began at Babel. Translated from the German by James Kirkup. Published by Delta Publishing Co. Inc. 1964.*

The Paleontologist seems to veer away from the parallel situations that are apparent on our planet today and perhaps existed in the distant past. The picture we have of our ancient ancestors is speculative hypotheses and conjecture.

The description of mans progress over the aeons of time reads like a stage play, in which one species appears upon the worlds stage for a period of time, to completely disappear and be replaced by the next species. Too many gaps and inconsistencies exist that would substantiate the findings propounded by the experts. It will require a considerable amount of work on the part of historians and anthropologist to lay a firm foundation to support their theories regards the history of man.

However, the description that has been given of the species known as the Neanderthal man who inhabited this earth between 100,000 and 40,000 years ago is not in accordance with what is known of this maligned race of men. The cave paintings, discovered at Lascaux in France, and Altamira in Spain, are landmarks in the history of art, being equal to anything produced by our modern society.

These beautiful drawings clearly indicate a sensitivity and appreciation for form and symmetry. A people described did not carry out these wonderful drawings "as nasty, brutish and short, a shambling lumbering stooped creature, with a heavy brutish face, clad in a loin skin and tugging his mate along with her hair."[1]

This description developed by our 17th and 18th century Anthropologist is how the average person sees our Neanderthal ancestor today. Yet this picture is far from the truth, perhaps, a figment of the imagination of our early Anthropologists.

If these drawing were truly the work of this early race, it depicts a person who had the ability and geometric skills to create such precise drawings on a rock surface that were a reflection of scenes drawn from everyday life that was part of the harsh existence lived by these people.

Rather then, accept that these drawings were art for art's sake; the vivid imagination of our scholars creates all manner of scenarios to explain the purpose, largely attributing them to religious or magical rites.

Drawings by these ancient people are not limited to Europe, but were discovered as far away as Australia, Asia, and the Middle East. Their religious beliefs in the afterlife by his love and compassion for the dead are an attribute that is characteristic of modern man that makes him more human in our eyes.

However, the scientific community has "brought to light the enormous antiquity of human lineage and must take particular care not to project modern mans philosophies or ideas on the distant past, their point of departure should be in prehistory itself."[2]

The scientific community should accept the fact that this planet, and the surrounding universe has existed since time immemorial. When did man, and all animal life first occupy

1   Hobbs. Thomas. Anthropologist.
2   Larousse. World Mythology.

this 'Garden of Eden' is conjectural. What can be said with some degree of certainty is that man, and all species now existing, have occupied their place on this planet for just about the same period. Is there any way in which science can determine when this occurred, sadly, no? Anytime frame offered by the scientific community is pure speculation, and not based on sound reasoning.

Nevertheless, there is sufficient evidence that clearly indicates the cataclysmic and catastrophic upheavals have occurred on this planet over aeons of time. The evidence suggests that these events had a devastating effect upon the human race, and all living species, which may at times, brought on the total extinction of some species. There is no reason to doubt that humanity equally suffered during these catastrophes, however, had the ability to overcome his adversities. Moreover, there is every reason to belief that the species of human remains discovered by our Paleontologists, may have been members of another race.

Chapter 17

Our world and universe abounds in mysteries that at times appear to be beyond the comprehension, of those who, professing to be experts, are prone to supposition in order to support their many theories. This approach to their work may perhaps be due to the lack of spiritual sterility of our age. What can be said is that the mechanistic mind of today is incompatible with the spiritual mind of our ancestors.

We see on all continents, traces of civilizations and cultures, whose achievements in construction, techniques leave us with a sense of admiration. When analyzed, it is found that despite the best efforts of our modern day experts, a multitude of unanswered questions remain.

As was expressed many years ago, "our age cannot look back to see what came about before this stage, except in so far as its traces can be uncovered by reason".[1] However, when it comes to finding answers to the most vexing questions, reason, it would appear plays little part in the explanations offered by the experts.

The majestic Temples and buildings left by these ancient civilizations, long since vanished, are a marvel of artistic skills incorporated into the stonework of these beautiful structures. The intricacy of their artwork and paintings, the methods, used to achieve this high standard are a mystery waiting to be solved. However, it is a sad reflection of our times that in the majority of cases the responses received are suppositions based upon the need to find an explanation to explain the unexplainable.

That a high degree of engineering skills was required in the construction process is beyond doubt. The size and weight of the monolithic units incorporated into the structures would be sufficient reason for our experts to hesitate before entering an opinion. Lacking the fundamental knowledge of the 'how' and the 'when' how can they therefore offer an opinion based upon faulty science.

Of the many structures on this planet, one of interest is the ancient Inca city of Machu Picchu, located in the Andes Mountains in Peru, South America.[2] This is only one of the many ancient ruins located in this region that leave nothing but question marks.

---

1   Lucretius, Titus. 'On the Nature of the Universe' Translated by R. E. Latham. Published by Penguin Books.
2   Bingham. Hiram. 1875- 1956. American Archaeologist. Located the Lost City of the Incas, Machu Picchu, in 1911.

Machu Picchu is situated high in the Andes Mountains at an elevation of seven thousand, seven hundred feet (7,700'), about fifty miles northwest of the city of Cuzco. This city was virtually inaccessible until re-discovered by an American, Hiram Bingham of Yale University in 1911. It is one of the few pre-Columbian towns found intact. Remote and inaccessible until its rediscovery, there is nothing known of its history for this reason, Archaeologist and Anthropologist are somewhat limited in their opinions regards its function and the date of its construction. However, this appears to be of little consequence to those with a vivid imagination.

Some have suggested a construction date of in the region of 1400 AD and "probably used as a home for members of the Inca Royal family".[1] How they reached these conclusions challenges reason when one considers the ruins and the manner of construction. The immense size of the masonry granite blocks incorporated in the structures would indicate a highly intellectual society, with the engineering skills to move and place such huge monoliths would belie such a date. The precision of the cutting of the monolithic blocks of granite and the dovetailing of the masonry joints is a mystery.

What tools did they use; not stone mauls as suggested by the experts. Stone mauls in the hands of the most expert of masons cannot cut angles of ninety degrees. Some experts whose imagination supersedes their intellectual skills have suggested that mirrors and the power of the sun accomplished the precision cutting of the stone while others suggests 'stone hammers and bronze crowbars'. Whatever the tools used to achieve such a high degree of engineering perfection is beyond the understanding of today's engineers.

Their use of weight, measure, and proportion, in all of their works denoted a high level of knowledge in engineering techniques. Most experts recognize that the knowledge of these ancient people in Astronomy, Geometry, and Mathematics was more advanced than our western civilization. Knowledge that existed in the South American cultures for perhaps thousands of years was unknown to our western civilization until the eighteen-century. Up to this time, the people of Europe were living in an age of religious darkness and superstitious beliefs grappling with the many theories inherited from the Greeks.

Perhaps it is for this reason our scholars prefer to concentrate upon the customary rituals of these ancient people, rather than their advanced knowledge. We are to believe, based on the findings of the experts that the intricate statuary and sculptures visible in all of these ancient cultures was accomplished by the use of the most primitive of stone tools. This would appear to be the accepted hypothesis put forward to explain the unexplainable.

Reason would suggest that the sophistication of the cutting of the stone would preclude any form of stone tool, perhaps to grind the face of the stone, but not for shaping. The masonry joints are too precise which would suggest that some form of a tool other than a stone hammer

---

1   *World Book Encyclopaedia Contributor: Susan A. Niles. Ph.D., Associate Professor of Anthropology, Lafayette Collage*

was used to cut and shape the granite blocks, but what? The intricacies of the statuary should give us reason to pause before offering an explanation.

The second part of the puzzle surrounds the cyclopean granite masonry monoliths that form part of the structures at Machu Picchu, some of which weigh up to 200 tons. These massive stone monoliths were not indigenous to this area, but transported over many miles and through extremely difficult terrain.

How a society who did not possess the wheel or roads on which to travel achieves these amazing accomplishments? These are but a few of the puzzling questions that face the experts when trying to find answers to this enigma.

When one is faced with such imponderable questions, speculation does not answer the questions, but tends to confuse rather than clarify. From the physical evidence, one can discount the theory that the native Inca people constructed these cities in the fifteenth century. They had many attributes more advanced than our Western culture, but the ability to move and erect such Impressive stone monoliths was far beyond their capabilities. This would lead one to believe that Machu Picchu buildings were constructed somewhere in the distant past, the question is when, most certainly not in 1423 AD as proposed by the experts.

The magnificent Temples of Central America, Greece, Egypt, and the Far East, though derelict and in ruin, still reflect a grandeur that is a mute testimony to the greatness of these ancient people. However, these are but a small percentage of the cultures waiting to be unearthed, from which, it is expected, some of the answers to these questions will be forthcoming. However, to accomplish their objective, our experts must approach the problem with an open mind, and not on preconceived ideas developed by antiquarians of the eighteen-century who had just emerged from an age of intellectual stagnation and religious superstition.

It is perhaps for this reason that, the diversity of opinions expressed by the experts when dealing with the pre-historic past is at times extremely confusing, as there appears to be no consensus in establishing the dates concerning these ancient cultures.

Had it not been for the wanton destruction of the written records by those who professed themselves as enlightened our library of knowledge would have been all the greater. Yet despite these shortcomings, Archaeologist and their associate disciplines continue to explore the past in the hope of finding answers to the most vexing questions that has defied the best minds of our century.

When we view the landscape of Central America, we see a culture that has defied its destruction and obliteration by the Church of Rome. An establishment that has over the centuries committed many crimes that still invoke a sense of revulsion but to condone and participate in the systematic destruction of a people and the accumulated knowledge of thousands of years was a crime unparalleled in the history of humankind.

That it was carried out in the name of a God, depicted as being a God of love and compassion, makes it all the more repulsive. Yet despite the persecution, the culture that once was, still exists today under a veneer of Catholicism interposed with the gods of ancient times.

The restoration of the Temples by the authorities to accommodate the tourist industry and the knowledge that has been assembled over the years from the meager amount of documents still extant; attest to the greatness of the ancestors of contemporary Mexicans and the people of South America.

Could modern man, using the same tools, and techniques attributed to these ancient people, achieve the high level of artistic and architectural beauty that is the hallmark of these cultures?

This question generates a myriad of excuses that range from the financial cost, the amount of time required, to the necessity of such structures, all quite valid. Nevertheless, the answer would be an emphatic; no, attempts have been made on a minor scale to emulate the work of these ancient people, and on each occasion resulted in failure.

Chapter 18

The Great Pyramid at Giza in Egypt has been an enigma that has baffled the best minds of our century. Again, the age-old questions, when was it built, how was it built, and why was it built are questions that have generated a myriad of theories ranging from the sublime to the ridiculous? The theories put forward are as varied as the theories concerning the formation of the Universe; each as preposterous as the next. Therefore, to find some reasonable explanation as to when it was built it may be necessary to remove extraneous misconceptions that have surfaced over the years and look at the few facts that are self evident.

First there is the belief that the Hebrew people were involved in its construction, wonderful if it was true, whereas it is nothing but a figment of the imagination of those who would support this spurious claim to enhance the Hebrews claim to antiquity. According to the best authorities Abraham did not arrive in Palestine until somewhere in eighteen hundred BC from Haren in Mesopotamia, therefore such a claim stretches the truths of history to the limits.

Secondly, it has been purported that it was built in the reign of the Pharaoh Cheops in the fourth dynasty (2613/2494BC). There is not sufficient evidence to support this supposition. The evidence available is flimsy and open to question. There is however, sufficient credible evidence to support the hypothesis that it was built sometime in the remote past before lands of Egypt was inundated by a major flood if we are to accept the geological evidence of the surrounding terrain.

We can also discount the theory that it was a means of alleviating the unemployment problem some say occurred during the seasonal flooding of the Nile including the theory that it was the work of extraterrestrials from outer space. There is no evidence that would support either of these theories.

Giving credit to our cousins from outer space sounds intriguing and fulfils the aspirations of those who look to the heavens for answers to the many ills that beset this planet. However, a theory that may have some credence when one considers the many great temples and structures found on other continents and the preponderance of evidence would suggest that these wonderful structures were the work of our ancestors.

Also the theory that the brick Pyramid at Saggara is the more ancient and the prototype of the Great Pyramids is also stretching the imagination to the limits. It's likely the Saggara brick Pyramids were an attempt to emulate the work so visible in the Great Pyramid, for that reason, lacking the knowledge and expertise, used the easier option and built in brick. Such being the case the Pyramid of Saggara is of a later date than the Great Pyramid which is the older of the two. Notwithstanding the statement made by the Egyptian Temple priest to Solon,[1] the Greek traveler, when he stated that Egypt had been protected by the Nile Delta from the many catastrophes that had inflicted the region in ancient times does not fit in with the facts as we know them today. The collective history of the many cultures in the Middle East would suggest that at sometime in the ancient past the region had suffered a calamitous flood that lived on in the memory of the people. Such being the case it is suggested from the evidence of marine fossils (Herodotus Book 11. Chapter 12) and the high salinity found in Egypt and mentioned by Herodotus would suggest that Egypt had been inundated by the sea during a calamity that destroyed the land and resulted in people suffering from famine conditions over many years.

If such an event did occur the inundation would leave its presence in the form of salt deposits at the lowest levels, especially in the subterranean passages which are extensive below the Saggara stone Pyramid. This however has not been reported as far as can be determined which lends support to the theory that the Great Pyramid of Giza is more ancient than that of Saggara.

On the question of 'How', Herodotus, the 4th century BC Greek historian provides us an explanation of how the Great Pyramid was built when he states the "Pyramid was built in steps, battlement-wise, as it is called, or according to others, alter-wise. After laying the stones for the base, they raised the remaining stones to their places by means of machines formed of short wooden planks. The first machine raised them from the ground to the top of the first step. On this there was another machine, which received the stone upon its arrival, and conveyed it to the second step, whence a third machine advanced it still higher. Either they had as many machines as there were steps in the Pyramid, or possibly they had but a single machine, which being easily moved, was transferred from tier to tier as the stones rose-both accounts are given, and therefore I mention both",[2]; a simple explanation to a complex problem from the mind of a man whose desire was to transmit knowledge.

We can be certain that Herodotus was standing gazing at a Pyramid that was intact and a wonder to see. How did he acquire this knowledge as to its inner composition? Was it from the Temple Priests? It is obvious that this was an occasion of logical reasoning, a bit of guesswork. What brings his description into question is the size and weight of the stone lintels over the Kings Chamber. These massive monoliths could not be moved by the methods, which he describes.

There is no doubt that he is referring to the limestone blocks that formed the central core of the Pyramid which weighted approximately 2.¾ tons each, This method of construction may be possible, but most unlikely when one considers the logistics involved. But as an explanation it fulfilled his inquiring mind and was accepted on face value.

---

1   *The Dialogues of Plato Translated by Benjamin Jowett Published by Sphere Books Limited London*

2   *Herodotus 'The Histories' Vol 1 1910 Translated by George Rawlinson Published by J.M. Dent and Sons Ltd. London.*

In his reference to the finished polished limestone blocks that formed the outer face of the Pyramid, he goes on to say that "The upper portion of the pyramid was finished first, then the middle, and finally the part which was lowest and nearer the ground".

It is apparent from his description that they had finished building the core, and then proceeded to cover the structure with polished limestone, starting at the top, and continuing to the bottom. A most unlikely method when one considers the weight and precision called for in the finished surface. Unlike Didodorus Siculus he fails to consider the use of a ramp therefore his description would be a natural assumption to make if one was looking at a structure that was complete, with the Pyramidion or capstone in place.

Therefore, if the method of placing the finished facing stones were carried out as described by Herodotus, it were natural for him to assume that the first stone placed at the pinnacle would be the capstone. This would be a logical conclusion to reach by a layperson when looking at the completed structure.

Again the simplicity of the explanation would appear to respond to his needs, but if one studies the logic of the method used in placing the outer facing stones to the precision achieved in the finished product the method he proposed is illogical and unworkable.

No doubt, the manner of raising and placing the finished stone facing blocks appears feasible to those who lack the basic knowledge of construction principals. However, this method of construction he describes does not take into account the limited working area on which the machines rested and the extraordinary precision required in placing the inner core blocks ready to receive the finished facing elements.

Lifting, and placing a stone block weighing in excess of five tons, on a platform approximately eight feet in depth, would prove extremely difficult to maneuver. Raising the same block to a height of hundreds of feet would be unworkable, arduous, dangerous, and extremely improbable when one considers the weight and size of the materials in question.

What is more extraordinary are the many theories put forward by the experts, is that there is no reference to the weights of the stone elements above the Kings Chamber. There is of course the few occasions when the total numbers of stone blocks have been calculated, and their weight, including the labor person-hours required fitting the theory put forward by Herodotus that the pyramid took twenty years to build. [1] However, the experts in their rush to find an explanation conveniently ignore those stone elements weighing 50-70 tons. To move and maneuver such large elements would require the construction of a ramp on which to move the elements to the elevation of the Kings Chamber, which leads one to the conclusion that a ramp was a prerequisite to construction as surmised by Diodorus Siculus.

---

1   Limestone facing blocks Weight of solid limestone 35.32 Lbs per cubic foot Weight of facing block uncovered by Pizza Smyth, 16.64 tons. Weight of core blocks, 2.76 tons. Possible weight of facing blocks above base course 5.5 tons. Weight of facing block described by Herodotus 60.33 tons. Weight of monoliths above the Kings Chamber 70. 0 tons

There is also the theory by some that a Zigzag ramp was used to transport the stone elements. In order to haul 50/70 ton blocks of granite to an approximate height of 200-250 feet precludes suggested theories that a zigzag ramp was the means of transporting the granite lintels;[1] this would require a straight ramp angled to a degree that would allow rest periods without fear of accidents.

The Egyptians have been attributed with many gifts and despite the high degree of engineering skills exhibited one major characteristic was that they were practical in their approach to their many tasks I therefore doubt if this would prove a problem to a people with the skills and dedication to their God. [2] The building of a straight ramp on which to transport the massive monoliths would be a major task. To suggest a zigzag ramp would be preposterous. Not only do we have the question of the amount of material required, there is also the question of the width to accommodate the maneuverability of the major elements when going around corners.

The ancient Egyptians were the most advanced people of their time. Their religious beliefs, their Temples, the writings left to us, bear testimony of a people who viewed themselves as being one step away from the God's. Above all they were assiduous in all their work. They were not in the habit of idly wasting time; the Temple priests approved nothing unless it had a purpose and conformed to the religious principals of the Kingdom.

The reality we must face is that they had a purpose behind their every action; and behind all their actions was a logic that defies the best minds of our century. Scholars have perused every conceivable hieroglyph found on stone and papyrus; yet found nothing in the writings that would suggest the Egyptians of 2400 BC were the builders of the Pyramid, therefore, the accepted theory that the Pharaoh Cheops or Khufu is pure supposition.

The crude hieroglyphics found painted on the stone lintels above the upper Kings Chamber purportedly naming the pharaoh 'Khufu' as the builder is insufficient evidence to suggest that it was constructed during the reign of the Pharaoh Cheops. However, as these are the only hieroglyphs found within the body of the Pyramid, one may surmise that the writer surreptitiously wrote without the permission of the authorities. I find it rather strange that nowhere in the research of the experts has there been a comment on the lack of hieroglyphic inscriptions within the many passageways, the Queens and Kings Chambers. The inner structure is devoid of any form of hieroglyph, which would give a clue to the people who erected this structure.

It is clear that these hieroglyphs found above the Kings Chamber were not the work of a royal scribe, but perhaps a person sufficiently educated in the sacred language. There is no reason to reject the theory that this may have been the case in Egypt. Who can disprove the theory of

1   Jackson., Kevin/Stamp., Jonathan *Building the Great Pyramid* Published by Firefly Books Ltd
2   Numerous theories have been put forward regards the method of construction, i.e. straight ramp, spiral ramp, zigzag ramp, envelope ramp multiple ramp, and the internal ramp. It is notable that in the many theories put forward logic appears to have been forgotten

there being a Pharaoh with the name of Khufu who lived in Egypt fifty thousand years ago or for that matter thirty thousand years ago?

Nevertheless, when the hieroglyphs were submitted to the British Museum for translation, there was no clear consensus. It was suggested one pictograph referred to 'King Suphis', or 'Shofo', or 'Khufu'.[1] Therefore, associating the Pharaoh Cheops with that of 'Khufu' is as been suggested, pure supposition.

The experts have however, associated the name 'Khufu' with that of the Pharaoh Cheops of the fourth Dynasty[2]. This appears to be grasping at straws in order to prove a point. The British royal house has had many George's, as did the Romans who had many Emperors by the same name. Who is to say that this was not the case within the royal house of Egypt?

It must also be understood that the Egypt of 4,000 BC was not the age at which this civilization began its climb to greatness, but most likely, when evaluated against its historical background the age at which it began its decline. There is very little knowledge of Egypt before the fourth millennia BC or for that matter before the time of the New Kingdom.[3] Our knowledge appears to bear fruit during the reign of the Pharaoh Akhenaton[4] when we are lead to believe that his attempt to bring Egypt back to its religious roots resulted in failure due to the power of the priesthood. The power struggle between Akhenaton and the Egyptian priesthood is a page in the history that brought on its decline but may have been for reasons that were not associated with religion or his move from Memphis but could have been more domestic than political.

Akhenaton inherited a land rich in assets and resources and at peace with its neighbors. His father Amunhotep 111 had been a wise benevolent King well loved by his people.[5] However it would appear that all of this was lost during the reign of Akhenaton whose preoccupation with the gods allowed the affairs of state to deteriorate to the detriment of his people.[6] However there was, a form of renaissance during the reign of the Pharaoh Ramses 11[7], but this was short lived. From this time on there was a rapid decline in the Egyptian social order until its death knell with the occupation by the Roman Authorities and the arrival of Christianity. It could be said that at this stage of its history even the memories of its past glories had been forgotten by the people.

The precision of the structures which remain from this long forgotten civilization demonstrates an extraordinary ability in mathematics. An age-old adage states, "Man is the measure of all things". [8] When one views the many human art forms, the mathematical attributes are all too discernable. Perhaps they did use the human form as a basis for developing

1   Thompkins. Peter. 'Secrets of the Great Pyramids Published by Harper Colophon Books. London.
2   2613 BC to 2494 BC.
3   Ibid
4   Akhenaten. 18th Dynasty 1558-1303 BC
5   Pharaoh Amunhotep 111 Ruled Egypt from 1386-1349 BC father of Akhenaton Wikipedia Encyclopaedia
6   The Amarna Letters The Decline and End of Akhenaton's Reform Britannic Encyclopaedia
7   Ramses 11 19th Dynasty 1303-1200 BC
8   Attributed to Protagoras Greek Philosopher

their standard of measure. This being the case the attributes of the personage would have to have godlike characteristics.

When one inspects the Royal Egyptian Cubit of Memphis, and the Egyptian measuring rule on display in the Turin Museum, each of the twenty-eight segments is dedicated to a particular God. One can understand the reasons behind this in a society whose lifestyle and future depended upon what they believed to be the gifts of the God's.

From its inscriptions, it is obvious that the Memphis cubit of black granite, as all-measuring instruments, were inviolable. It can be inferred that it was against this sacred stone that the priests of the Temple would at regular intervals, gauge all measuring cubit sticks in Egypt in order to avoid contamination. This would be much similar to the system that exists in today's society in which the Department of Weights and Measures police the various weighing and measuring systems in the business industry.[1]

It is against this background that if the mystery surrounding the Great Pyramid, is to be properly understood those who approach the problem must, by necessity put themselves in the place of the builders who planned and built this magnificent structure. What was their intent? For a people whose buildings and art, was carried out to an amazing level of precision, it would be naïve to suggest that an arbitrary method was the means by which they obtained their standard of measure. Did they use the human form as a prototype; it is quite possible when one considers how these people viewed the relationship between man and his God. One could appreciate the reasons why they invoked the presence of their God's in all of their actions

Therefore, if it were the Egyptians,[2] or their forebears, the dimensions at the base would be exact to a degree that would be equal to or better than the degree of error permissible in the building industry today. There would be no fractions of a cubit unless it was for a specific purpose.

A notable characteristic among those who have written extensively on the Great Pyramid is the tendency to increase or decrease its dimensions in order to suit a particular theory. This appears more prevalent among those who are religiously inclined, or who may have a particular axe to grind. This particular trait becomes quiet ludicrous when a millimeter is calculated to a forth decimal place in order to substantiate a theory.[3]

---

1   Ludwig Borchard. Director of Egyptology in Cairo, in 1925 established the dimensions of the base of the Great Pyramid to within a margin of error of plus /minus 6/10 mm.
    North Base line 230,253 mm = 755.42 feet = 438.77 Royal Cubits,
    South Base line 230,454 mm = 756.08 feet = 439.15 Royal Cubits
    East Base line 230, 391 mm = 755.87 feet = 439.03 Royal Cubits
    West Base line 230,357 mm = 755.76 feet = 438.97 Royal Cubits.

2   One could suggest that the methods of measure may have been more ancient than the Egyptians of the Old Kingdom 2686-2613 BC and possibly much older than the Pre-dynastic Period 5200 – 3050 BC

3   Tompkins. Peter. 'Secrets of the Great Pyramid' "Sir John Herschel, one of Britain's most eminent astronomers at the beginning of the nineteen century, had just postulated a unit of half a human hair's breadth longer than the British inch as the only sensible earth-commensurable unit, or unit based on the actual size of the earth".

Admittedly, the Great Pyramid has some attributes that appear puzzling; nevertheless, what is inescapable is that we have some facts on which to work.

a)   Among the many is the survey carried out by J.H.Cole on behalf of Ludwig Borchardt.[1]

b)   The facing stone uncovered by Howard Vyse, which gave an inclined angle of as 51°51° (51°30°36'). (See picture below).

c)   The black granite Royal Cubit of Memphis, the Cubit rules both presently on display in the Turin Museum in Italy. (See picture below.)

Rather than be bogged down in a quagmire of various methods of measure and theories developed by our modern and ancient historians, why not concentrate our efforts on the angle of incline, the results of the survey, and the Egyptian Royal Cubit and see where it leads.

Again it must be emphasized that if it were the Egyptians or their ancestors who were responsible for this magnificent structure they definitely did not build in feet or inches, nor meters, but in cubits of which there was a standard cubit of 17.72 inch's, and the Royal Cubit of 20.562 inch's (20 9/16"). [2]

Using the Royal Cubit of 20.5625" as our yard stick and the results of the survey carried out by J.H.Cole which established the following base measurements to within +/- 6/10 millimeters. The following calculations are within two decimal places.

North Baseline 230.253 mm÷0.3048 mm = (755'.43" feetx12"=9065.16"÷20.5625=) 440.86 Royal Cubits

South Baseline 230.454 mm÷0.3048 m = (756'.08" feet) =441.24 Royal Cubits

East Baseline 230.391mm÷0.3048 m = (755'.87" feet) = 441.12 Royal Cubits

West Baseline 230.357mm÷0.3048 m = (755'.76" feet) = 441.05 Royal Cubits

Within a reasonable degree of error, it is probable that the length of each side of the base was planned to be 756'0" (441 Royal Cubits), when considered the base length of 755'. 9⅝" feet, the margin of error is negligible. Accepting these dimensions as a working hypothesis we find that the actual height of the Pyramid to be by means of the trigonometric theorem.

North Baseline 756'.00"÷ 2 = 378'.00"= 220.43 Royal Cubits

Height a= Tan A x c=1.2576228 x 377.72 = 475'.03"x12=5700.36"/20.5625"= 277.22 Royal Cubits

Hypotenuse = (c=$\sqrt{}$ a² +b²) =$\sqrt{}$475'.03"²+ 377'.72"²=$\sqrt{}$225653'.5" + 142672'.4"=$\sqrt{}$368325'.9"=606'.89"x12= 7282.68"/20.5625"=354.17 Royal Cubits

---

1   *Ludwig Borchard 1863-1939 German Egyptologist*

2   *Scott Nora E Junior Research Fellow Department of Egyptian Art Metropolitan Museum*

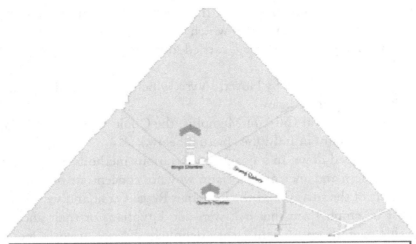

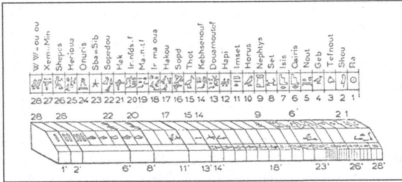

Summary;
Height is a= 475' 03"x12=5700.36"/20.5625"
a=277.21royal cubits
North Base Line 755'.43"÷ 2=377'72"x12=
4532.64"/20.5625"=
b= 220.43 x 2 = 440.87 royal cubits
Hypotenuse c=606'.89"x12 =7282.68"/20.5625=
C=354.17 royal cubits[1]

When one considers that there were only two established methods of measure in Egypt, as there is only the inch, foot, and yard in the Imperial system, any computation of numbers must by necessity, be based upon this system of measure prevalent at the purported time of construction. Additionally, we are encumbered with those who express various theories for the rationale behind this magnificent, structure, which, range from the sublime to the ridiculous. Whatever the rational it was important enough for these ancient people to devote time and effort into leaving this structure for posterity.

Peter Tompkins[2] writes an extraordinary dissertation on the dimensions of this amazing structure in his efforts to associate the dimensions with some hidden knowledge only known to the Egyptian's. However, to do so he has to ignore the results of the survey which was carried out by J. H. Cole and manipulate the dimensions to fit his theory. I very much doubt that these master builders paid much attention to the thickness of a finger over a distance of 441 royal cubits which is equal to the length of two football fields. If one concentrates on the information available it is obvious that there is hidden geometrical knowledge relative to the external dimensions. It is also probable that knowledge exists within the Queen's Chamber and the Kings Chamber and the famous granite coffer...

Built to last for aeons probably to await the coming of an intelligent race that would understand its hidden secrets they never envisaged a religion and culture that in their ignorance made every effort to destroy this work of art. So let's put aside the religious mumbo-jumbo that appears to dominate the mind and reasoning of those who wish to see a hand of some unknown god or extraterrestrial and center our thoughts on a common sense approach if one wishes to find answers.

Was it a depository of knowledge, most likely? Its orientation towards the four cardinal points of the compass and its location in the center landmass of the planet indicate a people of an advanced knowledge in geometrical proportions, this in itself is amazing.

There are those who say that its location was accidental suggesting that the builders were incapable of such advanced knowledge. This form of mentality belongs to the age when it was the belief that the earth was flat and the center of the Universe.

1
2   Ibid

Was it a tomb of a Pharaoh? There is no evidence to suggest this being the case. Those who first entered the room of the Kings Chamber found nothing, which would support this hypothesis. What they found was a lidless granite coffer.[1] No mummy, no wrappings, no gold no rewards for all their hard work, just a lidless empty stone coffer. What a disappointment for those who expected to find treasure beyond their dreams.

The granite plugs placed in the passageways leading to the 'Kings Chamber' to prevent entry would negate theory of it being a tomb for a future Pharaoh. These granite plugs were placed in position during the course of construction and not after as has been suggested.[2] It would be impossible to place these granite blocks in place after construction. To place the plugs after construction would prove an impossible task for the builders. Reaching such a conclusion is a futile exercise in logic. Such being the case one would ask 'why'? What was its purpose? What was it that had to be guarded and hidden away?

Was it, as some suggested, a make work project for an over populated country, absolute nonsense. This was no seasonal project but a project of major importance designed and constructed in one operation. Others have suggested that it holds the secrets to future events that will affect this planet. Only those who are religiously motivated believe such nonsense. No one can tell the future, they can however over a long period of time predict events that may happen based on the premise that nature in its wisdom repeats its actions subject to the earth's rotation. The arrivals of our seasons in due order comes as no surprise and are accepted as a normal occurrence in the life of the planet. Such an event is the approaching new Age of Aquarius a period which will see dramatic climate changes due to the earth's rotation. Sages of twenty-five thousand years ago having experienced such climatic changes may well have predicted the same occurrences at some future age. One does not have to be a God to fulfill such a function.

What is beyond doubt, the Great Pyramid was assembled to a precision that defies explanation. Its center sits exactly on the center of the planets known landmass, Latitude 30°00°, and Longitude 30 ° 00 °. In addition, each of its sides is orientated towards the four cardinal points of the compass. One has to dispense with the theory that this was by accident. What else can be found that adds to our knowledge?

In his writings on the subject, Peter Tompkins had this to say regards the builders of the Pyramid, "Whoever built the Great Pyramid knew the dimensions of this planet as they were not to be known again till the seventeenth century of our era. They could measure the day, the

1   *Tompkins Peter Secrets of the Great Pyramid Entrance to the Pyramid was first accomplished by Abdullah Al Mamun in 820 AD We can assume that the Pyramid was intact until this date*

2   *Tompkins Peter Secrets of the Great Pyramid On the question of the plugged passage ways Peter Tompkins outlines the many theories expounded by the experts Egyptologist is a puzzle yet to be solved It is foolhardy to suggest that monoliths were placed in position after the construction due to the many difficulties one would encounter*

year and the Great Year of the Precessions.[1] They knew how to compute Latitude and Longitude very accurately by means of obelisks and the transit of stars. They knew the varying lengths of a degree of Latitude and longitude at different locations on the planet and could make excellent maps, projecting them with a minimal of distortion. They worked out a sophisticated system of measures based on the earth's rotation on its axis which produced the admirably earth-commensurate foot and cubit which they incorporated into the Pyramid".[2]

This statement is correct in all respects with the exception of his contention that the British Imperial measurement of the "foot" is incorporated in the structural dimensions. As has been previously stated the British Imperial system of measure did not exist, nor that of the Greek foot, it is therefore foolhardy to suggest otherwise.

The structure was intact in its entire splendor at the time of Al Mamun's forced entry in the ninth century. When he eventually gained access to the King's Chamber there was no golden treasure waiting, in fact, nothing of any interest was found, except the stone coffer. Had it been the burial place of a Pharaoh one would expect to find some remnants of his body, clothing and jewellery, something that could identify the occupant. Nothing was discovered, the only places of interest were the Queens and Kings Chambers and of course the stone coffer.

What else can we look at? There is the inner dimension of the stone coffer, the King and Queens Chambers, they must be important to the puzzle. But what of the external dimensions of the Pyramid was there some cryptic knowledge hidden in these dimensions? One would like to believe so, however, in order to accomplish this requires the manipulation of the Pyramids dimensions.

If one accepts the dimensions established by J H Cole and the degree of 51.51 established by the facing block discovered by Howard Vyse the height of the Pyramid is 277.31 Royal cubits (475'16" feet).

However, the base dimensions established by J H Cole suggest that the length of the base on each side were, North 440.85, South 441.23, East 441.19, West 441.05 Royal cubits (an average length of 755'.81") It is evident from J H Cole's survey that each side measured 441.0 Royal cubits, a perfect square if one discounts the fractional differences which are but negligible when one considers the distance which in modern terms is equal to the length of two football fields.

It has been suggested that if one uses a baseline of 440 Royal Cubits the result is a remarkable sequence of mathematical formula suggesting that there were "three possible values of the Royal Cubit"[3]. Why not four or five to suit any given circumstance, one may well hypothesis that

---

1   Various numbers of years have been attributed to these marvelous phenomena, ranging from 25,000 years to 26,000 years. The actual number of years is 25,920, which comprises of twelve Zodiac cycles of 2,160 years. This is determined by the rotation of the planet earth when the North Pole moves within a half degree of star Polaris an event that occurs every 25,920 years. We are now entering the end of this cycle, which will occur on the 21st March 2028 of our common era.

2   Tompkins. Peter Secrets of the Great Pyramid Published by Harper Colophon Books NY.

3   Tompkins Peter Secrets of the Great Pyramid published by Harper Colophon Books NY

we have three possible values for the Imperial foot. Again it is a question of manipulating the dimensions to fit the theory.

It is hypothesized that an earthquake or minor tremor may have disturbed the structure after total completion; this theory is most unlikely. Had such an event occurred, it is logical to suggest that the precision of the exterior surfaces would have shown a degree of surface fracture? Any imperfection would have been noticed by our ancient historians, however this has not been the case, there is no mention of this in the writings of the ancient historians, which would support this hypothesis? One could assume that some form of settlement occurred after the construction of the Kings Chamber. As the passageways had been plugged there would be no way of reentering the Kings Chamber which required a second entrance to inspect the damage which would account for the tunnel which circumvented the plugged passageway and allowed entrance to the Kings chamber to repair the damage as evidence of the dabbed cement covering the cracks for future inspection a method of detecting miniscule movement in a structure which is still practiced today.

We can therefore assume that the outer surface of the Pyramid was intact and free of surface fractures during the visit of Herodotus in the 4th century and later Diodorus Siculus in the 1st century; otherwise they would have mentioned this surface anomaly in their writings.

The most likely explanation would suggest it was a slight settlement that alarmed the builders. It is therefore safe to assume that if such an event happened it was shortly after it was built and in the lifetime of its constructors. If it was a slight settlement how did the builders detect it? Perhaps they were aware that such an event would occur and took appropriate measures to detect the slightest movement.

Why was it so important to evacuate a secondary tunnel, to gain access to the Kings Chamber in order to inspect any possible damage? The time and effort expanded on this exercise would support the theory that the dimensions of the chamber and the stone coffer were important. To what extend would be mere speculation and subject all forms of imaginary theories. Evidence suggests that those who entered the chamber dabbed the fractures with a cement paste to detect any further movement. This action would be followed by prolonged inspections over a period of time. The practice itself is a function that is prevalent today as it was those many years ago.

This may be the only reasonable explanation for the shaft, which we surmise was excavated in order to access the Kings Chamber. Only those with a precise knowledge of the Pyramids construction could accomplish this feat, a conclusion reached by David Davidson a structural engineer from Leeds England when he inspected the structure. It was a joy to read the thoughts of a logical mind.

So it was with the inner rooms of the pyramid, there was nothing to see except the stone coffer.

We also have the question of the salt that encrusted the walls of the 'Queens Chamber, including Herodotus reference to the damage caused by salt to the base of the Pyramid. His observation is supported by the comments made by Plutarch the Greek historian when he states that "for Egypt used to be all sea, and, for that reason, even today it is found to have shells in its mines and mountains. Moreover, all the springs and wells, of which there are many, have saline and brackish water, as if some stale dregs of the ancient sea had collected there".[1] It can be deduced from the observations of these two noted historians that some time in its history the sea inundated Egypt.

If this mystery were investigated, it would bring into question, not only the age of the pyramid, but also the antiquity of the people who erected this structure. Additionally, it would answer the question relative to the Diaspora of the Egyptians under the leadership of Moses to alleviate the suffering of the people due to a widespread famine.[2]

Therefore, the lack of any hieroglyphs within the structure, and the presence of salt would lead one to believe that it was not the Egyptians of the history book, or those of the fourth dynasty who erected this structure, but a civilization who preceded the Egyptians by many thousands of years who were the actual builders of the pyramids.

It has been noted by Schwaller de Lubicz in his work 'The Temple in Man' that "no one would build such monuments, and in such great numbers, over thousands of years, for uncultivated peasants. This work is of necessity that of an elite, and, even more remarkably, an elite that never ceased to renew itself, an elite that seems to have been uniquely endowed with a wealth of scientific knowledge, including an understanding of the laws of Life".[3]

Those who built the Pyramid were highly intelligent with a plan of approach which would ensure the maximum of productivity for the minimum amount of labor to ensure success, Therefore, the explanation given to Herodotus by the priests as to the method of construction is such that it was sufficient to meet a need, and appeared reasonable, one could say a simple explanation to a complex problem.

However, to give some idea of what we are dealing with it is important that we have some knowledge of the elements that comprise the Pyramid.

Solid limestone weighs approximately one hundred and fifty two pounds (152.54 Lbs) per cubic foot. There are two types of stones, whose size and weight are verifiable. The existing stone blocks, which make up the core of the Pyramid, over which the tourist gambol, and the facing stone uncovered by Howard Vyse[4], from which the angle of degree of the Pyramid has been determined. There are also the facing stone blocks described by Herodotus, and the weight of the lintels that covered the roof of the 'Kings Chamber'.[5]

1   *De Lubicz R A Schwaller Sacred Science The King of Pharaonic Theocracy Plutarch, op cit p 40.Published by MacMillan and Company Limited London*
2   *Apion an ancient historian theorized that at some time in the ancient past Egypt suffered from severe drought and to alleviate the food shortage, the King had all the old and infirm dispatched into the Sinai desert under the command of a prince of the Royal House called Moses.*
3   *De Lubicz R A Schwaller 'The Temple in Man' Sacred Architecture and the Perfect Man' Published by Inner Traditions International Vermont USA*
4   *Vyse Colonel Howard.*
5   *Ibid*

In the case of the core stone blocks, whose size is 50"x50"x28" each weighting approximately 2.77 imperial tons (6,240 lbs).

The facing stone block at ground level uncovered by Howard Vyse weighed approximately 16.34 Imperial tons (36,600 lbs).

The facing stone blocks described by Herodotus approximate weight 40.86 imperial tons (91,526 lbs).

In addition, the nine roof lintels above the 'Kings Chamber' as 70 imperial tons each, (156,800 lbs) also, other stone elements incorporated in the structure weighing 50 imperial tons each (1122,000 lbs).

What is missing is any trace of the succeeding facing stone blocks above ground level. We can assume that the dimensions in height and width would be proportionate to the core blocks. These may perhaps have measured 28" x 8'. 0" x 5.'5", (three Royal Cubits) each weighting approximately 5.24 imperial tons, (117,376) the width and height remaining constant throughout the project, except in the area of the reducing angles.

It can be said with a level of certainty is that the facing stones of the pyramid would be laid with a symmetry that would be equal to or greater than we see in the many forms of work carried out by these people.

There have been many theories regards the method of construction, all of which have been speculative. The first of these was outlined in the writings of Herodotus Histories in which he states "that the pyramid was substantially completed with the rough core blocks in place as is seen today, after which the facing blocks were installed, starting from the top of the pyramid, continuing to the middle, down to ground level.

This would require the inner core blocks be laid with an accuracy that would leave no room for error when it came to installing the facing blocks. No doubt the manner of raising and placing the stone blocks appears feasible, however, does not take into account the size and weight of the stones elements, and the limited working area on which the machines rested. Working from a platform no more than eight feet in depth, raising a stone weighting approximately 16.34 tons, or for that matter, one weighing 5.24 tons in the manner described by Herodotus as the work progressed would be improbable. It is obvious from Herodotus description that the information by the priest is through an interpreter. It is also apparent that the Priest in question offered his explanation without having any knowledge of the Pyramids history, except through myth. Therefore, rather than admit to his ignorance, offered an explanation to suit the occasion, as I said a simple explanation to a complex problem.

It would also be implausible to apply the same methods to a monolith weighting 70 tons. Logic suggests that the only way move granite monoliths of this magnitude would be by the use of a ramp inclined to a degree that would enable the workers to move the monoliths with ease. This would apply to any units weighting in excess of two tons.

An incline of 1:10 feet as a slope sufficient to meet the needs of construction has been suggested, however, it is obvious that the author of this hypothesis lacks the necessary knowledge in moving elements 70 imperial tons. A more appropriate slope of 1:12 with a slope of 5° would make the work all that much easier. One ingredient I find missing in the many hypothesizes put forward by those who have written on the subject is the absence of the papyrus mats, which were used extensively by the Egyptians when moving large objects as we see in the many hieroglyphs adorning their temples. The use of these mats and oil as a lubricant would make the movement of seventy-ton monoliths an easy task on a ramp with an incline of 5°.

It would follow that, as the ramp is a necessity in the construction process, would require that the polished facing stone blocks be first positioned for accuracy, to be followed by the inner core filling. This method of construction was proposed by Flinders Petrie[1], however, like all men of his time goes off on a tangent by proposing that the work was carried out by the illiterate populations during the three month inundation of the Nile River suggesting a make work project.

It has however been argued that each time a course of facing stones were laid would require the incline of the ramp be modified to address the rise in elevation, resulting in long delays in construction. The use of two ramps to service the supply of stone and allow for uninterrupted construction would resolve this problem. However, I doubt if this was the case. The Egyptians had the manpower and ingenuity to accomplish the project with the use of one ramp.

Only those who have been exposed to the field of engineering can appreciate the difficulties encountered when moving elements of this magnitude. Even with today's mechanical technology, lifting and moving a stone element weighing 70 tons would be difficult. The problem would be more difficult if one attempted to lift such a monolith above ground level, especially to the elevation of the 'Kings Chamber'. Ignoring the theories, which state the work, was completed with the help of a people with magical powers, or a people from outer space; a more mundane explanation would explain their capabilities.

What is clear is that it was a project that was brought to total completion from start to finish; there was no interruption in the construction process or change of mind on the part of the builders as purported by some experts.[2] Logic suggests that before one piece of limestone was quarried a concept plan of the Pyramid was completed in its entirety, the method of construction determined, the templates for each piece of stone prepared, and the method of transportation established.

This was no catch- catch can operation but a carefully thought out plan itemizing the position, size, and placement of each piece of stone. Once the dimensions of the base had been determined, work would commence on the laying out of the foundation. These were a practical people who exercised a practical approach to this enterprise. Possessing these attributes they would find the most expeditious way to perform the work.

The two elements required to accomplish their task were readily at hand; a dedicated workforce, and an abundance of black clay from the banks of the Nile for the manufacture of clay bricks. Diodorus Siculus, a Greek historian of the 1st century BC was less gullible than

1   *Sir William Matthew Flinders Petrie 1853-1942 British Archaeologist and Egyptologist*
2   *Ibid*

Herodotus. He states. " The edifices were raised by means of earthen ramps, since machines for lifting had not yet been invented in these days: and most surprising it is, that although such large structures were raised in an area surrounded by sand, no trace remains of either ramps or the dressing of the stones---Now some Egyptians try to make a marvel of these things, alleging that the ramps were made of salt and natron and that, when the river was turned against them, it melted them clean away and obliterated their every trace without the use of human labor. But, in very truth, it most certainly was not done in this way! Rather, the same multitude of workmen who raised the mounds returned the entire mass again to its original place; for they say that three- hundred and sixty thousand men were constantly employed in the prosecution of the work, yet the entire edifice was hardly finished at the end of twenty years".[1]

We can see in his writings, like his predecessor, Herodotus, Diodorus was at the mercy of his translator when he alludes to the "sixteen hundred talents spent on vegetables and radishes for the workmen".

It should come as no surprise that this myth passed from generation to generation. What is a surprise is his references to the construction of the ramps, which he states, were made of "salt and natron". There is sufficient evidence to show how the Egyptians manufactured clay bricks from a mixture of straw and mud, and dried in the sun. Perhaps his reference to 'salt' was to account for the salinity in the soil surrounding the Pyramid as mentioned by Herodotus.

Why it was constructed is one of the world's greatest mysteries. What is certain is that it was not a tomb for a living Pharaoh, or for some future Pharaoh. What was it guarding? The only focal point was the coffer inside the 'Kings Chamber' and the 'Queens Chamber,' which were empty rooms.

Through brute force and ignorance entry was made to the 'Kings Chamber', but nothing was found of any interest, but a stone coffer, no lid, no bones, no bodies, no gold or ornaments, no hieroglyphs, and most importantly, no sarcophagus. This was one occasion when no grave robbers had made entry before Al Mamun.[2]

What was so important about the two rooms that warranted such a beautiful edifice was it as the experts say, a structure, which purportedly contains information for future generations. All very mysterious and open to discussion and depending upon your religious belief the answers are there. Nevertheless, "whoever built the great Pyramid---knew the precise circumference of the Planet and the length of the year to several decimal-data which was not rediscovered until the seventeenth century. Its Architects may well have known the mean length of the earth's orbit round the sun, the specific density of the planet, the 25,920 year cycle of the equinoxes, the acceleration of gravity, and the speed of light".[3]

---

1   *Siculus, Diodorus. 1St century BC Greek historian. The Antiquities of Egypt Translated by Edwin Murphy. Published by Transaction Publishers. London UK.*

2   *Abdullah Al- Mamun, Youngest son of Harun Al-Rashid, Caliph of Baghdad. Peter Thompkins. Secrets of the Great Pyramid*

3   *Thompkins. Peter. Secrets of the Great Pyramid. Published by Harper Colophon Books. N.Y.*

There is one mystery that requires an explanation, and it is to Herodotus we turn to for information, when he states. "I observed that there were shells upon the hills, and that the salt exuded from the soil to such an extent as even to injure the Pyramids".[1] There is also the question of the salt, which encrusted the walls of the 'Queens Chamber".

Where did this salt come from? This one fact would bring into question the purported age of the Pyramids. Even in the time of Diodorus Siculus there was various opinions regards the age of the Great Pyramid, some believing it was "no less than a thousand years old, (or as some writers have it, more than three thousand and four hundred years".[2] It is abundantly clear that the Egyptians in the days of Herodotus and Diodorus Siculus were as ignorant of the history of the Pyramids as our experts are today.

The presence of ground salt, which Herodotus states damaged the base of the Pyramid, and more importantly, the salt on the walls of the 'Queens Chamber", would suggest that at some time in its history the region was inundated with sea water. With the presence of seashells and salt there is no other possible explanation. Some experts allege that the contours of the base of the Sphinx are the result of the sand storms prevalent in this area. However, if one examines the contours it is obvious that the characteristics are more the wave action of water that had lapped against the sandstone surface over a long period, and not caused through the action of sandstorms, as postulated by the Egyptologist. Similar contour characteristics can be observed at the bend of rivers through the action of the water on the riverbank.

Those who have studied the Sphinx, have remarked on the high degree of salinity found in the area, which like the pyramids would indicate the presence of sea water at some time in the past. What has been determined if we accept the physical evidence is that the lands of Egypt were at some time in their historical past a fertile land and not the desert waste we see today.

Would this suggest a cataclysmic event occurred in the distant past? Is it possible? Suggesting such an occurrence would transport the mind back to the time of the Great Flood[3] and the myth surrounding Isle of Atlantis in 10,000 BC.[4] If the evidence of the salt is a lynch pin to the dating of the Great Pyramid, would suggest that the Pyramid was not built by the Egyptians of the 4th Dynasty but by a people of a much earlier date, a people with extraordinary intelligence and it is sad to say, destroyed by a people who were extraordinarily ignorant.

The presence of salt would also suggest that to find an answer it would not be by the imagination of those who have written extensively on the subject. Logic dictates that to find an

---

1   *The Histories of Herodotus. Book 11. Pg 115. Translated by George Rawlinson. Published by J.M.Dent & Sons. London*

2   *Ibid*

3   *Diodorus Siculus. 'The Antiquities of Egypt' Translated by Edwin Murphy. Published by Transaction Publishers. London UK.*
     "During the flood of Deucalions time, some say the in habitants of southern Egypt alone were saved,--"

4   *Plato. The Dialogues of Plato Timaeus.Vol 3 The story of Atlantis Translated by Benjamin Jowett. Published by Sphere Books Ltd. London.*

answer, the mind must expand beyond the limits imposed by our modern establishment. The mind of the experts appear to be caught up in a time warp that will not allow them to think back any further than five thousand BC, whereas there is sufficient evidence to suggest that this is but a fraction of Egyptian history.

What then is the rightful age of the Egyptian civilization? How do we reconcile the opinions of our twentieth century experts with those of the fourth and first century BC historians? As we read the works of Herodotus and Diodorus Siculus, we are amazed at the periods they speak off regards the age of Egypt. There is in the works of Herodotus a statement in which he expresses his opinion on the gods of Greece and of Egypt where his says.

"Seventeen thousand years before the reign of Amasis, (26th Dynasty 664-525 BC) the twelve gods were, they affirm produced from the eight. Next, they (the Priests) read me from a papyrus, the names of three hundred and thirty monarchs, who they say were his successors upon the throne. Thus I have spoken on the authority of the Egyptians and their priests. They declare that from their first King to the last mentioned monarch, the priest Vulcan (Sethós) was a period of three hundred and forty one generations; such, at least, they say, was the number both of their Kings, and of their high priests, during this interval. Now three hundred generations of men make ten thousand years, three generations filling up the century; and the remaining forty-one generations make thirteen hundred and forty years. The whole number of years is eleven thousand, three hundred and forty; --. They led me into the inner sanctuary, which is a specious chamber, and showed me a multitude of colossal statues, in wood, which they counted up, and found to amount to the exact number they had said, the custom being for every high priest during his lifetime to set up a statue in the Temple".[1]

Speaking on the subject of Egyptian history, Diodorus Siculus states, "The Egyptian priests, computing the time elapsed from the reign of Helios until Alexandria crossed into Asia, say it is about twenty-three thousand years".[2]

Although eleven thousand years would appear to be a long duration for a civilization to continue uninterrupted, it is still only a fraction of Egypt's historical past. Herodotus reference to the rising and setting of the Sun creates another mystery, which, appears to have been ignored by the experts when he relates a comment by the priest who states. "The sun, however, had within this period of time, on four several occasions, moved from its wonted course, twice rising where it now sets, and twice setting where it now rises. Egypt was in no degree affected by these changes; the production of the land and of the rivers remained the same; nor was there anything unusual either in the diseases or the deaths".[3]

1   Herodotus. 'The History of Herodotus' Book 11. Chapters 44-47 & 143-146 Translated by George Rawlinson Published by J.M.Dent & Sons London
2   Alexandria the Great 332 BC.
3   Herodotus. 'The history of Herodotus' Book 11. Translated by George Rawlinson. Published by J.M.Dent and Sons ltd. London

To explain these phenomena the experts have put many theories forward while others have elected to ignore it. And to add to the confusion there are those who have interjected religion into what should be a rational explanation to what would appear to be a complex problem.

The Egyptians were a people whose pre-occupation were the study of the surrounding universe and therefore would not be so gullible as to confuse the reality of the movement of the stars and planets to the machinations of some unseen god/s. In this regard, you cannot compare the mind of the Egyptians to that of the Greeks

Although Greek legends and their pantheon of gods make interesting reading, they have done more to confuse, rather than clarify history. This becomes evident in the writings of the early Greek historians, nevertheless, there is found in their writings a semblance of the truth regarding the age of the Egyptian civilization.

To find an answer to this phenomenon, several theories have been put forward. In his writings, Immanuel Velikovsky [1] offers a wide range of explanations taken from ancient sources to explain these phenomena. However what is most surprising is that those who have studied this question elected to concentrate on the first part of the statement by the priest, and not his following comments in which he stated that the event had "no effect upon the daily life of the people". This however does not remove the possibility that at some time in its ancient past Egypt suffered from some form of cataclysmic event that devastated the land and changed the face of Egypt.

If we accept the statement of the priest, it is seen that the events occurred within historical memory, negates the many theories regards the planet reversing its motion, or the poles reversing their positions. Had such an event occurred, not only would the planet suffer irreparable damage, but also the life of the world's communities would be in upheaval and face extinction? I am of the opinion that the two events must be separated if we are to have an understanding of what the priest was transmitting to Herodotus.

What was the priest alluding too? Is there another explanation? We must remember that Herodotus was a traveler and an historian, and not an Astronomer, or for that matter a Mathematician, very much dependent upon the help of translators. What then would satisfy a rational explanation, which would clarify the statement made by the priest? Did Herodotus misunderstand the priest? Was there a breakdown in translation between the three people? Were the priest really speaking of the processional Equinox and the appearance and position of certain stars, and not of the 'Sun'?

I doubt if this was the case, to explain the earth's wobble and the precession of the Equinox to the layperson results with a blank stare. Astronomy is more often than not, beyond the understanding of the average person today and is not a subject that comes up for discussion. There is every reason to believe that this was the case between Herodotus and the Priest. From the gist of the conversation, it is apparent that the Priest is intent on conveying to Herodotus the antiquity of Egypt, and in order to emphasis his point, remarks on the movement of the celestial

---

1   *Velikovsky. Immanuel. 'Worlds in Collision' Published by Pocket Books. NY.*

bodies believing that Herodotus is conversant with the subject. Therefore, there is every reason to suggest that Herodotus misinterpreted, or the translator, not understanding the meaning behind the priest's words injected the word 'Sun' into the explanation.

Immanuel Velikovsky[1] suggests a possible explanation in his reference to the "equinoctial points of the terrestrial orbit", that allows him to be drawn away from his opinion. Rather than question the priests truthfulness, it may perhaps lead to a better understanding of the problem were the wording attributed to an error in translation. However, Velikovsky goes on to reference an early Latin author of the first century AD who wrote; "The Egyptians pride themselves on being the most ancient people in the world. In their authentic annals---one may read that since they have been in existence, the courses of the stars have changed direction four times and that the sun has set twice in the part of the sky where it now rises today". [2]

He then goes on to quote from other ancient Egyptian hieroglyphic texts which reference the same subject, that if true, suggest that Egypt's historical past is not to be reckoned in the thousands, but in aeons of years. Alternatively, as was stated by Herodotus, "they have existed since man appeared upon the earth". However, the comment that this subject "has become the despair of the commentators" would be easier to understand if the experts were to place some trust in the statement imparted by the priest to Herodotus.

Determining the antiquity of Egypt can be a daunting task. As one reads the various modern authors, there appears to be selectivity in their work in order to prove a point. In the case of the ancient Greek authors, what can be said was their propensity to associate themselves with the God's. Such was the case of Solon[3] and Hecatæus[4], two men who figure prominently in the works of Herodotus and Plato.

Plato recounts in his work 'Timæus' of how the Greek traveler, Solon, on a visit to Egypt found that "neither he nor any other Hellene knew anything worth mentioning about the times of old".

Solon, in his efforts to extol the antiquity of Greece, was taught a lesson in humility by one of the senior priests who states. " O Solon, Solon, you Hellenes are never anything but children, and there is not an old man among you.---There have been, and will be again, many destructions of mankind arising out of many causes, the greatest have been brought about by the agencies of fire and water, and other lesser ones by innumerable other causes.---There is a story, which even you have preserved, that once upon a time Phaëthon, the son of Helios, having yoked the steeds in his father's chariot, because he was not able to drive them in the path of his father, burnt up all that was upon the earth, and was himself destroyed by a thunderbolt. Now this has the form of a myth, but really signifies a declination of the bodies moving in the heavens around the earth. As for those genealogies of yours, which you have just now recounted to us,

1   *Ibid*
2   *Velikovsky. Immanuel. Worlds in Collision. Published by Pocket Books NY.*
3   *Solon. 639-559 BC. Athenian statesman, lawgiver, and poet.*
4   *Hecatæus of Miletus. 6ᵗʰ century BC traveller and historian.*

Solon, they are no better than the tale's of children. In the first place, you remember a single deluge only, but there were many previous ones, and from this calamity, we were preserved by the liberation of the Nile. And whatever happened either in your country, or in ours, or in any other region of which we were informed – if there were any action noble or great or in any other way remarkable, they have all been written down by us of old, and are preserved in our Temple".[1] The priest's reference to the many deluges may account for the salinity of the soil mentioned by Herodotus, Plutarch, and Diodorus Siculus.

Herodotus is offered physical proof as to the antiquity of Egypt. Many opinions have been expressed by some regards the truthfulness of Herodotus, gullible perhaps, but not a liar. Diodorus Siculus had small regard for Herodotus when he said, "We shall omit from our history the stories invented by Herodotus---who deliberately prefer fables to facts".[2] Others have questioned his veracity forgetting that he was a man of his time and prone to religious superstition. Not only is this characteristic found in the writings of Herodotus, but also more pronounced in the writings of Diodorus Siculus in his Antiquities of Egypt.

Be as it may, the Egyptian priests speak of a period of eleven thousand, three hundred and thirty (11330) years during which time the "sun on four several occasions moved from its wonted course". As the sun is stationary, logic requires that the rotation of the earth reverse its motion four times to meet this requirement. Such an event would have catastrophic results on the world's environment. Did such an event happen in the distant past, perhaps? Geologic evidence suggests that the earth has come through many phases of destruction over the many epochs of its existence. Nevertheless, as there is no solid evidence of the earth reversing its axis we can discount the theories of the reversal of the poles during this period.

Theories put forward by Immanuel Velikovsky, brings into question conditions that are beyond the imagination. A salient point that is irrefutable concerns the rotation of the earth and the speed at which it rotates within a cycle of time. During this present age the earth's axis is within one half a degree of the pole star Polaris. Approximately 12960 years from now the earth's axis will line up pointing at the star Vega. It will not return to the position it now occupies until the year 27,948 AD to complete its full cycle of 25,920 years.

The precession of the Equinox is a fact and not the workings of an over hyped imagination. Considering the thousands of years we are working on, to suggest that the earth has reversed its axis twice in a period of 11,340 years is preposterous. What then were the priests referring too?

A theory proposed by Schwaller de Lubicz suggests a more reasoned solution to the problem without the histrionics of the imagination. He suggests that the rising may refer to the Vernal Point, meaning" that the vernal point had twice been located in the same constellation of Aries, and that it had also passed twice in the opposing constellation of Libra. This would grant the

1   Plato. 428-348 BC. Greek Philosopher. 'The Dialogues of Plato. Vol 111. Timaeus and Other Dialogues. Translated by Benjamin Jowett. Published by Sphere Books Ltd. London.
2   Siculus. Diodorus. 'The Antiquities of Egypt' Translated by Edwin Murphy. Published by Transaction publishers. London.

duration of one and a half processional cycles to the entire historic and prehistoric periods, or approximately 39,000 years".[1]

In his book 'Secrets of the Great Pyramid' Peter Tompkins speaks of a find by Soviet Archaeologists during the work that was carried out on the Aswan Dam. The inscriptions appear to cover periods of 35,525 years, "which would be equivalent of 25 cycles of 1461 years. The apparent discrepancy of one year in this recording of cycles is due to the Sothic cycle of 1460 years being the equivalent of a civil cycle of 1461 years. According to Muck there were three main cycles; one of 365x4=1460; another of 1460x 25=36,500; and a third of 36,500 x 5 = 182,500 years".

The Royal Papyrus of Turin lists the kings from early times up to the reign of Ramses 11 (1279-1213 B.C). This is the most detailed and reliable of the Egyptian list of Kings. Although it suffered irreparable damage during transit to Italy, there remain sufficient pieces of fragments that give an insight into ancient Egypt. Compiled during the reign of the Pharaoh Ramses 11, one has to accept its authenticity. Unlike most ancient societies, especially the Greeks, the Egyptians were not interested in developing a pseudo relationship with the gods, as was the case of Hecatæus, the Greek historian, when he was at Thebes, attempted to trace his ancestry back sixteen generations to a god. Truth was all-important to the Egyptians. This fact alone should compel our scholars to accept the list and the years attributed to the respective reigns as fact and not as "exaggerated, and dismissed as fabulous".

Therefore, accepting the Royal Papyrus of Turin as a true record, Egypt can trace her history back 40,000 years.[2] Successive ancient authors have, within their limitation, ascribed great antiquity to Egypt.[3] It is left to the modern scholars of Egyptology, who suffer from a form of myopia, to reject the truths of history.

If the astronomical progression of the planetary system is an unchanging fact it follows that the past is a reflection of an unchanging future, therefore the theory suggested by Schwaller de Lubicz is easily put to the test. Within this wonderful unchanging universe, the precession

---

1   Lubicz. Schwaller de. *Sacred Science. 'The King of Pharaonic Theocracy" Published by Inner Traditions International. N.Y. "The Royal Papyrus of Turin give a complete list of kings who reigned over Upper and Lower Egypt from Menes to the New Empire, including the duration of each reign.—among which the Venerable of Memphis, the Venerable of the North, and finally the Shemsu-Hor. Fortunately, the last two lines have survived almost intact, as have indications regarding the number of years. ---the venerables Shemsu-Hor 13,420 years. Reigns up to Shemus-Hor, 23,200 years. King Menes" (total 36,620 years).*
2   *Ibid*
3   *Diodorus of Sicily reports that according to several chroniclers, gods and hero's ruled Egypt for 18,000 years. Therefore, the land was governed by mortal Kings for 15,000---33,000.*
    Manetho. Egyptian priest, 300 BC wrote a history of Egypt for Ptolemy 1. 305-282
    BC in which he grants 15,500 to the divine dynasties and 9,777 to all kings having reigned before Menes. A total of 24,927 years.
    According to George the Syncellus. Te Egyptians possessed a certain tablet ---comprising a period corresponding to twenty-five Sothic cycles of 1,461 years that is 36,525 years.

of the Equinox's an unchanging phenomenon that influences all life on this planet. With the technology available we have the means of tracing the movements of the universal bodies over long periods of time.

Tracing the movement of the constellation Aries, between 28,080 BC to 27,341 AD, it is seen that the constellation Aries has passed twice in the constellation of Libra, once in 10,800 BC and will again in 14,988 AD, a period of one full processional cycle of 25,920 years.

In addition, the movement of the constellation Libra and its rising in the vernal point has been traced over a period of fifty-one thousand years. During this period, Libra has passed through the vernal point on five occasions, 27,344 BC, 14460 BC, 1583 BC, 11032 AD, and 24202 AD.

Each of these readings was taken on the 21ˢᵗ March at midnight, from the vantage point of the pyramid of Giza. In order to eliminate the possibility of major errors, an imaginary co-ordinate line was taken between the stars Zubeneschemale, and Sig Lib in the constellation Libra. This was co-ordinate with the vernal point, ensuring that the reading would be within acceptable norm for the constellation Aries the star Del Air. Using this method as the yardstick the following positions of the constellation Libra and its relationship to the constellation Aries were established.

Constellation Libra	Constellation Aries
27340 BC	
12h03 +-00°.06°	00h03 +00°03
Location North °	South
14460 BC.	
00h02 +00°03°	12h03 -00°05°
Location West	East
1580 BC.	
12h01+00°01°	00h01 01°57°
Location South	North
11310 AD.	
00h02 +00°00°	11h53 +08°47°
Location North	South
24200 AD.	
12h03 -00°10°	23h31 +04°54°
Location West	East

It can be seen that there are intervals of approximately twelve thousand, eight hundred (12,800) years between each ascension. So it is highly probable that Schwaller de Lubicz is correct in his hypothesis, proving that the Egyptian civilization is somewhat older than the experts would have us believe.

How old was this civilization? No one really knows. The limitations of the minds of contemporary scholars will not acknowledge the possibility of the existence of a people who perhaps had survived for hundreds of thousands of years. There is sufficient evidence in their knowledge of the Universe, and the planet on which we live to support such a hypothesis.

By the time Herodotus reached Egypt in 460-455 BC, the Egyptian Empire, as we know it, had long since vanished and those from whom he was seeking information were to a large extend, like our present day scholars in their mind set, ignorant of their more ancient past.

We have to accept his statement that there were hieroglyphic inscriptions written on the base of the Pyramid within reasonable distance from ground level to be discernable. His statement that "An inscription is cut upon it in Egyptian characters recording the amount spent on radishes, onions, and leeks for the laborers, and I remember distinctly that the interpreter who read me the inscription said that sum was 1600 talents of silver".

If these inscriptions were inscribed with sacred hieroglyphics, they would not be of a frivolous nature, but more than likely, in keeping with the peoples religious beliefs, sacred in nature, and not graffiti, as purported by some. It is doubtful if the priests of the temple would use the sacred writings for such a commonplace subject. However, the statement by Herodotus as to the meaning of the hieroglyphs would suggest that his interpreter lacked the ability of understanding the sacred hieroglyphic inscriptions.

It would be natural to reach such a conclusion in light of the explanation given by the interpreter as to the amounts of "radish's, onions, and leeks" consumed by the laborers. It is likely that Herodotus did not speak or understand the Egyptian language, and it is doubtful if the Egyptian priest understood or spoke the Greek language. In between was a translator, who being aware of the situation, took advantage of Herodotus' ignorance and offered an explanation to suit his needs. Furthermore, his many conversations with the priests is indicative of how far Egyptians had fallen into a society of superstitious fables of an imaginary past that bore no relation to the historic fabric of ancient times.

Nevertheless, what is of importance, Herodotus was physically at the Pyramids and speaking from visual knowledge? This is corroborated by his reference to one of the littlest of the three pyramids, purportedly built by the Pharaoh Chephren of which he states. "Chephren imitated the conduct of his predecessor (Cheops) and, like him, built a Pyramid, which did not, however, equal the dimensions of his brother's. Of this I am certain, for I measured them both myself".[1]

What we see today is a pile of stones, yet we marvel at the structure. This was not the case in the days of Herodotus. During his visit, all the Pyramids were intact and presented a wonderful sight to

---

1 Herodotus. *The Histories' Book 11. Pg 180. Translated by George Rawlinson.*

the visitor. He tells us "the pyramid itself was twenty years in building. It is square, eight hundred feet each way, and the height is the same, built entirely of polished stone, fitted together with the utmost care. The stones of which it is composed are none of them less than thirty feet in length".[1]

Although both modern day translators state the same dimensions, there exists a discrepancy of fort-five (45' 0") feet between the actual length of approximately seven, hundred and fifty-five (755' 0") [2] and the length of eight hundred (800' 0") as mentioned by Herodotus. It is obvious he did not measure in Egyptian cubits, perhaps in Greek feet? It is however, likely that he may have paced out the distance. Had he done so, his measurement may have been much closer to the actual length. Perhaps, this may just be one of the many questions that will remain unanswered. However, his statement that the Pyramid was eight hundred (800'. 0") in height is exaggerated, but understandable.

Any tourist viewing this massive structure for the first time would find it difficult to estimate its height. Even those with a trained eye would find it so. What we have is a simple statement from a man who was a seeker of knowledge. If the translation of his work is accurate, and I have no doubt that it is, we can dispense with all the theories regarding the properties of phi and the golden section which were properties purported to have been transmitted to Herodotus by the temple priest.(η/φ)

In his work, 'Secrets of the Great Pyramid' Peter Thompkins states, "The key to the geometrical and mathematical secret of the Pyramid, so long a puzzle to mankind, was actually handed to Herodotus by the temple Priest when they informed him that the pyramid was designed in such a way that the area of each of its faces was equal to the square of its height".[3] How Peter Tompkins arrived at this conclusion is in itself a mystery but could be attributed to an over active imagination. Herodotus was quite unequivocal when he stated, "It is square, eight hundred feet each way, and the height the same, built entirely of polished stone". [4]

If the translation of his works is correct, it is difficult to reconcile the mathematical hypothesis with the information supplied to Herodotus by the Temple priest. However, if later research into the properties indicated such advanced knowledge, it proves how advanced were those who built this magnificent structure.

It is also doubtful if Herodotus or the Egyptian priest was interested, or conversant with the mathematical properties of the pyramid. As a seeker of knowledge, he would be more interested in the history behind the creation of such a structure and not in its mathematical

---

1   "To build the Pyramid itself took twenty years; it is square at the base, its height (800) feet equal the length of each side; it is of polished stone blocks beautifully fitted, none of these blocks being less than thirty feet in length", Translator. Aubrey de Selincourt.

2   Thompkins. Peter. The secrets of the Great Pyramid Chapter XV The Golden Section. Pg 189. The actual dimensions of the Great Pyramid are as follows North Base Line 755'. 42". South base line 756'. 08". East Base Line 755'. 87". West Base Line 755'. 76". Height 475'. 5". Angle of Incline 51º30º36' Reference Ludwig Borchardt. Director of Egyptian Archaeology 1925.

3   Ibid

4   The History of Herodotus Translated by George Rawlinson
     Herodotus The Histories Penguin Classics Translated by Aubrey de Selincourt

properties. However, the information he bequeaths of its size and height are at variance with the information published today.

It's been suggested, "That not all of his information be taken on face value".[1] As our only source from those bygone days, we are left with little choice but to accept his words. Like all tourists and those seekers of knowledge, Herodotus would be curious as to how the Pyramid was built, and his only source of information would be the priests of the Temple. As a seeker of knowledge he would naturally turn to many sources for his information, but the many tales he tells attributing their source to the priests of the temple leaves one to question their authenticity.

The story he relates concerning the Pharaoh "Rhampsinitus" and his treasure house is such a case. From his description, we can assume that the Pharaoh is Ramses 11 of the nineteen dynasties, (1303-1200 BC). In his description of the statues he states that they were located "At the western gateway of the Temple of Vulcan, and the two statues that stand in front of the gateway, called by the Egyptians, one 'summer', and the other 'winter', each twenty-five cubits in height. The statue of 'summer', which is the northernmost of the two, is worshipped by the natives, and has offerings made to it; that of 'winter', which stands towards the South, is treated in exactly the contrary way".

It is surprising that the Temple priests would impart a fable of this nature. There is no reason to doubt Herodotus. What is suggestive is that Egyptian religion had deteriorated into superstition and idolatry. The same can be said of the tale in which 'Rhampsinitus' descended into Hades, "and played dice with Ceres".[2] Accepting the information as factual, he names Cheops, Pharaoh of the 4th Dynasty, (2613-2494 BC) purportedly the builder of the Great Pyramid, as successor to the Pharaoh Ramses 11 of the 19th Dynasty, (1303-1200 BC). He is being truthful in making this statement believing the information he received from the priests to be true. But, it is obvious that the priests lacked any knowledge of his countries past, except in myth and fable.

As the oldest account of Egypt, one would be inclined to believe what he imparts, but there are times when what he relates appears to be beyond logic. His description of the polished facing stone block as being thirty (30'.0") feet long and weighting approximately forty (40) tons would appear to be an exaggeration. However, because of our limitations in moving such a large stone object over a long distance, and moving it into its position without injuring its surface, doubts are cast upon his integrity. Our failings should not be reason to reject his description.

The facing stone block uncovered by Howard Vyse weighted approximately sixteen (16) tons.[3] Therefore, Herodotus description of the facing stone block may appear to be an exaggeration,

---

1   Ibid

2   Ceres. Roman Goddess of grain. Identified with the Greek God Demeter. Earth Goddess of fertility rites and of the dead.

3   Thompkins. Peter. Secrets of the Great Pyramid Solid limestone weights 152.84 Lbs per cubic foot. Dimension of stone blocks are as follows; Polished facing block uncovered by Howard Vyse, (5'0" x 8'.0" x 12'. 00")-(5'0" x 4'.0" x 12'.0")= 240 cubic feet. Inner core blocks. 2'.4" x 4'. 2" x 4'.2". =40.71 cubic feet. Polished stone block described by Herodotus as being thirty (30) feet long, 600 cubic feet.

but not impossible. We are at times amazed at the many cyclopean structures erected by ancient civilizations in honor of their god's, therefore, the moving and erecting of stone monoliths weighting thirty to seventy tons should come as no surprise.

There is sufficient physical evidence available on which to base a reasonable hypothesis. The weight of the stone monoliths incorporated into the structure of the pyramid. Those that make up the core, the polished facing block uncovered by Howard Vyse, the lintels above the 'Kings Chamber, and the polished stone facing block described by Herodotus as being thirty feet in length.

Like any gullible tourist Herodotus was prone to believing any tale told to him by the priests, believing them to be the truth. It would however, be wrong to dismiss all that he tells us. There is truth in his writings to which we must pay attention if we are to have any understanding of his times.

What is clear is that his informants are apparently of the priestly castes, which because of their position lend truth to the matters under discussion. From these discussions, it is obvious that those to whom he was speaking were less knowledgeable regards the antiquity of their country than the purported experts of the eighteen century and those of today.

What was the purpose of those early explorers of the Great Pyramid? For the early Greeks it was a structure to be admired, and studied. For the early Arabs of the eight-century it was a place to be plundered for a treasure that never existed except in the imagination of storytellers, for the Englishman John Greaves, a place where one could obtain knowledge and for the French, a place of wonder and mystery to be recorded for posterity.

However, for the English who followed, were more bent on destruction in order to satisfy their curiosity rather than for scholarly pursuits. The tourist who out of ignorance continued the work of destruction that was commenced by the early English and Italian explorers followed these.

The gravediggers and robbers have gone and Archaeology has matured to being a profession and not a holiday pursuit for the rich. Discoveries continue to be made that at times result in history having to be rewritten. And as each new piece of evidence emerges, our admiration for these people increases. Nevertheless, from the ongoing excavations, it is evident that our Archaeologist is only scratching the surface of what was once a great civilization. Who knows what lies beneath the sands of Egypt? Will our experts ever penetrate the many mysteries of these ancient people? Only time will tell.

What can be ascertained is that longevity this great civilization can be attributed to their religious belief in a god who was all purity and truth. This profound belief enabled this culture to bridge each age uninterrupted by political or religious turmoil until the reign of the Pharaoh Akhenaton. From the events that followed his downfall, it is evident that the priest of the temple had become a corrupt institution, more politicized in their religious practice. The brief renaissance experienced in the reign of Ramses 11, was not religious, but political and self-serving, therefore, unsustainable. Our Western culture had to wait until the twelfth century to see an upsurge in religious fervor in the construction of the many Cathedrals' dedicated to this God of purity and truth, initiated by the Cistercian Order of Monks. But like all organizations there existed an element of self-serving political and financial gain.

Will our culture experience a repeat of such a program? I very much doubt if he would be capable of producing buildings. Modern man lacks the discipline of mind and dedication of purpose for an undertaking of this magnitude. The sterile mediocrity of our present day Art and Architecture is an indication of modern mans inability to carry out such works and a legacy bequeath to future generations.,

Chapter 19

in addition to the great Pyramid, there is another mystery that has generated more than enough interest in the Western hemisphere and that is the Temple of Stonehenge, located on the Salisbury Plain, just outside the town of Amesbury, Wiltshire, England.

This recumbent group of stones has been the subject of prolonged controversy over the years by the academic world and those who see in Stonehenge some mystical spiritual force. The opinions expressed from the minds of academia and those with an avid interest in the occult have been many and varied, and like those of the Great Pyramid, rang from the sublime to the ridiculous. There are also those, who suffering from an overextended imagination, suggests Stonehenge was a cenotaph built at the behest of the King of Britain who "commanded his magician Merlin should bring great stones from Ireland to build Stonehenge".[1] While some would suggest that the "first stones were set up in about 1,900 BC by primitive farming communities living on the Wiltshire Downs for the purpose of burials"[2]

It's fascinating[3] how definitive is the many and varied theories put forward by the experts. Rather than prefix their theories with "I don't know but" having no other explanation they would have us believe that these ancient people possessed telekinetic powers, which enabled them to move these huge stone monoliths.

It's also strange that the theories offered are in general without a valid explanation and inclined to stretch the imagination.[4] However, one critic has the answer to those who involve themselves in the conundrum that is Stonehenge when he states, "Most of what is written about Stonehenge is nonsense or speculation—No one will ever have a clue what its significance was"[5]; so speaks academia.

Nevertheless, his statement may have some merit when one considers the amount of speculation that surrounds Stonehenge. Nonetheless, when the hyperbole and exaggerations are

---

1   *Burl Aubrey Rings of Stone Published by Frances Lincoln London.*
2   *The Last Two Million Years Published by the Readers Digest Association Ltd*
3
4   *An example of which is the stone lintels of the Sarsen Circle. It is naïve to believe that such precision was achieved by the use of stone mauls.*
5   *Atkinson R.J.C Archaeologist of the University College, Cardiff*

removed what is left is that Stonehenge was constructed for a defined purpose. The extensive survey carried out by Professor Gerald Hawkins proves beyond doubt that it is an Astronomical structure. Therefore the question of 'why' it was built has been answered; the how it was built remains a mystery. The remaining question of 'when' it was built presents somewhat of a problem. It has been expressed that determining the age of a structure "cannot be accomplished by Astrology, but by Archaeology". This is in my opinion unsound reasoning, especially in the case of Stonehenge and does nothing to arrive at the truth.

The Egyptians were noted for their reliance on Astronomy in locating their Temples. Therefore, determining the age of a structure within reasonable limits by the use of Astronomy has been the determining factor in dating some of the more ancient Temples in Egypt, therefore there is no reason why the same principals cannot be applied to the structure that is Stonehenge. Archaeology is a tool, which has its limitations and is prone to preconceived ideas dictated by ones environment and religious beliefs and doctrinaire their views to the detriment of reason.

If the structure was constructed for the purpose of determining the rotation of the seasons for the benefit of an agrarian culture there were much simpler ways of watching the arrival of the seasons as we see from the many stone circles across Europe. Why such a sophisticated structure that by itself would be of little use to the farmers of Scotland or for that matter anyone outside the environs of Wiltshire.

Logic suggests that there had to be another reason for such an extraordinary structure. One can envisage the many years spent watching the heavens gathering information, and the many years spent in construction and on completion its workings and purpose only known to a few; for what purpose? Who would benefit from this information? And why Salisbury Plain, why not North Africa where the weather is clear, free of heavy clouds and variable weather patterns as one finds in England. It would suggest that location was all important and that there was a higher purpose behind the construction and may perhaps be more related to time and the earth's rotation than agrarian purposes.

Today the arrival of the seasons comes like clockwork, spring Equinox March 21st, Mid-Summer Day June 21st, Autumn Equinox September 21st, Mid-Winter Day December 21st, as their arrival can fluctuate between the 20th and the 22nd we will use the 21st for ease of explanation.

Having established that important point it would suggest that the same conditions that exist today would have to be in place at the time of Stonehenge construction for it to fulfill its function of predicting the seasons. This however presents a problem.

Checking the movement of the Sun back to the year 2,600 BC the arrival of the Equinoxes did not occur on the dates mentioned as we experience to day. The conditions that exist today at Stonehenge did not manifest themselves until the year 200 AD; it would therefore be foolhardy to suggest that Stonehenge was built in the year 200 AD.

Is it a coincidence that Stonehenge manifests the attributes of the seasonal rotation we experience today; I very much doubt it. The precision to which it was built negates such a theory. So the question remains, when was it built? It has been suggested that Stonehenge was constructed in three phases over a period of 650 years, phase one is said to have occurred between the years 2,350-1900.BC. Speculation regards the date is of no matter, it is safe to assume that during this period the construction of the outer bank would be a priority, which would be followed by the tracking of the Moons cycle as evidenced by the 56 Aubrey Holes. The seasonal rotation of the Equinoxes and Solstices would be deferred to another day.

However, during this period between 2,350 and 1900 BC the Spring Equinox arrived between the intervening years ranging from April 7th to the 13th; Summer Solstice from July 10th to the 16th, Autumn Equinox on from October 9th to the -14th and the Winter Solstice from January 5th to the 10th therefore would not be favorable to establishing the seasonal cycles as we recognize today.

Phase two is purported to have occurred during the period 1,900-1,700 BC. In this cycle as it was during the period between 2,350-1,900 BC the Spring Equinox appeared during the month of April from the 5th to the 7th, the Summer Solstice from July 8th to the 10th, Autumn Equinox from October 7th to the 9th, and the Winter Solstice from January 4th to the 5th.

Phase three is purported to have occurred between 1,700-1,350 BC, again as in the previous years the arrival of the Equinoxes and the Solstices arrived in the months of April, July, October and January. Months which are not conducive to the planting and harvesting of crops?

At no time over this long period could those who constructed this marvelous structure been capable of laying out their work to predict the seasonal cycles in which the Equinoxes arrive on March 21st and September 21st, and the Solstices arrive in June 21st and December 21st if these conditions did not exist at the time of its construction. It would be foolish to suggest that these ancient people were knowledgeable enough to predict the movement of the Sun and the Moon thousands of years into the future. It therefore follows that if Stonehenge was constructed as a seasonal calendar, it cannot have been constructed between the years 2,600- 1750 BC the dates purported by the experts but at some early date when conditions existed as they do today, so let us discard this piece of antler horn and look to the planets for an answer.

The seasonal phenomenon that is unique to Stonehenge first manifest itself in the year 200 AD when the Spring Equinox and Autumn Equinox arrived on March 21st and September 21st respectfully and has continued down through time to the present and will continue until the year 7,500 AD at which time it will go into regression to begin another cycle of time.

Again it must be emphasized that if Stonehenge was constructed to act as a seasonal calendar, which unquestionably it is, its date construction had to be somewhere around 40,000 BC when the conditions that manifest themselves today were in extant and not 2,600 BC as hypothesized by the experts.

Among the many theories put forward one would appear to answer all questions when the author takes a quantum leap by attributing the dimensions of the circle at Stonehenge to that of the New Jerusalem as envisaged by St, John in the Book of Revelation, [1]suggesting "that of all

---

1   *New Jerusalem Bible John 21: 15-18*

the ancient monuments that which can be most certainly identified as an example of the cosmic temple is Stonehenge".[1] One could say as much for the Great Pyramid of Giza in Egypt.

Intriguing supposition if it were true, however, the dimensions of the New Jerusalem attributed to the Apostle John are simple and to the point. However, associating these structures with the geometrical ratio of the square and the circle has merit when examined

In the Book of Revelation it is written that the dimensions of the plan of the New Jerusalem is perfectly square and a cube, its length the same as its breath, "twelve thousand furlongs in length, and in breath, and equal in height.

The angel measured the wall and it was one hundred and forty-four

There is nothing mysterious or strange in the imponderable when reading the Bible regards the authorship of the Book of Revelations and the time in which it was written.[2]

The Imperial method of measure did not exist in the first century AD therefore the mention of the furlong in the description of the New Jerusalem brings the whole issue into question and would suggest that this piece of the New Testament was written at a much later date or a copyist error.

Taking these dimensions literally, we have a cube of one thousand, five hundred miles in length, breath, and height. Confusion is created when the Angel measure the height of the wall which is "one hundred and forty-four cubits high". Exegetes suggest that the dimensions are symbolic and have no meaning other than to suggest that they allude to "immensity"...[3]

The dimensions of the New Jerusalem and those of Stonehenge have nothing in common which would suggest a relationship with the exception that one is square and the other is circular. However, if one combines the two, a square and a circle which are commensurate it becomes clear that we are dealing with geometrical proportions.

It is only through the manipulation of numbers that one arrives at the esoteric knowledge associated with the squaring of the circle, suggested by the author. If one had to make a case any square superimposed on a circle will arrive at the same result but not necessarily the dimensions, which would develop the squaring of the circle?[4] However, the theory does deserve our admiration as it blends all that haunts the human psychic with religious overtones and satisfies the need for mystery when dealing with the ancient past. Once again, religion been allowed to take precedence over common sense. The only feature common to both is that they have been co-opted into the realm of mysticism to satisfy the need of those who need assurance to support their religious beliefs.

Individuals who indulge in looking for mysteries where none exist must be wary of those who insist on associating the writings of the New Testament with this ancient structure who like

---

1   *Ibid*

2   *There are doubts as to the year in which the Book of Revelations was compiled, however, it is the opinion that it could have occurred either in the year 70 AD, or 95 AD.*

3   *New Jerusalem Bible John 21: 15-18*

4   *A system of measure in which the circumference of the circle equals the sum of the four sides of the perimeter of the square*

all religious allow their minds to take flights fancy and develop theories which are at variance with the information available.

I very much doubt if the builders of Stonehenge looked upon their work as being associated with religious overtones or as being mysterious. It was a work of precision and a definitive purpose more associated with Astronomy than religion. Although Mr. Mitchell's book makes interesting reading, his many conclusions become irrelevant when he introduces Christianity and Judaism into his work, both of these religions were and are a myth based upon much older pagan cults, which were widespread in the Middle East and have corrupted rather than enhanced history. We must not however deny that our ancient ancestors were unacquainted with the geometrical properties of the square and the circle.

Nevertheless it is an interesting hypothesis, however, the conclusions arrived at would require a leap of imagination far beyond the capabilities of the average person.[1] Also associating Stonehenge with the Squaring of the Circle,[2] may at first appear fanciful, however, have merit if one, moves away from measuring with the foot and inch, a system of measure that did not exist in ancient times, to a system of measure that was extant during the purported time of construction.

In the time of which we speak there were other systems of measure extent in the sacred hieroglyphics of ancient Mycenae, Egypt and India. If we accept the idea that the builders of Stonehenge were conversant with the squaring of the circle, we must also accept that they were conversant with the cultures of Egypt, Sumeria, Mycenae, India and possibly China.

The Greeks and the people of the British Isles were not sufficiently advanced in Astrology and Mathematics to warrant consideration. It could be said that in the case of the British Isles, with the exception of the occasional tribal raid society was relatively serene and free of strife, however the many stone circles discovered across the British Isles the most notable of which New Grange in Ireland[3] would indicate a people who were thirsty for Astronomical knowledge and went to extraordinary lengths to determine the rotation of the seasons.

This would open up a case as to who were the builders of this magnificent structure and when it was built? The technology of the computer has put to rest the speculation as to its purpose. Accepting the work of Gerald Hawkins,[4] the why it was built is self evident to track the seasons and most importantly, to determine the movements of the celestial bodies, especially the Moon and the Sun. However, accepting the findings of Mr. Hawkins raises a multitude of questions that requires answers.

---

1   Mitchell. John. 'City of Revelation' Published by Ballantine Books. NY.
    A corpus of esoteric knowledge found in Hindu mythology, and in Sacred Geometry Mitchell. John. 'City of Revelation' Published by Ballantine Books. NY.
2   A corpus of esoteric knowledge found in Hindu mythology, and in Sacred Geometry.
3   Brennan Martin The Stars and the Stones Ancient Art and Astronomy in Ireland Published by Thames and Hudson London
4   Hawkins Gerald S Stonehenge Decoded Published by Fontana/Collins

One would question why our ancestors went to such lengths to build this magnificent dimensional structure when the same knowledge could have been achieved with a couple of stones located across the horizon, as we see in the stone circles of Scotland, Ireland, and other locations in Europe. It is an interesting phenomenon that the properties attributed to Stonehenge can be found at other Astrological ruins in the Americas. One such Indian ruin is located in the Chaco Canyon in New Mexico in addition to those Temples in South America.

The only conclusion one can reach concerning the 'why' is that the knowledge of the Moon cycles and the seasonal arrival of the Sun which determine the seasons was not known, and the calendar needed to be correlated, and transcribe in permanent stone for posterity. This information relative to the seasons would be vitally important to an agrarian culture, but more important would be the restoration of time, which for some reason had been disrupted by some cataclysmic upheaval. This theory may appear farfetched but is as valid as the many that have been put forward by the experts.

That it later became a Temple of worship would be a natural outcome to a people who, with the exception of the priests, had no understanding of its function. There is every reason to believe this may have been the case.

In this context the author may be correct in his surmise regards Stonehenge being a Temple, however, to associate Stonehenge with Christianity through the manipulation of numbers and the process of numerology is somewhat implausible. Nowhere in the Revelations of John is there a circle; this is left to the imagination of those who wish to see some form of esoteric knowledge in his writings.[1]

If one were to believe that there is a source of esoteric knowledge associated with the dimensions of the New Jerusalem, which is prefigured by the number, twelve they would enter into a world of myth and fantasy. There are those who see in the dimensions of the New Jerusalem hidden knowledge known only to a chosen few. It is only by a giant leap of imagination that they reach this conclusion.[2]

One has to be realistic when it comes to making claims based on a weak foundation. The introduction of the Christianity weakens, rather than strengthens Mr. Mitchell's hypothesis, the method of measure incorporated in the stone circles needs researching.

It would however be interesting to ask if the builders of Stonehenge were knowledgeable of the geometrical properties of the squaring of the circle.[3] If we allow our imagination to take flight and accept the Mycenaean foot as the method of measure, there are good grounds to

---

1   *New Jerusalem Bible John 21:16-17. 'The plan of the city is perfectly square 12,000 furlongs in length and breath, and equal in height. He measured the wall, and this was a hundred and forty-four cubits high- the angel was using the ordinary cubit'.*

2   *People will see what they wish to see, and hear what they wish to hear, so it is with the religious sect of the Jehovah's Witnesses who believe that the measure of 144 cubits high refers to the number of souls that will be saved come the end of the world.*

3   *Ibid*

belief so. Accepting such a hypothesis would require historians and Archaeologist to amend their thinking and revise what has been written regarding this structure.

No doubt the theory surrounding the "Squaring of the Circle' has transcended time and was known too many ancient societies, perhaps St John, having this knowledge, used its properties to pre-figure the 'New Jerusalem' to fulfill the expectations of the newly converted Jewish people to the new teachings developed by Paul and the Apostles. Therefore, to combine the many myths developed and perpetrated by the Catholic Church of Rome brings into question Mr Mitchell's proposition.

Moreover, the dimensions of the various elements of Stonehenge as suggested by Mr. Mitchell would indicate that these ancient people of Britain were conversant with the inch, the foot, and the yard as measuring tools, as this system of measure did not exist in 2,600 BC and if by chance it was extant in the British Isles, which is most unlikely it was not the system of measure incorporated into the Stonehenge structure.[1]

The measuring methods available during this period, were the Babylon cubit, the Egyptian Royal Cubit, the Egyptian Standard Cubit, and the Mycenaean foot?[2] Could any one of these systems have been used? Some may say it is unlikely, as none of these systems is proportionate to the surveyed dimensions, but would this be a correct conclusion. When one evaluates the dimensions of Stonehenge, of all the methods of measure available, only that of Mycenaean foot appears the most likely. The Greeks were not sufficiently advanced to warrant consideration. What was to become the Greek Foot was derived from the Babylonian and Egyptian Cubit. As regard to the English imperial system, although the inch may be classed as very ancient the imperial system of measure was derived from the Greek and Roman foot.

Those who built Stonehenge were exact in the design of the structure; each stone had its place and function, with no room for error. This was not a case of just inscribing a circle, and building accordingly. This circle had a purpose; therefore, the design had to project the sacredness of its dimensions to ensure success. It is therefore reasonable to suggest that the two important circles would be the 56 holes of the Aubrey Circle, and the Sarsen Circle. No doubt the Bluestone Circle and the Horseshoe semi circle have some significance, however, we will concentrate on the Aubrey and Sarsen circles.

Once again, religion been allowed to take precedence over common sense. The only feature common to both is that they have been co-opted into the realm of mysticism to satisfy the need of those who need assurance to support their religious believes. Those who indulge in looking for mysteries where none exist must be wary of those who participated in compiling the Books of the New Testament who like all religious allowed their minds to take flights of fancy

---

1   2,600 BC the purported date established by the experts as the date Stonehenge was built
2   The Babylon Cubit = (20³¹/³²) 20.97 "inch's. (532.64 mm) The Egyptian Royal Cubit = 20, 66"inch's. (525 mm) The Egyptian Standard Cubit = (17¾") 17.75"inch's. (450.85 mm) The Mycenaean Foot = 10.923"inch's. (277.4488 mm)

The survey carried out by Gerald Hawkins established the dimensions of the outer rim of the Sarsen Circle as being 100' 10" analogous with the dimension developed by Mr. Mitchell on which he based his New Jerusalem theory.[1] However, are not based upon the diameter of the inner circle, which one would assume would be the more important dimension, as would the dimension of the Aubrey Circle.

The care and precision extended on the shaping of the surface of the inner circle of lintels is an indication of how important the shaping of the circle was to this structure. Therefore, the dimension taken by Mr. Mitchell for the purpose of establishing the principals of squaring the circle is a little short of the mark. If one were to inspect the various methods of measure extant during the years in which Stonehenge is alleged to have been built, the systems prevalent during this period, only the Mycenaean foot of 10.93" (277.4488 mm) or the Egyptian Standard Cubit of 450mm fits the criteria. Nevertheless, it must be emphasized that even in this case the dimensions are not exact, a requirement if one were to present a case for consideration.

The survey gives the dimensions to be as follows, which are all within a reasonable tolerance. However in the case of the Aubrey circle of holes we have two measurements given 285' 00" feet and 288' 00" feet.[2] One would assume that the measured diameter of 288' 00" would be the more correct of the two; however, this may not be the case. Although it is the preferred measure by many, the survey by Gerald Hawkins suggests that 285' 00" is the correct measure. It may be prudent to work on both measures to ensure accuracy.

1) Aubrey Circle Diameter 288' 00" relative to the Egyptian Standard Cubit of 450 mm (17²³/₃₂").
   a) Diameter 288' 00" x 0.3048=877.83mm÷450mm = 195.07 Egyptian Standard cubits.
   b) Circumference 195 x 3.142 = 612.84 Egyptian Standard cubits

2) Aubrey Circle Diameter of 288'.00" relative to the Egyptian Royal Cubit of 20.5625"
   a) Diameter 288'.00"x12=3456"÷20.5625=168.07 Royal Cubits
   b) Circumference 168.07x3.1412=528.02 Royal Cubits

1

2   *Hawkins Gerald S Stonehenge Decoded Published by Souvenir Press Ltd. "They (the Aubrey Holes) formed a very accurately measured circle 288 feet in diameter"*
    Hawkins Gerald S beyond Stonehenge Published by Harper & Row NY "Stonehenge 1 is the earliest, crudest structure, yet it contains the perfect circle of the Aubrey Holes, 285 feet in diameter"

3) Aubrey Circle Diameter of 288'.00" relative to the Mycenaean foot of 277.4488 mm[1] (10.93")
   a) Diameter 288' 00" x0.3048 mm =877.824mm÷277.4488 mm= 316.39 Mycenaean feet
   b) Circumference 316.39 x 3.142 =993.97 Mycenaean feet

4) Aubrey Circle Diameter of 285' 00" relative to the Egyptian Standard Cubit of 450 mm
   a) Diameter 285'00" x 0.3048mm=868.68mm÷0.450 mm =193.04 Egyptian Standard cubits.
   b) Circumference 193.00 X 3.142 = 606.33 Egyptian Standard Cubit

5) Aubrey Circle Diameter of 285".00 relative to the Egyptian Royal Cubit of 20.5625"
   a) Diameter 285'.00" x12=3420"÷20.5625=166.32 Royal Cubits
   b) Circumference 166.32x3.1412=522.52 Royal Cubits

6) Aubrey Circle of 285' relative to the Mycenaean foot of 277.4488mm
   a) Diameter 285' 00"x0.3048mm=868.68mm÷277.4488mm =313.09 Mycenaean Feet,
   b) Circumference 313' 00" X 3.142 =983' 32" Mycenaean Feet

7) Sarsen Circle Inner Diameter 97' 4" relative to the Egyptian Standard Cubit of 450mm
   a) Diameter of Inner circle 97' 4" x 0.3048mm=2966.6mm÷ 450mm = 65.93 Egyptian Standard Cubit
   b) Circumference 66.00 X 3.142=207.35 Egyptian Standard Cubit

8) Sarsen Circle Inner Diameter of 97'4" relative the Egyptian Royal Cubit of 20.5625"
   a) Diameter 97'4"x12=1168"÷20.5625=56.81 Royal Cubits
   b) Circumference 56.81x3.1412=178.45 Royal Cubits

9) Sarsen Circle relative to the Mycenaean foot of 277.4488 mm
   a) Diameter 97' 4" x 0.3048mm=296.67mm÷277.4488mm = 106.93 Mycenaean Feet.
   b) Circumference 107.00 X 3.142 =336 15 Mycenaean Feet

---

1   *Tompkins Peter. Secrets of the Great Pyramid Publish by Colophon Books NY*

10) Diameter to the center of the Sarsen stone lintel 99' 1" relative to the Egyptian Standard Cubit of 450mm
   a) Diameter 99' 1" x 0.3048mm=301.99÷450mm = 67.11 Egyptian Standard cubits.
   b) Circumference 67.11 X 3.142 = 210.86 Egyptian Standard Cubits

11) Diameter to the center of the Sarsen stone lintel 99'.1" relative to the Mycenaean foot
   a) Diameter 99' 1" x0.3048mm=302mm÷277.4488 = 108.85 Mycenaean feet.
   b) Circumference 109. 00 X 3.142 = 342.43 Mycenaean Feet

12) Diameter of the outer rim of the Sarsen Stone circle 100' 10"relative to the Egyptian Standard Cubit
   a) Diameter 100' 10" x 0.3048mm=307.34mm÷450mm = 68.302 Egyptian cubits.
   b) Circumference 68.3 X 3.142 =21.457 Egyptian Standard Cubits

13) Diameter of the outer rim of the Sarsen Stone circle relative to the Egyptian Royal Cubit
   a) Diameter 100'.10" x 12=1210"÷20.5625=58.84 Royal Cubits
   b) Circumference 58.54x3.1412=184.86 Royal Cubits

14) Diameter of the Sarsen Circle relative to the Mycenaean foot[1]
   a) Diameter 100' 00"x0.3048mm=307.34mm÷277.4488mm=110.77 Mycenaean feet
   b) Circumference 110.77x3.142=348.00 Mycenaean feet

It may have no significance, however, if one considers the rules of Gematria as outlined by Mr Mitchell the circumference of Aubrey Holes in Mycenaean feet 313' 0" X 3.142= 983.0[2] may take on an important nuance.

Allowing our imagination to lead us we see that if we multiply each of these numbers, 9 X 8 X 3 = we have a total of 216, adding a Zero gives 2160 which is the diameter of the moon in miles. This may be of some significance when one considers that the 56 Aubrey Holes are the different phases of the moon in its 18.6-year cycle.

As it will be seen we have a choice in our selection between the Egyptian Standard Cubit, and the Mycenaean Foot relative to the diameters of the Aubrey and Sarsen Circles.

If we accept the Mycenaean foot as the method of measure, it is seen that of the methods mentioned, this meets the need of complete measure within reasonable tolerance i.e., diameter

---

1   *Lawlor Robert. Sacred Geometry "Squaring the Circle" To construct a square which is virtually equal in perimeter to the circumference of a given circle, which is virtually equal in area to the area of a given circle Because the circle is an incommensurable figure based on (3.1415927), it is impossible to draw a square more than approximately equal to it.*

2   *Aubrey Holes 56 holes, diameter 5'.00", 11'.00" c/c, 3'00" deep, diameter of circle 285' 0"*

to face of inner circle, 107 Mycenaean feet, diameter to center of Sarsen Lintel 109 Mycenaean feet, diameter of outer rim of Sarsen circle 111 Mycenaean feet, diameter of Aubrey holes, 313 Mycenaean feet.

Only the Mycenaean Foot gives the accuracy that is not evident in the other systems of measure. However, if one were to accept the theory developed by Professor Alexandria Thom that there existed in ancient times a measure which he classed as the megalithic yard of 2.72 feet. Accepting this method of measure, the outer rim of the Sarsen stone circle has a diameter of 37 megalithic yards.[1] However, when evaluated against other measures have no significance to the overall structure.

What has not been considered by those who use the dimensions of Stonehenge to create an aura of mystique, is that in the year 2600 BC, as we have already stated, there was no sophisticated English method of measure, it did not exist, the units of, the inch, the foot, and the yard, was a method later derived from the Romans.[2]

What was the form of measure used by our ancestors? Perhaps the crudest, based upon the basic measures found in the human frame? How often have we heard the expression relative to the 'rule of thumb', which measured approximately one inch? There are numerous areas of the human body, which were common among the people in determining every day measurements. However, what is certain is that in the year 2600 BC there was no standard measurement and there were no stone building or Temples in the British Isles, as one would find in Mycenae, and other cities of the Near and Middle East during the same period.

In general, the habitat of the people in Britain was of the most basic construction, mainly of wattles and mud. If Stonehenge could be classed as a building, it was the first constructed stone building in the British Isles. . It is probable that people of this period method of measure was by the rule of thumb, by pacing out the distance between two points, or as is used by those in the clothing industry, with arms outstretched, the width from finger tip, to fingertip

Exact measurements would be of little concern to these people in everyday life, the demarcation of the land would be more important; therefore, the precision of measure would be of little concern to our Neolithic ancestors. Therefore, the precision with which Stonehenge was built negates the theory of those who presume that a farming people of the Neolithic Age built Stonehenge

In addition, the dimensions established by the survey, are not conducive to the squaring of the circle if the imperial measure of the foot and inch are used. This can only be accomplished by whole numbers, which is more conducive to the Mycenaean foot.

In his book on Sacred Geometry, Robert Lawler expresses the circle circumscribing the square as $2\pi\sqrt{\Phi} = 2 \times 3.1415927 \times 1.272 = 7.992217$. Again not exact, but close enough to the perimeter of a square of eight inches. However, the picture changes if we, for a moment, give our

---

1   *Thom. Alexander 'The Megalithic Unit of Length' Journal of the Royal Society of Statistics*
2   *Understanding Weights and Measures in Archaeology*
      Anglo-Saxon Weights and Measures Classic Encyclopaedia

ancestors the benefit of the doubt and believe that they were conversant with the principals of squaring the circle, and incorporated this into the design of Stonehenge. Let us further suppose that the actual dimension was intended to be one hundred (100' 0") feet.

In the case of Stonehenge there would appear to be three major circles, with one half circle i.e. a horseshoe inclosing the 'alter stone'. However, were we to accept the outer diameter of the Sarsen Circle as being a hundred (100') feet the result becomes quite clear, in accordance with the squaring of the circle? Circumference = 100'. 0" x 3.1415927 = 314'. 1415927", (= 3.1415927).

When one evaluates the precision with which the Sarsen Circle was constructed, it is difficult to reconcile this hypothesis with a circle whose outer diameter is 100' 10" or for that matter 37 Megalithic yards.

However, were we to take 111.0 Mycenaean feet, as the outer diameter of the Sarsen circle and count it as one, the squaring of the circle becomes evident; $1x\pi = 3.1415927 = 3.1415927$, (circumference four hundred and forty four (444'0") Mycenaean feet).

This being so, it would open up a case as to who were the builders of this magnificent structure and when it was built; certainly not our ancient British farmer. Perhaps the outline of the Mycenaean dagger or sword head sculptured into the face of one of the monoliths was the signature of the builders. This one particular piece of evidence has been neglected by the many experts over the years.

Accepting this hypothesis makes a case in favor of our ancestors possessing the necessary knowledge regards the squaring of the circle. It must also be noted that within the inner embankment circle are positioned the fifty-six Aubrey Holes which appear to be all but forgotten by those who have written extensively on Stonehenge.

If we could but for a moment transport our minds back in time to that moment when this dedicated group of men arrived on Salisbury Plains to survey the landscape and chose the site for this marvelous enterprise. They were not ignorant of the task ahead; they knew that what they were about to accomplish would take generations of dedication and patience.

Putting aside the minutiae, which is the hallmark of the specialists we can with a little imagination, take part in their operation and become part of the specialized crew whose job would be to build the great ditch that would protect the chosen site. It would be safe to say that before the first shovel of chalk was moved, these amazing people had a finished plan ready to be executed.

Inscribing the circle for the protection of the Aubrey Holes had to be done to precision if it were to meet the need for the fifty-six holes. This was the beginning of an enterprise that would take perhaps hundreds of years to accomplish. There would be no positioning of the postholes until the cyclical rotation of the moon had been established. How long would this take, those of us who have been exposed to the vagaries of English weather appreciate the difficulty of following the Moons progress across the heavens? It has been suggested that to complete this one exercise may perhaps have taken from seventy-four to one hundred and eleven years.

We can infer from the precision of the structure that no work would commence until all information had been checked and crossed checked for accuracy. The rising and setting of the sun would be less arduous and be accomplished in less time than the moon cycles. But again no work would commence until the findings were checked and crossed checked, a slow and tedious process but necessary for the finished product. These were no ordinary men but an order of people who were well versed in Mathematics and Astrology.

Quite recently, attempts were made on a minor scale to emulate the work of the people who built these structures, and on each occasion resulted in failure. Of the many attempts, to which we can refer, was the attempted re-construction of the stones at Stonehenge by the Ministry of public works and Buildings[1].

One would assume that the setting up of a 40-ton irregular surfaced megalithic stone would be an easy task for the modern equipment then available. Such was not the case. The task proved extremely difficult for the equipment to handle, and despite the modern scientific instruments used in placing the monolith, "no guarantees were given that it was positioned as the ancient people had intended,"[2]

Also the attempts to demonstrate the methods by which the stones were transported from the stone quarries in Wales to Stonehenge proved quite difficult and not very successful, despite the stones being a fraction of the weight of the original.[3]

When one considers the difficulties encountered by those who participated in these exercises, brings into question the many theories of the experts that Stonehenge was during its history dismantled, rearranged, and re-modeled by our ancient ancestors on more than one occasion. Based on no discernable evidence other than conjecture, one such theory suggests that an ancient society whom Archaeologists refer to as the 'Beaker' people were responsible for these modifications. Traces of their presence have been found from the Isle of Malta in the Mediterranean, France, Spain, and Ireland.

The many locations give evidence of their presence; however, there is no evidence to suggest that these people involved themselves in building stone structures. Nor is there any available evidence, which would suggest their involvement in Astronomy. Therefore, to suggest that these people, on their return from Ireland, transported between sixty, to eighty Rhyolite, and spotted Dolerite Bluestones, each weighing four tons, over a distance of 180 miles is questionable.[4]

Why? What would be their purpose? The work had been completed. The various phases of the moon had been determined, as evidenced by the 56 Aubrey Holes. The arrival of the Mid-Summer Solstice had been determined. The original builders accomplished all this over

1   Hawkins. Gerald S. 'Beyond Stonehenge' Published by Harper & Row. London.
2   Ibid
3   A 1954 BBC Documentary showing a reconstruction of how these ancient people transported the massive stones across country by a group of senior schoolboys. Using wooden rollers, ropes, and brute strength, their task was to pull a stone weighing 112 Lbs. A futile exercise when one considers that the stones transported by our ancestor's weight 9000 lbs each.
4   Stonehenge Tourist Information, Amesbury and Stonehenge,
    Alaster Service/Jean Bradbury A Guide to the Megaliths of Europe. Stonehenge

a long period. Why the Beaker people or for that matter the local farmers go to the trouble of enhancing what was already a marvel of construction. Lifting, moving about, and rearranging irregular monoliths the size and weight we see at Stonehenge would be a horrendous exercise for a people who had little but the most rudimentary tools.

An exercise of a similar nature was carried out on Easter Island in the South Pacific where attempts were made by qualified Engineers, and trained manpower, to re-erect the statues, that are quite widespread on the island. Using tools and methods, which our modern day Archaeologist assumed were used by the ancient people their many attempts met with failure.

Similar attempts have been in Egypt by teams of professional Engineers from Japan and North America to determine the methods by which the Pyramids were constructed by the ancient Egyptians and failed. Evaluating the efforts of these trained professionals, one wonders if our experts are correct in the surmise regards the methods used by our ancestors in their construction practices. If our present day experts cannot perform to the same standards, how then did our ancestors accomplish these Herculean tasks?

Other then satisfying their curiosity, and gaining valuable experience that will be a rewarding memory for the future, those who participated in these exercises proved how advanced these ancient people were in the construction activities. The methods used, is a puzzle that has taxed the minds of the experts, and will continue to do so for a great many years to come.

As one prominent author stated, "The astronomical, mathematical, and geodetic science of the ancient Egyptians, their cosmology and theology are only beginning to be appreciated."[1] This expressed view could apply to all of the ancient civilizations known to us today.

In the case of Stonehenge it has been said, "That to see Stonehenge intelligently one should concentrate on the definite evidence which scientific exploration can lay before him to-day".[2] However, basing ones findings on the carbon dating of a piece of charcoal, and a segment of antler horn, that could have been discarded at a much later date, tends to confuse, rather than clarify the age of this structure.

There can be no doubt as to the true purpose of Stonehenge. Scientists tell us the rationale of Stonehenge. That it became a religious center in later years may be attributing to a people who were ignorant of its true purpose. However, like a great many ancient structures around the world, the 'why' the 'how' and the 'when' are answers that still elude our scientific community.

Extensive research has confirmed that it was constructed to act as an Astronomical Observatory. The work carried out by Gerald S. Hawkins[3] should leave no doubt in the minds of scholars as to the true purpose of this amazing structure. Although not all members of the scientific community are in agreement with his findings; basing their objections on the theory that, "it required too much sophistication in the accumulation and passing on of data for the

---

1   *Tompkins. Peter. Secrets of the Great Pyramid.*
2   *H.M Office of Works Official Guide Book*
3   *Hawkins. Gerald. S. Stonehenge Decoded.*

Bronze age culture that existed in England at that time.[1]" Opinions such as this prove the limitations of the experts mind set when speaking of the past.

If the survey proved the Astronomical properties found at Stonehenge is accepted, it raises more questions than answers, as it negates the theory of there being successive stages of construction, as has been advocated by the experts, also the theory that all the Astronomical properties found within the structure were purely accidental.

The question that requires an answer is, if the people of Britain did not build Stonehenge, and it was not built within the period as advocated by the experts, calculated as between 2600–1600 BC when was it built, and by whom? Why was it necessary to construct this amazing edifice? Who would benefit from this knowledge? It is constructed on a plain in the middle of nowhere, if one could use that expression. What other cultures existed during the periods attributed to the construction of Stonehenge that had the knowledge and expertise to carry out this project. It is obvious from the mathematical properties found within its environs that those who built Stonehenge came from an advanced culture.

If the construction was carried out in the manner and the years proposed by the experts why was it necessary to go to all this trouble when this knowledge relative to the motions of the Sun and Moon, was already known to the Egyptian and Mycenaean cultures, and was most likely available to the people of Britain?

As we have previously stated there is every reason to believe that a trade route existed between the Mediterranean and the British Isles for many thousands of years, especially in the export of tin, which was an important element in the manufacturing process of bronze for those countries in Europe and the Middle East.

The tin mines of Cornwall in the South of England was the principal source of supply during the Bronze age when metals were first used in the manufacture of tools and weapons, of which the earliest use was established in the Middle East around 4000 BC.

Attributing the construction to the 'Beaker' people whose presence ranged from "Iberia to Poland and from the Mediterranean Sea to the Baltic" is speculative thinking. Extensive evidence of these people was found at New Grange in Ireland, yet no one has suggested that it was the 'Beaker, people who constructed this magnificent structure.[2]

By the year 2600 B.C., the countries of the Middle East had reached a high level of knowledge in Astronomy, Mathematics, Geometry, and Astrology, and had been in possession of the calendar for thousands of years. "It is known that ancient Egypt possessed a very complete solar, lunar, and Sothic calendar in 4240 BC".[3]

---

1   *Ibid*

2   *O'Kelly. Michael J. Early Ireland. An Introduction to Irish Prehistory Published by Cambridge University Press. Cambridge. U.K.*

3   *De Lubicz. R.A. Schwaller. Sacred Science. The Sothic cycle is calculated on the coincidence every 1460 years of the vague year of 365 days with the Sothic year of 365¼ days. Calculations established by astronomers have demonstrated that between 4321 and 2231 BC, the Sothic year was almost identical to our Julian year of 365¼ days*

If Stonehenge was constructed to acquire Astronomical information, the whole project would be an exercise of futility, much as we would try to reinvent the wheel today or a calendar. Therefore, it is reasonable to suggest that the construction of Stonehenge was at a much earlier date than we are lead to believe and constructed in order to acquire knowledge relative to the movement of the Moon and its interaction with our planet, knowledge that may have been lost due to some major catastrophe that had inflicted the Planet.

Professor O'Kelly expressed that "in the older view, and indeed in the view still held by some archaeologists, the Beaker Folk migration theory could conveniently be used to explain a number of important changes in the archaeological record of the Late Neolithic/Metal Age transition. For instance, during the proposed Beaker Folk expansion and migration towards the end of the third millennium B.C, the building of megalithic tombs (i.e. constructed of large stones) ended in western Continental Europe. The knowledge of metallurgy began to spread widely there and eventually in Britain and Ireland, and in the latter there was a rapid development of this new technology. Because Beaker pottery was found at the great stone circle at Grange near the western shore of Lough Gur, it was tempting at that time to assume that the building of this impressive monument was inspired by the newly arrive Beaker people and carried into effect by the natives under the direction of the beaker Folk warrior aristocrats".

This same reasoning can apply to the commonly held views regards Stonehenge. The discovery of pottery in the environs of Stonehenge attributed to the 'Beaker' people does not necessarily endorse the claim that it was the Beaker people who constructed Stonehenge or carried out modifications.

There is also the question regard the artifacts purportedly used in the construction of the outer circular berm and excavations which were deer antlers which it is said acted as pickaxes for digging, and shoulder blades of oxen to act as shovels. However, the tools used to shape and dress the stone lintels are a matter of supposition. The precision by which the mortises and tendons were shaped negates the use of primitive stone tools.

We imagine and hypothesize as to the method and manner in which the works was executed and extrapolate on all off the different scenarios that our mind is capable of producing; however, the question is why?

Why build it at all to gain a knowledge that was already available. Why antler horns and oxen bones in an age of Bronze? Granting that the excavations were carried out in the method as postulated by the experts is correct. How did they shape the lintels so precisely? What technique did they use to shape the mortise and tendon joints by which the lintels were held to the uprights, in addition to forming tongue and grooved joints which held the circle of lintels together? We can discount the theory postulated by the many experts that sixty-pound stone mauls were the tools of preference. To achieve this precision would require knowledge of geometry to construct a template from which all of the 30 lintels that form the circle would be shaped, in addition to having knowledge of mathematics to lay out the site.

A very interesting anomaly was uncovered when the site was officially surveyed. It appeared the builders of Stonehenge did not grade and level the site before the commencement of construction activities which one would assume would be a requisite before commencing construction.[1] However, the survey carried out by Professor Hawkins highlighted an anomaly that had gone undetected over the years, readings taken showed an elevation drop of approximately eighteen (18") inches across the site.[2]

It was also detected that there was no common center point to the circles at Stonehenge. The center of the Sarsen Circle differs from the center of the Aubrey Circle by about two foot six inches (2' 6"). When one considers the interrelationship between the Sarsen Circle and the Aubrey Circle in determining of the various moon phases, the arrival of the Equinoxes, and the Solstices, again illustrates the advanced knowledge of these people.

The actual construction can only be appreciated by those who are conversant with building technologies that more than the academic are aware of the problem this would present to these ancient people. With modern instruments, this would present no problem, however, the positioning of forty-ton monoliths would. It is obvious that our ancestors overcame their problem, which increases our admiration for their engineering skills. Despite this anomaly the top of the lintels were level and in tangent with the horizon.

There is also the characteristics of the inner circumference of the support standing stones and lintels in that the inside face has been shaped to form a true circle, whereas in the case of the outer circumference, only the lintels have been shaped to form a true circle[3]. This should give us cause to wonder at the abilities of those who constructed this wonderful observatory.

What were the tools used to create the mortises, tendons, the tongue and groves to the standing stones and lintels with such precision? It has been suggested that this was accomplished by pounding the surfaces with stone mauls yet attempts to emulate these ancient builders has failed.

The shaping and placing of the uprights and lintels was an operation that precluded the practice of trial and error. Those who built Stonehenge "showed evidence of careful planning. Each stone was selected, shaped, dressed, and tailored to fit, making due allowance for the ground contours. It would not be an easy task even by today's standards. ---Somehow, by a technology unknown, the Stonehenge's figured out before hand the depth of the hole required to match up". [4]

Mr. Hawkins simplifies the matter by stating that in the construction process, the builders had to deal with a "collection of variables". Without the use of sophisticated equipment, the builders had to ensure that each stone when placed into position, level with the height of the preceding monolith, and the mortise joint exactly in position to receive the tendon of the lintel which would be placed later. To increase the degree of difficulty, the foundation of the 40-ton irregular monolith was of chalk.

1   *Hawkins. Gerald S. beyond Stonehenge.Published by Harper & Row NY*
2   *Ibid*
3   *Michell. John. The View over Atlantis Published by Ballantine Books NY*
4   *Ibid*

As was pointed out there was no room for error. What did they place at the base of the hole that would ensure the height would be consistent? It would be a major problem should the monolith be two or three inch too high, or too low. An occurrence such as this would be catastrophic. Putting it in and taking it out for adjustment was not an option.

Who were these people? Egyptologist tell us that the age of the Great Pyramids occurred in 2600 BC, coincided with the initial construction of Stonehenge, attributing the construction of the Step Pyramid of Saggara,(that was built by the Egyptian Architect Imhotep for King Djoser of the 3rd Dynasty 2686--2613 BC,[1]) as Egypt's first attempt to construct a Pyramid that would be used as the prototype for future pyramids, basing their hypothesis that this Pyramid was built in successive stages over an extended period of time. However, there is no evidence available that would indicate as to who the builders of the great Pyramids where and when they were built. "It is only on the basis of shrewd guessing that Egyptologists estimate the stepped pyramid of Saggara to be the oldest of the Egyptian pyramids."[2] The same criteria could apply to the building of Stonehenge.

However, who is to say that building of the Step Pyramid for King Djoser was not the beginning, but the end of the pyramid period, when the knowledge of the methods used to construct the great pyramid was lost in antiquity, much like the situation in which we find ourselves today. And as with the pyramids, the in-depth studies carried out, tell us what the Temple of Stonehenge is, however, like many ancient structures around our Planet, the how and when are questions that still elude the minds of our scientific communities when it comes to dating pre-historic times. The hypothesis postulated is, at best, conjectural, as the method of dating these ancient cultures is still a controversial issue among the experts.

---

1   *National Geographic. Ancient Egypt. Discovering it's Splendour.(1978)*
2   *Tompkins. Peter. Secret of the Great Pyramid.*

Chapter 20

We are about to enter the twenty first century, and with all of the Scientific and Technological advances made over the last one hundred years, it would appear that the minds of our scientific communities are set in a time lock when it comes to agreeing to the dates concerning these ancient cultures. I would venture to say, that this condition might be attributable to the religious and cultural heritage, based upon the concepts of the Judo-Christen religions.

It is within this Biblical period that the experts continue their efforts to unravel the past and find answers and it is in this time lock that they continue their efforts to find answers; however, can only assume and present a hypothesis on the information available.

Archaeology has, its limitations, despite its major successes over the years, as the experts in this particular field can only, in most cases assume and present a hypothesis, in evaluating a time and date of the artifacts discovered, based, upon the findings of their predecessors. However, due to the arbitrary system that was used in the past, there have been, and will be occasions when the scientific community will have to revise its dates as new methods are developed which may be more precise.

In the early years of Archaeology, it would appear that the common practice was to use the Bible as the criteria when evaluating ancient cultures and historical events and through a natural progression the dating of Archaeological artifacts was, subject to the times and dates outlined in the Hebrew Old Testament.

Due to this, the dates propounded by the experts vary to the extreme. It can be said that, in the majority of cases, the Bible is the yardstick by which ancient history is viewed, the premise being, that if the dates attributed to antiquity do not conform to those as stated in the Bible, and it must be in error.

In support of the above statement, we can cite the case of the eminent prelate and scholar Bishop James Ussher, who in his chronological study, The Annales Veteris, ET Novi Testament, arrived at a system of chronological dates, which set out the creation of the world as 4004. BC. A work that was so highly praised by his contemporaries, that his findings, relative to the creation, was incorporated into the Kings James Version of the Bible, which continued to be an article of faith within the Church of England until quite recently.

This is no isolated case, as we read in the works of Flavius Josephus, the Jewish historian, who wrote in the first century BC, states that the great flood, which engulfed the world, commenced on the twenty—seventh day of the month of Nisan, 2656 years from the time of Adam.[1] Logic would suggest that such a claim should be rejected due to the evidence to the contrary but there are those who accept this date as factual.

Therefore accepting this hypothesis as factual, it followed that all discoveries made in the early years of Archaeology, were required to be within this time frame and as all life had been destroyed upon the Earth (except for Noah and his family), all dating of artifacts were subject to this date. Once these criteria had been established, the dating that followed had by progression, to conform to this method. This date becomes the baseline for all other cultures that follows despite the discovery of cultures and civilizations whose existence dates back much further than these biblical dates, including that of Egypt. The knowledge available to modern scholars regards the ancient past would preclude the use of the Bible as a yardstick in determining the chronological sequence of the past has rather than clarify has created confusion in the dating of cultures and ancient historical events. History should not be evaluated against the events described in the Bible to prove their authenticity on the contrary; it is the Bible that should be evaluated against historical events and cultures that are known to have existed in the past.

As we now know, the events as described in the Bible are not always compatible with the knowledge that is known of these ancient civilizations. There is much within the Bible that is to be admired; however, there are many areas that do not conform to the historical facts as is known today.

This was the situation until the discovery of carbon dating in 1946 by W. F. Libby, an American chemist, an achievement for which he received the Nobel Prize for Chemistry in 1960.

This system of dating is based upon the presence of radioactive carbon 14 atoms (C^{14}), which is found in all organic matter. As these atoms disintegrate in dead organic material by radioactive decay, it is possible to determine the age of an object by measuring the amount of carbon 14 that remains.

Recent testing of this method, using known historical documents indicate that the system is flawed and can give incorrect readings, and as one goes back in time, the greater the error becomes.[2] For example, a date of 1500 BC should actually be 300 years earlier (1800 BC.); 3000 BC should be 500 to 1000 years earlier (3000 or 4000 BC).

This brings in to question the dating of artifacts and cultures, and may cause our experts to re-evaluate the dates that have been attributed to the civilizations and cultures of the past.

Other methods developed, such as growth rings in trees, or dendrochronlogy by which the age of the tree can be determined by counting the number of growth rings in its cross section.

---

1   Josephus. Flavius. Antiquities of the Jew's. Book 1.Chap, 3. Pg, 31. Translated by. William. Whiston. A.M.
2   Trento. Salvatore Michael. The Search for Lost America.Published by Penguin Books

The pattern is evaluated to other trees of a known age. By the use of overlapping patterns, dating can be traced back as far as 3,000 years. However, as with the Carbon 14 dating, this method has its limitations. One does not find trees 0f 3,000 years old in Egypt or the Middle East.

From this it can be seen how difficult it is for scholars to be definite regarding the age of ancient cultures. They are therefore, left with no other alternative than to follow in the footsteps of their predecessors, who through arbitrary dating methods and guesswork has led scholars to underestimate the age of ancient civilizations.

As case in point would be the questions surrounding the age of the Egyptian civilization there would appear to be reluctance on the part of our modern day Archaeologist to question the dates developed by the early Egyptologist. Among the many problems encountered and the most controversial is the dating established by the early explores.

Sir Cyril Fox commented by saying that "Archaeologist is incapable of dealing with myth". Yet, if we are to study ancient history, it is important that our scholars explore every avenue available, investigating every piece of evidence, whether in myth, or artifact which can pave a path into the past. How can a determination be made as to the age of these ancient cultures? What means are available by which a determination can be made? A mosaic of knowledge, the pieces of which can be gleaned from the myths of old may open our minds. But to be receptive, we must unlock the door to our minds and reject the restrictions, which have been placed by our religious, educational, and cultural environment, which has been the key that locked the minds of many.

What it does suggest is that we should question and seek out knowledge beyond that which has been taught in our establishments. It is by asking questions as to the 'when' the 'why', and the 'how' that we can open up a whole new world and a door of interest.

To illustrate a point concerns the Chinese Empire in the middle Ages. Of the many unanswered questions, is the case of the Chinese Astronomer, who in 1054 AD informed his Emperor of the birth of a new star, which he had observed in the heavens. But it has been determined that this major occurrence was also recorded by the Japanese, North American Indian tribes, and Persian/Arab Astronomers. Modern day Astronomers state that this supernova occurred in the Constellation Taurus, which we call today the Crab Nebula and was unknown to modern Astronomers, until catalogued in 1952.[1]

The question one would ask is how and by what means did this official observe this amazing event? What instruments allowed him to observe the phenomenon, and what knowledge did he possess to recognize it as an event to be reported, and recorded by the palace officials?

The system of recording unusual events, whether on land or in the heavens, was not unique to the Chinese culture history tell us that it was the practice of ancient societies to keep a daily record of unusual events which may impact upon their well-being. Would the observance of

---

1   *The Crab Nebula is reputed to be 6,300 light years away from Earth It is said that at the time of the occurrence it was bright enough to be seen in daylight and was visible in the night sky for 653 days Wikipedia Encyclopaedia*

this phenomenon be discernable by members of the public? Would it require a person who was dedicated to observing the heavens? This would require a person with the knowledge and experience, a position this responsibility entailed. By what means was this event detected? Galileo did not invent telescopes until the 17th century. We have to assume that it was by the naked eye. Is this possible? Lacking any further evidence, we have to believe that it was. On the other hand, was it possible that the Chinese had already invented an instrument with which they could view the heavens? The same reasoning can be applied to the Egyptians. How did they acquire the extensive knowledge they possessed on the planetary system?

There are numerous cases similar to the above, which cannot be adequately responded to by the experts. How and by what means did the ancient people achieve their knowledge of the planetary system? The Greek culture was fully cognizant of the system relative to the planets, Mars, Jupiter, Saturn, Venus, Mercury, Neptune, and Uranus, all of which are incorporated into their mythological tales. The ancient Greek's were not Astronomers; however, their astronomical knowledge was rudimentary compared to that of Egypt how did they come to this knowledge? What culture did they borrow from? By the time the early Greek historians reached Egypt, the heroic tales of Greek heroes were well established. This would indicate that the Egyptian culture was widespread in the early years of Greek development.

"The mythological tales of Greece were the result of a long tradition, developed by a guild of storytellers, and bards who would generally render their recitations with music. These people were held in high esteem by the rulers and general populace, and were the prime source of orally transmitting the traditions to each succeeding generation. The Bard choosing his successor at a very young age, in the majority, accomplished this; it would be the eldest son. The Bard would then pass on his storehouse of knowledge and wisdom to the next generation, of those bards who were part of the Royal household, or of the leading families. It was one of their prime duties to keep a record of the families genealogy, which would be recited on major occasions, such as births, marriages, and deaths, or on other auspicious occasions, on which he recount the deeds of the members of the household who had performed some feat of valor. It was by this means that the traditions of the past were passed from generation to generation".[1]

Perhaps the rudimentary astronomical knowledge acquired by the Greeks was the result of these ancient bards borrowing from the surrounding cultures. It would seem extraordinary that they would possess this Astronomical knowledge without the use of some form of optical instrument. Again the question must be asked, 'how' and from where?

It has been said, if a hypothesis appears plausible, it must be true, however illogical and against reason it may appear, and is quite often the means used to explain away the unexplainable. This form of logic has been the means by which the experts explain away the Temple at Stonehenge and many other ancient structures around the world.

---

1   Trypanis. Constantine. A. *Introduction to ' The History of Western Literature'*

Despite the overwhelming evidence, which proves, the people who built Stonehenge and the Great Pyramid were well versed in the principals of Mathematics and Geometry. the scientific community would have us believe that the people who built these magnificent structures were primitive farmers, who lacked "any degree of literacy, and any form of what we would consider a sophisticated culture."[1] Perhaps this view would apply to the general laborers involved in the construction, but not those who planned and executed the work.

This was also the view held by many regarding the early Egyptian civilization. In the embryonic years of Archaeology it was believed that the Egyptian people lacked the ability to write and record their history. As one famous author states, "The Egyptians, like all ancient peoples, contrary to our modern habits, did not leave us any history books, in the modern sense, there were in short, no historians. To overcome this problem, they conceived a method of pictographs as a means of communication."[2]

This view existed until the translation of the Rosetta stone by Jean Francois Champollion in 1822. Ensuing events have proved the opposite. The ancient Egyptians were highly developed in the Arts and Science. Herodotus, in his Histories states, "By their practice of keeping records of the past, have made themselves the most learned of any nation of which I have had experience."[3]

Obviously the writer did not avail himself to the writings of the early Greek historians when making his observation, or give consideration to the vast amount of historical documents destroyed by Julius Caesar and the Christen hordes that burned down the Library of Alexandria in Egypt. Who knows what information was in this body of documents?

History recounts the destruction to part of the library caused by Julius Caesar in 48 BC during his brief campaign in Egypt was accidental, and the damage was repaired, including the replacement of a 200,000-volume collection from Pergamum, which was given to Cleopatra by Mark Anthony. It is said that prior to the incident involving Caesar, the amount of scrolls or volumes ran into hundreds of thousands, being estimated in the region of 700,000 and was the greatest collection of scholarship in the ancient world.[4] There is no doubt that among this multitudinous library of documents many where of early Egyptian origin.

And so it is when we come to the question of Stonehenge There are no documents to which one can make reference. What we have is hypothesis and speculation by those who profess to be experts in their field. One of whom states, "There is no direct evidence of extensive theoretical geometrical knowledge, no archaeological remains that would suggest any degree of literacy. The conclusion reached by this observation, is the lack of any form of written records, either in stone or in some other form that would prove otherwise".[5]

1   *Newham C A. The Astronomical Significance of Stonehenge.Published by Moon Publications Wales*

2   *Ibid*

3   *Herodotus. The Histories. Trans; Aubrey de Selincourt Published by Penguin Classics*

4   *Quest for the Past. Readers Digest.*

5   *Newham. C A. The Astronomical Significance of Stonehenge. Published by Moon Publications Wales*

We are asked to ignore the sophisticated Astronomical Mathematical and Cosmic properties that exist within its fabric. The author goes on to state, "As far as Stonehenge is concerned, so far everything found there could have been accomplished using only the simple equipment of peg and line, a standard measure, and some form of tokens for numerical comparisons."[1] This form of sterile thinking does nothing to increase our knowledge of the past, nor that of our ancestors.

The authors reference to "the lack of any, archaeological remains," raises an interesting point. If we are to believe the experts that the construction of Stonehenge was carried out over a period of hundreds of years, between 2180--1550 BC, other than the finding of the antler pick, there exist no other artifacts by which the dating of Stonehenge could be determined.

Those who carried out the work were meticulous in their clean up operations, in that other forms of tools which may have been used in the construction process were not found within the precinct of the circle. This, I would say, is stretching the bounds of probability to the extreme. It is also highly probable that the carbon fragments that were found in the Aubrey holes and carbon dated as 1850 BC were deposited by some other culture that may have visited the site after its completion.

However, the basic principles of laying out the foundation and circles with peg and line are as valid today as it was when the foundations of Stonehenge were inscribed on the Salisbury Plains. Also to ascribe some form of "primitive measuring device by which they established their dimensions,"[2] Is to deny the precision by which the Temple was laid out, a precision that could only have been accomplished by a system of geometrical measure, equal to the systems in use today when setting out the foundations of any building.

If this is the criterion by which we view the builders of Stonehenge, we can ascribe the same reasoning to the builders of the great Temples of Greece the Middle East South America, including the great Temples of the Egyptian, and Babylonian civilizations.

The word illiteracy is defined as the inability to meet a minimum criterion of reading and writing skills, which has been defined by the United Nations as the inability to read and write a simple message in any language. They equate illiteracy, to an idea that has been developed in the twentieth century to the problems that affect our present day society where there exists a high degree of illiteracy among the less developed nations of the world.

The same can be said of the ancient civilizations, whereby the general population may have been illiterate, however, as like our present day society. There exists a vast population who does not fall into this category. In evaluating history, our historians appear to be looking into a one-way mirror from the wrong side.

Are the people who built the magnificent Temples of South America, China, Greece, and Egypt to be classed under the same heading or are our experts suffering from a mind blockage?

---

1   *Ibid*
2   *Ibid*

There are those who refuse to accept the fact that our ancient ancestors were advanced in Astronomy, Geometry, and Mathematics which is amply demonstrated by the many ancient structures found don this planet.

Logic dictates that to build a Temple or Church or any type of a building requires, in the initial stage of development, a concept, and a plan with which the project can be executed. To achieve these aims requires a high degree of Engineering, Architectural and Artistic skills, by which the structure can be completed to the satisfaction of the Master builder or Architect.

The advancement of Man has not removed the need for Engineering Design and Architectural plans, including specifications, to execute the construction of a building. These requirements are as valid today as they were 4000 years ago.

That these builders of the past did not leave any written records behind which would prove to modern man that they were a highly developed culture, should not diminish their stature in the eyes of our historians.

The Great Cathedrals of Europe built between the 11th and 13th century should give us pause to think. There exist very little written records of how these marvelous structures were constructed or who the individual Master builders were

We should remove the idea from our minds the idea that a group of illiterate primitive farmers was the builders of Stonehenge. This may apply to the general labors, who were perhaps involved in the general construction, as was the case in England during the early part of the 19th century, in the construction of the canals and railways that we know to-day, but not for those who were the master minds behind the planning and execution of the project.

When one looks at the Continent of Africa and the greater part of Asia, where the majority of the population are illiterate and agrarian in their culture. Their major cities are equal to those that are to be seen in our Western society. Supplied and furnished with the most modern and sophisticated equipment.

Given the same circumstances, regarding the lack of written records, how would future historians view the histories of these cultures? Would they say that primitive illiterate farmers built these cities, or reach the right conclusion, that these cities and major projects were planned and executed by expatriate Engineers and Architects of another cultural background.

Chapter 21

One of the many mysteries left to us by our ancestors is the Temple of Stonehenge located on the Salisbury Plain in Wiltshire England. The people who built this amazing structure and their place of origin are still a mystery. We can discount the theory that they were primitive farmers and illiterate. To achieve the level of proficiency required in the construction of the observatory would require an extensive knowledge of Astronomy, Geometry and Mathematics, including the necessary Design and Engineering skills. Also to complete a task of this magnitude would require a preconceived master plan, and the dedication and patience to carry out the project over an extensive period.

The Astronomical properties discovered would suggest that the initial work was determining the Moon cycles, which occurs every 18, 6 years. To carry out this task would require a period, as suggested by some experts, of more than 56 years, some suggesting "a period of six cycles for a total of 110 years" During this time, the movement of the Sun would be determined.

There was no confusion in the minds of these master builders. The actual construction would not begin until all information was collected and correlated. Therefore the theory that Stonehenge was built in stages over hundreds of years, and by different cultures lacks merit.

As to the actual construction, this was no haphazard exercise; the materials were carefully chosen and constructed to a preconceived plan that would reflect its cosmic properties[1].

Stonehenge was built to perfection, a masterpiece of architectural beauty. Only a cult of Priests would possess the knowledge and continuity to carry out such a task. As the Catholic Religious Order of the Knight Templers, did in constructing the medieval Gothic Cathedrals of Europe that were carried out over a period of 150 years, - should we class these master builders of the Cathedrals in the same category as being "intelligent though illiterate."?

It is said that the majority of people involved in the construction of these beautiful Church's were in the most part illiterate, who were uneducated when judged by to-days standards, Obviously, there must have been an educational system in place by which these people acquired the knowledge to carry out these monumental tasks?. According to what is known they were master craftsmen of a high order, Experts in Engineering Design, Architectural Concept,

---

1   Michell. John. *City of Revelation ,Published by Ballantine Books NY*

Sculptures and glass making. An art that, even today with all of our technological advances "no chemical analysis has penetrated,[1]"

Out of all the beautiful Cathedrals constructed, one has only to gaze upon the Cathedral of Chartres[2] in France to appreciate the Mathematical and Geometrical-engineering principals incorporated into its design. A structure built in number, weight, and measure, where harmony and proportion are a language that is hidden within its fabric. This masterpiece of medieval art was supervised and controlled by the Master Mason who, with his square, compass, straightedge, and plumb bob, laid the foundations for these wonderful structures that we admire today.

Modern man can only gaze upon the external shell and admire its beauty, however, lacks the spirit to discern the mysteries that is hidden within its fabric.

The overseers of the Cathedrals of Europe were far from being illiterate. As with the builders of Stonehenge, we have no knowledge of who these builders were, we can only guess and speculate. They were not interested in leaving their names to posterity. Their first duty was to ensure that the cosmic principals embodied in the structure was for future generations to discern for their well-being. The Cathedrals that grace the face of Europe are a testament to their knowledge and dedication. And like the Cathedrals, it follows that the construction of Stonehenge was carried out on a continuous basis over a period and not in a sporadic manner, some experts have advocated.

Academics allow their intellectual prowess to overcome their common sense when it comes to evaluating the purpose behind Stonehenge. They appear to spend an inordinate amount of time and effort looking for that which is not there. They also appear to find it difficult to face the obvious. Stonehenge was not constructed to act as a religious center, but as an Astronomical center in order to determine the flow of the seasons, and develop a calendar of time. Accepting this hypothesis would lead one to the conclusion that this planet had come through some form of catastrophic upheaval that had thrown the seasons out of order.

There would appear to be repetitiveness in the writings dealing with Stonehenge. Not only do they tell of the date in which it was built, but the dates for each successive stage and the people who were responsible, in addition, the manner of construction. All of which is based on speculation with no evidence to support their theories.

Among the many experts there are also those whose theories range from Stonehenge being built by extraterrestrial? While there are those who say that the Blue stones were magically transported and erected by the magician Merlin, a reputed, seer, and teacher at the court of King Vortigerm, a 5th century tribal King in the South of England.

There are also those who suggest that it was built to act as a market place, "Where assemblies of people could meet, not only for trade, but for seasonal rituals and the use of human bones.

---

1   Charpentier. Louis. The Mysteries of Chartres Cathedral. Translated by Ronald Fraser Published by Avon Books

2   Ibid.

It was for this consideration and not for Astronomy that decided the location of Stonehenge."[1] What those who have written extensively on this subject do not understand is that the location of Stonehenge was carefully chosen. Had it been located further north, or south, would have impaired its Astronomical function.

It is obvious that the author has very little knowledge of the environs of Salisbury Plain. It is outlandish claims of this nature that brings confusion to the minds of those who seek to understand the past.

The experts have proposed many theories, some suggesting a temple constructed by the Druids for offering human sacrifice. While others suggest its function was primarily religious. Each opinion is as valid as the next depending upon your beliefs. Nevertheless, what it was, and what it became is now self-evident.

The limitations of our minds prevent us accepting the amount of time spent by these people in collecting all the information necessary to construct the structure, perhaps generations. Mr. Hawkins states "hitherto, the construction was regarded as separate units by different invading cultures. The Astronomical results indicate some continuity of purpose either by cultural mixing or by transference".

The sophisticated knowledge required to bring the structure to fruition rules out the local population, as it would for invading cultures whose religious beliefs may have been totally different from the local populace. What can be said with some certainty is that there was "continuity of purpose" and transference of knowledge. Only a dedicated Priesthood would be capable of such a monumental task.

Although all are not in agreement, the survey carried out by Gerald Hawkins the computer readout of its attributes, is indisputable, and should leave no doubt in the minds of those interested in Stonehenge as to its true purpose. We can tell why it was built, and speculate on the how it was built, when it was built is open to question?[2]

This presents somewhat of a problem. If it was for the purpose of determining the arrival of the seasons the problem is more complex. Logic suggests that the conditions that exist today, where the seasons arrive in due order, were evident during the durations of the construction period. We could therefore assume that its purpose was for the tracking of the seasons over an extended period of time.

What can be stated with certainty is that those who built Stonehenge did not do so as a make-work project, or as a means of alleviating their boredom between planting seasons. Theirs was for a higher purpose for the benefit of society that by determining the positions of the moon, and sun in their travels across the heavens would allow the correction of a calendar that may have been disturbed by some form of catastrophic upheaval that had upset the balance of the planet and chaos within the natural order.

---

1   Burl. Aubrey. *Rings of Stone. Published by Frances Lincoln Publishers Limited London*
2   Hawkins. Gerald. *Beyond Stonehenge, Published by Harper & Row. N.Y.*

The only conclusion one can reach concerning the 'why' is that the knowledge of the Moon cycles and the seasonal arrival of the Sun which determine the seasons was not known, and if it was, needed to be correlated, transcribed in permanent stone for posterity. However, one has to be realistic when it comes to making claims based on a weak foundation. The introduction of the Christianity weakens, rather than strengthens Mr. Mitchell's hypothesis, nevertheless, there is a mystique surrounding the method of measure incorporated in the stone circles that needs some research.

No doubt the theory surrounding the "Squaring of the Circle' has transcended time and was known too many ancient societies, perhaps St John, having this knowledge, used its properties to pre-figure the 'New Jerusalem' to fulfill the expectations of the newly converted Jewish people to the new Christian teachings developed by Paul and the Apostles. Therefore, to combine the many myths developed and perpetrated by the Catholic Church of Rome brings into question Mr Mitchell's proposition.[1]

There are various opinions as to why it was built, as there is as to how? The opinions expressed are many and varied, each of which is as valid as the next. Nevertheless, what appears to be missing is any form of logic to explain these ancient people's abilities.

Extensive research has confirmed that it was constructed to act as an Astronomical Observatory. The work carried out by Gerald S. Hawkins[2] should leave no doubt in the minds of scholars as to the true purpose of this amazing structure. But there is still a puzzle to be solved as to when it was built.

Nevertheless, if the extensive survey carried out by Gerald Hawkins proved the Astronomical properties and if accepted, raises more questions than answers, as it negates the theory of there being successive stages of construction, as has been advocated by the experts, and that the ancient people of Britain were incapable of constructing such a structure, also the Astronomical properties found within the structure were purely accidental.

Therefore, the question is, if the people of Britain did not build Stonehenge, and it was not built within the period as advocated by the experts, calculated as between 2600--1600 BC when was it built, and by whom? Why was it necessary to construct this amazing edifice? What other cultures existed during the periods attributed to the construction of Stonehenge that had the knowledge and expertise to carry out this project. It is obvious from the mathematical properties found within its environs that those who built Stonehenge came from an advanced culture.

If the construction was for Astronomical purposes and accumulation of knowledge relative to the motions of the Sun and Moon, why was it necessary to go to all this trouble when at this phase in history this knowledge was already known to the Egyptian and Mycenaean cultures, and available to the people of Britain.

As we have previously stated there is every reason to believe that a trade route existed between the Mediterranean and the British Isles in the export of tin, which was an important

1 *2,600 BC the purported date established by the experts as to the date Stonehenge was built*
2 *Hawkins. Gerald. S. Stonehenge Decoded Published by Fontana Collins London.*

element in the manufacturing process of bronze for those countries in Europe and the Middle East.

Attributing the construction to the 'Beaker' people whose presence ranged from "Iberia to Poland and from the Mediterranean Sea to the Baltic" is speculative thinking. Extensive evidence of these people was found at New Grange in Ireland, yet no one has suggested that it was the 'Beaker, people who constructed this magnificent structure.[1]

If Stonehenge were constructed to acquire Astronomical information, the whole project would be an exercise of futility, much as we would try to reinvent the wheel today or a calendar. Therefore, it is reasonable to suggest that the construction of Stonehenge was at a much earlier date than we are lead to believe and was constructed in order to acquire knowledge relative to the movement of the Moon and its interaction with the rotation of the planet.

This hypothesis is not without foundation as by the year 2600 B.C., the countries of the Middle East had reached a high level of knowledge in Astronomy, Mathematics, Geometry, and Astrology, and had been in possession of the calendar for thousands of years. "It is known that ancient Egypt possessed a very complete solar, lunar, and Sothic calendar in 4240 BC".[2]

Professor O'Kelly expressed that "in the older view, and indeed in the view still held by some archaeologists, the Beaker Folk migration theory could conveniently be used to explain a number of important changes in the archaeological record of the Late Neolithic/Metal Age transition. For instance, during the proposed Beaker Folk expansion and migration towards the end of the third millennium B.C, the building of megalithic tombs (i.e. constructed of large stones) ended in western Continental Europe. The knowledge of metallurgy began to spread widely there and eventually in Britain and Ireland, and in the latter there was a rapid development of this new technology. Because Beaker pottery was found at the great stone circle at Grange near the western shore of Lough Gur, it was tempting at that time to assume that the building of this impressive monument was inspired by the newly arrived Beaker people and carried into effect by the natives under the direction of the beaker Folk warrior aristocrats".[3]

This same reasoning can apply to the commonly held views regards Stonehenge. The discovery of pottery in the environs of Stonehenge attributed to the 'Beaker' people does not necessarily endorse the claim that it was the Beaker people who constructed Stonehenge or carried out modifications.

---

1   O'Kelly. Michael J. *Early Ireland. An Introduction to Irish Prehistory. Published by Cambridge University Press. Cambridge. U.K.*

2   De Lubicz. R.A. Schwaller. *Sacred Science. The Sothic cycle is calculated on the coincidence every 1460 years of the vague year of 365 days with the Sothic year of 365¼ days. Calculations established by astronomers have demonstrated that between 4321 and 2231 BC, the Sothic year was almost identical to our Julian year of 365¼ days*

3   O'Kelly *Michael J Early Ireland An Introduction to Irish Prehistory Published by Cambridge University Press Cambridge UK*

There is also the question regard the artifacts purportedly used in the construction of the outer circular berm and excavations which were deer antlers that acted as pickaxes for digging, and shoulder blades of oxen to act as shovels. The tool used to shape and dress the stone lintels is a matter of supposition.

We imagine and hypothesis as to the method and manner in which the work was executed and extrapolates on all the different scenarios that our mind is capable of producing, however, the question still remaining is why?

Why build it at all to gain a knowledge that was already available. Why antler horns and oxen bones in an age of Bronze? Granting that the excavations were carried out in the method as postulated by the experts is correct. How did they shape the lintels so precisely? What technique did they use to shape the mortise and tendon joints by which the lintels were held to the uprights, in addition to forming tongue and grooved joints which held the circle of lintels together? To achieve this precision would require knowledge of geometry to construct a template from which all of the 30 lintels that form the circle would be shaped, in addition to having knowledge of mathematics to lay out the site.

We can cite the case of the eminent prelate and scholar Bishop James Ussher, who in his chronological study, The Annales Veteris, ET Novi Testament, arrived at a system of chronological dates, which set out the creation of the world as 4004. BC. A work that was so highly praised by his contemporaries, that his findings, relative to the creation, was incorporated into the Kings James Version of the Bible, which continued to be an article of faith within the Church of England until quite recently.

This is no isolated case, as we read in the works of Flavius Josephus, the Jewish historian, who wrote in the first century BC, that the great flood, which they say engulfed the world, commenced on the Twenty—seventh day of the month of Nisan, 2656 years from the time of Adam.[1]

Based upon this hypothesis, all dates arrived at in the early years of Archaeology, were required to be within this time frame and as all life had been destroyed upon the Earth (except for Noah and his family), all dating of artifacts were subject to this date. Once these criteria had been established, the dating that followed had by progression, to conform to this method. Hence the dating of the Egyptian Early Dynastic Period has been determined by the experts to be 3050-2890 BC. This date becomes the baseline for all other cultures that followed yet there have been traces found of cultures and civilizations whose existence dates back much further than these dates, including that of Egypt. Reason would suggest that our experts dispense with dating world history against the bible.

Using the Bible as a yardstick has created confusion in the dating of cultures and ancient historical events. History should not be evaluated against the events described in the Bible to prove their authenticity. On the contrary, it is the Bible that should be evaluated against historical events and cultures that are known to have existed in the past.

---

1 *Josephus. Flavius. Antiquities of the Jew's. Book 1.Chap, 3. Pg, 31. Translated by. William. Whiston. A.M.*

The events as described in the Bible are not always compatible with the knowledge that is known of these ancient civilizations. There is much within the Bible that is much admired; however, there are many areas that do not conform to the historical facts as is known today.

It can be seen how difficult it is for scholars to be definite regarding the age of ancient cultures. They are therefore, left with no other alternative than to follow in the footsteps of their predecessors, who through arbitrary dating methods and guesswork has led scholars to underestimate the age of ancient civilizations.

As case in point would be the questions surrounding the age of the Egyptian civilization there would appear to be reluctance on the part of our modern day Archaeologist to question the dates developed by the early Egyptologist. Among the many problems encountered and the most controversial is the dating established by the early explores.

What it does suggest is that we should question and seek out knowledge beyond that which has been taught in our establishments. It is by asking questions as to the 'when' the 'why', and the 'how' that we can open up a whole new world and a door of interest.

To illustrate a point concerns the Chinese Empire in the middle Ages. Of the many unanswered questions, is the case of the Chinese Astronomer, who in 1054 AD informed his Emperor of the birth of a new star, which he had observed in the heavens. Astronomers tell us that this supernova occurred in the Constellation Taurus, which we call today the Crab Nebula. This occurrence was unknown to modern Astronomers, and was not catalogued until 1952.

The question one would ask is how and by what means did this official observe this amazing event? What instruments allowed him to observe this phenomenon, and what knowledge did he possess to recognize it as an event to be reported, and recorded by the palace officials?

The system of recording unusual events, whether on land or in the heavens, was not unique to the Chinese culture history tell us that it was the practice of ancient societies to keep a daily record of unusual events which may impact upon their well-being. Would the observance of this phenomenon be discernable by members of the public? Would it require a person who was dedicated to observing the heavens? This would require a person with the knowledge and experience, a position this responsibility entailed. By what means was this event detected? Galileo did not invent telescopes until the 17th century. We have to assume that it was by the naked eye. Is this possible? Lacking any further evidence, we have to believe that it was. On the other hand, was it possible that the Chinese had already invented an instrument with which they could view the heavens? The same reasoning can be applied to the Egyptians. How did they acquire the extensive knowledge they possessed on the planetary system?

There are numerous cases similar to the above, which cannot be adequately responded to by the experts. How and by what means did the ancient people achieve their knowledge of the planetary system? The Greek culture was fully cognizant of the system relative to the planets, Mars, Jupiter, Saturn, Venus, Mercury, Neptune, and Uranus, all of which are incorporated into their mythological tales. The ancient Greek's were not Astronomers; however, their astronomical knowledge was rudimentary compared to that of Egypt how did they come to this knowledge?

What culture did they borrow from? By the time the early Greek historians reached Egypt, the heroic tales of Greek heroes were well established.

"The mythological tales of Greece were the result of a long tradition, developed by a guild of storytellers, and bards who would generally render their recitations with music. These people were held in high esteem by the rulers and general populace, and were the prime source of orally transmitting the traditions to each succeeding generation. The Bard choosing his successor at a very young age, in the majority, accomplished this; it would be the eldest son. The Bard would then pass on his storehouse of knowledge and wisdom to the next generation, of those bards who were part of the Royal household, or of the leading families. It was one of their prime duties to keep a record of the families genealogy, which would be recited on major occasions, such as births, marriages, and deaths, or on other auspicious occasions, on which he recount the deeds of the members of the household who had performed some feat of valor. It was by this means that the traditions of the past were passed from generation to generation".[1]

Perhaps the rudimentary astronomical knowledge acquired by the Greeks was the result of these ancient bards borrowing from the surrounding cultures. It would seem extraordinary that they would possess this Astronomical knowledge without the use of some form of optical instrument. Again the question must be asked, 'how' and from where?

This was also the view held by many regarding the early Egyptian civilization. In the early years of Archaeology it was believed by the experts that the Egyptian people lacked the ability to write and record their history. As one famous author states, "The Egyptians, like all ancient peoples, contrary to our modern habits, did not leave us any history books, in the modern sense, there were in short, no historians. To overcome this problem, they conceived a method of pictographs as a means of communication."[2]

This view existed until the translation of the Rosetta stone by Jean Francois Champollion in 1822. Ensuing events have proved the opposite. The ancient Egyptians were highly developed in the Arts and Science. Herodotus, in his Histories states, "By their practice of keeping records of the past, have made themselves the most learned of any nation of which I have had experience."[3]

Obviously the writer did not avail himself to the writings of the early Greek historians when making his observation, or give consideration to the vast amount of historical documents destroyed by Julius Caesar and the Christen hordes who burned down the Library of Alexandria in Egypt.

The destruction to part of the library caused by Julius Caesar in 48 BC during his brief campaign in Egypt was accidental, and the damage was repaired, including the replacement of a 200,000-volume collection from Pergamum, which was given to Cleopatra by Mark Anthony. It is said that prior to the incident involving Caesar, the amount of scrolls or volumes ran into

1   Trypanis. Constantine. A. Introduction to 'The History of Western Literature'
2   Ibid
3   Herodotus. The Histories. Trans; Aubrey de Selincourt. Published by penguin Classics

hundreds of thousands, being estimated in the region of 700,000 and was the greatest collection of scholarship in the ancient world.[1]

If this is the criterion by which we view the builders of Stonehenge. There is no written documentation and the legends surrounding this magnificent structure are comparatively recent and of no great age. It would be speculative to suggest that among the many thousands of scrolls would be some which may have had information relative to Stonehenge. The same reasoning can be ascribed to the builders of the great Temples of Greece the Middle East South America, including the great Temples of the Egyptian, and Babylonian civilizations.

The construction of Stonehenge was carried out in a systematic and methodical manner. Each stage being checked and crossed checked to ensure accuracy before construction commenced. It was not constructed in long protracted stages, as some experts would have us believe[2] it was a well planned and executed project from start to finish.

There was no confusion in the minds of these master builders. The actual construction would not begin until all information was collected and correlated. Therefore the theory that Stonehenge was built in stages over hundreds of years, and by different cultures lacks merit.

The actual construction was no haphazard exercise; the materials were carefully chosen and the constructed to a preconceived plan that would reflect its cosmic properties[3].

Stonehenge, was built to perfection, a masterpiece of architectural beauty. As the Catholic Religious Order of the Knight Templers, did in constructing the medieval Gothic Cathedrals of Europe that were carried out over a period of 150 years, - should we class these master builders of the Cathedrals in the same category as being "intelligent though illiterate."?

The majority of people involved in the construction of these beautiful Church's were in the most part illiterate, who were uneducated when judged by to-days standards, Obviously, there must have been an educational system in place by which they acquired the knowledge to carry out these monumental tasks?. According to what is known they were master craftsmen of a high order, Experts in Engineering Design, Architectural Concept, Sculptures and glass making. An art that, even today with all of our technological advances "no chemical analysis has penetrated,[4]"

Out of all the beautiful Cathedrals constructed, one has only to gaze upon the Cathedral of Chartres[5] in France to appreciate the Mathematical and Geometrical-engineering principals incorporated into its design. A structure built in number, weight, and measure, where harmony and proportion are a language that is hidden within its fabric. This masterpiece of medieval art

1   *Quest for the Past. Readers Digest.*
     Newham. C A. The Astronomical Significance of Stonehenge.Published by Moon Publications Wales UK
2   *Atkinson. Professor R.J.C 'Stonehenge'.*
3   *Michell. John. City of Revelation, Published by Ballantine NY*
4   *Charpentier. Louis. The Mysteries of Chartres Cathedral. Translated by Ronald Fraser Published by Avon Books NY*
5   *Ibid.*

was supervised and controlled by the Master Mason who, with his square, compass, straightedge, and plumb bob, laid the foundations for these wonderful structures that we admire today.

Modern man can only gaze upon the external shell and admire its beauty, however, lacks the spirit to discern the mysteries that is hidden within its fabric.

The experts have put forward many theories. Some suggesting a temple constructed by the Druids for the purpose of offering human sacrifice to the god's, others suggesting a place for burials and a religiously center for pagan worship. We can discount the theory propounded by the historians of the 18th century as it being a place for human sacrifice.

This form of antiquated thinking created confusion in the minds of those who were endeavoring to find answers to this enigma. There is no solid evidence to suggest that the inner precinct was a graveyard to accommodate the dead. Although signs of cremations were found near the Aubrey holes, and surrounding area, these could have been placed there by later generations.[1]

Situations of a similar nature occurred in the Cathedrals and Church's of Europe. It was never the intent of the master Builders in the middle Ages or their religious masters that the inner sanctum should become graveyards for Kings and Nobles; the Cathedrals and Church's were built to honor God and be centers of spirituality for the people. This however has not been the case. Over the years has become a place for the dead. When you enter you are walking in a graveyard with bodies buried in the floors and walls. In the hope that they would benefit from the prayers of the faithful, and be forgiven for their past transgressions, Kings, nobles, and people of note were interred in the inner sanctum of the Church.

There was also the ancient ceremonial ritual sacrifice, whereby, it was the common practice that a solemn human sacrifice be performed at the time of laying the foundation stone of the Temple or building. From what is known of this practice, the body was burned and the ashes deposited under, or in some cases under each corner stone, the purpose was for the protection of the building or Temple by the spirit of the deceased person/s. This form of ritual was not unique to any one culture, but was the general practice in many cultures.

It has been the strong belief of many ancient cultures that "to be burned alive was a great honor, regarded as a solemn sacrifice, an apotheosis, which it was believed, raised the victim to the rank of a God".[2] The ancients believed that the fire acted as a purgative so powerful that it could burn away all that was mortal in man, leaving only the divine and immortal spirit behind.[3]

Something of a similar practice of invoking the dead is an integral part of the Christian doctrine. Each Church Alter contains a cavity in which the relics of at least two Saints are encased. These relics usually consist of bone fragments of martyrs who had died for the faith

---

1   Newham. C.A. *The Astronomical Significance of Stonehenge Published by Moon Publications Wales UK*

2   Frazer. J.G. *The Golden Bough. The Roots of Religion and Folklore. Part IV. Published by Crown Publishers, Inc.*

3   *Ibid*

and are usually procured from the Catacombs in Rome. No Church Alter can be without these relics, as they are essential in the ceremony of consecration. There is a striking similarity between this practice and that of our pagan ancestors. In each the spirit of the departed is invoked to protect and guard the Temple or Church. The finding of cremated remains within the monolithic left to us by our ancestors are prevalent in Europe and the British Isles, and if researched, in many other cultures on this planet.

On the rediscovery of Newgrange in Ireland, cremated remains were found within the structures, which erroneously lead the Archaeologists to class Newgrange as a burial mound. However, recent research indicates that Newgrange and its environs was and is a large-scale solar construct.[1] Built much earlier than Stonehenge, (some estimates around 3,700 B.C) Newgrange performs the same functions as that of Stonehenge, however, where Newgrange differs from Stonehenge is the extensive burial mounds found around the environs of Stonehenge. Gerald Hawkins remarked in his writings it appeared that Stonehenge was a "focal point for departing souls".[2] This intuitive reasoning by Mr. Hawkins, may be the clue that will take us down the path as to the purpose, and the high place of honor in which this structure was held, by later generations, not only the Greek people, but by the people of Europe in general.

That Stonehenge later became an important religious center there can be no doubt, however, was initially constructed to act as an instrument that could measure the movement of the Moon and Sun, and Earths relationship to the planets. Possessing all of these attributes, we would be on safe ground in stating that it was an Astronomical Observatory, whose prime purpose was that of a time clock and calendar, and to ensure its continuity, and protect it from the profane, a major center of religion, a sacred temple dedicated to the sun God Apollo, around which the life of the people evolved.

Whether, this religious concept developed over time or was initiated at the onset, is difficult to determine, and may never be answered. But the dedication of the structure to the Sun God Apollo is significant, as it would imply that it was the Greeks who dedicated Stonehenge to the God Apollo. Stonehenge was built to withstand the ravages of time, but not of ignorance, what a wonderful sight had it remained intact.

Once it had served its purpose, our ancestors, being the clever people they were, made this temple into a religious center, dedicated to the god's in order to ensure its continuity, around which the life of the community evolved. What proof can be offered to substantiate the assertion that it was a temple of worship, not in the sense of being a place of human sacrifice, but a Temple dedicated to the sun God Apollo? In order to determine the validity of this statement we must refer to the writings of the early Greek historians.

There is no mystery. It is what it was meant to be, an Astronomical Observatory, judiciously located, and constructed to determine the cycles of the moon, the rising and setting of the sun in relation to the earth's circular motion, and most importantly, the duration of the seasons of the

---

1   Brennan. Martin. *'The Stars and the Stones' Ancient Art and Astronomy in Ireland. Published by Thames and Hudson Ltd. London.*

2   Hawkins. Gerald. *Beyond Stonehenge. Published by Harper & Row London.*

year, which was an important element in the life of the people. However, experts have made it an object of mystery due a lack of understanding and a common sense approach to the obvious. In their efforts to outdo each other in intellectual prowess, they argue ad nauseam regards its purpose, injecting Biblical, and Christian myth to support their various theories.

What is most extraordinary is the lack of information one finds in the writings of the ancient writers, especially those Roman historians on whom we place so much reliance for our information of the early centuries. None speak of the Temple at Stonehenge. It appears more than strange that the existence of such a wonderful structure, which we believe was intact in the first century, should have escaped the notice of historians down through the ages. One would assume that such an exposed pagan center of worship would find a place in the works of the Venerable Bede, but this has not been the case. Nor is there found any reference in Ecclesiastical History of the English Church, all are silent regards Stonehenge.

There is however a reference made by Diodorus Siculus, the Sicilian historian where he states, " The moon viewed from this island appears to be but a little distance from the earth, and to have it prominence like those of the earth which are visible to the eyes. They say that the God visits the island every nineteen years.[1] There is also on the island both a magnificent sacred precinct of Apollo and a notable Temple".

There have also been earlier writers, notably the Greek historian Hecataeus who states that "in the regions beyond the land of the Celts there lies in the ocean an island no smaller than Sicily.—There is also on the island both a magnificent sacred precinct of Apollo and a notable temple which is adorned with votive offerings and is spherical in shape. The Hyperborean also have their own language and are the most friendly disposed towards the Greeks…the moon as viewed from the island appears but a little distance from the earth…the god visits the island every nineteen years and the nights of the full moon are sacred to Apollo".

We must however, reach back further in history to the writings of Herodotus, the Greek historian of the 4th century BC, and the major cultures of Egypt and Greece, which existed side by side during this period. Both of these cultures were extremely religious. Herodotus tells us the Greeks adapted the Gods of Egypt, changing their names to align with the Greek religious beliefs. History also narrates that to the Egyptian and Greeks cultures, their mythical Gods ruled every facet of their lives, what the sun God Ra was to the Egyptians, the sun God Apollo was to the Greeks. Did they also adopt the Temple at Stonehenge, or did a people from Mycenae build it, long before the Greek culture developed?

Were the people of Britain known to the people of Greece? Of course they were. From the works of the great writers of Greek mythology, we can conclude that the people of Greece as Hyperborean intimately knew English people.

Reading the mythological tales of Greece, we find interwoven with the imagination of those who penned these tales, frequent mention of a people called the Hyperborean who lived beyond

1   *This is an obvious reference to the full Moon cycle, which occurs every 18.6 years.*

the Pillars of Hercules, which we know today as the Straits of Gibraltar. One such tale relates how Silenus told King Midas a wonderful tale of an immense continent lying beyond the oceans stream---where splendid cities abound, peopled by a gigantic, happy, and long lived inhabitants, and enjoying a remarkable legal system. A great expedition set out across the ocean in ships to visit the Hyperborean; but on learning that theirs was the best land that the old world had to offer, retired in disgust.[1] One cannot brush aside such an assumption as being fanciful thinking. In Homers 'Odyssey', though a work of fiction indicates the extent of his knowledge regards the British Isles.

Relating the travels of Odysseus, Homer speaks of a land "where a man who could do without sleep might earn double wages, once as a herdsman of cattle, and another as a Shepard of sheep, for the paths of night and day are close together". A fitting description of Scotland where night and day appear to mingle which leads Odysseus to say, "We have no idea where the sun sets or rises, so that we do not know east from west".

One does not have to be an expert to conclude that they are speaking of the British Isles. However, in order to substantiate this theory one has to look further into the writings of the early Greek poets, who wrote on the aftermath of the Trojan War.

How old are the Greek myths? The common belief is that they had their beginning in the 8th century B C, but would this be a correct assumption. In all probability they are memories from a long distant past, resurrected by the poets of the eight-century. The cult of the Sun God Apollo was not confined to Greece, but widespread throughout the Mediterranean area. Therefore it is reasonable to suggest that the Greeks, but also the people of Britain did not only revere the sun god Apollo. We find in the works of Herodotus, that the Hyperborean revered Apollo, and the Temple of Delos in Greece was the center for this cult.

It is sad to say that there is no true history of early Britain. A blanket of darkness covered the British Isles until the arrival of the Romans under the Emperor Claudius in the first century AD, until the Venerable Bede wrote his history of the English-speaking people in the 7th century AD. It would be true to say that the people of the British Isles have been deprived of their historical heritage.

The hybrid cultural heritage they profess today is the outcome of what has been given by the cultures of Europe. One would expect the writers of Rome would have much to say about this new colony, but we find very little. It would appear that it was treated as a backwater, not worthy of mention. Except for the military battles and skirmishes, little is known of Britain before their arrival.

What was Britain was eradicated by its occupation by the Romans, and later the Normans. This has been the natural outcome of any conflict between peoples in ancient days, and is as true today as it was in the past. The victor relates the historical events, which may, or may not be true, but are meant to enhance the reputation of both himself and his country, as was the case of Julius Caesar and his incursion into Britain in 55 BC.

---

1   *Graves Robert. The Greek Myths Vol 1 Published by Penguin Books. London.*

Are the people who built the magnificent Temples in South America, China, India, Greece, and Egypt, to be classed as being illiterate, or is it that we suffer from a mind blockage, our academics refusal to accept the fact that a people with advanced knowledge in Astronomy, Geometry, and Mathematics, existed in the past. Therefore, when we truthfully evaluate the people who built Stonehenge we find a people with all of these attributes, with a dedicated purpose.

These people were not confused with the task to which they were assigned. There was no question of them changing their minds, endeavoring to find answers through trial and error. Those who postulate such a theory lack the fundamental knowledge regards the principals required for such an enterprise. Were these a special group of people sent to England for the sole purpose of carrying out a specific task?

Stonehenge was built in stages, but not as postulated by the experts. If we follow the sequence of construction we can see that the first order of business was to build the outer circular ditch, to protect stage two, which was to determine the Moons cycle, over a period of 18.6 years. This exercise would only result in preliminary findings, as before one can rightly track the moons movements, they first must know a starting point from which to commence. Having acquired this information and roughly marking out the various positions, the real work of tracking the moons cycle would commence. This exercise would be carried out on more than one occasion, perhaps four or five to enable the Astronomer Priests to cross-reference their findings and to ensure accuracy. The importance of this work left no room for error. The approach to their work would be methodical, each stage checks, and crossed checked before being implemented. It is probable that this work lasted over a period of seventy four to one hundred and eleven years.

Logic suggests that the second phase would be determining the suns position as it traveled across the heavens. How many years would it take to establish the various seasons, winter Solstice, spring Equinox, summer Solstice, autumn Equinox? Would this work be carried out in tandem with the moon phases, most likely? However, one could theorize and say that the preparations of the stonework would be well in hand during this period.

Like any major project, whether in five thousand BC, or the twenty-first century, no work would commence until all information had been collected and evaluated. For the duration of this time no work would commence on the actual stone structure until this second stage had been completed as evident by the fifty (56) six Aubrey Holes. Therefore, the construction of the actual temple was not carried out in long protracted stages, as the experts would have us believe. This was a well-planned, executed project meticulously carried over a long period of time out by a dedicated priesthood.

Chapter 22

Reading the religious history of ancient civilizations, we find their gods were few in number and generally their functions limited.

In the case of Egypt, their functions were clearly defined. In contrast, in Greece, where we are presented with a myriad of gods whose capricious behavior leaves one to wonder as to how a people who professed advanced intelligence, believed such nonsense, but believe it they did.

No other people wrote so extensively of a world peopled by a retinue of imaginary gods and supernatural being, who controlled the lives of the human family. How and when it had its beginning is lost in the far distant past. It is all most certain that the poets of the 8th century BC had access to a corpus of mythological knowledge that had transcended time. Nevertheless, those who penned these tales would, in order to make their stories believable to the general audience, incorporate actual place names, known to their audience, in order to give credence to their narratives. Nevertheless we can be certain that, there is in every myth a grain of truth that can be weeded out if only we take the time.

Therefore, it is reasonable to ask, at what stage in their cultural development the Greeks referred to the British Isles, as the 'Isles of the Blest'. What attributes did these islands and its people possess to warrant such a title? In seeking an answer to this question we are dependent on the works of the Greek poets of the 8th century BC. The most famous of this select group was the poet, Homer and his famous tales outlined in the Iliad, in which he relates the battles fought at the siege of Troy,[1] and the Odyssey, that relates the famous travels of Odysseus.

In these tales of adventure, Homer makes numerous references to what we can only assume is the British Isles. However, the much earlier tale of Jason and the Argonauts, from which Homer may have borrowed some of his material, also alludes to the British Isles. So when we say that the Greek people knew the British Isles in the 8th century BC, we are stating a truth.

There are of course other sources, which allude to the relationship that existed between the British Isles and Greece. We find mentioned in the Epic Myths of Ireland of how Ireland was first inhabited by Queen Cessair and her female companions after the great flood,[2]

---

1   *Purportedly occurred in 1200 BC*
2   *Larousse. The Book of Invasions the Mythological Tales of Ireland World Mythology The Epic Myths of Ireland.*

This may be a reference to the goddess Circe, daughter of the sun god Helios, who settled on the island of Aeaean, which would be Ireland. The goddess Circe figures prominently in the tale of Odysseus and his encounter with the goddess when they "came to the island of Aeaean where Circe lives, a great and cunning goddess who is sister to the magician Aeëtes—for they are both children of the sun by Perse, who is daughter to Oceanus".

The next settlers, we are told, was the prince Partholon of Greece who in 2640 BC, arrived in Ireland with twenty-four couples. On their arrival the land was a smooth plain, broken by three lakes, and watered by nine rivers. Over a period of 300 years, their numbers increased to 5000, however, on the feast of Beltane, an epidemic killed all the inhabitants.

It is notable that the feast of Beltane was at this early date important in the Irish calendar. It is doubtful if the Greeks worshiped the God Bel who was primarily a god of the Semitic people, and one who demanded human sacrifice.[1]

Even though we read in the Greek myths occasions when human sacrifice was offered, they were on the whole, sun worshipers, as were the Egyptians. The next races of people to come to Ireland it is said were the Sons of Nemed, from Scythia around 2600 BC.

Elsewhere in Greek mythology, we find reference to the British Isles as recounted in the birth of the God Apollo. This tells the story of Leto who had been ravished by Leus, and was about to give birth, but the goddess Hera in her jealousy had forbidden Leto to take shelter anywhere on earth. The goddess wandered about until she was welcomed on a floating island that was barren and rocky. There the children of Zeus were born, Artemis, and Apollo. When Apollo came into the world, sacred swans circled the island seven times, Leus commanded the swans to take Apollo to Delphi and found a sanctuary. However, before taking Apollo to Delphi, the swans flew with him to their own country where the Hyperborean people lived, "A happy race, for which life was sweet. Apollo was their high God and went there at fixed times to receive their homage".

In the myth involving the tale of Prixus and Helle, we are told that Prixus went east, where Helios the sun god settled his son Aeëtes, and Helios daughter; Circe has her home where the sun sets in the west, on the island of Aeaea.[2] From these tales we can conclude that within the myth our attention is directed towards the islands in the west, England and Ireland.

In the adventures of Jason and the Argonauts in their quest for the Golden Fleece, we read that after seizing the Fleece, and the death of Apsyrtus, the brother of Medea, the Argonauts would have to wander over the gulfs of the sea, unless Medea was cleansed of her brother's blood. However, there was only one who could cleanse Medea---Circe, the daughter of Helios, and Perse.

Following their journey, we can with a little imagination place our self on their ship and travel the rivers mentioned in the narrative. Leaving the Black Sea they travel up the Danube

1   Graves Robert The Greek Myths Vol 2 Iphigeneia among the Taurians 'an oracle, advised the Spartans to propitiate the image of Artemis, by drenching the alter with human blood, they cast lots for the victim, and sacrificed him; and the ceremony was repeated yearly until King Lycurgus forbade it---.

2   Ibid

River. Reaching the end, they transship across land to the Rhine River, which exits at the port of Rotterdam in Holland. Sailing up the river Ister they come to the Eridanus; they then enter the Rhodanus, a river that rises in the extreme north, where the night itself has her habitation, and after voyaging up the river they come to the stormy lakes. A mist lay upon the lakes night and day, voyaging through them the Argonauts at last brought out their ship upon the sea of Ausonia and so came to Aeaea, and escaped to Circes Island where Jason and Medea was purified by Circe for the murder of Apsyrtus.

As this is a tale of adventure set in a mythological background, it is obvious that the author takes free license in his description of place names and events. In this instance he describes a journey across Europe by way of its two main rivers, the Danube, and the Rhine. Transferring their craft across land from the Danube to the Rhine would present no problems to these stalwart warriors. Traveling up the Rhine they would enter the North Sea by way of what is now Rotterdam, in Holland. They would then have to sail down through the English Channel, circumvent Penzance on the South coast of England, thence to Ireland.

On their return journey they come to the island of Thrinacia, which we assume was England. Upon that island "the cattle of the sun pastured, and if one of the cattle perished through them, their return journey home might not be won. Orphus would not have them land, and they saw the cattle of the sun feeding by the meadow streams, all were white as milk".

We find similar events when we read the adventures of Odysseus in Homers 'Odyssey' and his many references to Circes Island in which he states. "Thence we sailed on, glad to have escaped death, though we had lost our comrades, and came to the Aeaean Island where Circe lives, a great and cunning goddess who is the sister to the magician Aeëtes for they are both the children of the sun by Perse".[1]

Leaving Circes Island Odysseus remembers the warning given by the blind Theban, "When your ship reaches the Thrinacian Island, where you will find the sheep and cattle belonging to the Sun God, seven herds of cattle, and seven flocks of sheep, with fifty head to each flock. And the Goddesses, Phaethuse, and Lamptie, who are the children of the sun god Hyperion, tend them. While at sea in my ship, I could hear the cattle lowing as they came home to their stalls, and the sheep bleating. And then I remembered what the blind Theban had told me and how carefully Aenean Circe had warned me to shun the island of the Blessed Sun God".[2]

When the tales of Jason and Odysseus are compared there is a striking similarity in the descriptions of their journeys across the rivers of Europe. Therefore, based upon the works of the Greek mythological storytellers, there is sufficient evidence to suggest that the Greeks were acquainted with England and Ireland in the eight century BC, as the Isles of the Blessed, or "that happy land beyond the North Wind".

---

1   Homer 'The Odyssey' Book X. Pg102 Translated by Samuel Butler published by Washington Square Press NY.
2   The Odyssey Book X11 254-304 Translated by Samuel Butler Published by Washington Square Press. NY

What are of interest are the place names we find in these ancient narratives. Without stretching our imagination to the limits, it is easy to associate the names described in their journeys with that of Britain, Ireland, Scotland, Lands End, the Straits of Gibraltar, the Cliffs of Dover, and of course, Stonehenge, as the Gates of Helios.

We must however be careful to differentiate between fact and fiction. It is important that we recognize that in the most part we are dealing with fiction. However, in the case of the 'Iliad', which deals with the destruction of the city of Troy, we are dealing with an historical fact, which has been substantiated by Archaeological excavations.

How its destruction was brought about is still being researched. Was its downfall due to the battle described by Homer, by natural events, or by trade wars, has yet to be determined. But it is history and formed the basis for the epic tales penned by Homer.

It is likely that the events that occurred before, and after the fall of Troy are imaginary, developed by Homer to embellish his stories surrounding the 'Iliad' and the 'Odyssey' is imaginary. Storytelling was a profession in ancient Grecian society in which the God's played an important role in the life of the people. But like all good storytellers, it was important that Homer should have an in-depth knowledge of the Geographical locations relevant to his story. And what must also be remembered is that the people to whom he was relating his tales would consist of the educated rich families. Generally, it was customary to invite your friends to your home for supper, and be entertained by the storyteller. He would also relate his stories to the ordinary folk in the market place, where he had a willing audience, and as one would say, pass around the hat.

But a most important point to be considered, the Greek people were not isolated from the surrounding nations. Extensive trade was carried out with other nations. Despite, the lack of documentary evidence, there is sufficient evidence to suggest that their trade routes extended beyond their own boundaries as far as the British Isles. The Greeks were manufactures of Bronze and would require quantities of tin in the metallurgical processes. The nearest deposits of tin in the western hemisphere were to be found in Cornwell on the south coast of England. Coming closer to our time we have the works of Herodotus, the Greek historian, who wrote of his travels in the fourth century BC. Unlike those who wrote in the eight century, Herodotus was a traveler who recounted his experiences. In book four of his histories, he speaks of a people who lived beyond the Pillars of Hercules, (Gibraltar) known to the Greeks as the Hyperborean's. Of these people he states that there is mention of them in the Hesiod, and in Homers Epigone. He then goes on to recount the information, which he received from a people called the Delians regarding the religious practices of the Hyperborean's and their relations to the people of Greece.

He relates that it was the habit of the Hyperborean's to send a sacred offering to the Temple of Apollo at Delos in Greece. In reading his account we can only be amazed at the fervor of the people of Britain in those bygone years. He relates how the Hyperborean's brings the sacred offerings to Scythia.[1]

---

1   *Scythia Ancient region of Eurasia The Scythians flourish from the 8th to the 4th century BC*

"But the people who tell us by far the most about them are the Delians; for according to them, certain sacred offerings wrapped in wheat straw come from the Hyperborean's into Scythia, whence they are taken over by the neighboring peoples in succession until they get as far as the Adriatic. From there they are sent south and the first Greeks to receive them are the Dodonaeans. Then continuing southward, they reach the Malian gulf, crosses to Euboea, and are passed from town to town as far as Carystus. Then they skip Andros, the Carystians take them to Tenos, and the Tenians to Delos. This is how things are said to reach Delos".

It is significant that at each place named in his narrative, a temple dedicated to the God Apollo was located. It would also appear that the offering was passed from temple to temple, on its journey to the Temple of Apollo at Delos. But what is most interesting is that this ceremony was still being performed in the lifetime of Herodotus.

From his account traveling the waterways of Europe carried out part of the journey. His statement that the offerings were received by the Scythians, "whose country boarded the Black Sea, into which the mouth of the Danube completes its journey, where a temple of Apollo was located at Mount Olympus".

However, his reference to the Scythians raises some questions, as these people were not worshippers of the Sun God Apollo, but very well versed in the arts of sorcery, and witchcraft, alters, and temples were not part of their religious practice. However, it is not beyond the bounds of probabilities that they were in their own way as religious as the Greeks and carried out this service for the Greek people. One can assume that in those far off days there existed religious tolerance among the people of Europe.

Herodotus goes on to say, " on the first occasion they were sent in charge of two girls, whose names the Delians say were Hyperoche, and Laodice. To protect the girls on the journey, the Hyperborean's sent five men to accompany them – the people now known as Perpherees, and greatly honored in Delos. Later, however, when the Hyperborean's found that their messengers did not return, they changed their plans, and disliking the idea that they might always lose whoever it was they sent away on this long journey, began the practice of wrapping the offerings in straw, and taking them to the border, with instructions to their neighbors to see them conveyed to their destination by a process of relay, from one nation to another. And that is how they arrive at Delos to-day".

It is obvious that this was a ceremony performed each year and of deep religious significance to the people. Also, if this process of travel was to be successful, it had to involve the religious priests of each community on its way to Delos, which would suggest a common religious belief, or a high level of respect for the belief of others. It would also require stable religious societies within the different cultures. This would lead one to belief that the history of England, like that of Europe, is seen through the eyes of the Romans, which may not reflect the true conditions that existed prior to the suppression of the Celts.

The temple at Delphi in Greece was the pre-eminent shrine of the Sun God Apollo, as the Vatican in Rome is to the Catholics today. We read in Greek mythology of how in winter when the God Apollo was absent among the Hyperborean's, the shrine at Delos became sacred to the Goddess Dionysus.[1]

It is therefore clear that Stonehenge and the English people were well known to the Greeks of the 8th century BC. It is almost certain that Stonehenge, the Temple of Apollo, dedicated to the Sun God Helios, was functioning as a major religious center during the lifetime of Herodotus in the 4th century BC, and during the lifetime of Diodorus Siculus who wrote in the 1st century BC. Conceivably, the suppression of the Celts by Julius Caesar in 100 BC, and the arrival of the Romans into Britain in 100 AD, the Temple of Apollo at Stonehenge ceased to exert its influence in the life of the British people.

The sacred offerings sent to the Temple at Delos were purely symbolic, representing the presence of their supreme God, and to these people, it was the personification of their God.

To have an understanding of what this ceremony had on the life of the people, we have to compare it with the practices of the Catholic Church. It's ironic that this icon of religious orthodoxy would deride these ancient people as pagans unworthy of the grace of God, yet carry out a similar ceremony for much the same purpose. In the case of our ancestors it was a bundle of straw, in the case of the Catholic Church it is a wafer of wheaten flour.

One being as equally pagan as the other, however, there is a subtle difference between the two approaches. In the case of the Catholic Church your love for your god is an enforced love, with an attending threat of punishment should they falter in their belief? If the believer should accept the doctrine whole heartily, his/her reward is a place in heaven. However, should the question and disbelieve the doctrine, the punishment is a place in hell and everlasting fire. For most the choice is too stark to question what the church say's is the truth.

We have on the other hand our pagan ancestors who willingly loved their God unconditionally. There were no rewards or punishment for their failures. If punishment was meted out it was through the actions of nature, storms, crop failure, decease of livestock, or any of the many natural occurrences that inflict the farming communities to day. There was no hell fire to receive their souls when they departed this life; fear was not a tool used to garner love.

In the ceremony of the Mass, the people believe that the body of Christ is present in the Blessed Sacrament. The similarity between the two festivals is to striking to be ignored, however, church history states that it was the universal practice of the early Church to co-opt pagan festivals, and with minor modifications, adapt them and develop their own religious ceremonies. Because of this practice, one could say that the church is the embodiment of pagan believes.

There is also the ceremony of Corpus Christi, which is performed during the Spring Equinox. This ceremony bears all the hallmarks of the ancient ceremonies and of the god Apollo. During this festival, the blessed sacrament is exposed to the faithful, to be adored and venerated, believing that the body of Jesus Christ, the living God, the light of the world, is truly present in the sacrament. This circular piece of thin unleavened wheaten flour is exposed

---

1   *The Winter Solstice 21st/22nd December*

in a vessel called a Monstrance, which is usually made of gold or silver. Its construction is such that it is made to appear like the sun, with the sacred Host in the center, surrounded with the rays of the sun.

If we were to appreciate the importance this ceremony had to the ancient people of Britain, would require that we allow our imagination to travel into the past to witness this wonderful ceremony. Ceremonies carried out today by the various religious groups dim into insignificance in comparison.

How old are the ancient myths of Greece and how much credence can be placed upon these ancient tales? Had it not been for those ancient poets and storytellers, our knowledge of the ancient past would have been lost. Although these tales may have been the product of a vivid imagination, and embellished over the years, we can however, be certain that the essential body of the story remains intact. Further evidence exists in the tales of Ireland and Greece, which would support the theory that the Greeks were cognizant of the British Isles.

What I have found interesting is that the multitudinous articles written on Stonehenge I don't believe that there has appeared any reference to the relationship that existed between the Greek people and those of Britain, It would be interesting if more research were carried out which would determine the depth of this relationship.

Chapter 23

It has been expressed that "Egyptology can be a profession for gravediggers and tomb vandals, or else the most marvelous source of knowledge for the world to come".[1] However, in this search for knowledge it has been the predisposition by some to ignore the obvious and put forward preconceived opinions that do nothing for those who try to understand this wonderful civilization.

Notable is a tendency to associate the tenets of Judaic/Christianity with those of Pharaonic Egypt. How they arrive at this conclusion is difficult to understand, as there is no historic evidence to suggest that the early church fathers were aware of ancient Egypt, or its philosophy.

This lack of knowledge could also be attributed to the early Roman historians. Much like what is being experienced today with the American society, which manifests inclusiveness regards surrounding cultures?

The remnants of this ancient civilization lay dormant, unknown to our western culture until the seventeenth century when the English man, John Greaves, astronomer and mathematician, arrived in Egypt in 1638.

What followed was initially a search for knowledge by these early explorers, however, those who followed in their footsteps were far removed from seekers of knowledge and could only be classed as "gravediggers and vandals" until a semblance of order and discipline was created in the twentieth century when Archaeology gained a level of respect in academia.

Providentially, archaeology developed into a science that has imparted a corpus of information regarding these ancient people, increasing the general public's knowledge. Yet, despite the work that has been carried out over the years we are no closer in our understanding of these people and their times. What we do know is meager, built mainly upon "guesswork and speculation".[2] Those who have written extensively on this subject cannot be held at fault for approaching their subject from this direction as speculation and conjecture has been the tools of historians over the years. As a result history is being modified and rewritten, as new evidence is unearthed. Perhaps as modern methods of investigation improve our knowledge of the past will increase to the point that the conjectures arrived at by the experts may astonish our perception of Egypt

---

1   *De Lubicz R A Schwaller 'The Egyptian Miracle' Published by Inner Traditions International Ltd. NY.*
2   *An opinion expressed by French scientist, Lauert, who spent 60 years in Egypt trying to unravel its mysteries.*

It has been much to our advantage that there exists a body of information in the hieroglyphic inscriptions found on the walls, of the ruined temples and burial tombs unearthed over the years that has allowed the experts to leave the world of "speculation and guesswork" and enter a world of reality. To some extent, the translation of these writings has allowed a better understanding of Pharaonic Egypt that is nearer the truth. Those who entered this field of research did so with a reverence not found among the many explorers digging among the rubble of Egypt.

Among the many important finds unearthed in the early years of exploration was "the Royal Papyrus of Turin" which gave a complete list of Kings who reigned over Upper and Lower Egypt from Menes (3050 BC) to the New Empire (1303 BC) including mention of the duration of each reign".[1]

What is absent is how the line of accession was accomplished over the thousands of years in the life of the Empire. Was it hereditary, or a system whereby the Temple Priests selected the candidate who would occupy the royal throne? The diversity of those who occupied the throne would suggest that the latter might have been the case. However, this may not have been the case in all situations, in what has been classed as the new kingdom (1558-1303 BC), there were listed fourteen kings, eight of whom were related.[2] Perhaps over its long history it was a combination of both. It is a reflection of the power of the Temple Priests that harmony and stability was maintained in the land for thousands of years until the reign of Pharaoh Akhenaton. The disappearance of his family and the death of Tutankhamon was the harbinger, which eventually led to the downfall of the Empire.

It was during his reign that the affairs of state and the country suffered from the neglect of the Pharaoh. Archaeological correspondence discovered indicates the neglect Egypt suffered under his reign. It could be surmised that Akhenaton was so engrossed in the worship of his god that he forgot about the realities of life.

His domestic and foreign policies created an environment of instability, which made Egypt open to attack by age-old enemies. From discoveries made over the years, it appears that the family of Akhenaton was so detested by the Priests and people; that a program of destruction was carried out to eradicate and erase his name and image from the face of Egypt.

Among the major Temples destroyed was the new city of Tel El Amarna, which had been built by Akhenaton to honor the sun god Aton.

The downfall of Akhenaton and the destruction of his family was the beginning of the decline of the Egyptian civilization cumulating in the occupation by Rome in 30 BC. There were periods during this gradual decline when it appeared that a resurgence of its past glories were possible, especially during the reign of Ramses 11, however, this was of a short duration and it was not long before the decline continued. It was a sad reflection of the times that the

1   Ibid
2   New Kingdom Dynasty 18 (1558 – 1303 BC) Amunhotep 1, Thutmose 1, Thutmose 11, Queen Hatshepsut, Thutmose 111, Amunhotep 111, Akhenaten, Smenkhkare, and Tutankhamon Ancient Egypt national Geographical Society

actions of one man could bring an end to a civilization that had lasted all these thousands of years, Whereas in the past the ability to overcome change had been the hallmark of these people, this was one occasion when their way of life changed which deprived them of the ability to handle change.

Today the land, once occupied by these great people has been and continues to be a gravedigger's paradise. We can however be certain that the present generations of Archaeologists are far more knowledgeable and less influenced by religious doctrine than their predecessors of the early nineteenth century; however, they continue to allow their thinking to be influenced by the opinions of those early explorers.

Despite evidence to the contrary they continue to propagate the belief that this civilization existed for a mere four thousand years whereas this is only a fraction of their cultural existence. As was said, modern man lacks the depth of mind to appreciate the Egyptian civilization.

We should not be surprised at this as religious principals influenced those who first made a study of this ancient civilization. Because of this presumption, nothing they found could come into conflict with the Biblical teachings of the Judaic/ Christian concept of time. The result has caused incalculable damage to history.

What do we really know of Egypt? They were meticulous in keeping track of time is demonstrated by the multitudinous hieroglyphics that adorn the many Temples and the Horoscope of Dendara. There is also the famous Giza Pyramid purportedly constructed in 2,600 BC, in addition to the many sarcophagi of dead kings and nobles. Egypt did not evolve as purported by the many experts, but an entity complete from its inception. Where did they have their origins is speculative and an exercise in futility, the long list of Kings from the early dynasties (3050 BC) to the late dynasty (527 BC) gives prove of a lineage extending over thousands of years. How was this accomplished? Was it hereditary or was it the Temple Priests who selected the candidate, or a bit of both. If it were the Temple Priests it gave them supreme power over the Pharaoh, and the conduct of the people?

What was this link that enabled the Egyptians to maintain religious stability over eons of time? It could be presumed that they possessed the ability to adapt and absorb change without conflict was an obvious trait, which ensured stability and harmony in society, unlike to-days society which has seen no rest from conflict for two thousand years due to religious turmoil.

What is ascertainable is the longevity of this great civilization, which can be attributed to their religious belief in a god who was all purity and truth. The Egyptians were not fearful of death, they rather looked forward to the occasion by preparing for the day when they would at long last appear at the gate and be ushered into the presence of their god. There was no fear in their religious believes, but love and expectation; they were the most religious of people, their daily life was centered on the knowledge of a divine presence in all their actions.

Putting aside the Mythological concepts that evolved over the thousands of years, which differed from district to district, their primary belief in the one god and the resurrection of the soul was paramount. This profound belief enabled their culture to bridge each astronomical age uninterrupted by political or religious turmoil. In this respect the actions of the Pharaoh Akhenaton conformed to the age-old rite of moving the religious center of worship therefore could not be attributed to his downfall. Consequently, there must be other profound reasons why this man's family was eradicated from the pages of Egyptian history.

In his work 'Sacred Science' Schwaller de Lubicz states "A perennial concern for remaining in harmony with the heavens amply justifies events such as the displacement of the cult canters or the accentuation of the dominant character of the epoch as well as many modifications in the monuments and figurations for which there is no other explanation".

The displacement of the cult centers had been an ongoing practice from time immemorial that maintained the harmony and stability of Pharaonic rule, until the reign of Akhenaton.

From the events that followed his downfall, it is evident that the priestly function of the Temple had become corrupt; more politicized in their religious practices, self-serving their own interest, rather than the state. As long as the Pharaoh was subordinate to the Temple Priests, carrying out his functions to their dictates, social stability was maintained. However, when the Pharaoh believed he was God, rather than his representative, circumventing the rules of natural law, it was inevitable that the Temple Priests would rebel. A similar situation existed in the case of Jesus the Nazarene. His position was secure as long as he spoke on behalf of God, but when he took on the role of God, his mission was doomed to failure.

Notwithstanding, the circumstances surrounding the relocation of the Temple worship from Memphis to Karnak, it was not his religious beliefs that caused his conflict with the temple priests but his personal behavior that may have came into question, this being the case, it was a battle he could not win and doomed to failure a situation that ultimately resulted in the loss of his crown and the destruction of his family; it is here that a small segment of Egyptian history takes on a new dimension and becomes interesting.

A controversial subject among the experts has been the death of the young Pharaoh Tutankhamon. Of all the many puzzles left to us by this ancient civilizations that of the young King is the most intriguing. By his death we see the disappearance of a Royal family from the annals of Egyptian history and would have continued had it not been for Howard Carter.[1]

The story of Tutankhamon has been one of conjecture. The best that can be said is that he lived and died under mysterious circumstances and for one so young who we believed led uneventful life was awarded the most opulent funeral yet unearthed in Egypt, but why?

Up to recently there have been no clear consensus regards his death except all agrees he was in his seventeenth or eighteenth year, this much is beyond dispute. From this point onwards we enter into the realm of speculation[2]. Some say he died from natural causes, while some say his uncle treacherously murdered him. Recently, Zahi Hawass, Director of Egyptian Antiquities put the matter to rest stating that the young Pharaoh death was due to him breaking one or

---

1   Carter, Howard. *The Tomb of Tutankhamon Published by Excalibur Books*
2

two of his legs, which resulted in the legs becoming infected. Was this an attempt to end the controversy regards his death. As there is so little information scholars cannot rightfully tell the story of Tutankhamon, they can only piece together what information is presently available and speculate.

Finding simplistic answers to complex problems in order to bring an end to research does a disservice to history. If an answer has to be found to this complex problem it lies within the family of the Pharaoh Akhenaton, if not his father, Amunhotep 111, somewhere within this dysfunctional family can be found a reasonable explanation which would account for the young Pharaoh's death, but first we must look at the life styles of the Royal House, the role of the Temple Priest in the life of the Pharaoh, the rituals and religious beliefs. Unless we are conversant with a limited knowledge of these aspects of Egyptian life we will be unsuccessful in understanding the circumstances behind the untimely death of this young Pharaoh.

It must also be understood that the life of the Pharaoh was not one of ease and leisurely pursuits. Far from it, his every moment was taken up with ritual and ceremony with every waking moment controlled by the temple priests. Not even the royal bedchamber was immune from their presence as is seen by the pictures discovered at Luxor and Deir el Bahari; and the inscriptions attached to the paintings" leave no doubt as to the meaning of the scenes. The pictures at Deir el Baheri represent the begetting and the births of Queen Hatshopsitou are the more ancient, and have been reproduced with but little change at Luxor, where they represent the begetting and birth of King Amenophis 111."

It is also important to remember that the Egyptian artist did not involve himself with the abstract, but with reality. What is seen on the walls of Deir el Bahari and Luxor is the realities that existed in the Egyptian royal house and were the enactment of events that may have existed for thousands of years. We can surmise that the act of intercourse between the King and the Queen was not an arbitrary act subject to the whims and fancies of the King but a union that was controlled by the Temple Priests. Therefore what is seen on the walls of the Temple is the reality of the carnal union between the royal consorts.

In describing this J G Frazer states "the nativity is depicted in about fifteen scenes, which may be grouped in three acts; first, the carnal union of the god with the Queen; second, the birth; and third, the recognition of the infant by the gods. The marriage of Ammon with the Queen is announced by a prologue in heaven; Ammon summons his assessors, the gods of Heliopolis, revels to them the future birth of a new Pharaoh, a royal princess, and requests them to make ready the fluid of life and of strength, of which they are masters. Then the gods are seen approaching the Queen's bedchamber; in front of him marches Thoth, with a roll of papyrus in his hand, who to prevent mistakes, recites the official names of the Queen, the spouse of the reigning King (Thothmes 1 at Deir el Bahari, Thothmes 1V at Luxor), the fairest of women. Then Thoth withdraws behind Ammon lifting his arm behind the god in order to renew his vital fluid at this critical moment. Next, according to the inscription, the mystery of incarnation takes place. Ammon lays aside his godhead and becomes flesh in the likeness of the King, the human spouse of the Queen. The consummation of the divine union follows immediately. On the bed of state the god and the queen appear seated opposite each other, with their legs crossed. The queen receives from her husband the symbols of life and strength, while two goddesses, Neith and Selkit, the patronesses of matrimony, support the feet of the couple and guard them from harm. The text, which encloses the scene, sets forth clearly the reality of this mystic union of the human with the divine."[1]

A notable characteristic of all living species on this planet is the sacredness of the genetic pool; this applies to all life, especially to Homo sapiens, as a result all ancient cultures looked upon incest as the most heinous of crimes which generally resulted in the death of the perpetrator. We can look at the spectrum of all ancient tribal societies and find that the act of incest was an act that was not tolerated; the purity of the tribe was all-important. To a lesser extent the act of adultery was thought to be detrimental to the well being of the social order, but punishment was not as severe as that of incest. However, there have been recorded cases in history in which the King/Emperor has stepped outside the natural law.

One such case involved the King of Persia, Cambyses, who during the invasion of Egypt married both his daughters taking them to be his wives.[2]

The other case involved the Roman Emperor Claudius who when he had his wife, Messalina executed for her infidelity, married his niece, which was against Roman law. [3] However, being Emperor rescinding this age-old law presented no problems. I have no doubt that there have been other rulers of societies who circumvented the natural laws to their advantage. It has been purported by some that incest was a general practice among the Egyptians; however, there is no evidence, which would support this hypothesis.

The Book of Leviticus implies that the Egyptians were the most irreligious people, which is far from the truth. In fact quite the opposite as we now know from the many hieroglyphs adorning their temples.[4] It is worth remembering that it was the custom of the Semitic people to offer human sacrifice to the God Moloch, usually the first born, a practice that continued for many hundreds of years into the third century BC. It could be conjectured that in addition to human sacrifice, the ancient Semites would equally practice incest. However, it would be naïve to believe that those cultures that looked upon incest with horror, a crime punishable by death did not have the occasional incident, much as we in the west experience to day.

Nature in its wisdom has imbued all living species with the inherent aversion to the mixing of species through sexual intercourse. One will not find a lion mating with a leopard, or for

1   Frazer J C D C L., LLD., Litt D The Magic Art and the Evolution of Kings Vol 11 The Sacred Marriage Published by Macmillan & Co Ltd London

2   Herodotus., The History of Herodotus, Chap 10-31., Cambyses Conquers Egypt., Translated by George Rawlinson., Published by J M Dent & Sons Ltd London 1942.

3   Tacitus., The Annuals of Imperial Rome., The Fall of Messalina., Published by Penguin Classics

4   The New Jerusalem Bible The Book of Leviticus 18- 1-30.

that matter, a chimpanzee with a gorilla. A notable characteristic of the human family is its abhorrence to sexual relationship between Mother/ Son/Father/ Daughter/Brother/Sister and those directly related to each other. This taboo is also evident in all aspects of nature and applies to all life, whether on land, sea, or air.

All life through some unknown code look upon incest as a most heinous crime, we can look at the spectrum of all ancient cultures and find that incest was an act punishable by death. Not only was incest detrimental to the well-being of the people, but also considered an affront to the god's. In the minds of our ancestors, there was an interconnecting relationship between the sexual act and nature's cycle of growth. It was a firmly held belief that an incestuous act would have an adverse effect upon all life and bring a pestilence upon the land.[1]

Sophocles, the Greek poet speaks of this when he wrote, "a plague is on all our people, and thought can find no defense. The fruits of this famous earth do not grow, nor do women rise from the crying agony of childbirth with their children alive. One after another, like the swift winged birds, and faster than irresistible fire, you see them hurrying to the shore of the western god. By such countless deaths the city is ruined; her children lie unburied on the ground, with no one to mourn them, spreading death. And the wives and gray haired mothers wail at the altar steps on every side, begging for an end to their bitter pain".[2]

When he wrote these verses it was in regard to the incestuous relationship between Oedipus and his Mother,[3] a Greek tragedy based upon a long held belief of a similar incident said to have occurred in Egypt's royal house during the reign of the Pharaoh Akhenaton. Whether this calamitous of natural events ever occurred is again a matter of conjecture, nonetheless, it was the fear of such happenings that made people look upon such relationships with dread, therefore, to forestall such happenings, insured that the ultimate penalty was paid by the perpetrator".

The belief that incest had the power to effect the fruits of the earth probably go back to a remote antiquity. ---Conceived as an unnatural union of the sexes, incest was thought to subvert the regular processes of reproduction, preventing the earth from yielding its fruits and

---

1   Frazer, J, G. D.C.L., LL.D., Litt.D. The Golden Bough A study in Magic and Religion 3rd Edition 1911 The Magic Art and the Evolution of Kings Vol 11 Published by Macmillan and Co., Ltd London.

2   Sophocles 'Oedipus' Thebes in Time of Pestilence Greek Verse Published by Penguin Books by Constantine A. Trypanis.

3   The story of King Laius of Thebes, and his Queen, Jocasta who bore a son whom the oracle predicted would kill his father. Tying his feet together they abandoned the baby to the elements on Mt. Cithaeron. Found by a shepherd in the employ of King Polybus of Corinth the child was brought up as their own. However, being told by the oracle at Delphi that he would kill his father and marry his mother he left home never to return. On his travels he encountered King Laius, whom he killed in a quarrel. In keeping with tradition, he received the throne of Thebes and married the widow with whom he had four children. When the truth was divulged, Queen Jocasta committed suicide; Oedipus went into exile accompied by two of his daughters, leaving his kingdom in the hands of his brother-in-law, Creon. It is said that Oedipus died at Colonus near Athens.

hinder animals and men from propagating their kind".[1] Did such an incestuous act occur in the reign of the Pharaoh Akhenaton? There is sufficient evidence to suggest that the myth of Oedipus was based upon fact and related to events that may have occurred before and during this Pharaoh's reign?

---

1   *Frazer J G. D.C.L., LL.D., Litt.D. The Golden Bough A Study in Magic and Religion The Magic Art and the Evolution of Kings 3rd Edition Vol 11 Macmillan and Co Ltd London.*

Chapter 24

It's important that we dispel the views of others relative to the question of incest in the ancient Kingdom of Egypt. Writing on the subject, Professor Frazer expressed the opinion that incest between brother and sister was the norm and not the exception among ancient Egyptians. His statement that "in the eyes of the Egyptians marriage between brother and sister was the best of marriages, and it acquired an ineffable degree of sanctity when the brother and sister who contracted it were themselves born of a brother and sister, who had in their turn also sprung from a union of the same sort. Nor did the principal apply only to gods and Kings. The common people acted on it in their daily life. They regarded marriages between brother and sister the most natural and reasonable of all."[1]

However, what he describes relates to the Macedonians who conquered Egypt under Alexandria the Great in 300BC suggesting that they had borrowed the practice from their predecessors. That it occurred within the family of Akhenaton is amply documented, and perhaps within his father's household is highly possible, but was it the general practice among the population? Highly unlikely when one views the Egyptian culture and its longevity. If such a practice were the general rule over the millennia it would be devastating in a society that was all-inclusive. The dilution of the genetic pool would result in a population of imbeciles, genetic misfits and as science have shown a high proportion of malformed births in each generation.

We cannot let our imagination run away with us and depict the Egyptians as population of sexual deviants. It is however possible that like contemporary society sexual intercourse between siblings did occur occasionally but not the norm and the same may be said for ancient Egypt. The picture however changes when we come to the reign of Akhenaton and his family.

For one of whom little is known the prolific amount of literature regarding his life is amazing. It clearly demonstrates the creative ability of our academics and historians. There is "almost nothing known about Akhenaton childhood. He was the son of Amenhotep111 and Queen Tiy---but where he grew up---even the dates of his birth are questions that perhaps no amount of scholarly work will ever be able to resolve".[2] To our modern historians Akhenaton

---

1   Frazer J C., D. C. L., L L D., Litt D *The Magic Art and the Evolution of Kings The Sacred Marriage*
2   Russman Edna R *Change in a Changeless Land National Geographic*

is a man of mystery and will remain so, however, the little information available allows many writers the opportunity to offer conjectural opinions on his life and time. Among which can be counted the work by Immanuel Velikovsky[1], but again like all who their own axe to grind he tends to subvert history in order to mould his own agenda as it impacts the Jewish view as regards their purported past. However he does bring to light many of the vexing questions surrounding the young King Tutankhamon and his father. He questions as to why "this (young) monarch, who ruled only a very short time died young, was honored to such an extent after his death". There is a mystery here and it can only be answered by the events surrounding the household of his father Akhenaton.

To have an understanding of this man we must see him as he is and not as we would wish him to be, not based upon conjecture, but regards his family, the customs relevant to the times in which he lived, and the disappearance of him and his family from the annuals of Egyptian history. Had it not been for the discovery of the tomb of Tutankhamon an important page of Egyptian history would have been lost.

It is however important to understand that when we view the paintings and statuary of the Egyptians we are looking at reality and not an embellishment of the artistic mind. Therefore, when we view the paintings and statuary depicting Akhenaton we see him as he was and the same can be said for those around him. The same principal applies to the paintings at Deir el Bahari and Luxor. This was the reality of life re-enacted in stone for posterity. So when viewed the scenes depicting the Royal Wedding is an actual event that may have been carried out over the millennia.

However, in the reign of Akhenaton this was to change. A tableau depicting the royal family is revealing. In it we see the King, his wife Nefertiti, and three of his children. When we look closely we see that the facial and bodily features of the Royal couple are very similar, including the facial features of the children. In contrast a bust of Nefertiti shows her to be the most beautiful of women whereas in the tableau her features are those of her husband. It is also strange that the bodily characteristics of the King are similar to that of the Queen. The Kings bodily features are more female rather than male; in fact his figure is grotesque. The experts have suggested that he suffered from a genetic disorder known as 'Marfan's Syndrome' a hereditary disease, which is manifested by the characteristics observed in the tableau. The most striking feature is the elongated skull formation of the family, which is similar to that of Tutankhamon, and the two children discovered in his tomb. This striking deformity would suggest that there was a genetic relationship between all the members of the royal household thus reinforcing the theory that all of these children were the result of an incestuous relationship.

For that reason there is sufficient evidence to suggest that incest played a major role in the family of Akhenaton, and may have been practiced in the reign his father, of which he was a product. Also the characteristics of the family would suggest, despite her beauty, Nefertiti

---

1   *Velikovsky Immanuel 'Oedipus and Akhenaton' Myth and History Published by Doubleday & Company Inc NY*

may have been the sister of Akhenaton. When considered, anything was possible within this dysfunctional family. However, a major obstacle facing all those who write on this subject is the lack of dates. When was he born and where? When did he ascend the throne and at what age? How old was he when he died? In between he fathered six daughters, whose names were Merytaten, Meketaten, Ankhesenpaaten, Neferneferuaten-tasharit, Neferneferure, and Sotepenre. What happened to this family is unknown but many have speculated, some saying that four of the children died from the plague, including Akhenaton's concubine, Kiya,[1] a simple explanation to a difficult problem. These were children of the royal household and had they died of the plague would have had full burial honors afforded to them yet no traces of their burial tombs have been discovered. Could there be another explanation that would be more appropriate to the events that followed. Would be reasonable to suggest that when Akhenaton went into exile he was accompied by Nefertiti her four youngest children in addition to Kiya acting as their nurse?[2] Those other members of remaining of the family were the two sons, Smenkhkare and Tutankhamon, the eldest daughter Merytaten, and Ankhesenpaaten, the wife of Tutankhamen Again conflict arises as to the relationship of the two young men to Akhenaton. Who was their mother? It has been speculated that the two boys were the offspring of one of his concubines, which is highly unlikely when one considers the anatomical characteristics of the skeletal remains and the view of this family left to us on the many tableau. As the Temple Priests controlled the heirs to the throne, children of the harem did not have access, however if Smenkhkare and Tutankhamen were the offspring of Akhenaton's mother Queen Tiy would be accepted?[3] When one considers the times of which we speak and the propensity of the Royal household to indulge in the act of incest it is not an impossible theory, actually may be nearer the truth than some of the harebrained theories put forward by the experts. We are however at a disadvantage surrounding the question of age of those involved. Had Tiy given birth to these two boys before Akhenaton ascended the throne the events that followed would be clarified. Was this the catalyst that set off a chain of events that saw to destruction of the entire family? It is supposition on the part of the experts relative to the age of these two young men. It is assumed that Smenkhkare was 18/20 years when he died and Tutankhamen was 8/10 years when he ascended the throne.[4] It is arguable that they may have been a lot closer in years than it has been theorized. If they were the offspring of Akhenaton's mother Tiy it is possible that they may have been less than two years between the brothers. Lacking dates makes any attempt to follow this line of reasoning difficult. Perhaps the destruction of the family had nothing to do with him changing the seat of government to the new city of Amarna, or as some has suggested converting Egypt from Polytheism to Monotheism, but rather the behavior of the royal house? Egypt had believed in the concept of one supreme God thousands of years before Judaism saw

1   *Lorenz Megeara An Analysis of Akhenaten's Familial Relationships*
2   *If this theory has any credence it would account for the lack of Archaeological evidence*
3   *Ibid*
4   *Lorenz Megaera An Analysis of Akhenaten's Familial Relationships*

the light of day. Therefore any relationship between Judaism and Egyptian concept of God has no bases in fact.

Let us add another dimension to the many speculative opinions that has been offered concerning this family. Evidence suggests that on the death of his father Amunhotep 111 Akhenaton inherited a land rich and prosperous[1] and a stable society in which the people were at peace. One would assume that under these circumstances the future reign of the Pharaoh would be assured but this was not the case, as future events would show. Therefore, it is important that we bring into focus the role of the King in this ancient society if we are to have an understanding of his times.

Although the Egyptians believed in a supreme God they also had panoply of gods, which they invoked in their prayers, much the same as the Christians do to day except that Christians have panoply of saints to which they direct their prayers. In this respect they were as superstitious as our present day religious in the wearing of amulets and charms in which they believed brought them good luck. This habit is more pronounced among Catholics and those of the Muslim faith and extends too many other pagan cultures on this planet.

In ancient societies "the King/High Priest was thought to be endowed with supernatural powers" He was also thought to be the incarnation of God and with this belief the course of nature is supposed to be under his control, and he would be held responsible for bad weather, failure of the crops, and similar calamities. It appears to be assumed that the King's power over nature, like that over his subjects and slaves is exerted through definite acts of will; and therefore if drought, famine, pestilence, or storms arise, and the people attribute the misfortune to the negligence or guilt of their King, and punish him accordingly and if he remains obdurate, with death. He is the point of support on which hangs the balance of the world, and the slightest irregularity on his part may overthrow the delicate equipoise. The greatest care must, therefore, be taken both by him and off him and his whole life, down to the minutest details, must be so regulated that no act voluntary or involuntary may disarrange or upset the established order of nature".[2]

Modern people may look upon this as being preposterous but it was the glue that held ancient societies together. Such a case existed in Japan until its defeat by America in 1945/46. This was a society, which treated its Emperor as a "God who governs the universe". In much the same fashion the Pharaoh "of Egypt were worshipped as God whose life was fixed for them by law, not only their official duties, but even the details of their daily life, not only were the times appointed at which he should transact public business or sit in judgment; but the very hours for his walking and bathing and sleeping with his wife, in short, performing every act of life was settled".[3]

Recognizing the importance of the Pharaoh's well-being to that of the people it is reasonable to suggest that the tableau's portraying the young Tutankhamon in the heat of battle can be dispelled as being more symbolic rather than factual; this can also apply to the reign of Ramses

---

1   *Ibid*
2   *Frazer J G 'D C L LL D Litt D The Golden Bough' Taboo and the Perils of the Soul*
3   *Ibid*

11, who it is said fought many battles fraught with danger to his person. The holiness of the Pharaoh's person was too important to the stability of the country to be placed in danger.

The Priests of the Temple were not impotent, in fact they were all powerful having control over every aspect of Egyptian life, therefore moving the seat of government from Thebes to El Amarna had to be with their consent, for this reason it is doubtful if this was the reason for Akhenaton's downfall and possible exile. Whatever the crime of which he was guilty it was not associated with the relocation of the center of worship Thebes but something of deeper significance which resulted in the destruction of the family.

During his reign we see the disappearance of the Queen Nefertiti from the royal household. The reason for her disappearance has never been fully explained. Some suggest she changed her appearance to that of a man and became co-regent with her husband. A theory of this nature lends itself to pulp fiction rather than contributing to history. Also suggested is theories that on her departure Akhenaton choose one of his concubines as his wife with whom he had additional children. Again the imagination of the author is more fantasy than reality. It is doubtful if the Royal priesthood would allow such to happen. To have them as bedmates was permissible, but not as a Queen and royal consort. As we read the various theories propounded by the multitudinous array of experts we are confronted with imaginary speculative vague opinions that confuse rather than clarify the issues.

Among the many theories are those that suggest shortly after Nefertiti's departure the King himself was stripped of his authority and sent into exile to be replaced by his son Smenkhkare whose reign was short lived. Archeological evidence suggests that this young man's funeral was not one of opulence as was his brother, Tutankhamon. In fact, the discovery of what is purported to be his sarcophagus gives one the impression that he was buried without the usual ceremonies befitting a King. Actuality the discovery of his sarcophagus created confusion among the experts in there hast to associate the sarcophagus with Akhenaton. The confusion found in the tomb, if it was his tomb, would suggest a burial carried out in secrecy and hast.[1] Associate this with the disappearance of the family. What was the time spans between the disappearances of Nefertiti, and her children, Kiya, the concubine and the possible exile of Akhenaton, the death of Queen Tiy, the mother of Akhenaton, the death of Smenkhkare, and the disappearance of his sister Merytaten, and that of Tutankhamen's wife, his sister Ankhesenpaaten did these occur in a short space of time? Would this indicate a consorted effort to rid the land of this accursed family? One could suggest that there was a sequence of events that was planned and executed by the royal priesthood and Ay, the uncle of Tutankhamen. Also the conditions that existed in Egypt during Akhenaton's reign create another mystery that remains unanswered that may have been the catalyst that initiated the events that lead to Tutankhamen's sacrificial death

Interesting descriptions of these conditions give us some idea as to the depth and degradation the lands of Egypt had fallen into during Akhenaton's reign that may help us to arrive at the

1   *Velikovsky Immanuel Oedipus and Akhnaton Published by Double Day and Co Inc NY*

conclusion that the young King Tutankhamon being the last of his family was sacrificed remove the wrath of the god's and restore the lands of Egypt, hence the opulence of his burial.

It was written in ancient text that "the good ruler, performing benefactions for his father (Amon) and all the gods, for he has made what was ruined to endure as a monument for the ages of eternity and he has expelled deceit throughout the Two Lands, and justice was set up so that it might make lying to be an abomination of the land, as in the first time. Now when his majesty appeared as King, the temples of the gods and goddesses from Elephantine down to the marshes of the Delta had fallen into neglect. Their shrines had become desolate, had become mounds over grown with weeds. Their sanctuaries were as if they had never been. Their halls were a footpath. The land was topsy-turvy and the gods turned their backs upon the land, if the army was sent to Djahi to extend the frontiers of Egypt, no success of theirs came at all. If one prayed to a god to seek council from him, he would never come at all. If one made supplication to a goddess, she would never come at all".[1] (Ancient Near Eastern Texts, Tutankhamen)

A land bereft and forgotten by the gods or so it would seem. One could construe that the relocation of the seat of government from Thebes to El Amarna and the construction of a new city so engrossed Akhenaton that the affairs of state were neglected to the extent the temples of the gods in Thebes and throughout the whole of Egypt fell into disrepair. It has also been established by recent discoveries that Egypt was suffering from a period of desolation among the general population.

It is obvious from the description the conditions described was long in the making and may perhaps have commenced shortly after Akhenaton ascended the throne. How long a situation of this nature would last without the Royal priesthood taking action would be speculative but from the events that followed it is clear that they did take action of the most drastic measures in order to rid themselves of this curse that covered to land by the age of ritual of sacrificing the life of the King. "The tradition that associated the sacrifice of the King or his children with a great dearth points clearly to the belief, so common among primitive folk, that the King is responsible for the weather, and the crops, and that he may justify pay with his life for the inclemency of the one or the failure of the other".[2] "For we must not forget that the King is slain in his character of a God, his death and resurrection, as the only means of perpetuating the divine life unimpaired, being deemed necessary for the salvation of his people and the world"[3]

Under these circumstances we can find reason for the opulence afforded to the young Kings burial. It would also be true to say that no other pharaoh in the history of Egypt, as far as it can be determined, had a burial of such magnificence.

What form did the ritual killing of the young King take and who would be involved in the sacrificial rite? We can be certain that it would be carried out with all due religious solemnity; a

1   *Pritchard James Ancient Near Eastern Texts Princeton 1969 Tutankhamon Restoration after the El Amarna Revolution*

2   *Frazer J G The Dying God Published by Macmillan & Co Ltd London 1911*

3   *Frazer J G The Golden Bough The Roots of Religion and Folklore Published by Gramercy Books NY*

ceremony of this nature would require nothing less. We can also be certain that a ceremony of such importance to the people would not be carried out in secret but in full view of the public with the high priest of the temple and full panoply of attending priests. As to the actual death of the young King one can only speculate. But if we are to offer a hypothesis it would follow the age old ritual we read off in the works of J G Frazer in which he outlines the manner by which the ritual killing were carried out which involved strangulation in order to avoid spilling the royal blood which would be profane. Who would be delegated with this holy sacrifice? Again one could speculate and hypothesis that a priest of the temple would be given this task considering its importance.

Watching this tableau play itself out would be two personages that had important roles to play in future events, Ay the brother of Akhenaton's mother Tiy, and the army general, Horemhab both of whom were later to occupy the throne. What is most strange is what was found in the tomb of Tutankhamon in tableau depicting the ceremony relative to the 'Opening of the Mouth'[1] a most important ceremony which involved the soul of the deceased in the netherworld. The Egyptians truly believed in the immortality of the soul and that this particular ceremony enables the soul of the deceased to transverse the worlds of the living and of the dead. Thus the soul will live into eternity in the abode of the God's

Ordinarily, this important ceremony was the function of the SEM priest who carried it out in the tomb of the deceased, assisted by an assemblage of priests, each of whom takes on the role of a particular god. A full and comprehensive description of the ceremony can be found in the Egyptian Book of the Dead.[2] However, in the tableau found on the walls of Tutankhamon tomb, the person administrating this most important rite is Ay, Tutankhamen's uncle dressed in the leopard skin robe which is customarily worn by the SEM priest as an insignia of his office. Additionally, Ay is wearing the blue crown of the reigning monarch which would indicate that the young Queen, Ankhesenpaaten the wife of Tutankhamon was in all likelihood dead thus enabling Ay to usurp the crown and assume the role of Pharaoh. However, when one reads the many experts it is the general opinion that it was the army general Horemheb who succeeded Tutankhamen which is obviously not the case, rather General Horemheb was to succeed Ay to the throne and who early in his reign had all traces of the Akhenaton dynasty effaced from the Temples and monuments across the land.

Nonetheless, what we see and what we speculate leads us to question and seek answers to some puzzling aspects of the tableau. There is no Archeological evidence which would suggest that Ay was a member of the priesthood, therefore taking the role of the SEM priest for the most important ceremony of the funeral is rather strange. Also, the theory put forward by some experts that it was tradition for succeeding Pharaoh to administer the funeral rites is a theory that lacks foundation as again there is no Archeological evidence which would support

---

1   *Budge E A Wallis The Egyptian Book of the Dead The Papyrus of Ani Published by Dover Books Publications INC NY*

2   *Ibid*

this hypothesis.[1] Both theories are put forward for the want of a more logical explanation. But if the death of Tutankhamon was a sacrificial death Ay's presence and the role he played in administrating these age old religious rites would be logical. This may have been the one occasion when a society reverted to age old customs in the hope of bringing about change.

1   *Fox Penelope Tutankhamon Treasure Published by the Oxford University Press "The scene is without precedent, a succeeding pharaoh never before or after being depicted in a former rulers tomb"*

Chapter 25

Despite the many contradictory theories put forward by the experts, the Egyptian people were deeply religious with a belief that had sustained their civilization over thousands of years. Suddenly this once prosperous land begins to experience conditions never before known in their long history. As long as the priests of the temple controlled the behavior of the Royal household peace and stability reigned throughout the land. But when this priestly power was subverted by the Pharaoh the moral behavior of society disintegrated creating instability throughout the land. It could be said that "the life of the Pharaoh is only valuable so long as he discharges the duties of his position… So soon as he fails to do so, the care the devotion the religious homage, which they had hitherto lavished on him, ceases and are changed into hatred and contempt; he is dismissed ignominiously, and may be thankful if he escapes with his life".[1] From this description it can be construed that in ancient societies it was the norm that when society was sick the people looked to their king, from whom all good and evil transcends.

We must also consider the role of those within the royal circle and the Temple priests. The Priests were not impotent, but all powerful and as long as they controlled the daily behavior of the royal household peace and stability reigned throughout the land. But when this authority was usurped by the Pharaoh and the behavior of the Royal house became lax contravening the natural law, the tranquility of the land came to an end and the people suffered. Given these conditions it was only a matter of time before the priests of the temple set in motion a chain of events in order to correct the natural balance.

Notwithstanding the many theories put forward by panoply of experts, with the limited information available what conclusions can be reached devoid of imaginary fantasy? A major obstacle surrounds the question of time frames to which we can make reference to guide us through the labyrinth of history. We can however, be certain that the events surrounding the family of Akhenaton's were not of a long duration but were a sequence that saw the demise of the whole family in a very short space of time.

Therefore, assuming that the decision was made by the Temple priests to remove the Pharaoh from power, it would be one requiring immediate action. So let us add one more theory to many that has been circulated around this unfortunate family.

---

1   Frazer J G D.C.l., LL.D., Litt.D., *The Golden Bough Taboo and the peril of the Soul The Burden of Royalty*

In developing this theory there is the obstacle regards the age difference between the brothers Smenkhkare and Tutankhamen. It is speculation on the part of the experts regards the age when Tutankhamen became Pharaoh. However, bridging the years between the brothers allows us to make certain assumptions to fit the picture and bring what knowledge we have into focus.

We now come to the final act that brought on the total destruction of this unfortunate family and the beginning of the end of a civilization that had lasted over forty-millennium. In outlining this scenario we must consider that no traces of the family have been discovered, except that of Tutankhamen and the bodies of the two infants discovered in his tomb. However, skeletal remains were discovered that may have been those of Smenkhkare based upon the age of the remains and a striking likeness to Tutankhamen. No remains have been located of Akhenaton, Nefertiti, her four children, their nurse Kiya, Tutankhamen's wife Ankhesenpaaten, or his two eldest daughters, Merytaten, and Meketaten. It has been the theory that the four children and their nurse died from the plague if this were the case they would[1] as children of the Royal household be entitled to a royal burial irrespective of the manner of death. There is no evidence to support this supposition therefore the theories put forward to explain the disappearance of the family is pure speculation. There is however the theory put forward by Immanuel Velikovsky regards the demise of one of the daughters which one could assume was the eldest that has a ring of truth and would be in line with the events surrounding the sacrificial death of Tutankhamen[2] Blending legend and archeological discoveries he weaves a poignant tale of love and devotion that may account for the death of one of the sisters of Smenkhkare. One would surmise from the chain of events that the daughter involved in this sad tale would be Akhenaton's eldest daughter, Merytaten?

One last point that may need clarification surrounds the death of Smenkhkare which has been attributed to a battle of rival factions, or as some have purported between the brothers Smenkhkare and Tutankhamen. Such a theory is more suited to the middle Ages than that of the Egyptian 18th dynasty. The discovery of his remains and the impoverished manner of his burial may suggest that his death was no accident, but may have been arranged to be followed by his sister who as suggested by Immanuel Velikovsky may have been entombed alive to die a slow death?

1   *Lorenz Megaera Akhenaton*
2   *Velikovsky Immanuel Oedipus and Akhenaton Published by Doubleday& Co Inc NY*

Chapter 26

It has been some weeks now and my mind is still stagnant for the want of words. This is the last chapter and I just cannot put what I want to say into comprehensive words that would bring this chapter to a close. However, what I am convinced of is that the downfall of the Egyptian pharaoh Akhenaton was not through his preoccupation with the solar god nor was it due to moving his capital to Tel Amarna which was a custom that had been in vogue for many thousands of years.[1]

Egypt had throughout its known history been engrossed with the Solar Disk as an emblem of their God who was met with daily adoration on his rising in the morning and his setting in the evening. So we can debunk the theory as put forward by some as this being the reason for his downfall.

There is more than significant evidence to confirm that Egypt was a truly monotheistic throughout its long history. Nor can we accept the theory that his moving the capital from Thebes to Tel Amarna as a contributing factor as it had been the practice of the Egyptian Royal priesthood over aeon's of time to move the seat of power in line with the universal clock.[2]

So what are we left with that would support the theory that the demise of this dysfunctional family in what was a very short period of time. If we follow the reasoning of the experts we stumble along trying to fix dates to fit the many theories which in the end leave us back where we started. There are so many with different theories each a contradiction creating a maze of thoughts which do nothing but confuse the mind.

However, when we bring the cast of characters into perspective and their possible motives we can discern a situation that reads like the Greek tragedy it became with the writings of the Greek dramatis Sophocles when he penned the story of 'Oedipus' and his tragic end.[3]

Was this a figment of Sophocles imagination or was it based upon a more ancient tale concerning the Egyptian Royal House that may have been prevalent during his life time? I would rather be inclined to believe that this may have been the case. Incest in any age revolts the senses and has been taboo in most cultures on this planet, but we must however recognize

---

1   *Lubicz R A Schwaller 'Sacred Science' Published by Inner Traditions International N Y*
2   *Ibid*
3   *Graves Robert 'The Greek Myths 2; Sophocles 'Oedipus at Colonus' Published by Penguin Books*

the in some of the more ancient royal families incest was the accepted norm when it came to heredity succession which may have been the case with the parents of Akhenaton , Amenhotep 111 and his wife Tiy. Was Akhenaton himself a product of an incestuous relationship? There is that possibility when one considers what followed with Akhenaton and his family; it is reasonable to suggest that this may have been a family trait. We know relatively nothing about his father's family other than he was a great ruler bequeathed a prosperous land to his son. Did he have other brothers and sisters, or was he the only child, perhaps, but there appears to be no record of an extended family. His deformed body would lead one to belief that he may have been incestuously conceived but such an idea would be speculative, however, not unreasonable.

The disappearance of Akhenaton and his family, and the death of Tutankhamon is an undisputed fact it is the circumstances surrounding the events that has created the many controversial opinions expressed by a myriad of experts. What is undeniable are the circumstances surrounding the family and the pitiful plight of the Egyptian people during his reign which has been amply attested by the Archaeological discoveries at Tel Amarna; the major problem is the sequence of events relative to the family's demise.

It has been hypothesized that four of the children of Akhenaton's family died at an early age from the plague.[1] This opinion is conjectural and may or may not have been the case but construed from the conditions that the Egyptian's were suffering during Akhenaten's reign. It has also been hypothesized that Neferititi and her children were sent into exile, purportedly because she was unable to bear son's which was important to the Royal house, accompanied by their nurse, Kiya. This theory has a ring of truth to it when one considers the conditions then prevailing in Egypt and would account for the lack of information regarding the family's whereabouts. One could also speculate and suggest that Akhenaten accompanied his family into exile.

So what of the remaining members of the family, Smenkhkare, his sister Merytaten who perhaps was his wife, Tutankhamen and his wife Ankhesenpaaten? And all but forgotten by the many experts the two infant bodies found in the tomb of Tutankhamen, who were most assuredly the off spring of Tutankhamen.[2] The death and burial of Tutankhamon brother Smenkhkare was not one of pomp one would associate with the death of a King, it is doubtful if he ever attained the throne however the circumstances surrounding his burial would indicate that he had not, therefore there is every possibility that he was murdered hence the lack of ceremonial trappings to his burial. The death of Merytaten, his sister/wife, may have occurred simultaneously if we accept the hypothesis put forward by Immanuel Velikovsky[3] who based his theory upon the discoveries made by the American explorer, Theodore Davis who in his ignorance failed to appreciate the importance of his discovery.

We now come to what remains of this family, Tutankhamen, his wife Ankhesenpaaten and the mummified bodies of two children found in Tutankhamon tomb, one a fetus and one of

---

1   *Lorenz Megaera Akhenaten An analysis of Akhenaten's Familial Relationships*
2   *Carter Howard The Tomb of Tutankhamon Published by Excalibur Books*
3   *Velikovsky Immanuel Oedipus and Akhnaton Published by Doubleday & Company Inc NY*

a premature baby. How old were these two little bodies? There appears to be no information, they have been forgotten, overshadowed by the greater treasures discovered in the tomb. Whose children were they? It was the opinion of Howard Carter that these were the off spring of Tutankhamon and his young wife, Ankhesenpaaten. Recent medical examination of the two bodies has confirmed that they were in fact the offspring of the royal family, but which member? As the findings were based upon the cranium characteristics so pronounced in the Royal family it was the opinion of Howard Carter that they were the children of Tutankhamen's sister/wife Ankhesenpaaten but as one considers this theory it becomes most unlikely . It is possible that they could be the off spring of either Merytaten or Ankhesenpaaten. Who was the mother?

All of this is academic and may never find an answer; however, the events that occurred at the opening of the tomb perhaps would indicate that the little coffin with these two bodies may have been placed in the tomb after the main entrance door was sealed but not before the entrance was completely filled over obliterating the mortuary site.

We can only rely on the word of those who participated in this marvelous discovery. Howard Cater states that on exposing the entrance doorway "there had had been two successive openings and re-closing of a part of its surface; furthermore, that the sealing originally discovered, the jackal and the nine captives, had been applied to the re-closed portion, whereas the sealing's of Tutankhamon covered the untouched part of the doorway and were therefore those with which the tomb had been originally secured. The tomb then was not absolutely intact, as we had hoped. Plunders had entered it, and entered more than once-from the evidence from the huts above.....but that they had not rifled it completely was evident from the fact that it had been resealed". Further on in his narrative he states "Then in the middle of the afternoon, thirty feet down from the outer door we came upon a second sealed doorway, almost the replica of the first. The seal impressions in this case were less distinct, but still recognizable as those of Tutankhamon and of the Royal necropolis. Here again the signs of the opening and the resealing were clearly marked upon the plaster". On examining the door between the statues guarding the tomb it was noted that "a small breach had been made near the bottom, just wide enough to admit a boy or a slightly built man, and that the hole made had subsequently been filled up and resealed"

However, what gives food for thought is his statement that "in the anti-chamber there had been some sort of attempt to tidy up after the plunder's visit. Was this an action on the part of the temple priests or the thieves? What thief would take the trouble to clean up and reseal his point of entry? Also what thief worth his salt would forgo such riches in gold and jewelry? This would question Howard Carter's assertion that thieves had gained entry after the burial. What thief would go to the trouble of resealing his point of entry including the second entrance? I doubt if thief's had possession of the royal seals. However, as Tutankhamon has already been placed in the tomb and the entrance door sealed it was necessary to create a second entrance just sufficient to accommodate the small coffin containing the little bodies. Having accomplished their task the priests withdraw and resealed the second entrance.

The placing of the little coffin in the tomb of their father brought an end to this unfortunate family and brought to an end to thousands of years of stability.

What followed the removable of this family was the beginning of the end of this great empire. As there was no family members remaining to inherit the throne, Ay (the uncle of Nefertiti) became Pharaoh as successor to Tutankhamon and reigned for a short period of four years (1323-1319). Ay was followed by Horemheb the army general who reigned from 1319-1292, who during his reign erased the names of Akhenaton, Smenkhkare, Tutankhamon and Ay from the royal list and publicly condemned them, this final act brought to an the royal House of Egypt. From this date forward Egypt was ruled by commoners beginning with the army General Horemheb.

I would in conclusion take free license and borrow from Immanuel Velikovsky, who in his work 'Oedipus' made mention of a stylized writing on a piece of gold foil found under the feet o f the mummy of a young man whose remains has been Identified as that of Smenkhkare, the brother of Tutankhamen which reads.

I inhale the sweet breeze that comes from your mouth
I contemplate your beauty every day
It's my desire to hear your lovely voice
like the norths wind whiff
Love will rejuvenate my limbs
Give me thy hand that holds thy soul
I shall embrace and live by it
Call me by name again, again, forever
and never will it sound without response.

One can only wonder at the love and devotion that inspired such beautiful words. Who among us can hope for such love to enter our life?

APPENDIX 1

The following information is from the Sky globe program developed by Mark A. Haney involving the earth's rotation over a period of fifty-six, thousand, one hundred and sixty (56,160) years. This comprises two full precessions of the equinox cycles commencing in the year 23,760 BC to 2028 AD, to 27776 AD, to determine the position of the planet Aries and the constellation in which it ascended.

The reading is taken from the position of the Giza Pyramid, facing south, looking east towards the horizon. Each reading is taken on the 21st March, the day of the Equinox at midnight. This is not an exact science, but sufficient to determine the location of the planet Aries, and the constellation in which it rises. The purpose of this exercise was to check a theory postulated by R.A.Schwaller de Lubicz that the Egyptian priest in conversation with Herodotus was referring not to the Sun, but probably to the position of the planet Aries.

From the following readings it is seen that in one processional cycle of time the planet Aries ascended in the constellation of Libra.

Summer Solstice	Jun 21st	06h00	23.27	31.48 83	
Year Month Day Time					
28080 BC March 21st 00.00.	22h53	+00º50º	+58º47º	202º12º	South.
Constellation of Pisces					
(1)25920 BC.	00h44	+12º44º	+72º44º	165º34º	South.
Constellation of Pisces					
(2)23760 BC.	02h42	+23º29º	+69º32º	103º41º	East.
Constellation of Aries					
(3)21600 BC	04h53	+30º01º	+55º55º	79º14º	East.
Constellation of Taurus					
(4)19440 BC	07h12	+29º55º	+35º39º	72º50º	East.
Constellation of Gemini					

(5)17280 BC	09h22	+23°11°	+17°03°	72°30°	East.
Constellation of Cancer					
(6)15120 BC	11h20	+12°21°	-01°19°	74°44°	East.
Constellation of Leo					
(7)12960 BC	13h10	+00°28°	-19°09°	77°39°	East.
Constellation of Virgo					
(8)10800 BC	15h03	-09°41°	-36°18°	79°14°	East.
Constellation of Libra					
(9)8640 BC	17h04	-15°30°	-52°14°	75°47°	East.
Constellation of Ophiucus					
(10)6480 BC	19h08	-15°12°	-68°54°	58°28°	East.
Constellation of Sagittarius					
(11)4320 BC	21h08	-08°52°	-67°42°	19°45°	North.
Constellation of Aquarius					
(12)2160 BC	23h00	+01°33°	-58°04°	350°32°	North.
Constellation of Pisces					
(13)2028 AD	02h42	+23°29°	-13°19°	318°35°	North.
Constellation of Aries					
(14)4188 AD	04h53	+30°01°	+01°57°	303°57°	W/North.
Constellation of Taurus					
(15)6848 AD	07h12	+29°53°	+28°20°	290°03°	West.
Constellation of Gemini					
(16)8508 AD	09h23	+23°09°	+52°22°	269°45°	West.
Constellation of Cancer					
17)10668 AD	11h20	+12°19°	+67°52°	220°14°	S/West.
Constellation of Leo					
(18)12828 AD	13h11	+00°27°	+58°45°	158°56°	South.
Constellation of Virgo					
(19)14988 AD	15h04	-09°40°	+37°16°	133°07°	E/South.
Constellation of Libra					

(20)17148 AD Constellation of Ophiucus	17h05	-15°25°	+13°29°	117°07°	E/South.
(21)19308 AD Constellation of Sagittarius	19h09	-15°03°	-08°39°	102°36°	East.
(22)21468 AD Constellation of Aquarius	21h09	-08°41°	-27°52°	83°59°	East.
(23)23628 AD Constellation of Pisces	23h01	+01°46°	-41°14°	56°48°	East.
(24)25788 AD Constellation of Pisces	00h53	+13°40°	-43°51°	21°56°	N/East.
(25)27948 AD Constellation of Aries	02h51	+24°11°	-35°12°	349°24°	North.
(26)30108 AD Constellation of Auriga	05h04	+30°15°	-20°17°	326°24°	W/North

Then draw a circle by using the centre of the initial circle as centre, and the distance to the tip of the vesica as radius. This circle will be equal in circumference to the perimeter of the square which is tangent to the initial circle.

7.3

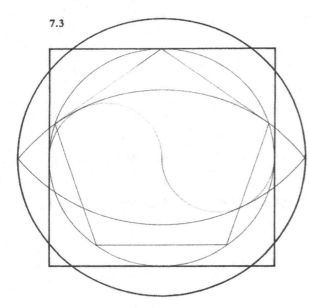

Drawing 7.4. This is based on the following:
The radius of the circle circumscribing the mouth of Rê, by Pythagoras:

$$\phi^2 = 1 + r^2$$
$$r = \sqrt{\phi - 1}$$
$$r = \sqrt{\phi}$$

and the circumference equals $2\pi\sqrt{\phi}$, with $\sqrt{\phi} = 1 \cdot 272 \ldots$ and

$$\pi = 3 \cdot 142 \ldots$$
$2\pi\sqrt{\phi} = 7 \cdot 993$ for the circumference, or approximately 8.

original circle whose radius is 1, has a side of 2. Thus the perimeter of this square is 8, and therefore approximately equal to the circumference of the large circle, 7·993.

This leads to the value of π which is believed to have been used by the ancient Egyptians for the construction of the Great Pyramid:

$$2\pi\sqrt{\phi} = 8$$
$$\pi\sqrt{\phi} = 4$$

then,

$$\sqrt{\phi} = \frac{4}{\pi} = 1 \cdot 272 \ldots$$
$$4\sqrt{\phi} = \pi = 3 \cdot 1446056 \ldots$$

Whereas true π is 3·1415926 .... A nearly exact π using the Golden Mean is $\phi^2 \times 6/5 = 3 \cdot 1416404 \ldots$. The ratio 5:6 or 1:1·2, incidentally, is the function which relates ϕ to π, and 1·2 equals the relationship of 12 to 10. Twelve is the number of the circles of cosmic time, it is the number of completion, and as the ratio 6 to 5 it relates the hexagon to the pentagon.

To return to our figure, by using the side of one quarter of the square (which is identical to the radius of the first circle) as Unity, we can determine these values:

$$pn = \frac{\sqrt{5}}{2} = 1 \cdot 118 \ldots = \frac{1}{2} + \frac{1}{\phi}$$
$$B'n = B'K = A'M = \phi = 1 \cdot 618 \ldots$$
$$OD = On = \frac{1}{\phi} = 0 \cdot 618 \ldots$$
$$AD = \frac{1}{\phi^2} = 0 \cdot 3819 \ldots$$
$$OM = \sqrt{\phi} = 1 \cdot 2720196 \ldots$$
$$AF, HG = \sqrt{(1 + 1/\phi^2)} = 1 \cdot 1756 = \text{side of pentagon}$$
$$DM = \sqrt{2} = 1 \cdot 4142135 \ldots$$

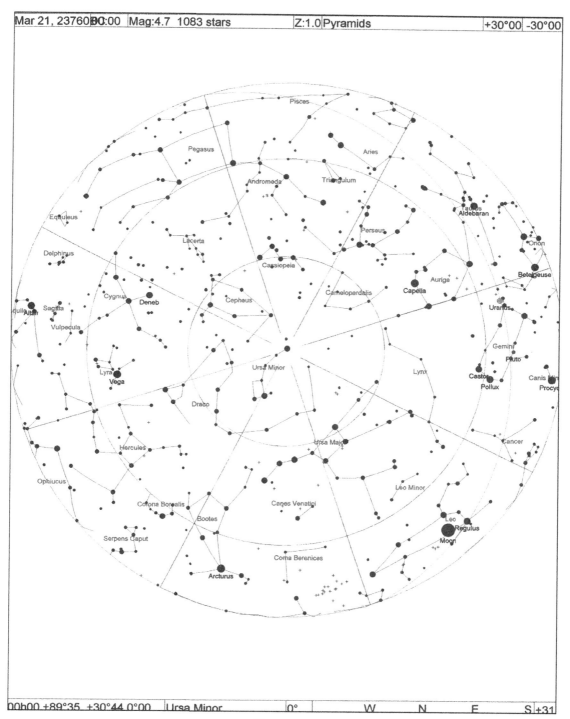

Figure 1.

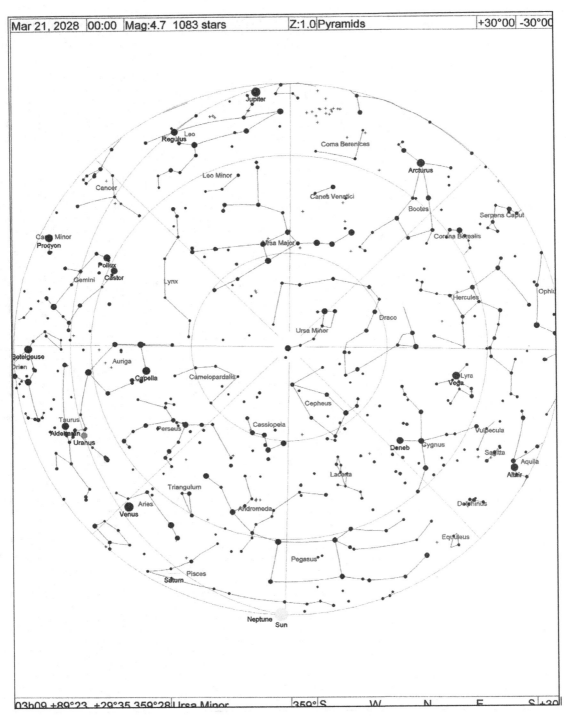

Figure 2.

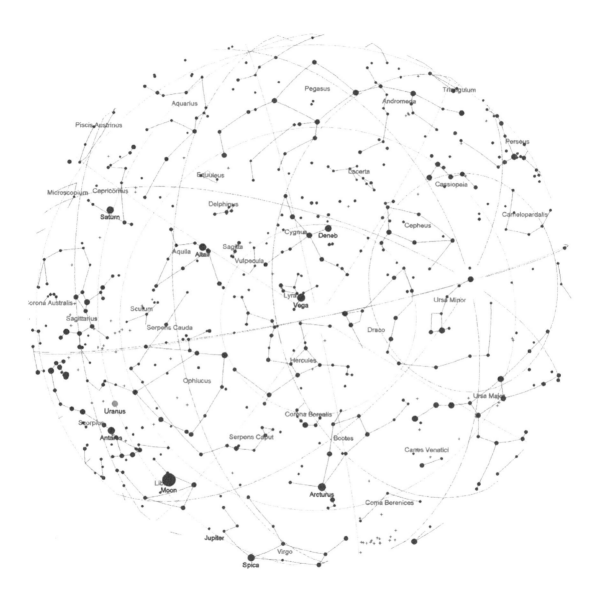

Figure 3.

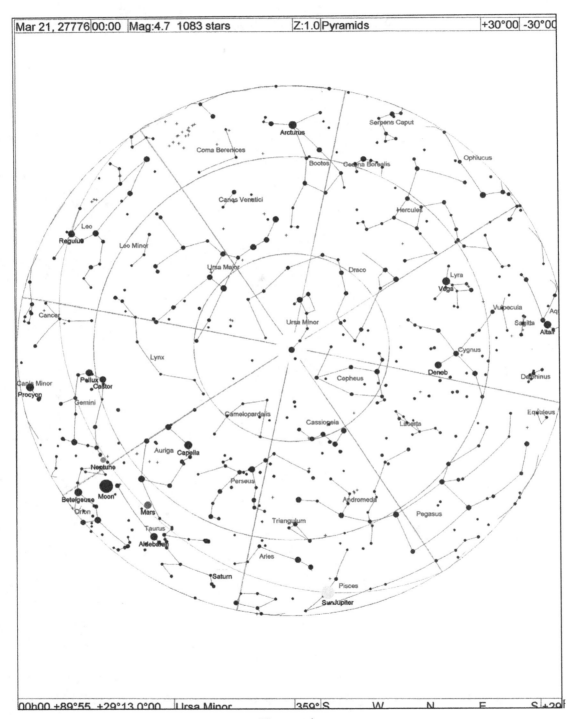

Figure 4.

Wednesday, February 16, 2005

Reading the various authors opinions proffered on the year the Astronomical structures at Stonehenge, located on the Salisbury Plains in England and that of New Grange located on the Boyne River in Ireland were built. It was the general consensus that in the case of Stonehenge this structure was constructed in the year 2,600 BC while that of New Grange was of a much earlier date.

It was also the opinion that the arrival of the Winter Solstice and the Summer Solstice was a permanent feature of these two ancient structures, however as one travels back in time it appears this may not be true.

The following readings are taken at one hundred year intervals from the year 30,000 BC. To 3,100 AD

It will be shown the belief that the precession of the seasonal Equinox's and Solstice's arrived on the same day, of the same month, of each year ad infinitum may not correct. In some cases the Summer Solstice arrives in the month of December and not in the month of June, as is now the case

From the chart it is seen that the seasons arrive in due order but on different days and dates over the course of time until a full cycle of time is complete.

If we take the year 2,000 AD as an example the Winter Solstice arrived on Dec 21st to be followed by the Spring Equinox on March 20th, the Summer Solstice on June 21st and the Autumn Equinox on September 22nd. These dares would coincide with the annual phenomena, which are presently experienced at Stonehenge and New Grange.

However if we look at the year 10,000 BC we see that the Winter Solstice arrived on March 9th, the Spring Equinox on June 8th the Summer Solstice on September 4th Autumn Equinox on December 4th.

And as we travel back through in time we see that the arrival of spring, summer, autumn, and winter dates change not to reappear until a cycle of time has been completed.

In this case the time span taken is from the year 30,000 BC to 3,001 AD.

The following readings are taken at one hundred year intervals at 8.00 AM from the vantage point if one were standing at the Giza Pyramid in Egypt.

The readings are not exact but are within a margin of +/-3 minutes of sidereal time.

The software astronomical program used to establish the following conclusions was developed by Mark A. Haney of Ann Arbor Michigan. U.S.A.

Spring Equinox		Mar 21st	00h03	00.36	57.31
Summer Solstice		Jun 21st	06h03	23.27	83.26
Autumn		Sept 22nd	11h59	00.06	59.55
Winter Solstice	3001 AD	Dec 22nd	18h01	23.27	34.00
Spring Equinox		Mar 21st	00h0	00.22	57.15
Summer Solstice		Jun 21st	06h03	23.26	83.26
Autumn Equinox		Sept 22nd	11h59	00.01	59.53
Winter Solstice	2901 AD	Dec 21st	11h58	23.27	34.04
Spring Equinox		Mar 20th	00h01	00.04	57.24
Summer Solstice		Jun 20th	06h00	23.27	83.24
Autumn Equinox		Sept 21st	11h57	00.01	59.53
Winter Solstice	2801 AD	Dec 21st	17h59	23.23	4.05
Spring Equinox		Mar 21st	00h02	00.10	57.35
Summer Solstice		Jun 21st	06h01	23.27	83.24
Autumn Equinox		Sept 22nd	11h57	00.16	60.14
Winter Solstice	2701AD	Dec 22nd	18h00	23.27	34.27
Spring Equinox		Mar 21st	00h02	00.16	57.41
Summer Solstice		Jun 21st	06h01	23.27	83.24
Autumn Equinox		Sept 22nd	11h58	00.12	60.09
Winter Solstice	2601 AD	Dec 21st	17h57	23.27	34.26
Spring Equinox		Mar 21st	00h0	00.21	57.46
Summer Solstice		Jun 21st	06h00	23.27	83.25
Autumn Equinox		Sept 22nd	11h59	00.08	60.05
Winter Solstice	2501 AD	Dec 21st	17h58	23.27	34.27
Spring Equinox		Marc 20th	00h01	00.03	57.31
Summer Solstice		Jun 21st	00h03	23.27	83.25
Autumn Equinox		Sept 22nd	11h59	00.03	60.00
Winter Solstice	2401 AD	Dec 21st	11h59	23.27	34.29

Spring Equinox		Mar 21st	00h02	00.29	57.58
Summer Solstice		Jun 21st	05h59	23.27	83.25
Autumn Equinox		Sept 23rd	12h00	00.01	59.56
Winter Solstice	2301 AD	Dec 22nd	18h00	23.27	34.30
Spring Equinox		Mar 21st	00h02	00.14	57.42
Summer Solstice		Jun 21st	06h00	23.27	83.26
Autumn Equinox		Sept 22nd	11h57	00.18	60.15
Winter Solstice	2201 AD	Dec 21st	17h57	23.27	34.30
Spring Equinox		Mar 21st	00h03	00.20	57.47
Summer Solstice		Jun 21st	06h01	23.27	83.26
Autumn Equinox		Sept 22nd	11h58	00.13	60.10
Winter Solstice	2101 AD	Dec 21st	17h58	23.27	34.31
Spring Equinox		Mar 20th	00h00	00.01	57.31
Summer Solstice		Jun 21st	06h01	23.27	83.26
Autumn Equinox		Sept 22nd	11h59	00.09	60.06
Winter Solstice	2001 AD	Dec 21st	17h59	23.27	34.32
Spring Equinox		Mar 21st	00h00	00.07	57.37
Summer Solstice		Jun 21st	05h58	23.37	75.23
Autumn Equinox		Sept 23rd	12h00	00.03	56.01
Winter Solstice	1901 AD	Dec 22nd	18h00	23.27	34.33
Spring Equinox		Mar 21st	00h02	00.13	57.41
Summer Solstice		Jun 21st	05h5	23.2	75.21
Autumn Equinox		Sept 23r	12h00	00.01	55.56
Winter Solstice	1801 AD	Dec 22nd	18h02	23.27	34.35
Spring Equinox		Mar 20th	23h59	00.05	57.26
Summer Solstice		Jun 21st	05h59	23.27	75.18
Autumn Equinox		Sept 23rd	12h01	00.06	55.51
Winter Solstice	1701 AD	Dec 21st	17h58	23.27	34.34

Spring Equinox		Mar 20th	00h00	00.00	57.31
Summer Solstice		Jun 21st	06h00	23.27	75.16
Autumn Equinox		Sept 22nd	11h58	00.12	56.09
Winter Solstice	1601 AD	Dec 21st	18h00	23.27	34.36
Spring Equinox		Mar 11th	00h01	00.05	57.36
Summer Solstice		Jun 12th	06h01	23.27	75.13
Autumn Equinox		Sept 13th	11h59	00.07	56.03
Winter Solstice	1501 AD	Dec12th	18h01	23.27	34.37
Spring Equinox		Mar 12th	00h02	00.11	57.44
Summer Solstice		Jun 13th	6h01	23.27	75.11
Autumn Equinox		Sept 14th	11h59	00.03	55.58
Winter Solstice	1401 AD	Dec 13th	18h02	23.27	34.38
Spring Equinox		Mar 12th	23h59	00.08	11.25
Summer Solstice		Jun 14th	06h02	23.27	75.08
Autumn Equinox		Sept 15th	12h01	00.03	55.53
Winter Solstice	1301 AD	Dec 13th	17h59	23.27	34.38
Spring Equinox		Mar 13th	23h59	00.02	11.33
Summer Solstice		Jun 15th	06h03	23.27	31.28
Autumn Equinox		Sept 16th	12.01	00.08	13.42
Winter Solstice	1201 AD	Dec 14th	18h00	23.27	-6.56
Spring Equinox		Mar 14th	00h01	00.03	11.38
Summer Solstice		Jun 15th	05h59	23.27	31.32
Autumn Equinox		Sept 17th	12h02	00.13	13.38
Winter Solstice	1101 AD	Dec 15th	18h01	23.27	-6.54
Spring Equinox		Mar 15th	00h02	00.08	11.43
Summer Solstice		Jun 16th	06h00	23.27	31.34
Autumn Equinox		Sept 17th	11h59	00.06	13.51
Winter Solstice	1001 AD	Dec 16th	18h03	23.27	-6.56

Spring Equinox		Mar 16th	00h02	00.13	11.48
Mid-Summer Solstice		Jun 17th	06h00	23.27	31.36
Autumn Equinox		Sept 18th	12h01	00.01	13.48
Winter Solstice	901 AD	Dec 16th	18h00	23.27	-6.55
Spring Equinox		Mar 16th	23h59	00.05	11.31
Summer Solstice		Jun 18th	06h01	23.27	31.38
Autumn Equinox		Sept 19th	12h01	00.05	13.44
Winter Solstice	801 AD	Dec17th	18h01	23.27	-6.58
Spring Equinox		Mar 17th	17h59	00.18	11.58
Summer Solstice		June 19th	06h02	23.27	31.40
Autumn Equinox		Sept 20th	12h01	00.08	14.01
Winter Solstice	701 AD	Dec 18th	18h02	23.27	−7.01
Spring Equinox		Mar 18th	00h01	00.05	11.43
Summer Solstice		June 20th	06h02	23.27	31.42
Autumn Equinox		Sept 21st	12h03	00.16	13.36
Winter Solstice	601 AD	Dec 19th	18h03	23.27	-7.04
Spring Equinox		Mar 19th	00h02	00.10	11.47
Summer Solstice		Jun 21st	06h03	23.27	31.44
Autumn Equinox		Sept 21st	11h59	00.03	13.49
Winter Solstice	501 AD	Dec 19th	18h00	23.27	-7.03
Spring Equinox		Mar 20th	00h03	00.15	11.52
Summer Solstice		Jun 21st	06h00	23.27	31.48
Autumn Equinox		Sept 22nd	12h01	00.03	13.45
Winter Solstice	401 AD	Dec 20th	18h02	23.27	-7.05
Spring Equinox		Mar 21st	00h04	00.20	11.58
Summer Solstice		Jun 22nd	06h00	23.27	31.50
Autumn Equinox		Sept 22nd	11h58	00.15	13.57
Winter Solstice	301 AD	Dec 21st	18h03	23.27	-7.08

Spring Equinox		Mar 21st	00h01	00.02	11.41
Summer Solstice		Jun 23rd	06h01	23.27	31.52
Autumn Equinox		Sept 23rd	11h59	00.09	13.53
Winter Solstice	201 AD	Dec 21st	18h00	23.27	-7.07
Spring Equinox		Mar 22nd	00h02	00.07	11.46
Summer Solstice		Jun 24th	06h03	23.27	31.54
Autumn Equinox		Sept 24th	11h59	00.04	13.48
Winter Solstice	101 AD	Dec 23rd	18h00	23.27	- 7.10
Spring Equinox		Mar 23rd	23h59	00.01	
Summer Solstice		Jun 25th	05h59	23.47	32.00
Autumn Equinox		Sept 26th	12h02	00.08	13.39
Winter Solstice	100 BC	Dec 23rd	17h59	23.27	-7.12
Spring Equinox		Mar 24th	00h01	00.02	11.40
Summer Solstice		Jun 26th	06h00	23.27	32.02
Autumn Equinox		Sept 26th	11h58	00.10	13.51
Winter Solstice	200 BC	Dec 24th	18h00	23.28	- 7.14
Spring Equinox		Mar 25th	00h0	00.03	11.46
Summer Solstice		Jun 27th	06h00	23.27	32.04
Autumn Equinox		Sept 27th	11h59	00.03	13.46
Winter Solstice	300 BC	Dec 24th	17h57	23.27	-7.13
Spring Equinox		Mar 26th	00h02	00.07	11.52
Summer Solstice		June 28th	06h01	23.28	32.06
Autumn Equinox		Sept 28th	12h01	00.03	13.41
Winter Solstice	400 BC	Dec 25th	18h00	23.28	-7.16
Spring Equinox		Mar 27th	00h03	00.12	11.57
Summer Solstice		Jun 29th	06h02	23.27	32.08
Autumn Equinox		Sept 29th	12h02	00.09	13.35
Winter Solstice	500 BC	Dec 26th	18h00	23.27	-7.18

Spring Equinox		Mar 27th	23h59	00.06	11.41
Summer Solstice		June 29th	05h59	23.27	32.12
Autumn Equinox		Sept 29th	11h59	00.09	13.48
Winter Solstice	600 BC	Dec 27th	18h01	23.28	-7.21
Spring Equinox		Mar 28th	00h01	00.02	11.47
Summer Solstice		Jun 30th	05h59	23.28	32.14
Autumn Equinox		Sept 30th	12h01	00.03	13.42
Winter Solstice	700 BC	Dec 28th	18h01	23.28	- 7.23
Spring Equinox		Mar 29th	00h01	00.03	11.52
Summer Solstice		Jul 1st	06h00	23.28	32.16
Autumn Equinox		Oct 1st	12h02	00.04	13.36
Winter Solstice	800 BC	Dec 28th	17h59	23.28	-7.22
Spring Equinox		Mar 30th	00h02	00.07	11.58
Summer Solstice		Jul 2nd	06h01	23.28	32.18
Autumn Equinox		Oct 1st	11h58	00.14	13.49
Winter Solstice	900 BC	Dec 29th	18h00	23.28	-7.25
Spring Equinox		Mar 30th	23h59	00.11	11.42
Summer Solstice		Jul 3rd	06h03	23.28	32.19
Autumn Equinox		Oct 2nd	11h59	0.07	13.43
Winter Solstice	1000 BC	Dec 30th	18h00	23.28	-7.27
Spring Equinox		Mar 31st	23h59	00.07	11.48
Summer Solstice		July 3rd	05h58	23.28	32.23
Autumn Equinox		Oct 2nd	11h59	00.07	13.37
Winter Solstice	1100 BC	Dec 30th	18h02	23.28	-7.27
Spring Equinox		Apr 1st	00h01	0002	11.54
Summer Solstice		Jul 4th	05h59	23.28	32.25
Autumn Equinox		Oct 4th	12h01	00.06	13.31
Winter Solstice	1200 BC	Dec 31st	18h00	23.28	-7.28

Spring Equinox		Apr 3rd	00h05	00.25	12.22
Summer Sol		Jul 5th	06h00	23.28	32.26
Autumn Equinox		Oct 4th	11h58	00.11	13.42
Winter Solstice	1300 BC	Jan 1st	18h01	23.28	-7.31
Spring Equinox		Apr 3rd	00h02	00.06	12.06
Summer Sol		Jul 6th	06h00	23.28	32.28
Autumn Equinox		Oct 5th	11h59	00.05	13.36
Winter Solstice	1400 BC	Jan 2nd	18h02	23.28	-7.33
Spring Equinox		Apr 3rd	23h58	00.12	11.49
Summer Sol		Jul 7th	06h01	23.28	32.29
Autumn Equinox		Oct 6th	12h02	00.02	13.30
Winter Solstice	1500 BC	Jan 2nd	17h59	23.28	-7.32
Spring Equinox		Apr 4th	00h01	00.08	11.56
Summer Sol		Jul 8th	06h02	23.28	32.31
Autumn Equinox		Oct 7th	12h02	00.09	13.23
Winter Solstice	1600 BC	Jan 3rd	18h01	23.28	-7.34
Spring Equinox		Apr 5th	00h01	00.04	12.02
Summer Sol		Jul 8th	06h01	23.28	32.35
Autumn Equinox		Oct 7th	11h59	00.06	13.35
Winter Solstice	1700 BC	Jan 4th	18h00	23.28	-7.36
Spring Equinox		Apr 6th	00h01	00.01	12.08
Summer Solstice		Jul 9th	06h00	23.28	32.36
Autumn Equinox		Oct 8th	12h01	00.01	13.28
Winter Solstice	1800 BC	Jan 4th	17h59	23.29	-7.34
Spring Equinox		Apr 7th	00h01	00.23	12.36
Summer Solstice		Jul 10th	05h59	23.28	32.37
Autumn Equinox		Oct 9th	12h02	00.06	13.21
Winter Solstice	1900 BC	Jan 5th	18h00	23.29	-7.36

Spring Equinox		Apr 7th	23h58	00.13	12.41
Summer Solstice		Jul 11th	06h01	23.28	33.23
Autumn Equinox		Oct 10th	12h03	00.13	13.56
Winter Solstice	2000 BC	Jan 6th	18h01	23.29	-7.00
Spring Equinox		Apr 9th	00h03	00.13	13.09
Summer Solstice		July 12th	06h02	23.29	33.24
Autumn Equinox		Oct 10th	12h01	00.04	14.08
Winter Solstice	2100 BC	Jan 6th	17h58	23.29	-6.58
Spring Equinox		Apr 9th	23h59	00.05	12.53
Summer Solstice		Jul 12th	05h59	26.29	33.27
Autumn Equinox		Oct 11th	12h02	00.03	14.00
Winter Solstice	2200 BC	Jan 7th	17h59	23.29	-7.00
Spring Equinox		Apr 10th	00h01	00.01	13.00
Summer Solstice		Jul 13th	06h00	23.29	33.28
Autumn Equinox		Oct 12th	12h03	00.11	13.53
Winter Solstice	2300 BC	Jan 8th	18h00	23.29	-7.02
Spring Equinox		Apr 11th	00h01	00.14	13.19
Summer Solstice		Jul 14th	06h01	23.29	33.29
Autumn Equinox		Oct 12th	11h59	00.06	14.05
Winter Solstice	2400 BC	Jan 9th	18h02	23.29	-7.03
Spring Equinox		Apr 12th	00h02	00.07	13.13
Summer Solstice		Jul 15th	06h01	23.29	33.30
Autumn Equinox		Oct 13th	12h02	00.01	13.57
Winter Solstice	2500 BC	Jan 9th	18h00	23.29	-7.05
Spring Equinox		April 13th	00h03	00.12	13.19
Summer Solstice		Jul 16th	06h02	23.29	33.31
Autumn Equinox		Oct 14th	12h02	00.09	13.50
Winter Solstice	2600 BC	Jan 10th	18h00	23.29	-7.03

Spring Equinox		Apr 13th	23h59	00.07	13.03
Summer Solstice		Jul 16th	05h58	23.29	33.34
Autumn Equinox		Oct 14th	11h59	00.08	14.01
Winter Solstice	2700 BC	Jan 11th	18h01	23.29	-7.05
Spring Equinox		Apr 14th	00h01	00.03	13.10
Summer Solstice		Jul 17th	06h00	23.29	33.35
Autumn Equinox		Oct 15th	12h01	00.01	13.53
Winter Solstice	2800 BC	Jan 11th	17h58	23.29	- 7.03
Spring Equinox		Apr 15th	00h02	00.01	13.16
Summer Solstice		Jul 18th	06h01	23.30	33.36
Autumn		Oct 16th	12h02	00.07	13.46
Winter Solstice	2900 BC	Jan 12th	17h59	23.30	-7.04
Spring Equinox		Apr 16th	00h02	00.05	13.23
Summer Solstice		Jul 19th	06h02	23.30	33.36
Autumn Equinox		Oct 16th	11h58	00.10	13.57
Winter Solstice	3000 BC	Jan 13th	18h00	23.30	-7.05
Spring Equinox		Apr 17th	00h02	00.09	13.30
Mid-Summer Solstice		Jul 19th	05h59	23.30	33.39
Autumn Equinox		Oct 17th	12h01	00.02	13.49
Winter Solstice	3100 BC	Jan 14th	18h01	23.30	-7.06
Spring Equinox		Apr 17th	23h59	00.09	13.16
Summer Solstice		Jul 20th	06h00	23.30	33.39
Autumn Equinox		Oct 18th	12h02	00.06	13.42
Winter Solstice	3200BC	Jan 15th	18h02	23.30	- 7.07
Spring Equinox		Apr 18th	23h59	00.05	13.20
Summer Solstice		Jul 21st	06h01	23.30	33.40
Autumn Equinox		Oct 18th	11h58	00.11	13.52
Winter Solstice	3300 BC	Jan 15th	17h59	23.30	- 7.05

Spring Equinox		Apr 19th	00h01	00.01	13.27
Summer Solstice		Jul 22nd	06h02	23.30	33.43
Autumn Equinox		Oct 20th	12h02	00.04	13.45
Winter Solstice	3400 BC	Jan 16th	18h00	23.30	-7.06
Spring Equinox		Apr 20th	00h02	00.03	13.34
Summer Solstice		Jul 22nd	06h00	23.30	33.43
Autumn Equinox		Oct 20th	12h02	00.04	13.37
Winter Solstice	3500 BC	Jan 17th	18h02	23.30	-7.07
Spring Equinox		April 20th	23h58	00.16	13.18
Summer Solstice		Jul 23rd	06h00	23.30	33.43
Autumn Equinox		Oct 20th	11h58	00.12	13.48
Winter Solstice	3600BC	Jan 18th	18h03	23.30	-7.07
Spring Equinox		Apr 22nd	00h03	00.11	13.47
Summer Solstice		Jul 24th	06h01	23.30	33.42
Autumn Equinox		Oct 21st	12h02	00.03	13.32
Winter Solstice	3700 BC	Jan 18th	17h59	23.30	-7.05
Spring Equinox		Apr 22nd	23h59	00.08	13.32
Summer Solstice		Jul 25th	06h02	23.31	33.42
Autumn Equinox		Oct 22nd	12h02	00.03	13.32
Winter Solstice	3800 BC	Jan 19th	18h01	23.31	-7.06
Spring Equinox		Apr 23rd	00h01	00.03	13.39
Summer Solstice		Jul 26th	06h03	23.31	33.42
Autumn Equinox		Oct 22nd	11h58	00.13	13.42
Winter Solstice	3900 BC	Jan 20th	18h02	23.31	-7.06
Spring Equinox		Apr 24th	00h02	00.01	13.45
Summer Solstice		Jul 26th	06h00	23.31	33.44
Autumn Equinox		Oct 23rd	12h01	00.05	13.22
Winter Solstice	4000 BC	Jan 21st	18h03	23.31	- 7.06

Spring Equinox		Apr 25th	00h02	00.05	13.52
Summer Solstice		Jul 27th	06h01	23.30	33.44
Autumn Equinox		Oct 24th	12h02	00.03	13.26
Winter Solstice	4100 BC	Jan 21st	18h00	23.31	-7.04
Spring Equinox		Apr 26th	00h02	00.09	13.59
Summer Solstice		Jul 28th	06h02	23.31	33.43
Autumn Equinox		Oct 24th	11h58	00.14	13.37
Winter Solstice	4200 BC	Jan 22nd	18h01	23.31	-7.04
Spring Equinox		Apr 26th	23h59	00.01	13.44
Summer Solstice		Jul 28th	06h00	23.31	33.46
Autumn Equinox		Oct 25th	11h59	00.05	13.29
Winter Solstice	4300 BC	Jan 23rd	18h02	23.31	-7.04
Spring Equinox		Apr 27th	23h59	00.05	`13.51
Summer Solstice		Jul 29th	06h00	23.31	33.45
Autumn Equinox		Oct 26th	12h02	00.03	13.21
Winter Solstice	4400 BC	Jan 23rd	17h58	23.31	-7.01
Spring Equinox		Apr 28th	00h01	00.01	13.58
Summer Solstice		Jul 30th	06h01	23.31	33.44
Autumn Equinox		Oct 26th	11h58	00.14	13.32
Winter Solstice	4500 BC	Jan 24th	18h00	23.31	-7.01
Spring Equinox		Apr 29th	00h02	00.03	14.04
Summer Solstice		Jul 31st	06h02	23.31	33.43
Autumn Equinox		Oct 27th	11h59	00.06	13.24
Winter Solstice	4600 BC	Jan 25th	18h01	23.31	-7.01
Spring Equinox		Apr 30th	00h02	00.07	14.12
Summer Solstice		Jul 31st	06h01	23.32	38.49
Autumn Equinox		Oct 28th	12h02	00.00	13.16
Winter Solstice	4700 BC	Jan 26th	18h02	23.32	- 7.01

Spring Equinox		Apr 30th	23h58	-00.11	13.56
Summer Solstice		Aug 1st	06h00	23.32	33.44
Autumn Equinox		Oct 28th	11h58	00.14	13.27
Winter Solstice	4800 BC	Jan 26th	17h58	23.32	- 6.58
Spring Equinox		May 1st	23h59	00.07	14.03
Summer Solstice		Aug 2nd	06h02	23.32	33.43
Autumn Equinox		Oct 29th	11h59	00.06	13.19
Winter Solstice	4900 BC	Jan 27th	17h59	23.32	-6.57
Spring Equinox		May 2nd	00h01	00.02	14.10
Summer Solstice		Aug 2nd	05h58	23.32	33.45
Autumn Equinox		Oct 30th	12h02	00.02	13.11
Winter Solstice	5000 BC	Jan 28th	18h00	23.32	- 6.57
Spring Equinox		May 3rd	00h02	00.02	14.17
Mid Summer Solstice		Aug 3rd	06h00	23.32	33.43
Autumn Equinox		Oct 30th	11h58	00.14	13.22
Winter Solstice	5100 B C	Jan 29th	18h01	23.32	-6.56
Spring Equinox		May 4th	00h02	00.06	14.24
Summer Solstice		Aug 4th	06h01	23.32	33.42
Autumn Equinox		Oct 31st	11h59	00.07	13.14
Winter Solstice	5200 BC	Jan 30th	18h02	23.32	-6.55
Spring Equinox		May 4th	23h58	00.12	14.09
Mid Summer Solstice		Aug 5th	06h02	23.32	33.40
Autumn Equinox		Nov 1st	12h02	00.02	13.06
Winter Solstice	5300 BC	Jan 30th	17h59	23.32	-6.52
Spring Equinox		May 5th	23h59	00.07	14.16
Summer Solstice		Aug 5th	06h00	23.52	33.42
Autumn Equinox		Nov 1st	11h58	00.15	13.17
Winter Solstice	5400 BC	Jan 31st	18h00	23.32	-6.51

Spring Equinox		May 6th	00h01	00.03	14.23
Summer Solstice		Aug 6th	06h01	23.32	33.40
Autumn Equinox		Nov 2nd	11h59	00.07	13.09
Winter Solstice	5500 BC	Feb 1st	18h01	23.32	-6.50
Spring Equinox		May 7th	00h02	00.02	14.30
Summer Solstice		Aug 7th	06h02	23.32	33.38
Autumn Equinox		Nov 3rd	12h02	00.01	13.01
Winter Solstice	5600 BC	Feb 2nd	18h02	23.32	-6.49
Spring Equinox		May 8th	00h02	00.07	14.37
Mid Summer Solstice		Aug 7th	06h00	23.32	33.40
Autumn Equinox		Nov 4th	12h02	00.09	12.54
Winter Solstice	5700 BC	Feb 2nd	11h59	23.32	- 6.45
Spring Equinox		May 8th	23h58	0012	14.21
Summer Solstice		Aug 8th	06h00	23.33	33.37
Autumn Equinox		Nov 4th	11h59	00.07	13.05
Winter Solstice	5800 BC	Feb 3rd	18h00	23.33	-6.44
Spring Equinox		May 9th	23h59	00.04	14.41
Summer Solstice		Aug 9th	06h02	23.33	33.35
Autumn Equinox		Nov 5th	12h01	00.01	12.57
Winter Solstice	5900 BC	Feb 4th	18h01	23.33	-6.43
Spring Equinox		May 10th	00h01	00.02	14.36
Summer Solstice		Aug 9th	06h00	23.33	33.37
Autumn Equinox		Nov 6th	12h02	00.09	12.50
Winter Solstice	6000 BC	Feb 5th	18h01	23.33	-6.41
Spring Equinox		May 11th	00h02	00.03	14.43
Summer Solstice		Aug 10th	06h00	23.33	33.34
Autumn Equinox		Nov 6th	11h59	00.08	13.01
Winter Solstice	6100 BC	Feb 6th	18h02	23.33	- 6.40

Spring Equinox		May 12th	00h02	00.18	15.02
Summer Solstice		Aug 11th	06h01	23.33	33.31
Autumn Equinox		Nov 7th	12h01	00.00	12.54
Winter Solstice	6200 BC	Feb 6th	17h59	23.33	-6.36
Spring Equinox		May 12th	23h58	00.10	14.34
Summer Solstice		Aug 12th	06h00	23.33	33.22
Autumn Equinox		Nov 8th	12h02	00.08	12.47
Winter Solstice	6300 BC Feb 7th	18h00	23.33	-6.34	
Spring Equinox		May 13th	23h59	00.05	14.41
Summer Solstice		Aug 12th	06h00	23.33	33.30
Autumn Equinox		Nov 8th	11h59	00.08	12.58
Winter Solstice	6400 BC	Feb 8th	18h01	23.33	-6.33
Spring Equinox		May 14th	00h01	00.00	14.48
Summer Solstice		Aug 13th	06h01	23.34	33.40
Autumn Equinox		Nov 9th	12h01	00.01	12.51
Winter Solstice	6500 BC	Feb 9th	18h02	23.33	-6.31
Spring Equinox		May 15th	00h02	00.05	14.56
Summer Solstice		Aug 14th	06h03	23.33	33.24
Autumn Equinox		Nov 10th	12h02	00.07	12.45
Winter Solstice	6600 BC	Feb 9th	17h58	23.33	-6.27
Spring Equinox		May 15th	23h58	00.12	14.40
Summer Solstice		Aug 14th	06h00	23.33	33.26
Autumn Equinox		Nov 11th	12h03	00.15	12.38
Winter Solstice	6700 BC	Feb 10th	17h59	34.34	-6.25
Spring Equinox		May 16th	23h59	00.07	14.47
Mid Summer Solstice		Aug 15th	06h01	23.33	33.22
Autumn Equinox		Nov 11th	12h01	00.02	12.49
Winter Solstice	6800 BC	Feb 11th	18h00	23.34	- 6.25

Spring Equinox		May 18th	00h02	00.04	15.01
Summer Solstice		Aug 16th	06h00	23.34	32.21
Autumn Equinox		Nov 12th	11h58	00.1	12.54
Winter Solstice	6900 BC	Feb 13th	18h02	23.34	-6.19
Spring Equinox		May 19th	00h02	00.09	15.08
Mid Summer Solstice		Aug 17th	06h01	23.34	33.17
Autumn Equinox		Nov 13th	12h01	00.03	12.48
Winter Solstice	7100 BC	Feb 13th	17h59	23.34	-6.15
Spring Equinox		May 19th	23h59	00.00	14.53
Summer Solstice		Aug 17th	06h00	23.34	33.18
Autumn Equinox		Nov 14th	12h02	00.05	12.42
Winter Solstice	7200 BC	Feb 14th	7h59	23.34	-6.13
Spring Equinox		May 20th	00h01	00.03	15.00
Summer Solstice		Aug 18th	06h00	23.34	33.15
Autumn Equinox		Nov 14th	11h58	00.12	12.54
Winter Solstice	7300 BC	Feb 15th	18h00	23.34	-6.10
Spring Equinox		May 21st	00h02	00.03	14.25
Summer Solstice		Aug 19th	06h02	23.34	32.27
Autumn Equinox		Nov 15th	11h59	00.05	12.06
Winter Solstice	7400 BC	Feb 16th	18h01	23.34	-6.08
Spring Equinox		May 22nd	00h02	00.09	14.32
Summer Solstice		Aug 19th	06h00	23.34	32.28
Autumn Equinox		Nov 16th	12h02	00.03	12.00
Winter Solstice	7500 BC	Feb 17th	18h02	23, 34	-6.43
Spring Equinox		May 23rd	00h03	00.15	14.39
Mid Summer Solstice		Aug 20th	06h00	23.34	32.25
Autumn Equinox		Nov 17th	12h02	00.10	11.55
Winter Solstice	7600 BC	Feb 17th	17h59	23.34	-6.39

Spring Equinox		May 23rd	00h01	00.02	14.24
Summer Solstice		Aug 21st	06h02	23.34	32.09
Autumn Equinox		Nov 17th	11h59	00.07	12.07
Winter Solstice	7700 BC	Feb 18th	17.59	23.34	-6.37
Spring Equinox		May 24th	00h02	00.04	14.31
Summer Solstice		Aug 21st	06h00	23.34	32.22
Autumn Equinox		Nov 18th	12h01	00.01	12.02
Winter Solstice	7800 BC	Feb 19th	18h00	23.34	-6.34
Spring Equinox		May 25th	00h02	00.10	14.38
Summer Solstice		Aug 22nd	06h00	23.34	32.19
Autumn Equinox		Nov 19th	12h02	00.08	11.56
Winter Solstice	7900 BC	Feb 20th	18h01	23.34	-6.32
Spring Equinox		May 25th	23h59	00.07	14.23
Summer Solstice		Aug 23rd	06h02	23.34	32.15
Autumn Equinox		Nov 19th	11h58	00.09	12.09
Winter Solstice	8000 BC	Feb 21st	18h02	23.34	-6.29
Spring Equinox		May 26th	00h01	00.00	14.30
Mid Summer Solstice		Aug 23rd	06h00	23.34	32.16
Autumn Equinox		Nov 20th	12h01	00.02	12.04
Winter Solstice	8100 BC	Feb 22nd	18h03	23.35	-6.26
Spring Equinox		May 27th	00h02	00.06	14.36
Summer Solstice		Aug 24th	06h01	23.35	32.12
Autumn Equinox		Nov 21st	12h02	00.05	11.59
Winter Solstice	8200 BC	Feb 22nd	18h00	23.35	-6.22
Spring Equinox		May 27th	23h58	00.11	14.21
Summer Solstice		Aug 25th	06h02	23.35	32.08
Autumn Equinox		Nov 22nd	12h03	00.12	11.55
Winter Solstice	8300 BC	Feb 23rd	18h00	23.35	-6.20

Spring Equinox		May 28th	23h59	00.04	14,28
Summer Solstice		Aug 25th	06h00	23.35	32.09
Autumn Equinox		Nov 22nd	11h59	00.05	12.07
Winter Solstice	8400 BC	Feb 24th	18h01	23.35	-6.17
Spring Equinox		May 29th	00h02	00.03	14.35
Summer Solstice		Aug 26th	06h02	23.35	32.06
Autumn Equinox		N0v 23rd	12h02	00.02	12.03
Winter Solstice	8500 BC	Feb 25th	18h02	23.35	-6.14
Spring Equinox		May 30th	00h03	00.15	14.47
Summer Solstice		Aug 26th	06h00	23.35	32.05
Autumn Equinox		Nov 23rd	11h58	00.09	12.12
Winter Solstice	8600 BC	Feb 25th	18h00	23.35	-6.10
Spring Equinox		May 30th	23h58	00.07	14.26
Summer Solstice		Aug 27th	06h00	23.35	31.59
Autumn Equinox		Nov 24th	11h58	00.08	12.12
Winter Solstice	8700 BC	Feb 26th	18h00	23.35	-6.07
Spring Equinox		May 31st	00h01	00.00	14.33
Summer Solstice		Aug 28th	06h02	23.35	31.59
Autumn Equinox		Nov 25th	12h01	00.02	12.09
Winter Solstice	8800 BC	Feb 27th	18h00	23.35	-6.05
Spring Equinox		Jun 1st	00h02	00.04	14.40
Summer Solstice		Aug 28th	06h00	23.35	32.00
Autumn Equinox		Nov 26th	12h02	00.05	12.05
Winter Solstice	8900 BC	Feb 28th	18h01	23.35	-6.02
Spring Equinox		Jun 1st	05h58	00.10	14.25
Summer Solstice		Aug 29th	06h00	23.35	31.56
Autumn Equinox		Nov 26th	11h58	00.12	12.18
Winter Solstice	9000 BC	Mar 1st	18h02	23.35	-5.59

Spring Equinox		Jun 2nd	23h59	00.02	14.32
Summer Solstice		Aug 30th	06h02	23.35	31.52
Autumn Equinox		Nov 27th	11h58	00.16	12.28
Winter Solstice	9100 BC	March 1st	17h59	23.35	-5.55
Spring Equinox		Jun 3rd	00h02	00.05	14.38
Summer Solstice		Aug 30th	05h59	23.35	31.53
Autumn Equinox		Nov 28th	12h02	00.01	12.12
Winter Solstice	9200 BC	Mar 2nd	18h00	23.35	-5.25
Spring Equinox		Jun 3rd	23h58	00.11	14.23
Summer Solstice		Aug 31st	06h01	23.35	31.50
Autumn Equinox		Nov 29th	12h02	00.07	12.09
Winter Solstice	9300 BC	Mar 3rd	18h00	23.35	- 5.50
Spring Equinox		Jun 4th	00h04	00.21	21.08
Summer Solstice		Sept 1st	06h02	23.35	31.59
Autumn Equinox		Nov 30th	12h02	00.03	12.19
Winter Solstice	9400 BC	Mar 4th	18h01	23.35	-5.47
Spring Equinox		Jun 5th	00h02	00.04	14.36
Summer Solstice		Sept 2nd	06h00	23.35	31.47
Autumn Equinox		Nov 30th	11h58	00.04	12.20
Winter Solstice	9500 BC	Mar 5th	18h02	23.35	-5.47
Spring Equinox		Jun 5th	23h58	00.12	14.21
Summer Solstice		Sept 2nd	06h01	23.35	31.43
Autumn Equinox		Dec 1st	12h02	00.02	12.17
Winter Solstice	9600 BC	Mar 5th	18h00	23.35	-5.42
Spring Equinox		Jun 6th	23h58	00.05	14.28
Summer Solstice		Sept 3rd	06h03	23.35	31.40
Autumn Equinox		Dec 2nd	12h02	00.08	12.15
Winter Solstice	9700 BC	Mar 6th	18h00	23.35	-5.38

Spring Equinox		Jun 7th	00h02	00.03	14.34
Summer Solstice		Sept 4th	06h02	23.35	31.38
Autumn Equinox		Dec 3rd	12h03	0014	12.13
Winter Solstice	9800 BC	Mar 7th	18h01	23.35	-5.36
Spring Equinox		Jun 8th	00h03	00.12	14.41
Summer Solstice		Sept 4th	06h02	23.35	31.38
Autumn Equinox		Dec 3rd	11h58	00.03	12.27
Winter Solstice	9900 BC	Mar 8th	18h02	23.35	-5.33
Spring Equinox		Jun 8th	23h58	00.04	74.22
Summer Solstice		Sept 4th	05h58	23.35	31.52
Autumn Equinox		Dec 4th	12h02	00.03	12.25
Winter Solstice	10000 BC	Mar 9th	18h03	23.35	-5.31
Spring Equinox		Jun 9th	00h02	00.04	16.36
Summer Solstice		Sept 5th	06h00	23.35	33.48
Autumn Equinox		Dec 4th	11h58	00.09	14.41
Winter Solstice	10100 BC	Mar 9th	18h00	23.36	-3.37
Spring Equinox		Jun 10th	00h03	00.12	16.43
Summer Solstice		Sept 6th	06h02	23.35	33.45
Autumn Equinox		Dec 5th	11h58	00.03	14.40
Winter Solstice	10200 BC	Mar 10th	18h01	23.36	-3.35
Spring Equinox		Jun 11th	00h04	00.21	16.08
Summer Solstice		Sept 6th	05h59	23.35	33.02
Autumn Equinox		Dec 6th	12h02	00.03	13.57
Winter Solstice	10300 BC	Mar 11th	18h02	2335	- 4.09
Spring Equinox		Jun 11th	00h02	00.05	15.53
Summer Solstice		Sept 7th	06h01	23.35	32.59
Autumn Equinox		Dec 7th	12h02	00.09	13.55
Winter Solstice	10400 BC	Mar 11th	18h00	23.36	-4.05

Spring Equinox		Jun 12th	00h03	00.14	16.00
Summer Solstice		Sept 8th	06h02	23.35	32.56
Autumn Equinox		Dec 7th	11h58	00.09	14.10
Winter Solstice	10500 BC	Mar 12th	18h00	23.36	-4.03
Spring Equinox		Jun 13th	00h04	00.23	16.06
Summer Solstice		Sept 8th	06h01	23.36	36.37
Autumn Equinox		Dec 8th	11h58	00.01	45.09
Winter Solstice	10600 BC	Mar 13th	18h01	23.36	-4.01
Spring Equinox		Jun 13th	00h02	00.07	15.51
Summer Solstice		Sept 9th	06h01	23.36	32.55
Autumn Equinox		Dec 9th	12h02	00.02	14.08
Winter Solstice	10700 BC	Mar 14th	18h02	23.35	-3.59
Spring Equinox		Jun 14th	00h03	00.16	15.16
Summer Solstice		Sept 9th	05h59	23.36	32.56
Autumn Equinox		Dec 10th	12h02	00.08	13.28
Winter Solstice	10800 BC	Mar 14th	17h59	23.36	-4.32
Spring Equinox		Jun 14th	00h02	00.00	15.01
Summer Solstice		Sept 10th	06h00	23.36	32.10
Autumn Equinox		Dec 11th	12h03	00.03	13.25
Winter Solstice	10900 BC	Mar 15th	18h00	23.36	-4.30
Spring Equinox		Jun 15th	00h02	00.09	15.07
Summer Solstice		Sept 11th	06h01	23.36	32.07
Autumn Equinox		Dec 12th	12h03	00.19	13.24
Winter Solstice	11000 BC	Mar 16th	18h01	23.35	-4.48
Spring Equinox		Jun 15th	23h58	00.06	14.52
Summer Solstice		Sept 12th	06h03	23.35	32.05
Autumn Equinox		Dec 12th	12h02	00.01	13.39
Winter Solstice	11100 BC	Mar 17th	18h02	23.36	-4.27

Spring Equinox		Jun 16th	00h02	00.03	14.59
Summer Solstice		Sept 12th	06h00	23.35	32.06
Autumn Equinox		Dec 13th	12h02	00.07	13.38
Winter Solstice	11200 BC	Mar 18th	18h03	23.35	-4.25
Spring Equinox		Jun 17th	00h03	00.12	15.05
Summer Solstice		Sept 13th	06h02	23.36	32.04
Autumn Equinox		Dec 14th	12h03	00.12	13.38
Winter Solstice	11300 BC	Mar 18th	18h00	23.36	-4.22
Spring Equinox		Jun 18th	00h04	00.21	15.12
Summer Solstice		Sept 13th	06h00	23.36	36.26
Autumn Equinox		Dec 14th	11h58	00.06	13.53
Winter Solstice	11400 BC	Mar 19th	18h01	23.36	-4.20
Spring Equinox		Jun 18th	00h02	00.06	14.42
Summer Solstice		Sept 14th	06h00	23.35	32.04
Autumn Equinox		Dec 15th	11h58	00.01	13.11
Winter Solstice	11500 BC	Mar 20th	18h02	23.35	-4.56
Spring Equinox		Jun 19th	00h03	00.15	14.21
Summer Solstice		Sept 15th	06h02	23.35	31.18
Autumn Equinox		Dec 16th	12h02	00.05	13.11
Winter Solstice	11600 BC	Mar 20th	17h59	23.36	-4.52
Spring Equinox		Jun 20th	00h04	00.25	14.20
Summer Solstice		Sept 15th	05h59	23.36	31.20
Autumn Equinox		Dec 17th	12h02	00.10	13.11
Winter Solstice	11700 BC	Mar 21st	18h00	23.36	-4.51
Spring Equinox		Jun 20th	00h02	00.10	14.12
Summer Solstice		Sept 16th	06h00	23.35	31.12
Autumn Equinox		Dec 18th	12h02	00.09	13.15
Winter Solstice	11800 BC	Mar 22nd	18h00	23.35	-4.50

Spring Equinox		Jun 21st	00h03	00.19	14.19
Summer Solstice		Sept 17th	06h02	23.35	31.17
Autumn Equinox		Dec 19th	12h03	00.15	13.15
Winter Solstice	11900 BC	Mar 23rd	18h01	23.35	-4.49
Spring Equinox		Jun 21st	00h02	00.04	14.04
Summer Solstice		Sept 17th	05h59	23.36	31.20
Autumn Equinox		Dec 19th	12h02	00.03	13.29
Winter Solstice	12000 BC	Mar 23rd	17h59	23.35	-4.46
Spring Equinox		Jun 22nd	00h02	00.14	14.10
Summer Solstice		Sept 18th	06h00	23.35	31.19
Autumn Equinox		Dec 20th	12h02	00.08	13.27
Winter Solstice	12100 BC	Mar 24th	18h00	23.35	-4.45
Spring Equinox		Jun 22nd	23h58	00.01	13.55
Summer Solstice		Sept 19th	06h02	23.36	31.17
Autumn Equinox		Dec 21st	12h03	00.13	13.28
Winter Solstice	12200 BC	Mar 25th	18h02	23.35	-4.45
Spring Equinox		Jun 23rd	00h02	00.09	14.01
Summer Solstice		Sept 19th	05h59	23.35	31.21
Autumn Equinox		Dec 22nd	12h03	00.18	13.28
Winter Solstice	12300 BC	Mar 25th	17h59	23.35	-4.42
Spring Equinox		Jun 24th	00h03	00.18	14.08
Summer Solstice		Sept 20th	06h00	23.35	31.19
Autumn Equinox		Dec 22nd	11h58	00.00	13.43
Winter Solstice	12400 BC	Mar 26th	18h00	23.35	-4.41
Spring Equinox		Jun 24th	00h02	00.03	13.53
Summer Solstice		Sept 21st	06h01	23.35	31.19
Autumn Equinox		Dec 23rd	12h02	00.05	13.44
Winter Solstice	12500 BC	Mar 27th	18h01	23.35	-4.41

Spring Equinox		Jun 25th	00h03	00.13	13.59
Summer Solstice		Sept 21st	05h58	23.35	31.22
Autumn Equinox		Dec 24th	12h02	00.10	13.44
Winter Solstice	12600 BC	Mar 28th	18h02	23.35	-4.41
Spring Equinox		Jun 26th	00h04	00.23	14.06
Summer Solstice		Sept 22nd	06h00	23.35	31.21
Autumn Equinox		Dec 25th	12h03	0015	13.45
Winter Solstice	12700 BC	Mar 28th	17h59	23.35	-4.38
Spring Equinox		Jan 26th	00h.02	00.08	13.57
Summer Solstice		Sept 23rd	06h01	23.35	31.21
Autumn Equinox		Dec 26th	12h03	00.21	13.45
Winter Solstice	12800 BC	Mar 29th	18h01	23.35	-4.38
Spring Equinox		Jun 27th	00h03	00.18	13.57
Summer Solstice		Sept 24th	06h02	23.35	31.21
Autumn Equinox		Dec 26th	12h02	00.03	14.01
Winter Solstice	12900 BC	Mar 30th	18h02	23.35	-4.39
Spring Equinox		Jan 27th	00h03	00.03	13.42
Summer Solstice		Sept 24th	06h02	23.35	31.21
Autumn Equinox		Dec 27th	12h02	00.08	14.01
Winter Solstice	13000 BC	Mar 30th	17h59	23.35	-4.36
Spring Equinox		Jun 28th	00h03	00.13	13.49
Summer Solstice		Sept 24th	06h00	23.35	31.24
Autumn Equinox		Dec 28th	12h03	0013	14.02
Winter Solstice	13100 BC	Mar 31st	18h01	23.35	-4.36
Spring Equinox		Jun 28th	23h58	00.02	13.34
Summer Solstice		Sept 26th	06h02	23.35	31.25
Autumn Equinox		Dec 29th	12h03	00.18	14.02
Winter Solstice	13200 BC	Apr 1st	18h02	23.35	-4.37

Spring Equinox		Jun 29th	00h02	00.08	13.40
Summer Solstice		Sept 26th	05h59	23.35	31.29
Autumn Equinox		Dec 30th	12h04	00.23	
Winter Solstice	13300 BC	Apr 1st	17h59	23.35	00.00
Spring Equinox		Jun 30th	00h03	00.18	13.47
Summer Solstice		Sept 27th	06h00	23.35	31.29
Autumn Equinox		Dec 30th	12h02	00.01	-4.18
Winter Solstice	13400 BC	Apr 2nd	18h01	23.35	-4.35
Spring Equinox		Jun 30th	00h02	00.03	13.32
Summer Solstice		Sept 28th	06h02	23.35	31.30
Autumn Equinox		Dec 31st	12h02	00.10	14.18
Winter Solstice	13500 BC	Apr 3rd	18h02	23.35	-4.36
Spring Equinox		July 1st	00h03	00.13	13.39
Summer Solstice		Sept 28th	05h59	23.35	31.34
Autumn Equinox		Jan 1st	12h02	00.25	14.18
Winter Solstice	13600 BC	Apr 4th	18h02	23.34	-4.37
Spring Equinox		July 2nd	00h0-4	00.23	13.46
Summer Solstice		Sept 29th	06h00	23.35	31.35
Autumn Equinox		Jan 2nd	12h04	00.22	14.19
Winter Solstice	13700 BC	Apr 4th	18h00	23.35	-4.35
Spring Equinox		July 2nd	00h02	00.00	13.31
Summer Solstice		Sept 30th	06h01	23.35	31.35
Autumn Equinox		Jan7th	12h02	00.05	14.35
Winter Solstice	13800 BC	Apr 5th	18h02	23.34	-4.37
Spring Equinox		July 3rd	00h03	00.18	13.37
Summer Solstice		Oct 1st	06h02	23.35	31.38
Autumn Equinox		Jan 3rd	12h02	00.10	14.34
Winter Solstice	13900 BC	Apr 5th	17h59	-23 35	-4.35

Spring Equinox		July 3rd	00h02	00.03	13.22
Summer Solstice		Oct 1st	06h03	23.34	31.39
Autumn Equinox		Jan 4th	12h03	0015	14.35
Winter Solstice	14000 BC	Apr 6th	18h01	-23.34	-3.46
Spring Equinox		July 4th	00h03	00.13	13.29
Summer Solstice		Oct 2nd	06h00	23.34	31.44
Autumn Equinox		Jan 5th	12h03	00.21	14.34
Winter Solstice	14100 BC	Apr 7th	18h02	-23.34	-4.38
Spring Equinox		July 5th	00h04	00.29	13.36
Summer Solstice		Oct 3rd	06h01	23.34	31.46
Autumn Equinox		Jan 5th	12h02	00.03	14.49
Winter Solstice	14200 BC	Apr 7th	18h00	-23.34	-4.36
Spring Equinox		July 5th	00h02	00.08	13.21
Summer Solstice		Oct 3rd	05h58	23.34	31.50
Autumn Equinox		Jan 6th	12h02	00.09	14.49
Winter Solstice	14300 BC	Apr 8th	18h01	-23.34	-4.40
Spring Equinox		July 6th	00h03	00.18	13.28
Summer Solstice		Oct 4th	06h00	23.34	31.52
Autumn Equinox		Jan 7th	12h03	00.15	14.48
Winter Solstice	14400 BC	Apr 9th	18h03	-23.34	-4.40
Spring Equinox		July 7th	00h04	00.27	13.36
Summer Solstice		Oct 5th	06h01	23.34	31.54
Autumn Equinox		Jan 8th	12h03	00.20	14.48
Winter Solstice	14500 BC	Apr 9th	18h00	-23.34	-4.38
Spring Equinox		July 7th	00h03	00.13	13.21
Summer Solstice		Oct 6th	06h02	23.34	31.57
Autumn Equinox		Jan 8th	11h58	-00.03	15.03
Winter Solstice	14600 BC	Apr 10th	18h02	-23.34	-4.20

Spring Equinox		July 8th	00h03	00.31	13.39
Summer Solstice		Oct 7th	06h03	23.34	31.52
Autumn Equinox		Jan 9th	12h02	-00.09	15.09
Winter Solstice	14700 BC	Apr 10th	17h59	-23.34	-4.39
Spring Equinox		July 8th	00h02	00.07	13.13
Summer Solstice		Oct 6th	05h59	23.34	32.01
Autumn Equinox		Jan 10th	12h03	-0015	15.01
Winter Solstice	14800 BC	Apr 11th	18h01	-23.34	-4.41
Spring Equinox		July 9th	00h03	00.17	13.21
Summer Solstice		Oct 8th	06h00	23.34	32.07
Autumn Equinox		Jan 11th	12h03	-0021	15.00
Winter Solstice	14900 BC	Apr 12th	18h02	-23.33	-4.44
Spring Equinox		July 10th	00.04	00.26	13.28
Summer Solstice		Oct 9th	06h02	23.34	32.09
Autumn Equinox		Jan 11th	12h02	-00.04	15.15
Winter Solstice	15000 BC	Apr 12th	17h59	-23.34	-4.42
Spring Equinox		July 10th	00h02	00.11	13.13
Summer Solstice		Oct 10th	06h03	23.33	32.12
Autumn Equinox		Jan 12th	12h02	-00.11	15.13
Winter Solstice	15100 BC	Apr 13th	18h01	-23.33	-4.45
Spring Equinox		July 11th	00h03	00.20	13.21
Summer Solstice		Oct 10th	06h00	23.34	32.17
Autumn Equinox		Jan 13th	12h03	00.17	15.12
Winter Solstice	15200 BC	Apr 13th	17h58	-23.33	-4.44
Spring Equinox		July 11th	00h02	00.05	13.06
Summer Solstice		Oct 11th	06h01	23.33	32.20
Autumn Equinox		Jan 13th	11h58	00.00	15.26
Winter Solstice	15300 BC	Apr 14th	18h00	-23.33	-4.47

Spring Equinox		Jul 12th	00h03	00.14	13.14
Summer Solstice		Oct 12th	06h02	23.33	32.24
Autumn Equinox		Jan 14th	12h04	-00.06	15.24
Winter Solstice	15400 BC	Apr 15th	18h02	-23.33	-4.49
Spring Equinox		July 13th	00h04	00.24	13.21
Summer Solstice		Oct 12th	15h59	23.33	32.29
Autumn Equinox		Jan 15th	12h03	-00.13	15.23
Winter Solstice	15500 BC	Apr 15th	18h00	-23.33	-4.49
Spring Equinox		July 13th	00h02	00.09	13.07
Summer Solstice		Oct 13th	06h00	23.33	32.32
Autumn Equinox		Jan 16th	12h03	-0019	15.20
Winter Solstice	15600 BC	Apr 16th	18h01	-23.33	-4.52
Spring Equinox		July 14th	00h03	00.17	13.15
Summer Solstice		Oct 14th	06h01	23.33	32.36
Autumn Equinox		Jan 17th	12h04	-0026	15.18
Winter Solstice	15700 BC	Apr 16th	17h59	-23.33	-4.51
Spring Equinox		July 15th	00h04	00.26	13.26
Summer Solstice		Oct 15th	06h02	23.33	32.39
Autumn Equinox		Jan 17th	12h02	-00.10	15.32
Winter Solstice	15800 BC	Apr 17th	18h01	-23.33	-4.54
Spring Equinox		July 15th	00h02	00.11	13.08
Summer Solstice		Oct 15th	05h59	23.33	32.44
Autumn Equinox		Jan 18th	12h03	-00.16	15.29
Winter Solstice	15900 BC	Apr 18th	18h02	-23.33	-4.57
Spring Equinox		July 16th	00h03	00.20	13.16
Mid Summer Solstice		Oct 16th	06h00	23.33	32.48
Autumn Equinox		Jan 18th	11h58	00.00	15.43
Winter Solstice	16000 BC	Apr 18th	18h00	-23.32	-4.59

Spring Equinox		July 17th	00h04	00.28	13.24
Summer Solstice		Oct 18th	06h02	23.33	32.56
Autumn Equinox		Jan 19th	12h02	-00.07	15.40
Winter Solstice	16100 BC	Apr 19th	18h02	-23.32	-4.59
Spring Equinox		July 17th	00h02	00.22	13.21
Summer Solstice		Oct 18th	06h02	23.32	32.56
Autumn Equinox		Jan 20th	12h03	-00.04	15.37
Winter Solstice	16200 BC	Apr 19th	17h59	-23.32	-4.59
Spring Equinox		July 18th	00h0	300.21	13.18
Summer Solstice		Oct 19th	06h03	23.32	38.44
Autumn Equinox		Jan 21st	12h03	-00.22	15.33
Winter Solstice	16300 BC	Apr 20th	18h.01	-23.32	-32.59
Spring Equinox		July 18th	00h02	00.06	13.04
Summer Solstice		Oct 19th	06h00	23.32	33.05
Autumn Equinox		Jan 21st	12h02	-00.06	15.46
Winter Solstice	16400 BC	Apr 21st	18h03	-23.32	-5.05
Spring Equinox		July 19th	00h03	00.14	13.12
Summer Solstice		Oct 20th	06h00	23.32	33.20
Autumn Equinox		Jan 22nd	12h03	-0013	15.42
Winter Solstice	16500 BC	Apr 21st	18h00	-23.32	-5.05
Spring Equinox		July 20th	00h03	00.22	13.20
Summer Solstice		Oct 21st	06h02	23.32	33.13
Autumn Equinox		Jan 23rd	12h03	-00.20	15.38
Winter Solstice	16600 BC	Apr 22nd	18h02	-23.32	-5.08
Spring Equinox		Jul 20th	00h02	00.07	13.07
Summer Solstice		Oct 22nd	06h03	23.32	33.17
Autumn Equinox		Jan 23rd	11h58	-00.05	15.51
Winter Solstice	16700 BC	Aug 22nd	18h00	-23.32	-5.08

Spring Equinox		July 21st	00h03	00.15	13.15
Summer Solstice		Oct 22nd	05h59	23.32	33.22
Autumn Equinox		Jan 24th	12h03	-00.12	15.47
Winter Solstice	16800 BC	Apr 23rd	18h01	-23.32	-5.11
Spring Equinox		July 22nd	00h04	00.23	33.26
Summer Solstice		Oct 23rd	06h02	23.32	39.2
Autumn Equinox		Jan 25th	12h03	-00.21	15.42
Winter Solstice	16900 BC	Apr 24th	18h03	-23.31	-5.14
Spring Equinox		July 22nd	00h02	00.16	35.04
Summer Solstice		Oct 24th	06h02	23.32	55.33
Autumn Equinox		Jan 25th	12h02	-00.08	35.50
Winter Solstice	17000 BC	Apr 24th	18h01	-23.31	12.12
Spring Equinox		July 23rd	00h03	00.18	58.35
Summer Solstice		Oct 25th	06h03	23.31	39.34
Autumn Equinox		Jan 26th	12h03	-00.16	35.42
Winter Solstice	17100 BC	Apr 25th	18h03	-23.31	12.11
Spring Equinox		July 24th	00h03	00.22	13.27
Summer Solstice		Oct 25th	06h01	23.31	33.38
Autumn Equinox		Jan 27th	12h03	-00.10	15.57
Winter Solstice	17200 BC	Apr 25th	18h00	-23.31	-5.17
Spring Equinox		July 25th	00h04	00.30	13.36
Summer Solstice		Oct 26th	06h00	23.31	33.44
Autumn Equinox		Jan 29th	12h07	-00.09	15.34
Winter Solstice	17300 BC	Apr 26th	18h02	-23.31	-5.16
Spring Equinox		July 25th	00h03	00.14	13.22
Summer Solstice		Oct 27th	06h01	23.31	39.54
Autumn Equinox		Jan 28th	12h03	-00.14	15.50
Winter Solstice	17400 BC	Apr 26th	17.59	-23.31	-5.19

Spring Equinox		July 26th	00h03	00.21	13.31
Summer Solstice		Oct 28th	06h01	23.31	33.35
Autumn Equinox		Jan 28th	11h58	00.01	16.02
Winter Solstice	17500 BC	Apr 27th		18h00	-23.31
Spring Equinox		July 26th	00h02	00.07	27.52
Summer Solstice		Oct 28th	06h01	23.31	40.05
Autumn Equinox		Jan 29th	12h02	-00.09	29.44
Winter Solstice	17600 BC	Apr 27th	17h59	-23.31	6.49
Spring Equinox		July 27th	00h03	00.24	28.00
Summer Solstice		Oct 29th	06h02	23.31	50.08
Autumn Equinox		Jan 30th	12h03	-00.18	29.37
Winter Solstice	17700 BC	Apr 28th	18h01	-23.31	6.47
Spring Equinox		July 28th	00h03	00.22	28.09
Summer Solstice		Oct 20th	06h02	23.31	50.11
Autumn Equinox		Jan 30th	11h58	-00.03	2950
Winter Solstice	17800 BC	Apr 28th	11h59	-23.31	6.48
Spring Equinox		July 25th	00h02	00.05	27.55
Summer Solstice		Oct 31st	06h03	23.30	50.14
Autumn Equinox		Jan 31st	12h02	-00.12	22.42
Winter Solstice	17900 BC	Apr 29th	18h00	-23.31	6.45
Spring Equinox		July 29th	00h02	00.25	28.17
Summer Solstice		Nov 1st	06h04	23.30	50.17
Autumn Equinox		Feb 1st	12h03	-00.21	29.34
Winter Solstice	18000 BC	Apr 30th	18h02	-23.30	6.43
Spring Equinox		July 30th	00h03	00.19	28.12
Summer Solstice		Nov 1st	06h02	23.30	50.21
Autumn Equinox		Feb 1st	12h02	-00.07	29.46
Winter Solstice	18100 BC	Apr 30th	18h00	-23.30	6.44

Spring Equinox		July 31st	00h04	00.26	28.21
Summer Solstice		Nov 2nd	06h01	23.30	50 24
Autumn Equinox		Feb 2nd	12h03	-00.16	29.38
Winter Solstice	18200 BC	May 1st	18h02	-23.30	6.42
Spring Equinox		Jul 31st	00h02	00.10	28.06
Summer Solstice		Nov 2nd	06h00	23.30	50.29
Autumn Equinox		Feb 2nd	11h58	-00.01	29.51
Winter Solstice	18300 BC	May 1st	17h59	-23.30	-6.42
Spring Equinox		Aug 1st	00h03	00.16	28.15
Summer Solstice		Nov 3rd	06h00	23.30	50.31
Autumn Equinox		Feb 3rd	12h02	-00.11	29.42
Winter Solstice	18400 BC	May 2nd	18h01	-23.30	6.40
Spring Equinox		Aug 2nd	00h04	00.23	28.24
Summer Solstice		Nov 4th	06h01	23.30	50.34
Autumn Equinox		Feb 4th	12h03	-00.20	29.33
Winter Solstice	18500 BC	May 3rd	18h03	-23.30	6.39
Spring Equinox		Aug 7th	00h02	00.07	28.09
Summer Solstice		Nov 5th	06h02	23.30	50.57
Autumn Equinox		Feb 5th	12h02	-00.10	29.41
Winter Solstice	18600 BC	May 3rd	18h00	-23.30	6.39
Spring Equinox		Aug 3rd	00h03	00.13	28.18
Summer Solstice		Nov 6th	06h03	23.30	50.39
Autumn Equinox		Feb 5th	12h03	-00.16	27.36
Winter Solstice	18700 BC	May 4th	18h02	-23.30	46.38
Spring Equinox		Aug 4th	00h03	00.20	28.27
Summer Solstice		Nov 6th	06h01	23.30	50.43
Autumn Equinox		Feb 6th	12h04	-00.26	29.27
Winter Solstice	18800 BC	May 4th	17h59	-23.30	6.38

Spring Equinox		Aug 5th	00h04	00.26	28.36
Summer Solstice		Nov 7th	06h02	23.29	50.46
Autumn Equinox		Feb 6th	12h02	-00.12	29.38
Winter Solstice	18900 BC	May 5th	18h01	-23.29	6.39
Spring Equinox		Aug 5th	23h58	-00.01	28,32
Summer Solstice		Nov 8th	06h01	23.29	42.36
Autumn Equinox		Feb 7th	12h02	-00.10	31.14
Winter Solstice	19000 BC	May 6th	18h01	-23.29	13.52
Spring Equinox		Aug 6th	00h02	00.05	28.42
Mid Summer Solstice		Nov 9th	06h02	23.29	42.48
Autumn Equinox		Feb 8th	12h03	-00.21	31.07
Winter Solstice	19100 BC	May 6th	17h59	-23.29	13.54
Spring Equinox		Aug 7th	00h02	00.12	28.57
Summer Solstice		Nov 9th	05h59	23.29	42.47
Autumn Equinox		Feb 8th	12h03	-00.07	31.12
Winter Solstice	19200 BC	May 7th	18h00	-23.29	13.51
Spring Equinox		Aug 8th	00h03	00.18	29.03
Summer Solstice		Nov 10th	06h00	23.29	41.51
Autumn Equinox		Feb 9th	12h03	-00.17	31.05
Winter Solstice	19300 BC	May 8th	18h02	-23.29	13.49
Spring Equinox		Aug 18t	23h58	00.01	28.55
Summer Solstice		Nov 11th	06h01	23.29	42.54
Autumn Equinox		Feb 9th	11h58	-00.03	31.10
Winter Solstice	19400 BC	May 8th	18h00	-23.29	13.51
Spring Equinox		Aug 9th	00h02	00.07	29.06
Summer Solstice		Nov 12th	06h03	23.29	42.57
Autumn Equinox		Feb 10th	12h03	-00.13	31.02
Winter Solstice	19500 BC	May 9th	18h01	-23.29	13.48

Spring Equinox		Aug 10th	00h03	00.13	29 .16
Summer Solstice		Nov 12th	06h00	23.29	43.04
Autumn Equinox		Feb 11th	12h04	-00.24	30.55
Winter Solstice	19600 BC	May 10th	18h03	-23.28	13.46
Spring Equinox		Aug 11th	00h04	00.25	29.38
Summer Solstice		Nov 14th	06h02	23.28	43.09
Autumn Equinox		Feb 11th	12h02	-00.10	30.59
Winter Solstice	19700 BC	May 10th	18h00	-23.29	13.49
Spring Equinox		Aug 12th	00h04	00.25	29.38
Summer Solstice		Nov 14th	06h02	23.28	43.09
Autumn Equinox		Feb 12th	12h03	-00.02	30.51
Winter Solstice	19800 BC	May 11th	18h02	-23.29	13.47
Spring Equinox		Feb 12th	12h02	00.02	30.56
Mid Summer Solstice		Nov 14th	05h59	23.28	42.12
Autumn Equinox		Feb 12th	12h02	00.02	30.56
Winter Solstice	19900 BC	May 11th	17h59	-23.28	13.50
Spring Equinox		Aug 13th	00h02	-00.20	29.52
Summer Solstice		Nov 15th	06h01	23.28	43.18
Autumn Equinox		Feb 13th	12h03	-00.18	30.48
Winter Solstice	20000 BC	May 12th	18h01	-23.28	13.48
Spring Equinox		Aug 14th	00h03	00.20	29.52
Summer Solstice		Nov 16th	06h01	23.28	43.20
Autumn Equinox		Feb 13th	12h02	-00.04	30.52
Winter Solstice	20100 BC	May 13th	18h03	-23.28	13.47
Spring Equinox		Aug 14th	23h58	00.03	29.45
Summer Solstice		Nov 16th	05h59	23.28	43.25
Autumn Equinox		Feb 14th	12h03	-00.15	30.44
Winter Solstice	20200 BC	May 13th	18h00	-23.28	13.50

Spring Equinox		Aug 15th	00h02	00.09	29.56
Mid Summer Solstice		Nov 17th	05h59	23.28	43.28
Autumn Equinox		Feb 14th	11h58	-00.02	30.48
Winter Solstice	20300 BC	May 14th	18h02	-23.28	13.49
Spring Equinox		Aug 16th	00h03	00.15	30.07
Mid Summer Solstice		Nov 17th	06h01	23.28	42.22
Autumn Equinox		Feb 15th	12h03	-00.03	30.40
Winter Solstice	20400 BC	May 15th	18h03	-23.28	13.49
Spring Equinox		Aug 16th	23h58	-00.02	30.00
Summer Solstice		Nov 18th	06h02	23.28	43.28
Autumn Equinox		Feb 15th	11h58	00.01	30.44
Winter Solstice	20500 BC	May 15th	18h01	-23.28	13.52
Spring Equinox		Aug 17th	00h02	00.04	30.11
Summer Solstice		Nov 19th	06h01	23.28	43.34
Autumn Equinox		Feb 16th	12h02	-00.10	30.35
Winter Solstice	20600 BC	May 16th	18h02	-23.28	13.52
Spring Equinox		Aug 18th	00h02	00.16	30.34
Summer Solstice		Nov 20th	06h02	23.28	43.35
Autumn Equinox		Feb 16th	11h57	00.10	30.57
Winter Solstice	20700 BC	May 17th	18h04	-23.28	1352
Spring Equinox		Aug 19th	00h03	00.15	30.34
Summer Solstice		Nov 20th	06h02	23.28	43.39
Autumn Equinox		Feb 17th	12h02	00.01	30.42
Winter Solstice	20800 BC	May 17th	18h01	-23.28	13.56
Spring Equinox		Aug 20th	00h04	-00.22	30.45
Summer Solstice		Nov 21st	06h01	23.28	43.59
Autumn Equinox		Feb 18th	12h03	-00.19	30.23
Winter Solstice	20900 BC	May 18th	18h02	-23.28	13.56

Spring Equinox		Aug 20th	00h02	00.05	30.37
Summer Solstice		Nov 22nd	06h03	23.27	43.49
Autumn Equinox		Feb 18th	12h03	-00.31	30.26
Winter Solstice	21000 BC	May 18th	18h00	-23.27	14.01
Spring Equinox		Feb 19th	12h02	-00.16	30.18
Summer Solstice		Nov 30th	06h04	23.27	43.35
Autumn Equinox		Feb 19th	12h03	-00.16	30.18
Winter Solstice	21100 BC	May 19th	18h01	-23.27	14.01
Spring Equinox		Aug 22nd	00h03	00.16	31.00
Summer Solstice		Nov 23rd	06h03	23.27	43.31
Autumn Equinox		Feb 19th	12h02	-00.03	30.22
Winter Solstice	21200 BC	May 20th	18h03	-23.27	14.02
Spring Equinox		Aug 22nd	23h58	-00.00	14.07
Summer Solstice		Nov 24th	06h03	23.27	43.42
Autumn Equinox		Feb 20th	12h03	-00.04	30.14
Winter Solstice	21300 BC	May 20th	18h00	-23.27	14.077
Autumn Equinox		Feb 21st	12h04	-00.25	30.06
Winter Solstice		May 21st	18h01	-23.27	14.08
Spring Equinox		Aug 23rd	00h02	00.06	31.04
Summer Solstice	21400 BC	Nov 24th	06h01	23.27	43.45
Autumn Equinox		Feb 22nd	12h04	-00.07	30.02
Winter Solstice		May 22nd	18h00	-23.27	14.15
Spring Equinox		Aug 24th	23h58	00.05	31.08
Summer Solstice	21500 BC	Nov 25th	06h00	23.27	43.47
Autumn Equinox		Feb 22nd	12h04	-00.12	30.02
Winter Solstice		May 22nd	18h00	-23.27	13.52
Spring Equinox		Aug 25th	00h03	00.18	31.26
Summer Solstice	21600 BC	Nov 25th	06h00	23.27	43.47

Autumn Equinox		Feb 22nd	12h03	00.03	29.55
Winter Solstice		Nov 25th	18h00	-23.27	14.17
Spring Equinox		Aug 25th	23h58	00.01	31.19
Summer Solstice	21700 BC	Nov 26th	06h02	23.27	43.45
Autumn Equinox		Feb 23rd	12h04	00.02	29.58
Winter Solstice		May 24th	18h03	-23.27	14.19
Spring Equinox		Aug 26th	00h03	00.17	31.30
Summer Solstice	21800 BC	Nov 27th	06h03	23.27	43.43
Autumn Equinox		Feb 23rd	12h02	00.06	29.01
Winter Solstice		May 27th	18h00	-23.27	13.33
Spring Equinox		Aug 27th	00h03	00.14	30.40
Summer Solstice	21900 BC	Nov 27th	06h0	23.2	42.42
Autumn Equinox		Feb 24th	12h04	00.01	28.54
Winter Solstice		May 25th	06h01	-23.27	42.42
Spring Equinox		Aug 27th	23h58	00.07	30.33
Summer Solstice	22000 BC	Nov 28th	06h03	23.27	42.39
Autumn Equinox		Feb 24th	12h02	-00.04	28.58
Winter Solstice		May 26th	18h02	-23.27	13 39
Spring Equinox		Aug 28th	00h02	00.04	30.44
Summer Solstice	22100 BC	Nov 28th	06h00	23.27	42.41
Autumn Equinox		Feb 25th	12h03	-00.18	56.45
Winter Solstice		May 26th	18h00	-23.27	34.32
Spring Equinox		Aug 29th	00h03	00.13	57.48
Summer Solstice	22200 BC	Nov 29th	06h02	23.27	77.39
Autumn Equinox		Feb 25th	12h02	-00.04	56.56
Winter Solstice		May 27th	18h01	-23.27	34.33
Spring Equinox		Aug 30th	00h04	00.19	57.57
Summer Solstice	22300 BC	Nov 29th	06h00	23.27	77.41

Autumn Equinox		Feb 26th	12h03	-00.14	50.07
Winter Solstice		May 28th	18h03	-23.27	30.09
Spring Equinox		Aug 30th	00h02	00.02	51.38
Summer Solstice	22400 BC	Nov 30th	06h02	23.27	77.38
Autumn Equinox		Feb 26th	11h58	00.00	50.11
Winter Solstice		May 28th	17h59	-23.27	30.13
Spring Equinox		Aug 31st	00h03	00.09	57.49
Summer Solstice	22500 BC	Nov 30th	05h59	23.27	67.14
Autumn Equinox		Feb 27th	12h03	00.10	38.33
Winter Solstice		May 29th	18h00	-23.27	21.51
Spring Equinox		Sept 1st	00h03	00.15	40.56
Summer Solstice	22600 BC	Dec 1st	06h01	23.27	53.11
Autumn Equinox		Feb 28th	12h04	-00.06	21.54
Winter Solstice		Dec 1st	06h01	-23.27	42.35
Spring Equinox		Sept 2nd	00h04	00.21	41.07
Summer Solstice	22700 BC	Dec 2nd	06h03	23.27	53.07
Autumn Equinox		Feb 28th	12h03	-00.06	38.33
Winter Solstice		May 3rd	18h03	-23.27	21.58
Spring Equinox		Sept 2nd	00h02	00.06	40.58
Summer Solstice	22800 BC	Dec 2nd	06h00	23.27	53.08
Autumn Equinox		Mar 1st	12h03	-00.16	38.26
Winter Solstice		May 31st	18h00	-23.27	22.03
Spring Equinox		Sept 3rd	00h03	00.12	41.09
Summer Solstice	22900 BC	Dec 3rd	06h02	23.27	53.04
Autumn Equinox		Mar 1st	12h02	-00.03	38.33
Winter Solstice		Jun1st	18h00	-23.27	22.07
Spring Equinox		Sept 4th	00h04	00.20	41.19
Summer Solstice	23000 BC	Dec 3rd	06h00	00.20	53.01

Autumn Equinox		Mar 2nd	12h03	-00.13	38.27
Winter Solstice		Jun 2nd	18h00	-23.27	22.10
Spring Equinox		Sept 4th	00h02	00.04	41.10
Summer Solstice	23100 BC	Dec 4th	06h02	23.27	53.01
Autumn Equinox		Mar 3rd	12h04	-00.23	38.21
Winter Solstice		Jun 2nd	18h00	-23.27	22.16
Spring Equinox		Sept 5th	00h03	00.11	41.20
Summer Solstice	23200 BC	Dec 4th	05h59	23.27	53.02
Autumn Equinox		Mar 3rd	12h03	-00.09	38.28
Winter Solstice		Jun 3rd	18h01	-23.27	22.20
Spring Equinox		Sept 6th	00h04	00.19	41.30
Summer Solstice	23300 BC	Dec 5th	06h01	23.27	52.57
Autumn Equinox		Mar 4th	12h04	-00.09	00.00
Winter Solstice		Jun 4th	18h02	-23.27	00.00
Spring Equinox		Sept 6th	00h03	00.03	41.21
Summer Solstice	23400 BC	Dec 6th	06h03	23.27	52.51
Autumn Equinox		Mar 4th	12h03	-00.05	38.30
Winter Solstice		Jun 5th	18h03	-23.27	22.28
Spring Equinox		Sept 11th	00h03	00.11	41.31
Summer Solstice	23500 BC	Dec 6th	06h01	23.27	52.53
Autumn Equinox		Mar 5th	12h03	-00.15	38.25
Winter Solstice		Jun 5th	18h00	-23.27	22.34
Spring Equinox		Sept 8th	00h04	00.19	41.41
Summer Solstice	23600 BC	Dec 7th	06h03	23.27	52.47
Autumn Equinox		Mar 5th	12h03	-00.00	38.33
Winter Solstice		Jun 6th	18h01	-23.27	22.38
Spring Equinox		Sept 8th	00h03	00.03	41.31
Summer Solstice	23700 BC	Dec 7th	06h01	23.27	52.40

Autumn Equinox		Mar 6th	12h03	-00.10	38.29
Winter Solstice		Jun 6th	17h58	-23.27	22.44
Spring Equinox		Sept 9th	00h03	00.11	41.41
Summer Solstice	23800 BC	Dec 7th	05h58	23.27	52.49
Autumn Equinox		Mar 7th	12h04	-00.09	38.25
Winter Solstice		Jun 7th	18h04	-23.27	22.46
Spring Equinox		Sept 10th	00h04	00.19	41.51
Summer Solstice	23900 BC	Dec 8th	06h01	-23.27	52.43
Autumn Equinox		Mar 7th	12h03	-00.09	38.21
Winter Solstice		Jun 8th	18h00	-23.27	22.52
Spring Equinox		Sept 10th	00h03	00.04	41.41
Summer Solstice	24000 BC	Dec 9th	06h03	23.26	52.36
Autumn Equinox		Mar 8th	12h03	00.01	38.38
Winter Solstice		Jun 10th	18h02	-23.27	23.11
Spring Equinox			Sept 12th		
Summer Solstice	24100 BC	Dec 10th		06h02	23.27
Autumn Equinox		Mar 8th	12h03	-00.18	55.50
Winter Solstice		Jun 9th	-18h00-	-23.27	32.56
Spring Equinox		Sept 11th	00h03	00.26	52.38
Summer Solstice	24200 BC	Dec 9th	05h59	23.27	69.49
Autumn Equinox		Mar 9th	12h03	-00.08	38.35
Winter Solstice		Jun 10th	18h02	-23.26	23.06
Spring Equinox		Sept 12th	00h03	00.06	41.50
Summer Solstice	24300 BC	Dec 10th	06h00	23.27	52.33
Autumn Equinox		Mar 10th	12h02	-00.18	38.32
Winter Solstice		Jun 11th	18h00	-23.27	23.11
Spring Equinox		Sept 13th	00h04	00.15	41.59
Summer Solstice	24400 BC	Dec 11th	06h02	23.27	52.27

Autumn Equinox		Mar 10th	12h03	-00.02	29,57
Winter Solstice		Jun 12th	18h02	-23.27	16.27
Spring Equinox		Sept 13th	00h03	-00.00	33.19
Summer Solstice	24500 BC	Dec 11th	06h00	23.27	42.57
Autumn Equinox		Mar 11th	12h03	-00.11	29.55
Winter Solstice		Jun 13th	18h03	-23.27	16.31
Spring Equinox		Sept 14th	00h03	00.09	33.27
Summer Solstice	24600 BC	Dec12th	06h02	23.27	42.51
Autumn Equinox		Mar 12th	12h04	-00.19	29.54
Winter Solstice		Jun 13th	18h01	-23.27	16.38
Spring Equinox		Sept 15th	00h04	00.18	33.36
Summer Solstice	24700 BC	Dec 12th	06h0	23.2	42.51
Autumn Equinox		Mar 12th	12h03	-00.04	30.03
Winter Solstice		Jun 14th	18h02	-23.27	16.43
Spring Equinox		Sept 15th	00h03	00.03	33.26
Summer Solstice	24800 BC	Dec 13th	06h02	23.27	42.46
Autumn Equinox		Mar 13th	12h03	-00.13	30.03
Winter Solstice		Jun 15th	18h03	-23.27	16.48
Spring Equinox		Sept 16th	00h03	00.13	33.35
Summer Solstice	24900 BC	Dec 14th	06h03	23.27	42.40
Autumn Equinox		Mar 14th	12h04	-0015	30.14
Winter Solstice		Jun 15th	18h00	-23.27	16.55
Spring Equinox		Sept 16th	00h03	-00.01	33.25
Summer Solstice	25000 BC	Dec 14th	06h02	23.27	42.40
Autumn Equinox		Mar 14th	12h03	-00.06	3012
Winter Solstice		Jun 15th	18h00	-23.27	16.55
Spring Equinox		Sept 18th	00h04	00.18	33.41
Summer Solstice	25100 BC	Dec 15th	06h01	23.27	42.36

Autumn Equinox		Mar 15th	12h04	-00.14	30.12
Winter Solstice		Jun 16th	18h01	-23.27	16.59
Spring Equinox		Sept 17th	00h03	00.15	33.44
Summer Solstice	25200 BC	Dec 15th	06h04	23.27	42.35
Autumn Equinox		Mar 15th	12h03	00.01	30.22
Winter Solstice		Jun 17th	18h02	-23.27	16.18
Spring Equinox		Sept 18th	00h03	00.04	33.31
Summer Solstice	25300 BC	Dec 16th	06h01	23.27	43.42
Autumn Equinox		Mar 16th	12h03	-00.07	30.23
Winter Solstice		Jun 17th	17h59	-23.27	16.21
Spring Equinox		Sept 19th	00h03	00.29	34.04
Summer Solstice	25400 BC	Dec 16th	06h01	23.27	43.42
Autumn Equinox		Mar 17th	12h04	-00.15	30.24
Winter Solstice		Jun 18th	18h01	-23.27	16.26
Spring Equinox		Sept 19th	00h03	00.0	33.29
Summer Solstice	25500 BC	Dec 17th	06h03	23.27	42.26
Autumn Equinox		Mar 17th	12h03	00.00	30.34
Winter Solstice		Jun 19th	18h02	-23.27	16.3
Spring Equinox		Sept 20th	00h03	00.11	33.36
Summer Solstice	25600 BC	Dec 17th	06h01	23.27	42.27
Autumn Equinox		Mar 18th	12h03	-00.07	29.35
Winter Solstice		Jun 20th	18h03	-23.27	16.56
Spring Equinox		Sept 21st	00h05	00.21	33.44
Summer Solstice	25700 BC	Dec 18th	06h03	23.27	41.17
Autumn Equinox		Mar 18th	12h03	-0.07	29.35
Winter Solstice		Jun 21st	18h00	-23.27	16.41
Spring Equinox		Sept 21st	00h04	0.02	32.43
Summer Solstice	25800 BC	Dec 18th	06h01	23.27	42.24

Autumn Equinox		Mar 19th	12h03	00.01	30.48
Winter Solstice		Jun 22nd	18h03	-23.27	16.63
Spring Equinox		Sept 22nd	00h04	00.18	33.41
Summer Solstice	25900 BC	Dec 19th	06h03	23.27	42.19
Autumn Equinox		Mar 20th	12h03	-00.07	30.51
Winter Solstice		Jun 22nd	18h03	-23.27	16.49
Spring Equinox		Sept 22nd	00h03	00.05	33.30
Summer Solstice	26000 BC	Dec 19th	06h00	23.27	42.20
Autumn Equinox		Mar 21st	12h04	-0015	30.57
Winter Solstice		Jun 22nd	18h00	-23.27	16.56
Spring Equinox		Sept 23rd	00h03	00.16	33.37
Summer Solstice	26100 BC	Dec 20th	06h02	23.27	42.16
Autumn Equinox		Mar 21st	12h03	00.01	31.04
Winter Sol		Jun 23rd	18h01	-23.27	16.59
Spring Equinox		Sept 23rd	00h03	00.03	33.27
Summer Solstice	26200 BC	Dec 20th	06h00	23.27	42.18
Autumn Equinox		Mar 22nd	12h03	-00.06	31.07
Winter Sol		Jun 24th	18h03	-23.27	17.0
Spring Equinox		Sept 24th	00h04	00.14	33.33
Summer Solstice	26300 BC	Dec 21st	00h02	23.27	42.14
Autumn Equinox		Mar 23rd	12h04	-00.13	30.09
Winter Solstice		Jun 24th	18h00	-23.27	17.09
Spring Equinox		Sept 24th	00h03	00.01	33.23
Summer Solstice	26400 BC	Dec 22nd	06h01	23.28	41.08
Spring Equinox		Sept 25th	00h04	00.12	32.29
Summer Solstice		Dec 22nd	06h02	23.28	41.08
Autumn Equinox		Mar 24th	12h00	-00.20	30.13
Winter Solstice	26500BC	Jun 25th	18h01	-23.27	17.12

Season	Year	Date	Time		
Spring Equinox		Sept 26th	00h05	00.2	32.35
Summer Solstice	26600 BC	Dec 22nd	05h59	23.28	41.11
Autumn Equinox		Mar 24th	12h03	-00.05	30.24
Winter Solstice		Jun 26th	18h03	-23.28	17.16
Spring Equinox		Sept 26th	00h04	00.10	32.25
Summer Solstice	26700 BC	Dec 23rd	06h01	23.28	41.08
Autumn Equinox		Mar 25th	12h04	-00.12	30.28
Winter Solstice		Jun 26th	18h00	-23.27	17.21
Spring Equinox		Sept 26th	00h03	-00.02	32.14
Summer Sol	26800 BC	Dec 24th	06h03	23.28	41.05
Autumn Equinox		Mar 26th	12h04	-00.19	30.31
Winter Solstice		Jun 27th	18h01	-23.28	17.24
Spring Equinox		Sept 26th	00h03	-00.04	53.06
Summer Sol		Dec 23rd	06h00	23.28	26.27
Autumn Equinox		Mar 25th	11h57	00.08	15.08
Winter Solstice	26900 BC	June 27th	17h58	-23.28	-00.08
Spring Equinox		Sept 27th	00h03	-00.10	59.17
Summer Sol		Dec 24th	06h01	23.28	79.09
Autumn Equinox		Mar 26th	11h57	00.16	59.17
Winter Sol	27000 BC	June 28th	17h59	-23.2	36.16
Spring Equinox		Sept 27th	00.h03	-00.03	59.04
Summer Sol		Dec 25th	06h03	23.28	79.07
Autumn Equinox		Mar 27th	12h03	-00.01	59.02
Winter Solstice	27100 BC	June 29th	18h00	-23.28	36.16
Spring Equinox		Sept 28th	00h03	00,05	52.47
Summer Solstice		Dec 25th	05h59	23.28	70.44
Autumn Equinox		Mar 28th	12h03	-00.04	53.47
Winter Solstice	27,200 BC	June 30th	18h01	-23.28	31.42

Spring Equinox		Sept 29th	00h04	00.17	52.58
Summer Solstice		Dec 26th	06h01	23.28	70.45
Autumn Equinox		Mar 29th	12h04	-00.18	53.36
Winter Solstice	27,300 BC	July 1st	18h03	-23.28	31.41
Spring Equinox		Sept 29th	00h03	00.05	52.50
Summer Solstice		Dec 27th	06h03	23.28	70.46
Autumn Equinox		Mar 30th	12h04	-00.18	53.25
Winter Solstice	27,400 BC	July 1st	18h00	-23.28	31.38
Spring Equinox		Sept 30th	00h05	00.30	53.17
Summer Solstice		Dec 27th	06h01	23.38	70.42
Autumn Equinox		Mar 30th	12h03	-00.02	53.36
Winter Solstice	27,500 BC	July 2nd	18h01	-23.28	31.37
Spring Equinox		Sept 30th	00h03	-00.01	52.48
Summer Solstice		Dec 28th	06h01	23.28	70.42
Autumn Equinox		Mar 31st	12h03	-00.03	53.30
Winter Solstice	27,600 BC	July 3rd	18h02	-23.28	31.36
Spring Equinox		Oct 1st	00h04	00.17	53.04
Summer Solstice		Dec 28th	06h00	23.29	70.38
Autumn Equinox		Apr 1st	12h04	-00.16	53.13
Winter Solstice	27,700 BC	July 3rd	18h00	-23.28	31.34
Spring Equinox		Oct 1st	00h03	00.04	52.56
Summer Solstice		Dec 29th	06h02	23.29	70.38
Autumn Equinox		Apr 1st	12h03	00.00	53.25
Winter Solstice	27,800 BC	July 4th	18h02	-23.29	31.33
Spring Equinox		Oct 2nd	00h04	00.16	53.07
Summer Solstice		Dec 30th	06h03	23.29	70.38
Autumn Equinox		Apr 2nd	12h04	00.01	53.29
Winter Solstice	27,900 BC	July 4th	17h59	-23.29	31.31

Spring Equinox		Oct 2nd	00h03	00.04	52.59
Summer Solstice		Dec 30th	06h01	23.29	70.33
Autumn Equinox		Apr 3rd	12h03	-00.05	53.01
Winter Solstice	28,000 BC	July 5th	18h01	-23.29	31.30
Spring Equinox		Oct 3rd	00h04	00.16	53.10
Summer Solstice		Dec 31st	06h02	23.29	70.32
Autumn Equinox		Apr 3rd	12h03	00, 02	53.12
Winter Solstice	28,100 BC	July 6th	18h03	-23.29	31.30
Spring Equinox		Oct 3rd	00h03	00.18	53.19
Summer Solstice		Dec 31st	06h00	23.29	70.27
Autumn Equinox		Apr 4th	12h03	-00.05	53.01
Winter Solstice	28,200 BC	July 6th	18h00	-23.29	31.28
Spring Equinox		Oct 4th	00h04	00.16	53.14
Summer Solstice		Jan 1st	06h02	23.29	70.25
Autumn Equinox		Apr 5th	12h04	-00.12	52.49
Winter Solstice	28.300 BC	July 7th	18h02	-23.29	31.28
Spring Equinox		Oct 4th	00h03	00.04	53.06
Summer Solstice		Jan 2nd	06h03	23.29	7023
Autumn Equinox		Apr 5th	12h03	-00.12	52.49
Winter Solstice	28,400 BC	July 7th	18h00	-23.29	31.26
Spring Equinox		Oct 5th	00h00	00.16	53.17
Summer Solstice		Jan 2nd	06h01	23.29	70.17
Autumn Equinox		Apr 6th	12h03	-00.03	52.48
Winter Solstice	28,500 BC	July 8th	18h02	-23.29	31.26
Spring Equinox		Oct 5th	00h03	00.04	53.09
Summer Solstice		Jan 3rd	06h02	23.29	70.15
Autumn Equinox		Apr 7th	12h04	-00.01	52.37
Winter Solstice	28,600 BC	July 9th	18h03	-23.29	31.27

Spring Equinox		Oct 6th	00h04	00.16	53.20
Summer Solstice		Jan 4th	06h01	23.29	70.13
Autumn Equinox		Apr 8th	12h04	-00.18	52.25
Winter Solstice	28,700 BC	July 9th	18h01	-23.29	31.25
Spring Equinox		Oct 6th	00h03	00.04	53.12
Summer Solstice		Jan 4th	06h01	23.30	70.06
Autumn Equinox		Apr 8th	12h03	-00.02	52.36
Winter Solstice	28,800 BC	July 10th	18h03	-23.29	31.26
Spring Equinox		Oct 7th	00h05	00.30	53.39
Summer Solstice		Jan 5th	06h03	23.30	70.03
Autumn Equinox		Apr 9th	12h04	-00.09	52.24
Winter Solstice	28,900 BC	July 10th	18h00	-23.30	31.24
Spring Equinox		Oct 7th	00h03	00.04	53.14
Summer Solstice		Jan 5th	06h00	23.30	69.56
Autumn Equinox		Apr 10th	12h02	-00.17	52.12
Winter Solstice	29,000 BC	July 11th	18h02	-23.30	31.25
Spring Equinox		Oct 8th	00h04	00.16	53.24
Summer Solstice		Jan 6th	06h01	23.30	53.24
Autumn Equinox		Apr 10th	12h03	-00.01	52.23
Winter Solstice	29,100 BC	July 11th	18h00	-23.30	31.24
Spring Equinox		Oct 8th	00h03	00.03	53.16
Summer Solstice		Jan 7th	06h03	23.30	53.16
Autumn Equinox		Apr 11th	12h04	-00.09	69.49
Winter Solstice	29,200BC	July 12th	18h02	-23.30	31.25
Spring Equinox		Oct 9th	00h01	00.15	53.26
Summer Solstice		Jan 7th	06h00	23.30	69.41
Autumn Equinox		Apr 12th	12h04	-00.17	52.00
Winter Solstice	29,300 BC	July 12th	18h00	-23.30	31 24

Spring Equinox		Oct 9th	00h03	00.03	53.18
Summer Solstice		Jan 8th	06h02	23.30	69.37
Autumn Equinox		Apr 12th	12h03	-00.01	52.10
Winter Solstice	29,400 BC	July 13th	18h02	-23.30	31.25
Spring Equinox		Oct 9th	00h03	-00.04	53.14
Summer Solstice		Jan 8th	06h00	23.30	69.30
Autumn Equinox		Apr 13th	12h04	-00.15	51.53
Winter Solstice	29,500 BC	Jul 13th	18h01	-23.30	31 25
Spring Equinox		Oct 10th	00h03	00.08	53.23
Summer Solstice		Jan 9th	06h01	23.30	69.26
Autumn Equinox		Apr 13th	12h03	00.00	52.04
Winter Solstice	29,600 BC	Jul 14th	18h03	-23.30	31.26
Spring Equinox		Oct 11th	00h05	00.20	53.33
Summer Solstice		Jan 10th	06h03	23.30	69.21
Autumn Equinox		Apr 14th	12h03	-00.07	51.52
Winter Solstice	29,700 BC	Jul 14th	18h00	-23.30	31.26
Spring Equinox		Oct 11th	00h03	00.07	53.23
Summer Solstice		Jan 10th	06h00	23.31	69.13
Autumn Equinox		Apr 15th	12h04	-00.15	51.40
Winter Solstice	29,800 BC	Jul 15th	12h03	-23.31	31.27
Spring Equinox		Oct 12th	00h05	00.18	53.23
Summer Solstice		Jan 11th	06h02	23.28	69.05
Autumn Equinox		Apr 15th	12h03	-00.01	51.51
Winter Solstice	29,900 BC	Jul 15th	18h00	-23.27	31.36
Spring Equinox		Oct 12th	00h03	-00.00	53.19
Summer Solstice		Jan 12th	06h02	23.27	69.02
Autumn Equinox		Apr 16th	12h03	-00.03	51.45
Winter Solstice	30,000 BC	July 11th	18h01	-23.27	31.28

Index

A

B

Baal 78, 79

Babylon 29, 36, 135

Babylonian 32, 210

Bedouin 22, 76, 77

Berytus 57

Bible 23, 27, 28, 29, 30, 31, 32, 33, 38, 39, 40, 41, 43, 52, 53, 69, 70, 72, 73, 74, 75, 76, 77, 78, 79, 80, 81, 83, 89, 90, 91, 93, 97, 116, 122, 124, 127, 130, 207

Biblical 53

Biological 66, 135

Biologist 92

Bologna 132

Book of Genesis 79, 90, 91

Book of Wisdom 69, 73, 79, 89, 97, 122, 124, 127, 130

Bosnia-Herzegovina 62

British Isles 25, 105, 205

British Museum 153

Bronze 136

C

Caesar 42, 43

Caesarea 43, 57

Calendar Stone 118

Cambridge 132, 140

Cambridge University 140

Canaan 75, 77, 78

Canaanites 77, 78

Canada xvii, 20, 31, 108

Captain Cooke 137

Caraja 118

Cassius 42

Catholic 53

Catholic Church 40, 52, 134

Caucasoid 120

D

E

Europe x, xiv, 2, 8, 14, 18, 25, 40, 52, 54, 62, 73, 93, 102, 104, 105, 126, 131, 139, 142, 143, 206, 210

Europeans 83, 99

Evangelical 62

Evolution 25, 95

F

Far East 7, 90, 147

Flavius Clemens 56, 57

Flavius Joseph 51

French 175

Fulvia 46

G

Galilel Galileo 132

Galileo 7

Garden of Eden 2, 10, 11, 144

Garden of Paradise 90

Geological 102, 108, 109, 110, 111

Geologist 98, 109, 110, 111, 119, 121

Geometry 90, 112, 134, 135, 139, 146, 206

George W. Bush x

German 40, 61, 66, 142

Germany 66, 105, 139

Ghana 12, 139

Giants 104, 105, 116

Giza 171

God 1, 8, 9, 12, 15, 17, 23, 27, 28, 29, 30, 32, 33, 34, 35, 36, 40, 41, 43, 45, 53, 54, 62, 69, 70, 71, 72, 73, 74, 75, 76, 78, 79, 80, 81, 82, 83, 85, 86, 89, 90, 91, 93, 94, 101, 104, 110, 124, 129, 130, 135, 147, 152, 154, 158, 174, 176, 211, 212, 213, 214, 217, 220, 221, 228

Gold 108, 136

Great Dialogues of Plato 3

Great Flood 165

Greek xi, xiv, 6, 8, 17, 34, 61, 77, 85, 103, 104, 112, 113, 115, 116, 129, 132, 150, 163, 164, 167, 168, 169, 170, 209

Q

Queens Chamber 164, 165

Queen Tiy 231, 235

Qumran 22

R

Ramses 77, 153, 170

Ramses 11 170

Reformation 131, 132, 133

Richard E. Leakey 93

Roger Bacon 132

Roman ix, 41, 42, 43, 45, 47, 48, 53

Roman Empire ix, 10, 18, 22, 29, 56, 57, 61

Rome 8, 33, 38, 39, 42, 44, 45, 46, 47, 49, 51, 52, 53, 55, 56, 57, 61, 62, 132, 133, 136

Ronald Reagan x

Royal Cubits 162

Royal Papyrus of Turin 170

Russia ix, xvi, 14, 62, 65

Russian Republic ix

S

Sahara Desert 136

Sam Teitel 131

Sanhedrin 38

Sanskrit 9, 65

Sardinia 46

Saturnius 45

Schwaller de Lubicz 6, 7, 117, 169, 170, 172, 245

Selene 116

Semite 74, 77, 78

Semites 77

Serbian 72

Sesostris 77

T

Titans 116
Tophet 78
Tutankhamen 233, 235, 236, 237, 240
Typhon 104, 116

U

United Nations x
Universe 3, 5, 8, 10, 11, 35, 64, 68, 69, 79, 86, 87, 89, 95, 96, 98, 123, 124, 129, 145
University of Paris 132
Ur of Chalda 75

V

Vedic 65, 66
Velikovsky 68, 102, 111, 112, 115, 167, 168
Vespasian 43, 47, 49, 50, 51
Vulcan 166

W

West Africa 99
William Whiston 39, 40, 41, 42, 43, 46, 48, 49, 50, 51, 57, 76

Y

Yahweh 74, 78
Yugoslavia 62, 72

Z

Zeus 104, 116

Bibliography

Agassiz, Louis. . . . .

Allegro. John. 'The Dead Sea Scrolls' . . . .

Alaster Service . . . .

Atkinson R.J.C . . . .

Apuleius Lucius The Golden Ass. 124 - 170? AD . . . .

Barbara Thiering. Jesus and the Riddle of the Dead Sea Scrolls. . . . .

Bernard of Clairvaux. . . . .*passim*

Tierney Brian / Painter Sidney. Western Europe in the middle Ages. 300-1475. . . . .

Brianton/Christopher/ Wolfl.

A History of Civilisation. Pre-history to 1715 AD. 5th edition. . . . .

. . . .

Balfour. Arthur James. . . . .

Bhagvad Gita The . . . .

Bingham. Hiram . . . .

Bord. Janet and Colin. . . . .

Brennan. Martin.. . . . .

Brinton . . . .

Brugsch. Dr . . . .

Budge.E.A.Wallace. 'The Egyptian Book of the Dead. . . . .

Burl Aubrey . . . .

Caesar. Julius The Conquest of Gaul . . . .

Columbia Encyclopaedia. . . . .

. . . .

Comptons Encyclopaedia. The Battle of Hastings Brinton Crane / Christopher John
    B. / Wolff.Robert Lee

A History of Civilization. Prehistory to 1715. 5th Edition . . . .

. . . .

Carter, Howard . . . .

Carus. Titus Lucretius . . . .

Castle Frank. . . . .

Charpentier. Louis . . . .